A History of Israel

PALGRAVE ESSENTIAL HISTORIES
General Editor: Jeremy Black

This series of compact, readable and informative national histories is designed to appeal to anyone wishing to gain a broad understanding of a country's history – whether they are a student, a traveller, a professional or a general reader.

Published

A History of the British Isles (2nd edn)   *Jeremy Black*
A History of Israel   *Ahron Bregman*
A History of Ireland   *Mike Cronin*
A History of the Pacific Islands   *Steven Roger Fischer*
A History of the United States (2nd edn)   *Philip Jenkins*
A History of India   *Peter Robb*
A History of China   *J.A.G. Roberts*

Further titles are in preparation

Series Standing Order

If you would like to receive future titles in this series as they are published, you can make use of our standing order facility. To place a standing order please contact your bookseller or, in case of difficulty, write to us at the address below with your name and address and the name of the series. Please state with which title you wish to begin your standing order. (If you live outside the United Kingdom we may not have the rights for your area, in which case we will forward your order to the publisher concerned.)

Customer Services Department, Macmillan Ltd
Houndsmill, Basingstoke, Hampshire RG21 6XS, England

A History of Israel

Ahron Bregman

First published 2003 by
PALGRAVE MACMILLAN
Houndmills, Basingstoke, Hampshire RG21 6XS and
175 Fifth Avenue, New York, N. Y. 10010
Companies and representatives throughout the world

PALGRAVE MACMILLAN is the global academic imprint of the Palgrave Macmillan division of St. Martin's Press, LLC and of Palgrave Macmillan Ltd. Macmillan® is a registered trademark in the United States, United Kingdom and other countries. Palgrave is a registered trademark in the European Union and other countries.

ISBN 0–333–67631–9 hardcover
ISBN 0–333–67632–7 paperback

This book is printed on paper suitable for recycling and made from fully managed and sustained forest sources.

A catalogue record for this book is available from the British Library.

Library of Congress Cataloging-in-Publication Data
Bregman, Ahron.
    A history of Israel/Ahron Bregman.
        p. cm.—(Palgrave essential histories)
    Includes bibliographical references and index.
        ISBN 0–333–67631–9—ISBN 0–333–67632–7 (pbk.)
        1. Palestine—History—1799–1917. 2. Palestine—History—
1917–1948. 3. Israel—History. 4. Zionism—History.
I. Title. II. Series.
DS125.B74 2002
956.94'03—dc21   2002072304

10   9   8   7   6   5   4   3   2   1
12   11   10   09   08   07   06   05   04   03

Printed and bound in Great Britain by
Creative Print & Design (Wales), Ebbw Vale

For my parents
Moshe and Ora Bregman

Contents

List of Maps

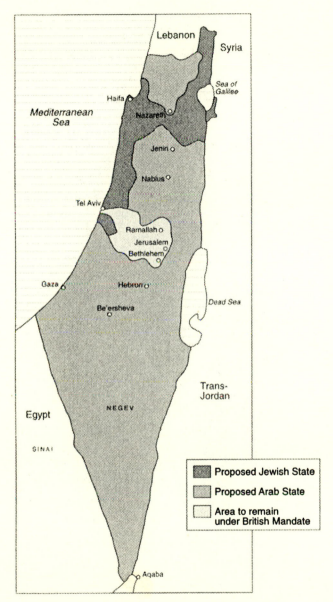

Map 1 Peel Plan for Partition of Palestine, 1937.

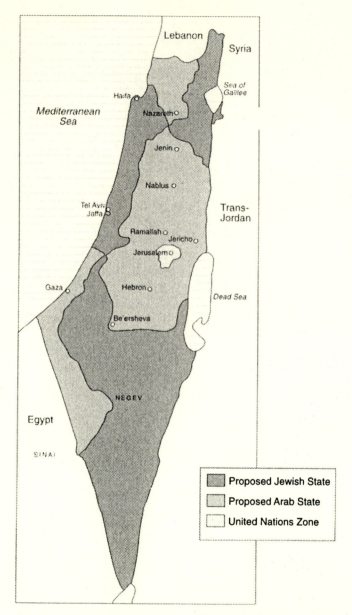

Map 2   UN Plan for Partition of Palestine, 29 November 1947.

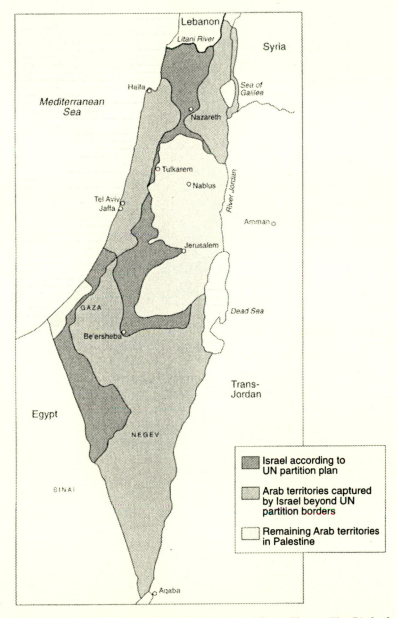

Map 3 Territories captured in 1948–49, adapted from Flapan, *The Birth of Israel: Myths and Realities* (Pantheon Books, New York, 1987), p. 50.

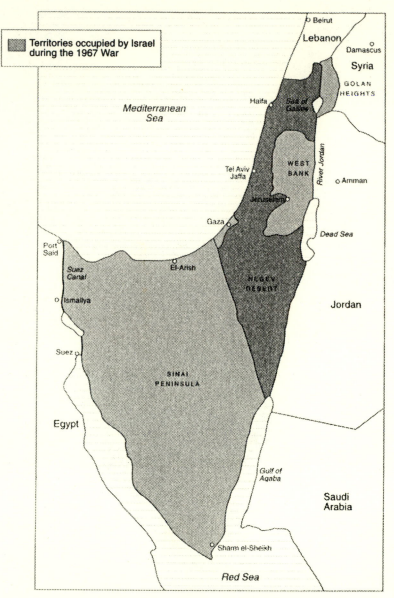

Map 4 Israel's Occupation in the Six-Day War, 1967.

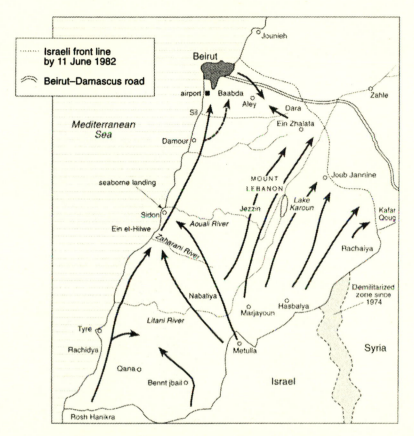

Map 5 Israel's Invasion of Lebanon, 6–11 June 1982.

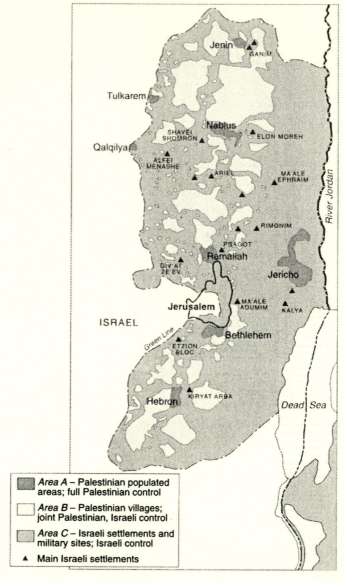

Area A – Palestinian populated areas; full Palestinian control

Area B – Palestinian villages; joint Palestinian, Israeli control

Area C – Israeli settlements and military sites; Israeli control

▲ Main Israeli settlements

Map 6   Oslo II, 28 September 1995.

Preface

A glance in the entries of a telephone directory and a visit to one of Israel's military cemeteries give the history of modern Israel in a nutshell. It is the story of Jewish immigration to the land of Israel and constant wars. It is also, particularly since the late 1970s, the story of attempts, some successful others less so, to forge peace between Israel and her neighbours on the principle of relinquishing land occupied by Israel in return for peace and recognition by Arabs and Palestinians.

Israel's past can be approached from many different angles for it is as much about the family, styles of music, sports and culture, as about issues of immigrations, wars and peace. For me, at least, a bird's-eye view is to see Israel's history as the gathering together of Jews from the four corners of the world into the piece of land which was once Palestine and then Israel; the struggle of these people to establish themselves in a hostile environment and expand the borders of the land allotted to them by the international community and, finally, their attempts to end the cycle of war by relinquishing some – though by no means all – the land they had occupied in previous wars and allowing some – though by no means all – Palestinian refugees of wars back home, in return for peace. The deeper levels of Israel's history are difficult, if not impossible, to fathom without a good understanding of these issues, and I have therefore reduced all other matters to a minimum and turned wars, immigration and the making of peace, into the driving themes of this work.

But where should one start? Surely at the beginning. But where *is* the beginning? Historians, mainly of Jewish stock, often range back to biblical times to begin the story of Israel, as if to assert that the development of modern Israel was a fulfilment of a biblical prophecy or, perhaps, the inevitable return of the Jewish people to the land of their fathers and the rebirth of a nation. This is not my approach. I do not regard the birth of Israel in 1948 as the fulfilment of a biblical prophecy nor as the continuation of any previous experience on this land, but rather as the outcome of two unfortunate causes. The first was the failure of nations to accept the Jews living among them as an integral part of society, and the second was the insistence of Jews – though by no means all of them – to lead their lives beside or on the fringe of societies and remain, as the saying goes, 'a people that dwelt alone', rather than being fully assimilated, both physically and culturally, into the people among whom they lived. These two elements – the unwillingness to absorb and to be absorbed – resulted in a situation, which has often been repeated in the history of nations, where, particularly in times of hardship, the non fully integrated segments of society have been made scapegoats.

It was, as I see it, the turning of Jews into scapegoats, mainly by European societies, and their persecution throughout many generations, reaching an appalling climax during the Second World War, that turned ideas of building a safe haven for the Jews and gathering them together, into reality. Rather than the fulfilment of a biblical prophecy or the rebirth of a nation, it was *harsh reality* that led to the birth and development of Israel on the land of Palestine. Hence my insistence that the story of modern Israel has little to do with biblical history and my starting it in 1897 with the launch of Zionism, the Jewish political movement for the establishment of a home for the Jewish people in Palestine.

Though written by a professional historian, this book is addressed not only to other academics, but as much to anyone seeking to make sense of Israel's recent history – how she came to be born and how she developed and established herself in the Middle East. My aim is to tell and, in the words of the historian A.J.P. Taylor, to help the reader 'understand what happened, and why it happened'. This is not an easy task for a writer of contemporary history who has to record events while they are still hot and lacks the luxury of being able to stand back and review events with the detachment possible to a historian who, say, chronicles the history of the French Revolution. Also, there is the daunting task of deciding what to leave out, for an event that now seems important may seem less so in, say, 100 years' time, when it can be put in a wider context. But selectivity is inherent in the task of telling history and must be employed vigorously and ruthlessly. In consequence, this work is far from being a full and comprehensive story of Israel's past.

Having said that, this relatively short volume contains much new, never before published material. Noteworthy are rare extracts from a radio exchange between air control and Israeli pilots on the fourth day of the Six-Day War, which shows that the Israelis did realize, quite early, that the ship they were bombing was indeed the

American USS *Liberty*, but nevertheless went on to attack her, the protocol of the secret meeting between Foreign Minister Moshe Dayan and President Sadat's emissary Hassan el-Tohami, in Morocco, in 1977 which shows that, contrary to common belief, no promise was made *a priori* to President Sadat, before his arrival in Israel a short time later, that he would get the Sinai back; and the Syrian Declaration of Principles of 1992 – the basis for talks between Israel and Syria – which appears here in its entirety for the first time. Even more notable are new exclusive revelations on the work of the most senior spy the Mossad ever had in Egypt and perhaps in the Arab world – a family relative of President Nasser as it is revealed here – and how, turning his back on the Mossad at the eleventh hour, he betrayed the Israelis and misled them, thus becoming the jewel in the crown of the Egyptian deception plan for the October 1973 war.

Those familiar with my previous works should immediately recognise that while the topic is different the method remains basically the same, namely a continuous narrative, though with occasional pauses for refreshment, which is based both on the written word and on oral history. For, as I have previously explained, although memory plays tricks with the past – events are sometimes remembered only in part, or in a jumbled order, or are used by witnesses to show their past in a better light – oral history is still an important complement to the written word and to our better understanding of the past. The list of those who helped me with their memoirs and gave so readily of their time is rather long, but I should like in particular to thank Meir Amit, Moshe Arens, Ehud Barak, Haim Bar-Lev, Mordechai Bar-On, Benyamin Begin, Yossi Beilin, Yossi Ben-Aharon, Benyamin Ben-Eliezer, Avigdor Ben-Gal, Yosef Burg, Warren Christopher, Ben-Zion Cohen, Avraham Dar, Robert Dassa, Uzi Dayan, Abba Eban, Rafael Eitan, Miriam Eshkol, Yeshayahu Gavish, Mordechai Gazit, Eli Geva, Benjamin Givli, Mordechai Gur, Eitan Haber, Yehoshafat Harkabi, Isser Harel, Yair Hirschfeld, Mordechai Hod, Yitzhak Hofi, Yehiel Kadishai, Lou Keddar, David Kimche, Tarje Rød Larsen, Yitzhak Levi-Levitza, Amram Mitzna, Yitzhak Molcho, Uzi Narkiss, Yitzhak Navon, Benjamin Netanyahu, Marcelle Ninio, Meir Pail, Dan Pattir, Matityahu Peled, Shimon Peres, Leah Rabin, Yitzhak Rabin, Itamar Rabinovich, Gideon Rafael, Ran Ronen (Peker), Elyakim Rubinstein, Yehoshua Saguey, Yossi Sarid, Uri Savir, Amnon

Lipkin-Shahak, Shlomo Shamir, Yitzhak Shamir, Ya'akov Sharett, Ariel Sharon, Yisrael Tal, Avraham Tamir, Ezer Weizman, Aharon Yariv, Danny Yatom, Re'havam Ze'evi and Eli Zeira. Finally, in a spotlight all of their own my three stars – Dana, Daniel and Maya – the most patient people in the world.

Ahron Bregman
London, 2002

I

The Road to Statehood, 1897–1947

THEODOR HERZL

It is fitting that a history of modern Israel should begin with the First
World Zionist Congress which was held at the concert hall of Basle's
Municipal Casino, Switzerland, on Sunday 29 August 1897. It was a
grand affair full of pomp and dignity attended by 197 Jewish delegates, who gathered to launch the Zionist movement. After three days
of deliberations, and not without much argument, a four-point declaration of principles, known thereafter as the Basle Programme, was
issued.

'The aim of Zionism', it went, 'is to create for the Jewish people a
home in *Palestine* secured by public law.' 'Home' was deliberately
used instead of 'state' for it was thought that the Ottomans, who then
ruled Palestine, would not relish the latter word. But there was no hesitation in signalling out Palestine as the site on which the Jewish home
should be established and the means of accomplishing this goal, that is
by 'the colonization of Palestine by Jewish agricultural and industrial
workers'.[1] Finally, went the Basle Programme, the Jewish home had to
be 'secured by public law', that is recognized by the family of nations.
The delegates at this extraordinary gathering at Switzerland also
decided to make the congress the supreme governing body of the new
Zionist Organization, to set up a Central Actions Committee consisting of 23 members to function as the governing body of the congress
and oversee activities between congresses, and to appoint five
members to act as a working executive. To become a member of the
Zionist movement, so it was agreed, candidates should be over 18,

abide by the Basle Programme and pay a yearly membership fee of one shekel, an ancient Hebrew coin, the equivalent of an Austrian schilling.

The Basle Congress was convened by 37-year-old Theodor Herzl. Born on 2 May 1860 in Budapest, he was given the Hebrew name Binyamin Ze'ev, along with the Hungarian Magyar Tivadar and the German Theodor. From the age of six to nine, young Theodor attended a Jewish parochial school, where he was exposed to some biblical Hebrew and religious studies. But he had, nevertheless, only the most superficial and distant acquaintance with Jewish history, literature, philosophy, law and ritual, and his bar mitzvah ceremony in the Budapest synagogue was, perhaps, his last dim memory of anything Jewish. In 1878, the Herzls moved to Vienna where Theodor studied law at the university. On completion of his legal studies he began to work for the Ministry of Justice, but soon bored he turned his back on the law and devoted himself to literary pursuits.

Strikingly handsome, sporting a full but perfectly trimmed beard, Herzl enjoyed the idle pleasures of a young man in peacetime Vienna, earning his living by journalism and the occasional writing of fashionable plays, moody travel pieces and feuilletons. He later became the Paris correspondent of the Austrian liberal *Neue Freie Presse,* and it was in France, while reporting, in December 1894, on the Dreyfus trial, that he was totally transformed.

Alfred Dreyfus was a Jewish French staff officer, who was court-martialled on a framed charge of high treason and espionage for Germany. He was found guilty, condemned to public degradation – his sword was broken and he was stripped of his uniform and insignia and taken away in chains – and imprisoned on Devil's Island, Guiana, for life. The scandalous anti-Semitism revealed during the course of Dreyfus's trial and the mob howling 'A mort, A mort les Juifs', shocked Herzl to the core and evoked in him memories of previous anti-Jewish sentiments, which he had himself experienced but had always brushed aside as isolated, random incidents rather than as a pattern. The fact that the whole Dreyfus episode had taken place in modern, cultured, civilized France, 100 years after the Declaration of the Rights of Man, tipped the balance within Herzl, and brought him to the conclusion that anti-Semitism was not merely religious but also racial and that the Jewish problem was intractable and that a new approach was needed. The result was *The Jewish State (Der Judenstaat)* which Herzl published in 1896 just a year before the

Zionist Congress of Basle. In the preface to this short, somewhat naive, work, some 500 copies of which were published by a small Viennese bookseller, Herzl said: 'The idea which I have developed in this pamphlet is a very old one: it is the restoration of the Jewish state.'[2]

It was, indeed, an old idea and Herzl, whose pamphlet eventually became the bible of the Zionist movement as he himself became its driving force was, by no means, the first to analyse the conditions of the Jews in their native lands, which were often appalling, and call for the establishment of a state as a solution to the Jewish problem. Earlier, Rabbi Zvi Hirsch Kalischer (1795–1848), after analysing the state of the Jews, came to the conclusion that the divine promise of restoring the Jewish people to their ancestral home should be ratified in an organized action and Eretz Yisrael – the Land of Israel – should become a Jewish 'settled land'. Moses Hess (1812–75), a German Jew, who had been through the whole gamut of assimilation and returned, in old age, to his own people, published *Rome and Jerusalem* in 1862 – it sold only 160 copies. In it he called for the establishment of a Jewish centre as a solution to Jewish suffering and discrimination. Arguing that the Jews had a considerable contribution to make to the whole of mankind and defining Judaism as an ethnic–spiritual entity which should be preserved and strengthened because it contained forces of the future, Hess linked this future to Eretz Yisrael, where the spiritual revival was destined to be fully realized. Leon Pinsker (1821–91), a physician of Odessa, in *Auto-emancipation: a Warning of a Russian Jew to his Brethren* (1882), analysed the psychological and social roots of anti-Semitism and defined the essence of the Jewish problem as emanating from the fact that, in the midst of the nations among whom the Jews reside, they form a distinctive element which 'cannot be assimilated'. Pinsker concluded that Jewry could liberate itself only if it took matters into its own hands, and he urged that all efforts should be concentrated on seeking Jewish emancipation from physical vulnerability by establishing a Jewish national centre – not necessarily in Palestine – which would convert the Jews into a nation among nations and restore their dignity. And there were many others who discussed the Jewish problem, as it was so often called, and offered their views on how this could be solved and how anti-Jewish prejudice and discrimination could best be dealt with.

What, however, distinguished Herzl from his predecessors was that whereas they were mainly *thinkers* Herzl was, first and foremost, a *leader, a man of action* committed to achieving practical results, and an *organizer,* who emphasized the need to build *institutions* to transform ideas into reality. And while the strength of Herzl's predecessors was mainly, though not exclusively, in offering a *diagnosis* of the Jewish problem, his was mainly in offering a detailed *prescription.*

At first, and even before convening the Zionist Congress in Basle, Herzl attempted to recruit prosperous Jews to the cause so that they would finance a mass Jewish emigration and the colonization of Palestine. He approached such people as Baron Maurice de Hirsch, a leading financial magnate, who had himself devised a programme to settle Jews in Argentina, a project into which he poured vast amounts of money. But the Belgian tycoon rebuffed Herzl by saying:

> All our misfortune comes from the fact that the Jews want to climb too high. . . . My intention is to keep the Jews from pushing ahead . . . after a few good years [in Argentina] I could show the whole world that the Jews make good farmers after all. As a result of this maybe they will be allowed to till the soil in Russia as well.[3]

Herzl's attempts with the head of the Viennese branch of the Rothschild family, Baron Albert von Rothschild, proved to be abortive as well and when his efforts to recruit the grandees all but failed, Herzl decided to turn to the little men – hence his decision to convene the Basle Congress.

After launching the Zionist movement, Herzl confided to his diary: 'At Basle I founded the Jewish state', and he lost no time in turning ideas into realities. Herzl strongly opposed piecemeal settlement in Palestine, or what he called 'gradual Jewish infiltration', which had already started even before the meeting of the first Zionist Congress at Basle, insisting that only a charter of settlement – a method which had been in use for nearly three centuries and had proved itself – will do. Knowing that Kaiser Wilhelm II of Germany had great influence with the Ottomans, who then ruled Palestine, Herzl, in a meeting with the German Kaiser on 18 October 1898, urged him that in his forthcoming audience with the Turkish Sultan he should make the Ottoman leader agree to a charter for a Zionist settlement in Palestine. A few weeks later, on 12 November, Herzl had a second meeting with the German Kaiser, who by then had already seen the Ottoman Sultan, but he found him reserved and cool. It later emerged that the Kaiser had not even raised the issue of Jewish settlement in Palestine with the Sultan but, instead, had pushed forward the Palestine colonization plans of the German religious Temple Sect. But even this failure did not, in any way, deter Herzl, or made him change track, and in the third Zionist Congress of August 1899, as well as in the fourth which met in London in 1900, Herzl continued to insist that the principal aim of Zionist policy was and remained the same, namely gathering the Jews and establishing a home for them on the land of Palestine, but not before acquiring a charter of settlement there.

With the conditions of the Jews, particularly in Russia and Romania, deteriorating by the day, Herzl decided to take the bull by the horns and ask for an official interview with the Sultan. The audience in Istanbul on 17 May 1901 did not, however, go well. Herzl was less than impressed with the 'small and shabby' Sultan of Turkey, whose beard, as he later recalled, 'was badly dyed', and who 'had long yellow teeth with a big gap on the upper right, and a bleating voice and feeble hands in white, oversize gloves'. He offered the Sultan financial help by which Jewish millionaires would assume responsibility for the huge national debt of the Ottomans and thereafter manage it, in return for a charter for the Jews to colonize Palestine. But, eager as he was to put his 'feeble hands' on Jewish money, the Sultan, nevertheless, insisted that all he could offer was permission for Jews to immigrate to Palestine provided that they became Turkish citizens, served in the Ottoman army and settled in scattered and dispersed fashion. This was definitely not what Herzl was after.

The shattering effect of his failed diplomacy turned Herzl – not immediately but gradually – towards England. Here, the expansionist and imaginative Colonial Secretary, Joseph Chamberlain, proved receptive to Herzl's advances and was to play a crucial role. In 1902, Chamberlain agreed to Herzl's proposal to settle Jews at El Arish, an oasis on the northern fringe of the Sinai Desert, a site which, in Herzl's view, had three main advantages. First, it had a very sparse indigenous population; second, it was quite unconnected politically with Egypt; third, and perhaps most importantly, El Arish was adjacent to and a step away from Palestine and thus the perfect jumping-off base to it. But Lord Cromer, the British Consul-General in Egypt, opposed the scheme on the ground that five times as much water would be needed for a Jewish settlement there as was available, and the Nile water, as his lordship put it, could not be spared. The plan fell through.

Chamberlain then offered Herzl the opportunity to establish a Jewish settlement in British East Africa, in areas of the Kenya highlands, bordering on Uganda, where the Jews could enjoy some measure of 'municipal autonomy' and could raise cotton and sugar. But while Herzl himself was inclined to accept this offer – he was looking for a *Nachtasyl*, an overnight, temporary refuge for the Jews who at this time suffered horrific pogroms in Kishinev, Bessarabia – this proposition met strong opposition especially – and ironically – from Zionist representatives of the persecuted Russian Jews, the very people whom such a settlement was primarily designed to help. They insisted that a Jewish home should be, as they put it, 'in Palestine or nowhere' and Herzl's argument that East Africa was not intended as a substitute for Palestine, and that like Moses he was leading his people to their goal, Palestine, in an apparent detour, could not convert them to his view. Anyway, the issue soon became academic, because English colonists in Africa strongly opposed a mass immigration of Russian Jews to the region and, as a result, Chamberlain dropped the idea.

Herzl's dream of living to see the day of a Jewish homeland being established was dashed. It all took longer than he had hoped and he was a very sick man. Worn out by his labours, he died at the age of 44 of a debilitating heart condition and was interred in Vienna next to his father's grave; 45 years later Herzl's remains were moved to a hill just west of Jerusalem which became Mount Herzl, later a large military cemetery containing fallen heroes of Israel's wars.

What was Herzl's legacy? With the benefit of hindsight we can say that his cardinal achievement, apart, of course, from his invention and creation of the Zionist movement as a political force during an effective public life of fewer than nine years, was his success in putting Zionism on the map of world politics. In crude modern terms – from a PR point of view Herzl's campaign was an extraordinary success in installing the Zionist idea in the minds of people – Jews and non-Jews alike. But perhaps his biggest failure was not to realize that the Jewish form of patriotism – especially its eastern European type – would never accept anything but Palestine as home for the Jews, and that his attempts to settle Jews in such places as El Arish or Africa were doomed and could only divide the Zionist movement. Indeed, Herzl left behind an organization which was torn and split between the Territorialists, who were eager to look for a land outside Palestine for the Jewish people, and the Zionists-of-Zion, who formed the majority of Zionists in the Congress and remained faithful to Eretz Yisrael as the one and only site where Jews should be settled. The Territorialists, led by the English writer Yisrael Zangwill, failed, however, to advance their cause beyond the stage of exploration of possibilities in Surinam, Libya, Iraq, Angola, Canada, Honduras, Australia, Mexico, Argentina and even Siberia, before they sank into insignificance. The Zionists-of-Zion, on the other hand, won the day, not only over the Territorialists but also over other Jewish groups, notably the Bund, which was founded in the same year as the Zionist organization, operated in Russia and eastern Europe and vehemently opposed Zionism on the ground that the Zionists were diverting Jewish energies to a hopeless dream to the detriment of the Bund's more realistic efforts to improve the lot of the Jews in the countries where they lived.

The idea of settling Jews on sites other than Palestine was officially killed by the seventh Zionist Congress which, meeting in Basle from 27 July to 2 August 1905, swore to remain devoted to Eretz Yisrael.

ERETZ YISRAEL

But what was Eretz Yisrael? In the mind of many Jews, it was the 'Promised Land' and the 'Land of Milk and Honey', but in reality it was a barren, rocky and obscure province which had been ruled by the Ottoman Empire since 1517. On this inhospitable little strip of land on the eastern littoral of the Mediterranean, Jews and Arab Palestinians lived side by side. By the time the first Zionist Congress met at Basle some 400,000 Arabs and a Jewish minority of 50,000 or so lived on this land. Most of the Jews were pious Orthodox who depended for their existence on charitable offerings of Jewish societies in Europe – *haluka* (division) as it was known – which were distributed to them by the communal organizations set up largely for that purpose which were known as *kolelim*. While the traditional motive for coming to Eretz Yisrael had been prayer and study, followed by death and burial in the holy soil, in the late nineteenth and early twentieth centuries a new type of Jew – secular and often idealistic – began to arrive in Palestine, many of them driven from their native lands by persecution.

The first Aliyah

They arrived not gradually but rather in a succession of immigration waves called *Aliot*, plural of the Hebrew word *Aliyah* which means 'to go up' or 'ascend'. The first *Aliyah* took place from 1882 to 1903 and was instigated by Storms in the South, the pogroms against Jews in the

spring of 1881, which followed the assassination of Tsar Alexander II
by revolutionaries. Spreading across the regions of permissible Jewish
settlement from Odessa to Warsaw, an area populated by 7 million
Jews, this wave of violence lasted eight months and caused thousands
of Jews to emigrate to western Europe, South America and, especially,
to the United States, where they founded the largest and most powerful
community in Jewish history. But about 25,000 of them, mostly young,
secular Jews who had received ideological instruction in the first organized nationalist Jewish groups such as Hovevei Zion (The Lovers
of Zion), which was set up in Odessa in the early 1880s, or in counter-
parts such as Bilu (from the Hebrew initials in the biblical phrase 'O
House of Jacob, come, let us go!', Isaiah 2: 5), which was set up in the
Kharkov region in January 1882, headed to Palestine. Those hardy and
dedicated Jews regarded themselves as pioneers rather than refugees
and they were determined to build up a new, modern Hebrew society in
Palestine, based on agricultural settlements and Jewish labour.

In Palestine, on 31 July 1882, newcomers of this first *Aliyah*
founded, on a stretch of uncultivated and uninhabited sandy land, just
eight miles south-east of Jaffa, a new settlement which they called
Rishon Lezion (First to Zion), and which became the first settlement
to be established by Jewish settlers from outside Palestine. In Rishon,
as this town came to be known, these Jewish pioneers established the
first Hebrew language kindergarten and elementary school in the
country and in honour of the founding of this town, a Romanian
Jewish poet, Naphtali Herz Imber, who later lived in America in
squalor, misery and alcoholism, wrote a poem, *Ha-tikvah* (The Hope)
which was to become the Zionist hymn, and later with a few alter-
ations, the state of Israel's national anthem. The poem went:

> As long as deep in the heart
> The soul of a Jew yearns
> And towards the East
> An eye looks to Zion
> Our hope is not yet lost
> The age-old hope,
> To return to the land of our fathers
> To the city where David dwelt.

But not all went well for the young Jewish pioneers of the first *Aliyah*.
For difficulties in adjusting to the climate of Palestine, illness, problems

of poor soil, lack of agricultural know-how, strong opposition from the Ottoman authorities and from local Arabs, and the need to employ guards, all diminished their resources, brought them to the threshold of bankruptcy, often even to starvation, and to the limit of their strength. We should remember that these pioneers had to fend for themselves because they had arrived in Palestine before the Zionist movement was even born.

It was Baron Edmond de Rothschild, head of the French branch of the House of Rothschild, who came to the rescue, practically adopting the Jewish villages in Palestine and saving their pioneers from total collapse. The Baron, who in spite of an eccentric, rather dictatorial character, came to be known among the Jews as 'the known benefactor', gave an immediate gift of 3000 francs to Rishon Lezion, and introduced vineyards into this town whose wine was so successful that it was awarded a gold medal in the Paris Exhibition of 1900, taking its place alongside the historically acclaimed 1899 vintages of Margaux and Château-Lafite.

For 16 years the Baron invested tremendous sums of money in direct support of the infant Jewish settlements – he built schools and hospitals and equipped the settlers with state-of-the-art agricultural equipment, training and other services. But the Baron was a businessman who regarded his colonies as a business proposition rather than as a charity, and saw his investment in Palestine in terms of costs and profits, which defeated the original purpose of the Jewish settlers which was the redemption of the land. Gradually tensions grew between the Baron's clerks and the settlers. In 1900, after noticing symptoms of eroded initiative among the Jewish farmers and growing dependency on Arab labour – by that time the 200 settlers of Zichron Ya'akov employed 1200 Arabs and the 40 Jewish families in Rishon Lezion employed 300 Arab families – Edmond de Rothschild announced that he would withdraw his patronage and stop channelling funds to the settlements. This led to such an appalling crisis that the settlements were soon floundering on the verge of ruin and by the year's end nearly a quarter of the Jewish families had departed.

The first *Aliyah* did not produce distinguished leaders or influential institutions to leave their mark on the future Jewish community in Palestine and historians still debate its real importance. Its claim that it instigated Jewish agricultural settlement in Palestine is not wholly true, for there had already existed agricultural settlements even before the arrival of the first *Aliyah*, notably the Mother of the Settlements,

Petach Tikva (Portal of Hope) which was founded in 1878 by a group
of veteran Jerusalemites led by Joel Moshe Salamon, and Rosh Pinna
(Cornerstone), in northern Palestine, which was built by Jews from
Safed. Nevertheless, it is undeniable that the settlers, who installed
themselves in Turkish-ruled Palestine at the end of the nineteenth and
the beginning of the twentieth century, managed to establish, in spite
of tremendous difficulties, 28 agricultural settlements with a total
Jewish population exceeding 5000, covering an agricultural area of
about 62,350 acres. More importantly, future waves of Jewish immigrants established their first foothold in the agricultural villages set up
by members of the first *Aliyah.*

The second Aliyah

The second *Aliyah* to Palestine started in 1904 and, like its predecessor, the first *Aliyah,* was instigated by pogroms in Russia where, in
1903, Jewish communities came under attack. Kishinev (Bessarabia),
in particular, was the scene of a violent pogrom where 45 Jews were
killed, more than 1000 wounded and 1500 houses and shops looted
and destroyed before the police intervened, on the afternoon of the
second day, to stop the violence. As previously shown, this pogrom
spurred Herzl, the energetic leader of the newly established Zionist
movement, to look for a temporary asylum for Jews in such places as
Africa and elsewhere. But Jews from these affected areas did not wait
and emigrated mainly to America but also to Palestine; 94.3 per cent
of the 35,000 Jews who arrived in Palestine in the decade before the
outbreak of the First World War came from such pogrom-ridden areas.

One of the most notable characteristics of this *Aliyah* to Palestine
was that it included the generation of the founding fathers of the future
Jewish state, notably its first three prime ministers: David Ben-Gurion
(Gruen), Moshe Sharett (Shertok) and Levy Eshkol (Shkolnik), as well
as Israel's second President Yitzhak Ben-Zvi, and the first Speaker of
the Knesset, Yosef Shprinzhak, among others. Of these, David Ben-
Gurion was perhaps the ablest and most important leader.

Born in 1886 in Plonsk, Poland, David Gruen, as he was then
known, arrived at the port of Jaffa on 7 September 1906. He was so
appalled by the dirt and poverty of Jaffa that he left immediately and
hastened on foot to Petach Tikva. He soon changed his name from
Gruen to Ben-Gurion (meaning son of Gruen) and became an agricultural labourer in, among other places, the vineyards of Rishon Lezion,

the settlement founded by members of the first *Aliyah*. Only five feet three inches tall with a granitic chin thrusting belligerently forward, Ben-Gurion was a tough and uncompromising, often single-minded, young man of superb organizational abilities.

He belonged to a group of young, secular and idealistic men and women, driven by a fierce sense of mission and bent on 'redeeming the land' and proving that they were fit not only for commerce, as their detractors often charged, but also for physical work. They adopted Spartan ideals and high standards of personal behaviour and rejected all emblems of comfort such as smart clothes, strong drink, tobacco and the ownership of personal possessions. They survived on a diet of lentils and bean soup and lived in mud huts, which often crumbled in summer heat, and in tents which leaked and were often washed away in winter rains. These young pioneers, who cut themselves adrift from home, family and a whole way of life, had to fight not only against nature – many of them contracted malaria and died – but also against members of the first *Aliyah*, who favoured Arab labour to the more expensive and less experienced and docile *chaluzim* (pioneers in Hebrew) of the second *Aliyah*. Life was such a grim struggle for these young people – by the time their feet touched the land of Palestine all notions of it as a land of milk and honey were dead and buried – that only three out of ten of them stayed in Palestine, while the rest returned to their countries of origin or emigrated elsewhere, to Europe or across the Atlantic.

Yet in spite of many difficulties, the ten years or so of the second *Aliyah* was a period of institutional and cultural development for the Jewish project in Palestine. The Zionist movement, which under Herzl and his successor David Wolffsohn was attempting to obtain a charter to settle Palestine, was by now fully engaged in 'penetration' into Palestine, precisely the policy which it had so much opposed a few years before. In 1908, the Zionist movement opened its first office in the country at Jaffa, and under the direction of a German economist and agronomist, Dr Arthur Ruppin, used a yearly budget of 30,000 francs to purchase tracts of land for new Jewish settlements from absentee Syrian, Lebanese and Palestinian landlords and from churches and foreign companies.

Greater political awareness and a desire to form organizations of their own which reflected their aspirations, led members of the second *Aliyah* to form political parties. In 1905 Ha'poel Ha'tzair (The Young Worker) was established. It stressed the need for collective settlement of the land as the foundation for the building of the Jewish nation, emphasized the importance of focusing on nurturing the Hebrew language and Hebrew labour and devoted considerable efforts to practical ways of assisting workers, such as by creating cooperative workshops, kitchens and stores, sick funds, labour exchanges and workers' libraries. A month later, in November 1905, Po'alei Zion (Workers of Zion) was established. This was more sectarian than Ha'poel Ha'tzair; one faction headed by Yitzhak Ben-Zvi, a future President of Israel, and buttressed by migrants from Rostov, insisted on the primacy of socialism, while the other, led by Ben-Gurion, placed more weight on nationalism. Also, and unlike Ha'poel Ha'tzair, Po'alei Zion considered itself as part of the international labour camp and celebrated May Day with the usual display of red flags.

Perhaps the most important achievement of Ha'poel Ha'tzair was its founding, in 1909, of Ha'shomer (The Watchman) which under Yisrael Shochat became the first defence organization of the Jewish community in Palestine. Members of Ha'shomer – their number never exceeded 90 of whom 20 were women – were a kind of Hebrew cowboy. They rode on horseback, wore Arab headgear and carried arms. Like many of their other colleagues of the second *Aliyah,* they wished to make a complete break with their Diaspora past and their representation as non-fighters, by taking new names for themselves: Barak (Lightning), Tsur (Rock), Eytan (Solid), Oz (Strength) among others. The importance of Ha'shomer was not so much in passing military experience on to the next generation as in generating a mental transformation by showing that Jews, who for generations had been the victims of violence and abuse, could fend for themselves and defend their lives and property by force.

In 1910, members of the second *Aliyah* settled on Um Juni, a tract of land on the southern shore of the Sea of Galilee, and formed the first kibbutz which they called Degania (Cornflower). This new form of agricultural settlement was based on full cooperation among its members in work and on equal profit sharing. By 1914, there were 14 such farms in Palestine. The urban Jewish sector in Palestine was also developing in earnest during this critical period and, with the endorsement of the eighth Zionist Congress, the Director of the Palestine Office, Arthur Ruppin, lent funds to a private development company which established a modest garden quarter on the sand dunes outside Jaffa. By 1914, this encompassed 139 houses and 1419 Jewish inhabitants. It was named Tel Aviv (Mound of Spring, from a site mentioned in the Bible) and under the firm direction of its first Mayor, Meir Dizengoff, it developed into the first all-Jewish city.

It was not, however, only the physical growth of the Jewish project in Palestine which characterized these years. There were also cultural developments, most notably the adoption of Hebrew as a daily language. This, in itself, was a revolution, for Hebrew, the language of the Bible, seemed by that time to be dead, buried and not suitable for daily use. But thanks to the efforts of the Russian-born philologist, Eliezer Perlman, better known as Eliezer Ben-Yehuda, and not without stiff resistance from the older, religious inhabitants of Palestine who held that the use of Hebrew for secular purposes was sacrilegious – Hebrew gradually came back to life. In 1904, Ben-Yehuda published the first volume of a Hebrew dictionary and went on to compose three more volumes. Like so many things in Palestine, the adoption of Hebrew as a daily language was not achieved without a fight, and in the period just before the outbreak of the First World War, the *Yishuv* was rocked by what came to be known as the War of the Languages. This reached its height in October 1913 when just a few months before the opening of the Haifa Institute of Technology (The Technion), the board of the Hilfsverein der Deutschen Juden, which financed the project, ruled that teaching should be in German rather than Hebrew. This decision produced a wave of protests from Jewish teachers throughout Palestine and, fortified by support from abroad, they forced the board to agree that within four years Hebrew, rather than German, should be exclusively used in this institute.

PALESTINE IN THE FIRST WORLD WAR

In August 1914 war broke out and Turkey, which then ruled Palestine, joined the Central Powers, Germany and Austria-Hungary, on 31 October. It then abolished the Capitulations regime which until that time had protected the Jews of Palestine as foreign nationals and decreed the expulsion of 'nationals of enemy states'. The first batch of Jews, 6000 in all, were expelled via the port of Jaffa to Alexandria on 17 December 1914 and by the end of the war the number of Jews expelled from Palestine reached 15,000.

For the remaining Jews in Palestine, many of whom applied for Turkish citizenship in order not to draw attention to themselves, the main concern was economic. For when war broke out most of them were still relying on funds collected in the Diaspora. These funds, which came principally from the countries considered enemy states, largely dried up as a result of the war. The Jewish agricultural settlers also suffered great hardships because their livelihood was dependent on exports of citrus and wine which ceased with the outbreak of war. A catastrophic locust invasion in 1915–16 caused colossal damage to fields and plantations. Jewish settlers struck out at the locusts with their brooms, swatted these insects with sacks, lit fires in the hope of smoking them off – all to no avail. Thus, general hardships, expulsions, persecutions and epidemics led to a dramatic reduction in the number of Jews in Palestine which fell from 86,000 to a mere 56,000 between the outbreak and the end of the war.

With Jews fighting on both sides, the leaders of the Zionist Organization, based in Berlin at the outbreak of war, declared neutrality, but many Jews, both in Palestine and elsewhere, concluded that they could benefit from the defeat of the Ottomans and they were determined to help the British win the war. One individual who took positive action in this direction was Vladimir (Ze'ev) Jabotinsky.

Born in the Black Sea port city of Odessa on 5 October 1880, Ze'ev Jabotinsky grew up in a secular Jewish home before studying in Berne and Rome. He was profoundly affected by the outbreak of anti-Semitism in eastern Europe and became interested in Zionism as a solution to anti-Semitism, taking part, aged 21, in the sixth Zionist Congress. In the Zionist movement Jabotinsky belonged to the right-wing faction, which was the main opposition to the socialist forces, seeing the main aim of Zionism as establishing a Jewish majority in Palestine, even against the wishes of the Arab majority, and creating an 'Iron Wall' of Jewish armed force to protect the Jewish project in Palestine. Jabotinsky was an impressive man, blessed by striking literary and linguistic talent, and he was a magnetic public speaker. In later years he became the spiritual father of Israel's right.

When the First World War broke out, Jabotinsky happened to be in Egypt as a correspondent for a leading Russian daily, *Russkiye Vyedomosti*, when chance brought him in contact with a certain Joseph Trumpeldor, formerly a Jewish Russian army officer and a remarkable soldier, who in 1904 had lost his left arm while fighting in the Tsarist army at Port Arthur. Having been expelled by the Turks from Palestine, Trumpeldor was living in Egypt, where with British permission he joined forces with Jabotinsky in setting up, in March 1915, Jewish military units – the Zion Mule Corps.

Members of these units, mostly raised from among the nearly 30,000 Jewish refugees interned at the Gabbari quarantine buildings outside Alexandria, were allowed to wear their own shoulder flashes bearing the Shield of David and they were trained by the British in transporting supplies and ammunition. When the Allies landed in Gallipoli, the Zion Mule Corps were also mobilized and were used to provide transport during the Gallipoli campaign. Whereas Trumpeldor himself served as a captain in this Jewish force, his co-founder of the Zion Mule Corps, Jabotinsky, declined to join because he regarded the task allocated to the Corps, transportation, as a humiliation.

In Palestine itself, Aaron Aaronson, a Zionist and the director of the experimental agricultural station at Athlit, northern Palestine, also concluded, along with his associate, Avshalom Feinberg, that there was no prospect for Jewish settlement in Palestine under the Ottoman regime, and that assisting the British to occupy Palestine could benefit the Jews. For this purpose Aaronson established a spy network which he called Nili (from the Hebrew *Netzach Yisrael Lo Yeshaker*, meaning The Eternal Jewish Shall Not Fail) and, taking advantage of the fact that as a respected agronomist he was allowed free movement in Palestine, he gathered important data which he then transmitted to a British frigate that anchored off the Athlit coast every two weeks at nightfall. To the British General Edmund Allenby, who was preparing to invade Palestine from the south, Aaronson's ring supplied data on Ottoman troop movements, defences around Beersheva, data on the weather, location of water sources and malarial swamps, and information on the condition of roads. But Aaronson's Nili ring did not survive for long. In September 1917, one of the ring's carrier pigeons fell into the hands of the Turks, who then rounded up the group, arrested its members, except for the leader Aaronson who managed to escape, and then tortured and killed them.

In response to pressure from Jewish elements, the British government, in August 1917, approved the establishment of a special Jewish infantry regiment, a Jewish Legion, to be assigned to combat duties on the Palestine Front to assist the British in liberating Palestine from the Ottomans. Called the 38th Royal Fusiliers, given the subtitle of The Judaeans, and nicknamed by the British army 'The King's Own Schneiders', the battalion was placed under the command of Lt. Col. John Henry Patterson, former commander of the Jewish Mule Corps. The first 120 recruits were veterans of the original Mule Corps, and with the active efforts of Jabotinsky, the driving force behind this initiative, who had volunteered as a private but later was promoted to lieutenant and became Patterson's aide-de-camp, the unit recruited from the immigrant Jewry of London's East End. In February 1918, the 38th Royal Fusiliers marched at its inauguration ceremony from the barracks in the Tower to Whitechapel in the East End with fixed bayonets, and the Lord Mayor took the unit's salute in front of the Mansion House. It was subsequently sent off to Palestine where it was joined by two other Jewish battalions, recruited in America and Canada, the 39th Battalion under Lt. Col. Eleazar Margolin, and the 40th Battalion commanded by Col. M. F. Scott and made up of volunteers raised in Palestine itself. None, however, saw active service.

The Balfour Declaration

While in Palestine the war significantly slowed down the development of the *Yishuv* and plunged the Jewish community into crisis, on the international arena the Zionist movement went from strength to strength. In a brilliant exercise of sustained persuasion, lobbying and influence, a small group of Zionists, in England, induced the British government, in the winter of 1917, to publish a declaration supporting the establishment of a 'national home' for the Jews in Palestine. It was the kind of international charter which, two decades before, Herzl had failed to obtain from Turkey. The prime mover and architect behind the Balfour Declaration was a Zionist by the name of Chaim Weizmann, later the first President of the state of Israel.

Of Russian stock, he was born in 1874 in the township of Motol, in the district of Kobrin close to the Polish border, the third of 12 children of a Jewish family, and he came to learn of the efforts of Theodor Herzl, whom he was later to criticize, while a student in the Berlin Polytechnic. At the turn of the century young Chaim came to Edwardian England to teach biochemistry at Manchester University. There, in 1906, destiny took a hand and led to a historic meeting between him and Arthur James Balfour while the latter was contesting a seat at Manchester in the general election. Balfour, we should recall, was Prime Minister when his Colonial Secretary, Joseph Chamberlain, made Herzl an offer, in 1902, to settle Jews in eastern Africa. Balfour was curious to know why elements in the Zionist movement, including Weizmann himself, were then opposed to the offer and he was keen to meet one of the opponents – hence his meeting with Weizmann. In his broken English Weizmann explained to Balfour why Jews could not accept the British proposal to have Uganda instead of Zion. 'Supposing I were to offer you Paris instead of London, would you take it?' Weizmann asked. 'But Dr Weizmann,' said Balfour, 'we have London.' To which Weizmann responded, 'That is true, but we had Jerusalem when London was still a marsh.' Balfour, as he later recalled, never forgot this encounter with Weizmann and he left the meeting knowing much more about the strong ties between the Jews and Palestine.

Weizmann was not Herzl's immediate successor – he would become the leader of the Zionist movement in 1920 and retain this office until 1946 – but he gradually became the leading voice of world Zionism, especially its East European branch. It was Weizmann who coined the term 'Synthetic Zionism', which called for the combination of two approaches as the way to build a Jewish state in Palestine: 'political' Zionism, which was aimed at giving priority to diplomatic activity to secure an international charter, and 'practical' Zionism which stressed land purchase and settlement in Palestine.

Like Theodor Herzl before him, Weizmann had given Zionism a personal image. But unlike Herzl who interacted only with world leaders but had no rapport with ordinary people, Weizmann was at ease in both worlds. He was suave – in spite of a tendency to pass from ecstasy to exaltation and back again – intelligent and a shrewd advocate of the Zionist cause. He always knew how to scale his demands to what was obtainable in practice and this was crucial to his success in obtaining the Balfour Declaration for the Jews.

This declaration of 2 November 1917 was contained in a letter from the British Secretary of State for Foreign Affairs, Arthur James Balfour (subsequently Earl of Balfour) to Baron Rothschild, a leader of English Jewry and the President of the British Zionist Federation. The letter was formally discussed by the British Cabinet on 3 September and 5 October, and it is curious that the issue of such a declaration was bitterly fought by the only Jew in the Cabinet at the time, Edwin Montagu, the Secretary of State for India, who was, nevertheless, in the minority for the Cabinet voted for and approved this declaration on 31 October.

Although short, a single 68-word-long sentence, the declaration was a highly significant statement, for it was the first time that a great power – and England was still a world power of the first rank – had openly pledged its full support to the idea of helping the Jews to have their 'national home' in the land of Palestine whose population, at the time this declaration was issued, was around 87 per cent Arab. Of course, Weizmann would have preferred to secure Britain's agreement to his more grandiose demand of support for 'the establishment *of* Palestine *as the* [italics added] national home of the Jewish people', rather than the hazy definition of British support for 'the establishment *in* Palestine of *a* national home for the Jewish people'. But it was still a great achievement and the declaration was received by Weizmann and his colleagues in Britain, America and, indeed, Palestine with great enthusiasm.

It is hard to say for sure why the government of Lloyd George authorized Balfour to write to Lord Rothschild as he did. One of the reasons, often put forward, is that Balfour himself regarded the Jews as the most gifted race to appear on earth since the ancient Greeks, but that without a territorial centre they lacked dignity and that this had to be put right – and by England. Another explanation is that the British government believed that a pro-Zionist declaration would swing American Jewish opinion towards the Allies and so influence President Woodrow Wilson to enter the war on the side of the Allies. Also suggested was that open support for Zionism would detach Russian Jews from the Bolshevik Party and so ensure that the revolution remained not only moderate but the belligerent ally of France and Britain. True or not, some of these often proposed attempts to explain why the British issued the far-reaching Balfour Declaration seem to be based on extremely exaggerated ideas of the extent of Jewish influence in the world.

Back in the Middle East, General Allenby invaded Palestine and on 11 December 1917 marched into Jerusalem. By 1918, the whole of Palestine was in British hands after General Allenby had defeated Gamal Pasha's fourth Turkish army, thus putting an end to four centuries of Ottoman Turkish rule in Palestine.

THE POST-WAR PERIOD

Militarily speaking, the assistance given by the Jews to the British occupation of Palestine was insignificant and the British army would have defeated the Ottomans with or without Jewish help. Nevertheless, the Jews did provide some assistance in recruiting people to serve in the British army and by spying on the Turks, and they expected that after the war, in return for their goodwill, the British would reward them by implementing the Balfour Declaration. Indeed, when in January 1918 the Middle East Committee of the British Cabinet resolved to send a Zionist Commission to Palestine to liaise between the administration there and the Jewish community and to prepare the way for the 'establishment of the Jewish national home', it seemed as if the Jews were about to get their reward. But when in April this Zionist Commission which was headed by Weizmann and came to be known as Va'ad Ha'tzirim arrived in Palestine it found that the British authorities on the ground were less cooperative than their masters in London. Perhaps to an objective observer the cold shoulder showed by the British in Palestine towards Weizmann's Jewish Commission was no surprise, for the last thing a freshly established administration needed was perpetual nagging and obstruction by a Jewish delegation, which was abrasive in demanding Jewish rights immediately. Indeed, given that at that time the Jews were a tiny minority in Palestine – 55,000 compared with some 560,000 Arabs – the demands of the Commission, such as granting the Hebrew language equal status with Arabic in all official proclamations, appointing a Jew as Mayor of Jerusalem, and ensuring that half the members of the municipal council of Jerusalem were Jewish, ending restrictions on Jewish immigration and employing Jews in the public service, could only be regarded as excessive. However, Weizmann was not an objective observer but rather the Zionist who had obtained for the Jews the Balfour Declaration in which the British pledged themselves to assist the Jews in setting a national home in Palestine, and he was disillusioned by what he regarded as the coldness and even hostility of many of the British, both military and diplomats, in Palestine. Weizmann's frequent attempts in London to countermand decisions made by the military administration in Palestine if he thought them unfavourable, did nothing to mend fences between his commission and the authorities in Palestine.

The third Aliyah

Disappointed as it was to be shown a cold shoulder by the British in Palestine, the Jewish leadership nevertheless hoped that the image of the British as liberal and their pledges as expressed in the Balfour Declaration would lure growing numbers of Jewish immigrants to Palestine, for this was crucial for the building of the national home. Jews did indeed come to Palestine after the war, though in smaller numbers than had been expected by the Jewish leadership; 26,900 Jewish immigrants arrived in Palestine between 1919 and 1923.

These newcomers of the, so-called, third *Aliyah*, came largely from Russia with the help of the Zionist emigration organization, He'chalutz (the Pioneer) and upon arriving they organized themselves into Gdud Ha'avoda, the Labour Battalion. By 1921, detachments of the battalion could be found throughout Palestine, cleaning swamps, building roads, living in tents and turning all their income over to a central committee. Another group of pioneers to arrive in Palestine in the post-war years came from Galicia and other regions of Poland, and like members of Gdud Ha'avoda they also took on any jobs Palestine required, especially the building of roads. And the legacy they left, apart from roads, was poetry. For the working groups engaged in road building proved a fertile ground for a unique cultural flowering which produced a new style of Hebrew poetry and literature, inspiring such poets as Avraham Shlonsky, Uri Zvi Greenberg and Alexander Penn, among others. Nowhere was the mood of the post-war settlers more apparent than in the literature of the third *Aliyah*, with its emphasis on self-sacrifice and national revival.

But Palestine – though a tough place – was never without people and its Arab population looked with growing dismay how European Jewish immigrants were building an infrastructure, which though it surely benefited them as well, was to all intents aimed at establishing an exclusive Jewish state on land which the Arabs fervently believed to belong to them alone. And fearing that Jewish immigration and land-purchasing would result in Jewish domination, the Arabs of Palestine resorted to violence to stop the Jewish project or, at least, to demonstrate their unhappiness with it. On 1 March 1920, Arab Palestinians attacked the isolated Jewish settlement of Tel Hai in northern Palestine and in the ensuing battle, Joseph Trumpeldor, who as previously mentioned, was the co-founder with Jabotinsky of the Zion Mule Corps during the First World War, was killed along with seven comrades. Trumpeldor was not the first to die this way, but he was the kind of awe-inspiring figure of whom national myths and legends are made and his last recorded words as he lay mortally wounded: 'It is good to die for our country' – or was it perhaps a hefty Russian curse? – entered Israeli mythology. Arab violence continued and, on 4 April 1920, which was the Jewish Passover, a Muslim religious procession broke into the Jewish quarter of Jerusalem killing 6 Jews and injuring 200; 6 Arabs lost their lives and 32 were injured.

But these tragic events did not, in any way, halt the build-up of the Jewish national home. On 19 April 1920, some 20,000 Jews, more than 70 per cent of all registered Jewish voters, elected members for Asefat Ha'nivharim (the Elected Assembly) which was a sort of electoral college and, on 7 October, the Assembly, 314 members belonging to 20 different parties, convened in Jerusalem to choose the Va'ad Leumi (the National Council), an executive of 38 members which undertook to represent the interests of the Jewish community before the British authorities. Then, in December 1920, the Labour movement in Palestine established the Histadrut, the General Federation of Labour for Jewish Workers, which under Ben-Gurion was, officially, to be a trade union. But it developed into something more than that, and it gradually became a large-scale owner of cooperative and industrial enterprises and became involved in stimulating Jewish immigration, employment services for immigrants and the actual creation of a broadly based working class.

Perhaps the most important achievement of the Histadrut during this period was the creation of the Haganah (Defence). It was essentially a clandestine organization operating without the approval of the British authorities in Palestine and dedicated to maintaining the security of Jewish settlements as seemed essential after the latest Arab violence. However, unlike Ha'shomer, which was established by members of the first *Aliyah* and which was a closely knit elite organization, the Haganah was intended to be a broad-based workers' militia. It recruited its members, among others, from veterans who had taken part in the First World War, notably Jews who served with the Zion Mule Corps and the Jewish Legion, and it produced some competent military leaders, notably Eliahu Golomb, an original tactician and future commander of the organization, and Yitzhak Sadeh, a burly Russian immigrant, Red Army veteran, poet and wrestler. In later years the Haganah would become the nucleus of the Israeli army.

THE BRITISH MANDATE

British forces had conquered Palestine and British arms were on the spot at the end of the war. Therefore, the San Remo Conference which decided, on 24 April 1920, to assign the Mandate of Palestine under the League of Nations to Britain – though formal ratification had to await a vote of the League of Nations on 22 July 1922 – did no more than confirm an accomplished fact.

For the Jews the Mandate document was a diplomatic victory, for it embodied a formal recognition of the principle of a national home for the Jews in Palestine as originally made in the Balfour Declaration of 2 November 1917. It was, in a sense, even more important than the Balfour Declaration, for unlike the latter which was a statement of policy that any subsequent British government could have ignored, the Mandate was an international engagement, signed and ratified by the principal Allied Powers acting through the League of Nations and, as such, it raised the Balfour Declaration, which was incorporated into it, to the status of a treaty.

Soon afterwards, the British military administration was replaced by a civil administration which assumed control of Palestine. Sir Herbert Samuel, a respected British Jew and Zionist, was appointed High Commissioner of Palestine. He was a distinguished statesman with many years' service in the British Cabinet behind him and bore a reputation for rectitude. Being a Jew, he was regarded by the Jews – at first at least – as the new Messiah leading them back to their ancient land under the Union Jack.

Continuing Jewish immigration and land purchase increased Arab indignation and by 1 May 1921 bloody communal disturbances broke out again in Palestine. They started in Jaffa, the gateway and the principal point of Jewish immigration into Palestine, where the friction between Arabs and Jews was most in evidence. From Jaffa the disturbances spread to the Muslim pilgrim shrine of Nevi Saleh near Ramleh, then northwards and southwards through the Jewish townships of the coastal plain. The casualties were appalling: 47 Jews were killed by Arabs and 48 Arabs were killed, mainly by the British police; 146 Jews and 73 Arabs were injured. Although the Arabs had been the aggressors, Herbert Samuel enforced a temporary ban on Jewish immigration – it would be lifted in July 1921 – for he rightly regarded Jewish immigration as the source of the troubles.

However, with enthusiastic Jews on the ground and the backing of the Zionist movement, the development of the Jewish centre continued unabated in spite of Arab violence and British restrictions. In London, a Zionist Conference convened and established Keren Ha'Yesod – the Palestinian Foundation Fund – which was to work side by side with Keren Ha'Kayemet, which had been founded at the fifth Zionist Congress in 1901. While the latter was dedicated to the redemption of the soil, the new fund was to be mainly used for building agricultural settlements. In 1921, Keren Ha'Yesod built ten new Jewish settlements on 17,500 acres in the valley of Jezereel. These included the first Moshav – smallholder's settlement – Nahalal. In the same year, Pinchas Ruthenberg, a Russian Jew who had settled in Palestine after the war and devoted his considerable energies to devising a plan for the electrification of Palestine with water power from the Jordan and Yarmuk rivers – received a concession from the Mandatory government to generate electricity in Palestine. In the next five years Ruthenberg set up power stations in Tel Aviv, Haifa and Tiberias which were to prove crucial for the industrial development of Jewish Palestine.

In London, in an attempt to assuage Arab fears, the British government issued, on 1 July 1922, a new statement of policy. Known as the Churchill White Paper, it excluded Transjordan from the Mandated area of Palestine, thus restricting the Jewish national home to the area west of the Jordan river, and it also rejected the notion of creating a predominantly Jewish state by limiting Jewish immigration thenceforth to the 'economic capacity of the country'.

The fourth Aliyah

This last restriction did not really matter. For with growing anti-Semitism in Poland, the imposition by the Polish government of a confiscatory income tax that bore heavily on Jewish businessmen, and the closing of America's doors to Jewish immigration, Palestine became the major outlet; 63,000 Jewish immigrants arrived in Palestine between 1924 and 1926.

These newcomers were very different from previous Jewish immigrants. They were not enthusiastic, pioneering Zionists prepared for personal sacrifice like members of previous *Aliyot*, but rather ordinary urban Jews who preferred city life to road works or agriculture in isolated settlements. Eighty per cent of them packed into the cities, primarily Tel Aviv, and their arrival led to an unprecedented construction boom, with housing being hurriedly thrown up and built at a staggering pace with no plan or sense of permanence. Tel Aviv expanded to north and east and in an 18-month period, beginning in mid-1924, its population nearly doubled from 21,500 to 40,000. In Haifa, northern Palestine, the suburb of Hadar Ha'Carmel was built, while in Jerusalem the new suburbs of Beit Ha'Kerem and Rehavia were established.

There were setbacks with a crisis in 1926 when new currency regulations in Poland, the country from where most Jewish immigrants came, prevented the export of capital and thus restricted departures. Between 1926 and 1927 the number of newcomers to Palestine dropped from nearly 14,000 to 3034 and by 1928 it was as low as 2178. Soon there was a surplus of apartments, a collapse of the building sector and, as a result, a dramatic increase in the number of unemployed. The Histadrut, the workers' trade union, which by now was also the biggest employer of Jews in Palestine, sought to ease the situation by setting up labour bureaux and bodies to provide social and economic aid. By 1929, immigration began to revive – 5249 Jewish immigrants came to Palestine – and there was clear evidence of a slow but steady emergence from the economic crisis.

That year in Zurich, the Zionist Congress set up the Jewish Agency under Weizmann's leadership with a headquarters in Jerusalem and a branch in London to represent world Jewry vis-à-vis the British administration in Palestine. This alarmed the Arabs of Palestine, who regarded the Agency as yet another step towards the realization of a Jewish state in Palestine, and with tensions running high an absurd dispute occurred when a Jewish demand for the erection of a light screen in the alley near the Wailing Wall to separate Jewish female worshippers from male worshippers, which gave rise to Muslim objections, lit the powder keg and led to the outbreak of a devastating wave of violence. From Jerusalem, where it started on 23 August 1929, violence spread south to Hebron and north to Safed, encompassing other Jewish settlements on the way. In a week of disturbances 133 Jews were killed by Arabs, 60 in Hebron alone, and 339 others were injured; the Jews killed 6 Arabs, and the British police killed 110 and wounded 232.

In what had by now become a pattern, the British government appointed a commission of inquiry which, headed by Sir Walter Shaw, a retired Chief Justice, was tasked to inquire into the immediate causes of the outbreak of violence and to propose policies to prevent any recurrence. After five weeks of hearings, the commission issued its report on 31 March 1930. It concluded that the Arab violence was a reaction to their sense that Jewish immigrants were taking control of Palestine and that the deep-seated reason for the disorders lay in the Arabs' fear for their economic future. Another commission, this time led by Sir John Hope-Simpson, a retired Indian civil service official and an authority on agricultural economics, was then sent out to Palestine to report on the likely effects of Jewish immigration on Arab rural life. After three months of travel investigation and aerial surveys of landholdings, Hope-Simpson issued a massive 185-page report on 20 October 1930. Its bottom line was that any further Jewish immigration to Palestine would, inevitably, be injurious to the Arabs and that there was no room for further agricultural development in the country. Later that month, on the basis of these findings, the British Colonial Secretary, Lord Passfield (better known as Sidney Webb), issued a White Paper which was a new statement of policy in Palestine. This not only foreshadowed severe restrictions on Jewish immigration to Palestine but also imposed an embargo on additional Jewish land purchases.

The Zionists raised an uproar and came up with their own data showing that Passfield's claim that, as he put it, there was no room 'to swing a cat in Palestine' was inaccurate and that, in fact, standards of living of the Arabs of Palestine shot up as a result of Jewish immigration and the infusion of Jewish capital in payments for land, wages, rents and services. Aghast at what they regarded as British capitulation to Arab violence, the violation of the letter and the spirit of the Mandate and repudiation of the very purpose of the Balfour Declaration, the Zionists pilloried Passfield as the worst enemy of the Jewish people since Haman. Worse still, Chaim Weizmann, in protest, resigned as President of the World Zionist Organization and the Jewish Agency and this was regarded as a blow to Zionist–British relations, for Weizmann, more than anyone else, symbolized the links of Britain with the Jewish people.

The Jewish outcry against the Passfield White Paper forced Prime Minister Ramsay MacDonald's hand and in a letter to Weizmann he simply reversed the policy expressed in the White Paper. He said that the obligation to facilitate Jewish immigration and make possible dense settlement of Jews on the land is 'still a positive obligation of the Mandate', and it can be fulfilled 'without jeopardizing the rights and conditions of the other part of the Palestine population'. By repudiating the Passfield White Paper – in fact, effectively killing it – MacDonald made the Jews happy, but he also proved to both Jews and Arabs alike that British policy in Palestine could be altered if enough pressure was applied.

Back in Palestine, in January 1931, Jews went to the polls to vote for a new Elected Assembly with two main parties in contention. The first was Mapai, which was a socialist party of the labour movement led by such people as Ben-Gurion, and which advocated the formation of a moderate socialist society with nationalization of the means of production and the ownership of land. The other was the Revisionist Party which, under the leadership of Jabotinsky, considered itself the representative of the bourgeoisie and capitalism. The two parties were in dispute over the preferable strategy for establishing a Jewish state in Palestine. While Mapai wished to build a Jewish state on only one side of the Jordan river, its western side, the Revisionists urged the immediate creation of a Jewish state on both sides of the river. In the elections Mapai won a landslide victory and the Revisionists, with 20 per cent of the votes, remained the second largest party in Palestine.

The fifth Aliyah

A wave of 175,000 Jewish immigrants, the so-called fifth *Aliyah*, arrived in Palestine between 1932 and 1939, mainly as a result of rising anti-Semitism in Europe. The great majority of the immigrants came from Poland, which still had the largest concentration of Jews in the world, with only 21 per cent from Germany. Nevertheless, this wave of immigration was dubbed 'The German *Aliyah*', perhaps because of the novelty of the arrival of German Jews in a country which was, so far, built on eastern European immigration. Thanks to a transfer agreement reached between Zionist leaders and the German Foreign Ministry, the German Jews were able to import part of their savings in the form of goods, and when this fully £63 million in imported capital was invested in Palestine, it led to a significant economic expansion, notably in the metal trades, textiles and chemicals; the number of industrial firms rose from 6000 in 1930 to 14,000 in 1937, and the workforce grew from 19,000 to 55,000 in the same period. As a result of the infusion of so much money into the economy there was a mini economic boom in Palestine, at a time when the world was suffering severe depression. Also, as many of the newcomers were professionals, they were a great boon to academic institutions, notably to the Hebrew University and to other research and medical institutes.

The German immigrants brought to Palestine not only money and professional skills, but also the seeds of cultural change, with greater emphasis on the field of classical literature and the development of musical creativity. Thus, with the arrival of players and music lovers and on the initiative of the famous violinist Bronisleb Huberman – in 1892 aged ten he had played the violin before the Emperor Franz Joseph in Vienna – the Palestinian Orchestra was established and became known all over the world.

Perhaps the main feature of this *Aliyah* was that it gave the growing Jewish community in Palestine a distinctly European veneer and brought about a change in norms as the tempestuous Russian pioneer, fired by his ideals, made way for a more measured settler, ready to devote himself to the cause only after calm consideration and precise planning. The German immigrants stood out and were very visible in the Palestinian scene. They were often called Yecke, the name apparently derived from *Jacke*, or jacket, and derived from the fact that they were highly genteel and clung to the garment in a warm country where Jews usually wore, not jackets, but open-necked, short-sleeved shirts. As these newcomers were mainly urban, they settled in the cities which led, in turn, to an even greater expansion of urban centres. Tel Aviv and its suburbs absorbed no less than half of the new immigrants, the number of Jews in Jerusalem shot up and Haifa's Jewish population nearly tripled between 1931 and 1935.

It was in this period that the rivalry between the socialist branch of the Jewish community in Palestine and the right-wing revisionist branch reached a shocking climax in the cold-blooded murder, on 16 June 1933, of Chaim Arlosoroff, one of Mapai's most outstanding and brilliant young leaders, who was shot at point-blank range on the shore of Tel Aviv. Arlosoroff's fault, in the eyes of some Jews, was that he was too much of a moderate, a disciple of Weizmann, and advocated the maintenance of good relations with the British Mandatory authorities. Nobody was indicted for the assassination, but suspicions were fastened on one of Jabotinsky's revisionist followers, Avraham Stavsky. This tragic episode was a shattering innovation, for although generous exchanges of insults were stock commodities of Jewish politics, killing was previously unknown.

THE ARAB REBELLION, 1936–39

In the mean time, Arab fears of being swamped by the growing tide of Jewish immigration drove them over the edge of despair into the abyss of an open rebellion. It was sparked, on 19 April 1936, by rumours in Jaffa that two Arab Palestinians had been killed by Jews in adjoining Jewish Tel Aviv. Arab mobs then turned on Jews and riots continued for three more days in which 16 Jews were killed and 5 Arabs were shot by British police intervening to stop the violence. A week later, on 25 April, in a rare display of unity, the usually feuding Arab factions in Palestine joined forces and set up the Arab Higher Committee. It was headed by the chief religious dignitary, the Mufti of Jerusalem, Hajj Amin el-Husseini, a man of talent and huge ambition, an uncompromising, stubborn and narrow-minded nationalist, who called a general strike which soon turned into a full-scale national uprising encompassing the whole of Palestine.

It was a genuinely popular uprising mainly of the *fellahin*, the Arab tenant-land workers who were systematically deprived of the land – which was theirs by work and birth – through its sale by rich landlords to the Jews. Stipulations in the Land Transfer Ordinance of 1920 required that in the event of the land changing hands, the Arab tenants should be left an area sufficient for their sustenance. But the Jewish purchasers wanted the land without tenants so they frequently had clauses inserted in the sales agreements stating that the property should be free of tenants when handed over to them.

The Arab Rebellion was directed against Jews but even more so against the Mandatory government which faced an Arab demand to end the Jewish immigration into Palestine. Arab bands attacked roads, bridges, telegraph lines, police stations and British officials and paralysed the smooth running of the Mandate.

Ironically, if by resorting to violence the Arab intention was to halt the development of the Jewish project in Palestine the result was the exact opposite, since the Jews were only pushed into ever growing self-reliance. For with the rebellion there came an acute shortage of Arab labour which was promptly filled by Jewish labour, and Jewish produce replaced Arab fruit and vegetables in markets. Also, with the Arab closure of the Jaffa harbour, the British allowed the Jews, on 15 May 1936, to build a jetty at Tel Aviv, thus enabling the Jews to realize an old dream of having their own independent port.

But perhaps more significantly, the Arab Rebellion accelerated the development of a Jewish military force in Palestine. In 1936, some time after the outbreak of the violence, the British recruited a first batch of 1240 Jewish supernumerary police – they were called Notrim – and later that year informed the Zionist leadership that a special force of constables would be permitted to remain in being with its arms, provided the already existing Haganah, which was formed back in 1920 as a clandestine self-defence Jewish organization, was disbanded and its weapons handed over. But with the growing Arab violence the British in Palestine tacitly dropped this demand, and in the following two years the Jewish force was further expanded until, by 1939, it totalled some 14,500 men, amounting to nearly 5 per cent of the total *Yishuv* population.

It was, however, in the guise of the Special Night Squads (SNS) that the Jews benefited most from the collaboration with the British during, and as a result of, the Arab Rebellion, and in particular from the military genius of an eccentric little Scotsman, a devout Christian who became a fervent Zionist of a mystical brand – Charles Orde Wingate.

When Captain Wingate arrived in Palestine as an intelligence officer in the British 5th Division, in September 1936, he obtained permission from General Sir Archibald Wavell, commander of British forces in Palestine, to recruit and organize members of Jewish Haganah for his SNS. His intention was to use these squads to lead his own guerrilla campaign against the rebellious Arabs, and, in particular, to protect the Iraqi Petroleum Company pipeline, which was a target for sabotage by Arab irregulars who used to wreck it by blowing holes in it and setting it alight.[4] Wingate personally trained his Jewish men and inculcated his squads with principles of offence, daring, surprise, deep penetration and high mobility, and he led them in operations against the Arabs of Palestine. Described by Weizmann as 'my favourite madman', Wingate became, after a few months in Palestine, the most popular British personality since Balfour among Palestinian Jews, a sort of Lawrence of the Hebrews. However, Wingate's tactics were little more successful than other British military methods in suppressing the Arab Rebellion and desperate to sort out this problem, the British government sent 70-year-old Lord Peel out to Palestine to investigate the causes of the riots and recommend a solution.

A man of strong personality and common sense combined with imagination, Lord Peel arrived in Palestine on 11 November 1936. He held 66 meetings, toured Palestine, returned to England and, on 7 July 1937, published his verdict – a massive, cool and balanced, 404-page-long report, which included maps and statistical indices. His Lordship reached the melancholy conclusion that the policy of conciliation, carried to its furthest limits, had failed, and pronounced that both the Jewish claim to Palestine on grounds of historical and religious connections and the Arab claim on grounds of 13 centuries of continuous occupation had validity and thus the conflict between Arabs and Jews in Palestine was not one of right against wrong but that of right against right. Lord Peel concluded that the Mandate was 'unworkable' and he proposed a bold solution to the strife along the lines of a judgement of Solomon, namely the reconstruction of Palestine through partitioning the land between Arabs and Jews. He proposed that the north-western part of Palestine, namely the coastal plain and Galilee, some 3125 square miles which accounted for about 20 per cent of Palestine – though its most fertile land – should be given to the Jews to become a Jewish state. The remaining land, proposed Lord Peel, should be given to the Arab Palestinians to become an Arab state which should then be united with the Emirate of Transjordan under Emir Abdullah. Jerusalem, Bethlehem and a corridor to the sea were to remain under British Mandatory control (see Map 1).

The Jews discussed the Peel proposal at the 20th Zionist Congress which was held in Zurich from 3 to 17 August 1937. Its passage through the Congress was stormy with Partitionists (the 'Jasagers', as they were called), led by Weizmann, Ben-Gurion and Moshe Shertok (then head of the Political Department of the Jewish Agency), and anti-Partitionists (the 'Neinsagers'), raging against each other. Weizmann argued that the Jews would be fools not to accept a state even if it were, as he put it, 'the size of a tablecloth', and that Lord Peel's proposal was a historic opportunity not to be missed and one which should be exploited to the full. The opposing point of view found an able spokesman in 74-year-old Menachem Ussishkin, a dynamic, stocky Zionist of the old guard, who was firmly opposed to acceptance of anything less than a Jewish state on the whole area of Palestine. Jabotinsky and the Revisionists, although no longer formally members of the Zionist Organization after breaking away from it and setting up an alternative organization, vehemently opposed the Peel Plan. In the end, however, the 'Jasagers' won the day and the principles of the Peel Plan were accepted as a basis for further negotiations with the British government on more favourable borders than those allotted.

A large part of the explanation why the Peel proposal was accepted by the Jews – even though the area proposed for them was minute and the plan as a whole was unsatisfactory in many other ways – may lie in the continuing deterioration of the Jewish situation in Germany, which gave any proposal for a safe haven in Palestine a compelling glamour which outweighed criticism in many minds. Another explanation lies in the view, shared by many, that the proposed scheme was to be regarded as a *temporary* arrangement, a stepping-off ground for further advance, and that after the formation of a large Jewish army, in the wake of the establishment of a Jewish state on the land allotted by the Peel proposal, the Jews could abolish partition and expand to the whole of Palestine.

However, the Arabs killed the Peel scheme. Their 400 delegates, representing all Arab states with the sole exception of Yemen and including a delegation from Palestine, gathered on 8 September 1937 at Bludan, Syria, and after lengthy, and often heated debate, rejected the proposal out of hand by declaring that Palestine was an integral part of the Arabian homeland and no part of it should be alienated.

The British government was faced with such a strong opposition by Arabs and, indeed, at home, that it simply shied away from the plan, justifying this on the basis of a report by yet another commission (the Woodhead Report) and saying that the difficulties in implementing partition were so great that the Peel solution was 'impracticable'. So the scheme was dropped – but not for long. Partition would come to life a decade later.

With no diplomatic solution to the troubles in Palestine, the Arab Rebellion was renewed and intensified and Palestine was ablaze from end to end. Arab guerrilla bands attacked Jewish settlements, buses and civilians, causing casualties and damage and leading to a heated debate in the *Yishuv* over how to react to Arab violence.

There were two schools of thought. The official policy maintained by most of the organized *Yishuv* was to adhere to a policy of self-restraint, of non-reprisal – *Havlagah* in Hebrew. This called on Jews to defend themselves by returning fire, holding their positions, but not engaging in counter-terror or in retaliation. The line of thought behind this policy was that Jewish restraint would keep the Mandatory authorities, to some extent, on the Jewish side, maintain British goodwill and that the Jews would eventually be rewarded for good behaviour. *Havlagah*, however, was extremely unpopular with some members of the Haganah, particularly among Haganah B, a splinter group which had already left the main organization in the spring of 1931 and which now urged a policy of reciprocating violence for violence and hitting back at the Arab attackers. Growing differences of opinions and clashes of temperament within Haganah B led to an eventual split with some members returning to the parent Haganah, but more than half forming themselves into a new organization, Irgun Zvai Leumi (Hebrew for the National Military Organization) commonly known as the Irgun.

In the mean time, in spite of continuous Arab violence, new Jewish settlements were set up at an ever-increasing pace using a unique method known as tower and stockade. The principle was simple: by nightfall, young Jews would venture on land, put up a prefabricated construction protected by an outer stockade and wooden tower with searchlight so presenting the British authorities and the Arabs with a fait accompli. Fifty-five such new settlements were built by this method during the Arab Rebellion and this, needless to say, did little to allay Arab anxiety or bring an end to the violence in Palestine.

In February 1939, in the shadow of growing tensions in Europe over Hitler's moves and fears over his intentions to annex the rest of Czechoslovakia, Britain convened a Round Table Conference of Arabs and Jews at St James's Palace in London. It was now essential for Britain to stop the violence in Palestine and quieten down the Middle East in order to channel all energies and free as many troops as possible to face the European war which seemed almost certain.

When the St James's Palace Conference opened, on 7 February 1939, the Arabs – members of the Higher Arab Committee, representatives of Egypt, Iraq, Saudi Arabia, Transjordan and the Yemen – refused to sit round the same table as the Jewish representatives. Chamberlain's address of welcome had, therefore, to be read twice, once to the Jews and once to the Arabs, and the British hosts had the daunting task of being the go-between between Arabs and Jews in futile attempts to reconcile the irreconcilable. When the parties failed to agree on anything, Britain, on 15 February, presented a series of final proposals to both sides. The Jews were asked to accept an immigration ceiling for several years and afterwards to base additional immigration upon Arab consent. The Arabs were requested to make special minority provisions for the Jews. Both Jews and Arabs, however, rejected these proposals out of hand, and with this impasse the conference fell apart, though negotiations continued until May 1939, against a background of dramatic international events, notably the setting up, on 7 May, of a formal German–Italian military alliance.

With the failure of the conference Britain produced her own solution which it was determined to impose on the parties by issuing a new Statement of Policy enshrined in the White Paper of 17 May 1939. This was the last pre-war landmark of British policy in Palestine and this time the Whitehall see-saw took the Arabs up, giving them more satisfaction than they had ever had before, and let the Jews down with the most violent jolts of all. It provided for the limitation of Jewish immigration to Palestine by placing a definite ceiling on the number of Jews allowed into the country – 75,000 over the next five years and thereafter only what the Arabs could be induced to accept. It also provided for Palestine to be divided into three zones in which the sale of land to Jews would be, might be, and would not be permitted, respectively, thus stringently limiting land transfers from Arab to Jewish hands.

It was a stunning reversal of policy which reinterpreted Britain's Mandatory obligations and seemed to guarantee an independent Palestine with an Arab majority and an end of all hopes of a Jewish state. It was a bitter blow for the Jews coming at a time when the Nazi persecution in Germany and Austria was becoming truly frightful. This new line of policy finally destroyed – though the process was gradual – the lingering reality of Anglo-Jewish cooperation which had had its ups and downs, was never happy, except in some early stages, but which nevertheless had achieved much. From now on, Britain was regarded by a growing number of Jews as the enemy of Zionism.

PALESTINE IN THE SECOND WORLD WAR

In Palestine, as in most places, Hitler's invasion of Poland on 1 September 1939, which was followed by the Anglo-French declaration of war on 3 September, was received with dumbfounded shock which was exacerbated by the sudden economic disaster which struck Palestine. For with the interruption of Mediterranean trade, a shut-down of the building industry and an immediate decline in the citrus industry, there came terrifying unemployment which saw half the labour force of Palestine out of work before the year's end.

With the outbreak of war, the leadership of the *Yishuv* was facing a dilemma. On the one hand the Jews were on a collision course with the British government because of her policies in Palestine, but on the other hand, Britain was fighting the Nazis. Treading a fine line, Ben-Gurion, the leader of the Jewish community in Palestine, proposed a complex political path, symbolized by his slogan: 'We shall fight with Great Britain in the war as if there were no White Paper, and we shall fight the White Paper as if there were no war.' Unlike most slogans it exactly defined policy and fighting Hitler *and* the White Paper became the two aims of mainstream Zionism which were carried out through-out the war years with neither aim ever laid aside.

Jewish scientific and medical centres were now placed at the disposal of the British forces and the *Yishuv*'s economy was progres-sively linked to Britain's war effort which, in turn, relieved the economic difficulties caused by the outbreak of war. About 85,000

Jewish men and 54,000 women registered for war service and approximately 250 Palestinian Jews volunteered for parachute drops into
Nazi-occupied Europe to organize resistance. On one occasion 32
Jewish volunteers were dropped but most of them were caught,
tortured and killed including a woman – Hannah Senesh – whose death
acquired legendary fame in Jewish history.

As in the First World War so in the Second, the Jews were anxious
to be embodied in the British army, not only to go down fighting the
Nazis, but also in the expectation that after the war they would be
rewarded whether in the form of further immigration to Palestine or in
some other way. In spite of strong opposition, especially from the
authorities in Palestine, to having an armed Jewish force, Churchill,
who replaced Chamberlain as Prime Minister, did not object and
thanks to his support a Jewish Brigade was established in September
1944. It came under the command of Brigadier Ernest Benjamin and
was a purely Jewish formation with its own Zionist banner and with a
blue and white shoulder flash inscribed with the Shield of David worn
by the troops. Early in 1945, some 3400 Jewish soldiers in the brigade
were shipped off for combat duty in Europe, where they were attached
to the British 8th Army and fought in battles in Italy. When the fighting ended, members of the Jewish Brigade took advantage of their
presence in Europe to rescue Jewish refugees and dispatch them to
Palestine, and they also formed a unit, called the Avengers, which took
upon itself to assassinate Nazis throughout Europe.

But parallel to their cooperation with the British and in line with
Ben-Gurion's policy, Jews in Palestine fought against the British
restriction on immigration, a fight which became violent at times. In
September 1939, the ship *Tiger Hill* succeeded in landing on the beach
of Tel Aviv, and most of the immigrants managed to land and hide
from the British police. On 11 November 1940, the ships *Pacific* and
Milos were intercepted by the British navy and escorted into Haifa
Harbour where their 1700 Jewish refugees were transferred to the SS
Patria, which was bound back for Mauritius. But on 24 November the
boat was blown up by the Haganah, which attempted to put the
vessel's engines out of order and leave it lying waterlogged in shallow
water, thereby forcing the British to permit the Jews to stay. But the
plan miscarried and 240 Jewish refugees and a dozen policemen were
killed by the explosion or died by drowning. During the war years, in
spite of immense practical difficulties, over 50,000 illegal Jewish
immigrants reached the shores of Palestine.

The Lehi and the Irgun

The British refusal to allow more than a mere trickle of Jewish immigration led to a revulsion of feeling among the Jews of Palestine and to a growing internal dispute between those who were willing to cooperate with the British against Hitler and those who insisted that the fight against the Mandate should not only be indirect, that is by bringing in illegal immigrants, but also physical, aimed at expelling the British from Palestine. The Irgun, like the Haganah, had refrained from attacking the British during the initial phases of the war; however, with a growing opposition within the organization to continuing the truce, a split occurred, in August 1940, and a group headed by Avraham Stern resigned and formed themselves into a new underground organization – Fighters for the Freedom of Israel, better known as the Lehi from its Hebrew initials or, by the British, as the Stern Gang.

Avraham Stern – Yair was his *nom de guerre* – who led this small band out of the Irgun was born in Poland in the part which was then Russian, in 1907 and settled in Palestine in 1925. He was exceedingly intelligent, a brilliant scholar, a poet, good-looking and always wore a suit with a tie even in Palestine at a time when the tone was set by men in shorts, open-necked rough shirts and sandals. Denouncing the Irgun's truce with the British as a capitulation, Stern and his followers went deeply underground and fought their illegal war against the British, hitting not so much at installations, but at servicemen. The anthem of the Lehi, written by Stern himself, was titled *Hayalim Almonim* (Anonymous Soldiers) and was a reflection of the single-mindedness of this small but determined organization:

> When we fall and we die
> Inside houses, on streets,
> We shall be buried quietly and in silence.
> But thousands and thousands of others shall vie
> For the right to fight and to die, for ever.

There were no officers, no hierarchy, no headquarters, just a Central Committee, but nevertheless discipline in the Lehi was extremely strict. So hostile was the Lehi to the British that it sought contact with the Axis powers and, in particular, with Fascist Italy in the hope that should Mussolini conquer the Middle East, he would allow a Jewish

state to be set up in Palestine. When Mussolini's troops were defeated
in North Africa, Stern attempted to establish contacts with Otto von
Hentig, the German emissary in Vichy Syria, in the hope of striking a
similar deal with Germany. But Stern's initiative came to nothing and
when details of it leaked to the press public opinion turned firmly
against his small band. On 12 February 1942, a detachment of CID
men under the command of a British officer, Jeffery Morton, broke
into Stern's garret in busy south Tel Aviv, where the underground
leader was hiding in a wardrobe. He was dragged out, his hands were
shackled and he was shot dead. This was the end of the Lehi for a time
though it was to rise again later in the war.

The Irgun underwent three changes of leadership during the Second
World War. Following the death of Jabotinsky in 1940, David Raziel
became the leader and his tenure was characterized by cooperation
with the British in the war effort. Raziel even undertook British-spon-
sored missions and was himself killed, on 20 May 1941, while participating with the British in an operation in Iraq to put down the
pro-Nazi rebellion of Rashid Ali el-Keylany. After Raziel's death a
new temporary leadership was appointed to lead the Irgun, until
command was finally transferred to Menachem Begin.

Begin was born in Poland, the son of a prosperous timber merchant,
and he was raised in the heavily Jewish city of Brest-Litovsk. He
completed his law studies at Warsaw University, where he met Ze'ev
Vladimir Jabotinsky, founder and leader of Revisionist Zionism and he
joined the movement. When the Soviet army occupied eastern Poland,
in September 1939, Begin was arrested and dispatched to a Siberian
prison camp. In 1942 he was released and less than a year later was
shipped to Palestine for advanced training under the British. There,
with the tacit approval of his police officers, he left his unit and joined
the Irgun.

Thin-faced, studious looking with nothing commanding about him,
Begin, nevertheless, was a charismatic leader and meticulous down to
the tiniest detail. He was also an exceptionally gifted propagandist.
Within a few months of taking over, he succeeded in resurrecting the
Irgun, which had been in a major crisis following the death of Raziel,
and in February 1944, in response to the continuing British policy of
restricting Jewish immigration to Palestine, Begin declared an end to
the truce. His rationale was that with the German defeat at El Alamein
(in November 1942) and the advance of British troops westwards
along the African shore, the danger of a German invasion of Palestine

and the destruction of the national home no longer existed and, there-fore, the Jews had to turn on the British, since they were the obstacle to the development of the national Jewish home. Under Begin, the Irgun blew up British government offices, police and military stations, and its people raided arms dumps. Assassination was not ruled out either. Thus, in August 1944, Begin's people carried out an abortive attempt on the life of the departing High Commissioner, Sir Harold MacMichael, whom the Jews held personally responsible for the *Struma* disaster on 24 February 1942; after Britain's refusal to allow this ship to land in Palestine, it sank in the Black Sea with 768 Jewish refugees on board.

The Lehi also recovered from the death of its leader Avraham Stern who was replaced by a Central Committee of three men. The chairman was Nathan Friedmann-Yellin whose *nom de guerre* was Gera and who was a ruthless man of brilliant mind. Then there was the scholar Dr Yisrael Eldad, and finally Yitzhak Yezernitzky (later Shamir), a broad-shouldered, bushy-browed man of secretive and retiring dispo-sition who took the *nom de guerre* Michael after Michael Collins, the Irish patriot and Commander in Chief of the Irish State Army who was shot dead in 1922. Gera was the planner, Eldad the propagandist and Michael – Shamir – in charge of military operations.

Under this new leadership and financing itself by occasional bank robberies and funds extorted from Jewish shopkeepers, the Lehi engaged in indiscriminate shooting at British police and assassina-tions. On 6 November 1944 in Cairo, two young members of the Lehi assassinated Britain's Deputy Resident Minister of State, Middle East, Lord Moyne. This murder not only staggered Britain but also the mainstream Zionism leadership which, fearing that such methods would turn world opinion against the Jews, instructed the Haganah, its militia in Palestine, to hand lists of Irgun and Lehi activists over to the British. This was done from November 1944 to June 1945 and came to be known as 'the Season'.

TURNING ON THE BRITISH

On 8 May 1945, Germany finally capitulated and in Britain, in July, the general election brought the Labour Party into office. Labour had always followed a pro-Zionist policy and in the elections the party had demanded that the 1939 White Paper be rescinded and pledged itself categorically not to prevent the Jews from achieving a majority in Palestine by bringing in more immigrants. In office, however, Ernest Bevin, Clement Attlee's Foreign Secretary, announced that the 1939 White Paper policy would be maintained and carried out. There are few cases in twentieth-century British history of a contrast between promise and performance so great as that shown by the incoming Labour administration, particularly by Bevin who, eager to remain on good terms with the Arabs whose oil Britain urgently needed, seemed to do his best from his first day in office to negate Balfour.

By adhering to the policies of the 1939 White Paper, the British government exposed its troops in Palestine to the rage of the Jews, and achieved the almost unthinkable in uniting Ben-Gurion's moderate Haganah with the two more violent organizations, the Irgun and the Lehi. The three organizations set up the Jewish United Resistance Movement which attacked and sabotaged British property and installations throughout Palestine. The British responded by bringing 80,000 extra troops to Palestine to put down Jewish opposition but to no avail. The violent Jewish campaign continued, reaching a high point on 22 July 1946, when the Irgun blew up a wing of the King David Hotel in Jerusalem, which housed the offices of the Mandatory government secretariat and its military headquarters. This act of terrorism, as the British rightly regarded it, in which 91 civilians including 15 Jews were killed, was devastating in both its symbolic aspect as well as its physical impact and profoundly shocked the British in Palestine and in England. The British in Palestine struck back, on Saturday 29 July 1946, by executing Operation Shark which was carried out by a massive military force. Some 787 people were arrested, some arms caches were discovered, but the prime target of the operation, Menachem Begin of the Irgun, could not be found.

In Europe, in the mean time, Jewish emissaries purchased ships and transferred survivors of the Holocaust to Palestine, mainly from French ports but also from Italy. By the beginning of 1946, the number of illegal immigrants entering Palestine was more than a thousand a month. The British made a sustained effort – in the countries of origin and transit, by naval action on high seas and by police action in Palestine – to stop this flow of refugees, but failed. And in Basle, when the Zionist Congress, in December 1946, convened, the anger of the delegates in the face of the British policy in Palestine could no longer be contained. The Anglophile Weizmann, who stood as President of the Jewish Agency and the Zionist organization, who, more than anyone had come to symbolize Jewish relations with Britain, was isolated as never before and was deposed.

PARTITION AND CIVIL WAR

Impatient of a commitment in Palestine which was losing valuable British lives, costing much and, so far as anyone could see, bringing Britain no benefit of any kind, the British government, on 14 February 1947, announced that it would refer the Mandate of Palestine back to the UN, which it did on 2 April 1947.

When the General Assembly of the UN discussed the Palestine Question, as it was known, at meetings on 28 April and 15 May 1947, it decided to set up an 11-member Special Committee on Palestine, UNSCOP, with the fullest powers to ascertain and record facts and investigate all questions and issues relevant to the problem of Palestine and decide what recommendations should be made to Britain as the Mandatory Power. The committee – six diplomats, four jurists and a professor – arrived in Jerusalem on 14 June, stayed for five weeks and met Jewish representatives. The Arab Higher Committee, the body representing the Arabs of Palestine, boycotted it on the ground that the UN was refusing to adopt the 'natural course', namely declaring independence for Arab Palestine. This was a grave error of judgement on the part of the Arabs, for with the absence of the Arab side it was easier for the Jews to put a forceful case before the UN committee in favour of partitioning the land with an independent Jewish state in part of Palestine. This stance, it is worth mentioning here, was a departure from the previous official policy of World Zionism, decided upon during the Second World War at a special conference at the Biltmore Hotel in New York, where 600 Jewish delegates called for an undivided Palestine to be reconstituted as a single 'Jewish Commonwealth', which was nothing less than a demand for a Jewish state in *all* parts of Palestine west of the Jordan river.

While the UN committee was carrying out its investigations in Palestine, the river boat *Exodus 1947*, creaking with its load of 4539 displaced persons, approached the shores of Palestine and attempted to break through the British blockade to bring its immigrants ashore. For the British, the clever thing would have been to allow the ship to land as an exceptional concession made in exceptional circumstances. But Bevin, in one of his notorious black rages, was determined to teach the

Jews a lesson and he ordered the boat back to her port of embarkation, Sete, a little town 85 miles west of Marseilles in France. The appalling scenes of British troops manhandling Jewish refugees, survivors of the Holocaust, to return them to Europe was witnessed, on 18 July 1947, by the UNSCOP delegation, and it left a strong impression on the committee's members, strengthening their resolve to recommend the end of British Mandate in Palestine.

On 31 August 1947, UNSCOP published its report. A majority of its members recommended that the Mandate for Palestine should be terminated at the earliest practicable date and that independence should be granted to the country with special safeguards for the holy places and partitioning the land between Jews and Arabs. A minority report, which was also published, advanced a federalist solution with immigration to continue up to the limits of Palestine's absorptive capacity. On Saturday 29 November 1947, in a dramatic session in New York, the General Assembly of the UN adopted UNSCOP's majority solution to partition Palestine between Jews and Arabs; 33 states voted for, 13 against and 13 abstained. Widespread Christian guilt over the fate of 6 million Jews in Europe, a feeling that at least the survivors should be given a fair chance and an effective Jewish diplomatic campaign to win the necessary two-thirds majority in the UN vote, worked in favour of the Jews. According to UN Resolution 181 Palestine, comprising some 10,000 square miles, was to be divided between the Arabs – then numbering 1,364,330 – who were to retain 4300 square miles, and Jews – then numbering 608,230 – who were allotted 5700 square miles. Jerusalem and Bethlehem were to become *corpus separatum* under UN control (see Map 2).

The Jews had not known a similar political victory since the days of the Balfour Declaration, for the UN partition resolution meant that they were now given independent control of three times more land than they had been given by the Peel plan in 1937. For the Arabs the partition resolution was a heavy blow, spelling the end of their hopes for an Arab state in the whole of Palestine. As they had refused to compromise in any way with the Jewish national home for nearly 30 years, it would have meant complete humiliation to accept the UN partition resolution and so, after the vote in the UN, the Arab Higher Committee proclaimed that 'to impose a solution contrary to the Arabs' birthright will lead to trouble, bloodshed, and probably a third world war'. And in Aley, Lebanon, the Arab League, which was set up during the war, met to reject partition and to set up a joint command to plan military intervention in Palestine in order to prevent partition of the land.

In Palestine, on 2 December 1947, Arabs embarked on a three-day strike to protest against the partition resolution and in Britain, on 11 December 1947, Colonial Secretary Arthur Creech Jones announced in the House of Commons that British forces would withdraw from Palestine on 15 May 1948. The British now concentrated on pulling out from Palestine with the minimum of casualties and took no responsibility for restoring order in Palestine where conditions deteriorated into anarchy with Jews and Arabs fighting out their differences. What had started as an Arab strike to protest against partition soon deteriorated into an all-out civil war between Arabs and Jews who rapidly turned from neighbours to sworn enemies. Like most civil wars it was vicious. In December 1947, 39 Jews were killed by Arabs in the oil refineries in Haifa; in January 1948, 36 Jews – a reinforcement to Gush Etzion – were killed, and in February 1948, following a killing by the Irgun of more than ten Arabs and two British soldiers, a group of British soldiers drove a car full of explosives to Ben-Yehuda street in Jerusalem where it exploded killing more than 60 Jews. On 9 April, 110 Arabs were massacred at the small village of Deir Yassin and in revenge the Arabs attacked a convoy of 77 Jewish doctors and nurses on their way to Hadasa hospital in Jerusalem, killing them all – to mention just a few atrocities.

However, the civil war in Palestine was more than the occasional killing – it was also a battle of organized forces. The Arab forces in Palestine were led by three principal commanders: Fawzi el-Kawakji, who acted with the authority of the Arab League; Sir John Bagot Glubb and his 45 British officers in command of the Transjordanian Arab Legion; and Abd el-Kader Husseini, who commanded Arab forces in the Jerusalem area and derived his authority from the Mufti's Higher Committee. On the Jewish side, the main militia force, the Haganah, was well organized and under the overall control of the Jewish civilian authorities in Palestine under Ben-Gurion's leadership. The Lehi and the Irgun were also fighting the Arabs, sometimes even coordinating their raids with the Haganah.

In the initial phases of the civil war the Arabs seemed to be in a much better military position than the Jews and this strongly influenced the attitude of the international community to the troubles in Palestine. For with the Arabs gaining the upper hand, the government of the United States began to wilt under an accumulation of pressures and began to have second thoughts about her Middle East policy. It is worth mentioning that in the very intense struggle that developed between supporters and opponents of partition in the last months of 1947, the United States not only backed partition but, in the crucial moments just before the decision, threw its full weight into the effort to mobilize the votes that were still needed for the resolution to pass. Without this US lobbying, it is doubtful whether the partition resolution would have obtained the statutory two-thirds majority in the General Assembly. But now, alarmed by the deteriorating situation in Palestine and the prospect of a full-scale war once the last British troops left the country and apprehensive that by supporting the Jews it would bring the USSR in on the side of the Arabs and thus enable it to penetrate into the Middle East, the United States began to back away from partition and move steadily towards the idea of replacing partition with trusteeship.

The Jewish leadership, alarmed by the dwindling of American support, became even more determined to achieve military success on the ground. Thus, on 10 March 1948, the Haganah launched Plan D, a large-scale offensive that eventually brought most of the territories assigned to the Jewish state by the UN in November 1947 under its control. At the same time, the Jews put enormous pressure on the American administration to reject trusteeship and with the Soviets also opposing trusteeship, Washington finally dropped the idea and turned all her attention to achieving a truce in Palestine.

In the mean time, the Jewish offensive was going from strength to strength. Operation Nachshon, launched on 3 April and continuing until 15 April, was successful in opening the road to Jerusalem and transferring food to the besieged city. In other parts of Palestine, Jewish forces occupied and gained control of four cities with mixed populations: Tiberias (18 April), Haifa (22–23 April), Jaffa (30 April) and Safed (10 May). By May, Jewish forces were in control of most of the areas assigned to the Jewish state by the UN, except for the Negev.

It was during the civil war in Palestine that what came to be known as 'the Palestinian refugee problem' began and gradually intensified. At first the Arab flight from Palestine was only a trickle, consisting mostly the inhabitants of isolated Arab settlements together with some of the more well-to-do Arab Palestinian families who, sensing trouble ahead, decided to move elsewhere until it blew over. But with the Palestinian leadership and the middle class leaving Palestine to take, what they believed to be, a temporary refuge in neighbouring Arab countries, and with the Jews 'advising' the poorer Palestinians to follow suit and often using force to expel them, and with rumours of ghastly massacres of Arabs, as occurred at the village of Deir Yassin where 110 civilians were killed by Jews on 8 April 1948, fear gripped Palestine and the trickle of Arab refugees became a flood. This departure en masse of the Arabs – 750,000 is the estimate of Arab Palestinians who eventually left Palestine – led to a situation where the demographic scales in Palestine were violently tilted in favour of the Jews. As the British Mandate in Palestine drew to an end the Jews were already the majority in the land.

2
The Birth of Israel, 1948–1949

FRIDAY, 14 MAY 1948

Friday, 14 May 1948, was a historical juncture when three critical events came together in a single day. The first was the proclamation of Israel's independence, the second was the end of the British Mandate, and the third was the advance into jumping-off positions of five regular Arab armies, supported by contingency task forces from Saudi Arabia and Yemen, in preparation to invading Palestine-Israel.

The ceremony inaugurating the state was attended by 200 people. It took place at four in the afternoon at the private house of the Mayor of Tel Aviv, Meir Dizengoff, at 16 Rothschild Boulevard, which was the only large hall in town. The ceremony was modest but significant, the culmination of a long and weary journey which had started 51 years before at Basle's Municipal Casino, where 37-year-old Theodor Herzl had launched the Zionist movement to create a 'home' for the Jewish people in Palestine.

Now, standing under a big portrait of Herzl, Ben-Gurion rapped a gavel as a signal to the Palestinian Philharmonic Orchestra, established in Palestine by members of the fifth *Aliyah*, to play *Ha'tikvah*, the national anthem which was written by Naphtali Hertz Imber in honour of the founding of Rishon Lezion in 1882. The second verse, however, which originally read:

> Our hope is not yet lost
> The age-old hope,
> To return to the land of our fathers
> To the city where David dwelt

was by now amended and read:

> Our hope is not yet lost
> The hope of two thousand years
> to be a free people in our land
> The land of Zion and Jerusalem

Ben-Gurion then read the 1027-word declaration. He opened by describing the land of Israel as the birthplace of the Jewish people where their spiritual, religious and national identity was formed and where they wrote and gave the Bible to the world. It was a land, said Ben-Gurion, to which Jews had never ceased praying and to where they had always hoped to return. He described the efforts of Theodor Herzl, mentioned the pledges made by the British government in the Balfour Declaration to assist the Jews to establish a 'national home' in Palestine, and the reaffirmation of this pledge by the League of Nations as expressed in the Mandate to Palestine. Ben-Gurion went on to mention the Holocaust which engulfed millions of Jews in Europe and proved the need to establish a state in order to solve the problem of the homelessness of the Jewish people. After alluding to the decision of the UN in November 1947 to allow the Jewish people to establish their independent state, Ben-Gurion declared:

> Accordingly we, the members of the National Council, representing the Jewish people in the Land of Israel and the Zionist movement, have assembled on the day of the termination of the British mandate for Palestine, and, by virtue of our natural and historical right and of the resolution of the General Assembly of the United Nations . . . we hereby proclaim the establishment of the Jewish state in Palestine, to be called Medinat Yisrael (The State of Israel).[1]

The state of Israel, Ben-Gurion assured his audience, would be open to the immigration of Jews from all countries, would promote the development of the country for the benefit of all its inhabitants, would be based on the principles of liberty, justice and peace, would uphold the full social and political equality of all its citizens, without distinction of religion, race or sex, would guarantee freedom of religion, conscience, education and culture, would safeguard the holy places of all religions and would uphold the principles of the UN Charter. Ben-Gurion then called upon the Arab inhabitants of the state of Israel to preserve the ways of peace and play their part in the development of the state on the basis of 'full and equal citizenship'. Israel, said Ben-Gurion, 'extends its hand in peace' to all the neighbouring states and their people. Significantly, however, Ben-Gurion failed to mention the boundaries of the Jewish state, presumably because he did not wish to rule out the possibility that Israeli forces would expand these boundaries beyond what the UN had allotted to the Jews in November 1947.

When Ben-Gurion finished reading the proclamation, he and 37 other signatories appended their signatures to a blank parchment scroll. For the Jewish leaders, who were so brilliant at founding a state, had failed to recruit in time for the ceremony a Torah scribe to scratch the text out with a goose quill in the ancient script. So the signatures came first and the text of the proclamation was added a week later.

The Jewish community in Palestine and Jews all over the world rejoiced over the formal establishment of the state, but Ben-Gurion, as he confided to his *War Diary*, was 'a mourner among the joyful', because he recognized that with the declaration of Jewish independence, war with the neighbouring Arab states was inevitable.[2]

The drama surrounding the birth of Israel was not, however, confined to Palestine. While the ceremony in Tel Aviv was still under way, across the Atlantic, the UN General Assembly which had proclaimed the Jewish people's right to statehood six months earlier, was debating a proposal to set up an international trusteeship instead of supporting the independence of a Jewish state.

In the mean time in Washington, after an acrimonious argument between Secretary of State George Marshall who opposed recognition of the Jewish state and President Truman, the President decided to recognize Israel. Truman was deeply affected by the plight of European Jewry and he was also well aware that to secure the Jewish vote in the coming elections he had to side with the Jews. Thus, just 11 minutes after Ben-Gurion declared independence Washington recognized Israel and in the UN Ambassador Warren Austin, the American representative, read a brief statement on President Truman's behalf, the gist of which was that a Jewish state has been proclaimed in Palestine, that it had asked Washington for recognition and that the government of the United States accepted the request and recognized the Provisional Government as the de facto authority of the new state of Israel. Shortly afterwards Russia and the government of Guatemala followed the US example in recognizing Israel.

The proclamation of the state and its recognition by members of the international community coincided with the second major event of the

day, which was the departure from Palestine, except for a small garrison at Haifa port to supervise last-minute evacuations, of the British.
Twenty-six years had passed since Britain was charged by a Mandate
of the League of Nations to 'facilitate the establishment of a Jewish
national home'. Visionary and unprecedented in law or history, it
carried radiant hopes for some years. Later, especially after 1939,
Britain gradually abandoned her own commitments as expressed in the
Balfour Declaration of 1917 and the pledges of the international
community to support the Jews in the building of their national home
in Palestine. This was not, however, as is often claimed, because of
British anti-Jewish prejudice, but simply because of strong opposition
by the Arab majority in Palestine to the Jewish project and subsequent
British attempts to pacify the Arabs and find some middle way
between Arab and Jewish demands and this, inevitably, resulted in a
watering-down of previous pledges to the Jews.

And so, on this Friday, just half an hour before midnight and a few
hours after the state of Israel had been proclaimed – the advent of the
Jewish Sabbath had made it necessary to advance the hour of the
proclamation ceremony – Lt.-Gen. Sir Alan Cunningham, the seventh
and last British High Commissioner for Palestine, left his official hill-
top residence in Jerusalem and set sail on board HMS *Euryalus* from
the bay of Haifa back to England. Thus ended three decades of British
presence in Palestine.

While a Jewish state was being proclaimed and recognized and the
British were departing, the last event of this dramatic Friday was under
way – preparations and actual movement of Arab armies for the invasion
of Israel-Palestine. Egyptian forces crossed the frontiers and advanced
into the southern Negev, the government in Cairo informing the UN
Security Council that her forces were entering Palestine 'to establish
security and order instead of chaos and disorder'. In the north of the
country, a small Lebanese force was ready to invade, an Iraqi column
advanced closer to the Jordan river, the Transjordanian Arab Legion was
arrayed along this river and a Syrian brigade was also ready to strike.

WAR

The Arab onslaught

Arab intervention in Palestine was triggered by Israel's proclamation
of independence. Could a postponement of Israel's proclamation have

averted this war? We will probably never know for certain the answer to this question but, given that a Jewish state was in being and existed de facto, it may well be that a change of the timing of the declaration, and an acceptance by the Jewish leadership of the US-inspired truce proposal which was on the table at that time, could have averted the coming war. Nahum Goldmann, one of the leading figures in Zionist diplomacy and an architect of the 29 November 1947 UN partition resolution, often claimed that Ben-Gurion's insistence on proclaiming independence just when he did was, in Goldmann's words, 'Israel's original sin'. It seems, however, that given a choice between having a de facto state without a war or declaring to the entire world the birth of a Jewish state and triggering an all-out war, Ben-Gurion preferred to opt for the latter. As revealed by an entry in his *War Diary*, he was well aware that choosing this route meant war. 'At four in the afternoon Jewish independence was proclaimed and the state [of Israel] was established', Ben-Gurion noted in his diary on 14 May, and added, as if knowing the implication of this, 'its fate is in the hands of the armed forces'.

From the south 15,000 Egyptian troops marched into Palestine-Israel in two main columns. The western, under Brigadier Muhammad Naguib, advanced northwards in the direction of Tel Aviv, hugging the coast and attacking on its way the Negev Jewish settlements of Nirim and Kfar Darom both of which survived the assault; but the settlement of Yad Mordechai fell after five days of resistance as did Nitzanim. The Egyptian column then reached Isdud (Ashdod), within 25 miles of Tel Aviv, where it was checked. In the mean time, the eastern Egyptian column, under Lt.-Gen. Abd el-Aziz moved to Nitzana and then advanced towards Jerusalem through Beersheva and Hebron, Bethlehem and Ramat Rachel.

In the north of Palestine, the Syrian assault opened on 16 May with forces advancing in two main columns, one to eastern Galilee in the direction of Mishmar Ha'yarden, the other towards kibbutz Degania (and its sister kibbutz, Degania B). Degania, the first kibbutz to be established by members of the second *Aliyah*, was regarded as the flagship of the kibbutz movement and had a symbolic significance for the Israeli farming community, and its fall could have caused morale to tumble. In the event, however, the use of two 65-millimetre light field guns, a relic of the French incursion into Mexico in the 1860s, even without aiming sights and which had arrived in Israel a few days before, crucially affected the result of the battle. As Moshe Dayan, a

young officer who played a leading role in this battle, later explained:
'The Syrian troops, who heard the shriek of the shells over their heads
... just took to their heels.'[3] The battle of Degania entered Israel's
history as a heroic moment. A knocked out Syrian tank still stands
close to the main gate of the kibbutz. For the next 20 days or so, the
Syrians caused little trouble from behind the international border to
which they withdrew. Then, on 10 June they launched a carefully
prepared surprise attack, seized land and established bridgeheads west
of the international border in areas allocated to the Jews by the UN in
November 1947. They managed to hold these for the remainder of the
war.

Also in the north of the country, an Iraqi force penetrated the Beit
Shean valley near kibbutz Gesher, but its siege of Gesher ended when
the two artillery pieces that had saved kibbutz Degania from the Syrian
onslaught were rushed there and opened fire on the Iraqis who scattered and retreated. Having failed to capture this area, the Iraqis under
the command of one General Tahir, concentrated their efforts on seizing the Arab triangle of Nablus–Jenin–Tulkarem, occupied this region
and dug in to defend it. Lebanese forces, composed mainly of volunteers, in the mean time started moving towards Nazareth and Shfaram
and the region of Malkia.

With the declaration of a Jewish state and the departure of the
British, Transjordan sent troops to cross the river Jordan into the sector
of Palestine allotted to the Arab Palestinians by the UN in November
1947. There was no need in shedding blood here for already in 1947
an agreement was reached between King Abdullah and the Jews to
divide Palestine between themselves, and now the area adjacent and
just west of the Jordan river went to Transjordan without them having
to fight the Israelis. Jerusalem, however, had been granted neither to
Jews nor to Arabs and here Israeli and Transjordanian troops clashed
fiercely, for both sides were eager to gain control of the city. The
Jordanians had the upper hand, at least in the initial stages of the battle.
On 19 May, they isolated Mount Scopus, and ten days later they seized
the Jewish Quarter of Jerusalem, took prisoners, transferred all able-
bodied fighters to Amman and expelled 700 women and children to
Jewish west Jerusalem. The defeat was militarily unimportant but
psychologically bitter, for the Jewish Quarter of the Old City was the
jewel of Jewish settlement in Palestine and the Wailing Wall was its
most treasured holy place, representing the spiritual centre of Jewish
Jerusalem.

Far more serious for the Israelis was that the Transjordanians held Latrun which sits atop the valley of Ayalon (where Joshua, by commanding the sun to stand still, had routed the Canaanites) and overlooks the road connecting Tel Aviv and Jerusalem. From this strategic location the Jordanians prevented convoys of food and arms from reaching Jerusalem. After disastrous failures with heavy loss of lives, attempts to seize Latrun from the Jordanians by force were abandoned in favour of hacking through the hills and transforming a sandy path, winding around the south of Latrun, into an alternative route to Jerusalem. This came to be known as 'the Burma Road' and later Kvish Ha'gevurah, (meaning the Road of Heroism) and through this route vital supplies entered besieged Jerusalem.

During these early and crucial days of the war, and under the command of the ailing Chief of Staff Ya'akov Dori, whose functions were discharged in practice by 34-year-old Yigael Yadin, Israeli forces were shifted between fronts to stem the invading Arab armies.

In the midst of the fighting, on 1 June, on the orders of the Provisional Government, the Haganah gave up its underground and clandestine status and became the nucleus of the Israeli army with its name incorporated into the name of the new organization – the Israel *Defence* Forces (IDF). Units of the Irgun and Lehi, the two underground organizations which had fought the British while they were still in Palestine, were invited to join the new army and an agreement reached between the Irgun's commander Begin and Ben-Gurion's people envisaged that Irgun units should be incorporated as organic units into the IDF.

The war was fought mainly on land, until in the last days of May and early June 1948, reconstructed Messerschmitts, Spitfires and Mosquitoes which had been purchased by Israeli emissaries in Czechoslovakia, were flown to Israel. Piloted largely by Jewish volunteers from England, America and South Africa, they bombed Egyptian troops at Isdud on 29 May, and throughout the rest of the war, acted as spotter aircraft for the ground forces, flying military supplies and food to isolated settlements and dropping bombs on Arab capitals.

Three weeks after the establishment of the state of Israel and the Arab invasion, Israel was in control of much more territory that she could have hoped for. Her forces had successfully consolidated their hold on the mixed Arab–Jewish towns which by now had lost most of their Arab inhabitants, and also controlled eastern and western Galilee, the Jezreel valley from Haifa to the river Jordan, the coastal plain down to a point just north of Isdud, and a large pocket in the central Negev. Jerusalem, however, was effectively cut in half. Roughly the side west of the dividing line came under Israel's control with the addition of Mount Scopus as an enclave. However, the Old City, including the Western Wall, as well as, the Jewish Quarter were held by the Transjordanians who also continued to control the Latrun salient overlooking the Jerusalem–Tel Aviv road.

The first truce and the Altalena *Affair*

On 21 May 1948, just six days into the war, the permanent members of the Security Council appointed Count Folke Bernadotte as a mediator for Palestine with a mandate to recommend a settlement to the crisis. Bernadotte was a member of the Swedish royal family, tall, slender, pleasant but also determined and energetic. He was well equipped for his new job for he had taken part in negotiations to end the Second World War, in April 1945.

Bernadotte's first preoccupation was to persuade Arabs and Jews to agree to a ceasefire, since continued fighting would make any mediation effort impossible. But the Arabs, although faced with an imminent shortage of ammunition, feared that a truce would benefit the Israelis by enabling them to regroup, strengthen their positions and obtain more arms. The Israelis, on the other hand, were eager for a truce for unlike the Arabs, who had been fighting for only a few days, were relatively fresh and unblooded, the Israelis had been fighting since December 1947 and felt that a ceasefire could enable them to snatch a breathing space, consolidate their achievements and reorganize. In spite of Arab insistence on continuing the fight, the Security Council met on 7 June and adopted a resolution to introduce a truce. Bernadotte then set 11 June as the date for the truce to start and both sides accepted.

By the truce provisions neither side was allowed to take any measures to change the military situation, in particular not to bring in any weapons or introduce 'fighting personnel and men of military age'. But both sides flouted the provisions whenever they had an opportunity and the Israelis, in particular, spent the weeks of truce in bringing in more weapons, regrouping and improving the organization of the armed forces, consolidating their hold on the occupied areas and widening the Burma Road, the bypass through which essential supplies reached Jerusalem.

It was during the truce that Israel experienced a traumatic event which came to be known as 'the *Altalena* Affair'. We should remember that although Ben-Gurion's government established the IDF as the sole legitimate armed force in Israel, and although Begin's Irgun units were incorporated into the IDF, the government was still not in full control of all Jewish armed forces, and in Jerusalem, in particular, which fell outside the official jurisdiction of the Jewish state, the Irgun and Lehi still operated independently of the IDF and the government. This anomaly of a divided military jurisdiction came to a head when the Irgun brought in a 5000-ton ship, called the *Altalena* – this was Jabotinsky's nom de plume – which had between 800 and 900 volunteers on board, 250 light machine guns and some 5000 rifles and ammunition. On 16 June, Ben-Gurion's and Begin's representatives agreed that the vessel should anchor off Kfar Vitkin, 23 miles north of Tel Aviv, where it thought it could unload far from the prying eyes of the UN truce observers, and that the weapons should be transferred to the IDF. But when the *Altalena* approached Israel's coast and anchored at Kfar Vitkin on the night of 20–21 June 1948, Begin had a change of heart and he insisted that instead of all arms being transferred to the IDF, 20 per cent of them should be given to the Irgun's units in Jerusalem. Begin then instructed his troops, most of whom were by now serving within the ranks of the IDF, to defect from their units and join in helping unload the ship's cargo of arms. This was a direct challenge to Ben-Gurion's government and after consulting his colleagues, Ben-Gurion issued unequivocal orders to the IDF to arrest the ship and the people on board even if force had to be used. Israel was on the brink of a civil war.

In the exchange of gunfire between Irgunists and Ben-Gurion's troops at Kfar Vitkin, two IDF soldiers and six Irgunists were killed. This was not to be the end of the drama, for on Begin's instructions the *Altalena* had weighed anchor and set sail for Tel Aviv where Begin hoped he could recruit more public support. With Begin himself now on board along with the ship's captain, 25-year-old Munroe Fine of Chicago, the *Altalena* arrived at Tel Aviv where a 10-hour battle ensued. A cannon was used – it was later dubbed the 'holy cannon' after Ben-Gurion's comment 'Blessed be the gun which set the ship on fire' – and it hit the ship. *Altalena* burst into flames, tilted on one side and the crew abandoned her and began to swim ashore. Among the Irgunists killed on this dramatic day was Avraham Stavsky, who had been one of those charged with the murder of Chaim Arlosoroff 15 years earlier to the day on the selfsame ill-fated spot. Begin, one of the last to abandon the ship, reached shore and broadcasted to his people to stop fighting. They obeyed and capitulated.

The '*Altalena* Affair' was one of the most painful experiences of the newly established state of Israel and it caused bitterness among Israelis for years to come. Nevertheless, it demonstrated that there was a government in Israel which was determined to impose its will and assert its authority, by force if necessary, and that the IDF would alone carry arms and no separate armies would be allowed to exist in the new state. Ben-Gurion's decision to use force and open fire on Jews must certainly be recorded as one of his most dramatic and formative acts.

The '*Altalena* Affair' was not, however, the only crisis to take place during this period. Another was the en masse resignation of the top IDF command on 2 July 1948. The resignations took place because of a row with Ben-Gurion about military appointments he wished to make, but also because of deep disquiet about his constant intervention in military affairs and his insistence on running the war down to its smallest details, often disregarding professional advice. Ben-Gurion's insistence, for example, on seizing the fortress of Latrun from where the Arab Legion blocked convoys travelling from Tel Aviv to Jerusalem, caused bitter resentment among military commanders who believed that since the site was held by a substantial and well-equipped Jordanian force, the Israelis stood no chance of seizing it. Indeed they proved right, for Ben-Gurion's insistence on throwing wave after wave of troops to seize Latrun came to grief as attacks were repeatedly thrown back with a heavy loss of young lives, mainly of men just liberated from internment in Cyprus. This crisis was eventually resolved when a committee of five ministers, rather than Ben-Gurion on his own, was appointed to oversee the conduct of the war.

The Bernadotte Plan

In the mean time, while the truce was still holding under the supervision of UN truce observers, and while Jew was fighting Jew, the Swedish mediator Bernadotte, who had established his headquarters at the Hôtel des Roses on the island of Rhodes, set himself to produce a plan to end the strife between Arabs and Israelis. His proposals – sent to the parties on 28 June 1948 – reflected, in large measure, the situation on the ground. He proposed that Palestine as defined in the original Mandate entrusted to Britain in 1922, namely with the inclusion of

Transjordan, should form a 'Union' of an Arab (effectively an enlarged kingdom of Transjordan) and a Jewish state. All, or part of, the Negev, assigned in the 29 November partition scheme to the Jews, and which was by now cut off by Arab forces, should be given to Transjordan. In return, so proposed Bernadotte, all, or part of, western Galilee, which had been awarded by the UN to the Arab Palestinians but which by now was mainly in Israel's hands, should be given to the Jews. A free port at Haifa and a free airport at Lydda, proposed Bernadotte, should be established. Regarding immigration, 'following a period of two years from the establishment of the Union either member would be entitled to request the Council of the Union to review the immigration policy of the other member and to render a ruling thereon'. If either side did not agree to this ruling, suggested Bernadotte, the matter would be referred to the Economic and Social Council of the UN, whose decision, taking into account the principle of 'economic absorptive capacity', would be binding on the member whose policy was at issue. Jerusalem, which according to the UN resolution of 29 November 1947 was to become an international city, was to be, according to the new Bernadotte plan, 'in Arab territory' with 'municipal autonomy' for the Jewish community and special arrangements for the protection of the holy places.

Bernadotte's plan was rejected out of hand by both Arabs and Jews. The Arabs thought that Bernadotte had allowed the Jews too much and replied to the mediator's proposals by proposing the creation of a unitary state of Palestine, a proposal which had been put forward repeatedly by the Arabs during the lengthy discussions which preceded the adoption of the 29 November 1947 resolution and was rejected. The Arab governments, particularly Egypt, Syria and Saudi Arabia, also felt that Bernadotte's proposals were favourable to Transjordan and opposed the plan, for they were jealous of an increase in the power of King Abdullah. The Israelis, for their part, regarded the plan as an attempt to redraw the map approved by the UN in November 1947, which by now had been modified in their favour by their military success on the ground and occupation of land allotted to the Arabs by the UN. In the UN, Israel's representative Abba Eban – his delegation was still called 'the Jewish Agency for Palestine' – said of Bernadotte's plan that, 'it was very much as though the surgeon went away with most of the patient's vital organs'.[4] The Israelis were upset that Bernadotte failed to recognize an independent Israel and that he allotted Jerusalem to the Arabs and suspected that the whole plan bore the fingerprints of Britain. In Israel, Bernadotte came under personal attack and was accused of having Nazi sympathies and of being a British agent. 'Those who suspected that Bernadotte is an agent of Bevin', noted Prime Minister Ben-Gurion in his diary, 'are not far off the mark'.[5] In some circles Bernadotte had become, after Ernest Bevin, the most hated man in Israel.

Thus, with Arabs, Israelis and even with some members of the international community, notably the Soviets who said of Bernadotte's plan that it bore the label 'made in Britain', rejecting his proposals, Bernadotte had to ensure that, at least, the truce, by now due to expire, was prolonged.

Fighting and a second truce

He was to be disappointed. The Arab League Political Committee meeting in Cairo to discuss the troubles in Palestine decided, under strong pressure from Egypt and Syria, not to prolong the truce. In his diary Bernadotte grimly recorded: 'They [the Arabs] totally rejected my proposal to prolong the truce'.[6] The Israelis, in turn, realizing that the truce would not be renewed, took the initiative and opened fire on 9 July. Now, as the Arabs had rightly feared when they had initially objected to having a truce, the Israelis emerged stronger, better organized and capable of going over to the offensive. It was, as Yigael Yadin, the acting Chief of Staff of the IDF commented, the turning point in the war. 'We took the initiative', he said, 'and after that we never allowed it to return to the Arabs.'[7]

Fierce fighting raged for ten consecutive days with the battle clearly going in Israel's favour. Operations were concentrated, in particular, in the centre of the country in the Lydda–Ramleh area, which formed a wedge only 11 miles from Tel Aviv. Led by Yigal Allon and Moshe Dayan, troops seized the Arab towns of Lydda (11–12 July), including its international airport, and Ramleh (12 July) which had been allotted to the Arabs in the UN partition plan. The 50,000 or so Palestinian inhabitants of these Arab towns were then expelled with the tacit approval of Premier Ben-Gurion who let his military commanders understand that he wished to see the Arab Palestinians go.[8]

Meanwhile, the Lebanese forces in the north were put out of action, but attempts failed to dislodge the Syrians from the strip of land west of the Jordan river, mainly from the areas of Mishmar Ha'Yarden and Al-Hama.

Now, Premier and Defence Minister Ben-Gurion instructed his military commanders to seize the Arab town of Nazareth, believing that taking this town would lead to the crumbling of the whole Arab war effort in western Galilee. But just before troops went into action Ben-Gurion sent messages urging commanders to take all necessary measures to prevent looting by their troops which had, by now, become a major problem within the ranks of the IDF. He warned, 'If you succeed in occupying the old town [of Nazareth] there is a serious danger of [your troops] pillaging . . . you have to ensure a special force . . . to shoot any Jew ruthlessly, particularly any Jewish soldier attempting to loot . . . any attempt at looting by our soldiers must be opposed by using machine guns without mercy. . . .'[9] On 16 July Nazareth fell into Israeli hands – looting was rife. No machine guns were used against the looters.

Count Bernadotte, the Swedish mediator, counselled the Arab League to accept another truce. King Abdullah agreed immediately, the Egyptians and the Syrians, on the other hand, rejected the proposal and the other League members, simply following the Egyptian lead, refused to stop the battle. The Israelis, like most of the Arab governments, were also reluctant to accept a truce at this stage for their military operations were very successful. In his *War Diary* on 18 July 1948 Premier Ben-Gurion noted, with much regret, that: 'it seems that [after all] a truce will [have to] take place'. How ironic it is that the international community was more keen to stop the bloodshed than were Jews and Arabs. On 15 July, the Security Council passed a resolution imposing a truce to remain in force without a time limit and continue until a 'peaceful adjustment' was reached. The parties agreed and the truce came into force on 18 July 1948.

As was the case during the first truce, a halt in the fighting enabled Israel to train new immigrants and, more crucially, acquire much needed weapons. Most of the arms came from Czechoslovakia where Ehud Avriel, a kibbutznik from lower Galilee, a brilliant mind and perhaps, the brightest of the young men whom Ben-Gurion gathered around him, was able to acquire arms and dispatch them to Israel. From Switzerland and Italy emissaries purchased artillery and anti-aircraft guns, from Mexico some field guns, from Europe and the United States surplus tanks, and from the United States' surplus in Hawaii, automatic weapons. Taking advantage of the halt in the battle, the Israelis also consolidated their hold on occupied territories, razing Arab villages to the ground so that their previous inhabitants who took what they believed to be a temporary refuge elsewhere, would have nowhere to return to. No less important, Israel continued, as it did throughout the war and in spite of the fighting, to absorb Jewish immigrants the number of whom reached some 123,999 in 1948 alone.

Bernadotte's final report and his assassination

Now, with the truce officially in place and holding, Bernadotte formulated a new plan which, when it emerged, differed from his previous one. Perhaps most notably, it explicitly recognized the existence of Israel – 'a living, solidly entrenched and vigorous reality' – without restriction on her foreign, defence or immigration policies. Bernadotte also dropped his idea, expressed in his first plan and which so much upset the Israelis, of handing over Jerusalem to the Arabs. Instead he recommended that Jerusalem should be placed under 'effective United Nations control', which was a return to the *corpus separatum* as foreseen in the 29 November 1947 resolution. The fate of Arab Palestine was, according to Bernadotte's new plan, to be decided by Arab governments in consultation with the Palestinians, although still with a recommendation that Palestine should be merged with Transjordan. With regard to the Palestinian refugees, Bernadotte now added a clause calling for them to be awarded compensation should they choose not to exercise their right to return to their homes in what used to be Palestine. Apart from these important changes the territorial provisions of the plan remained as in Bernadotte's first proposal. Thus, Galilee (originally given by the UN to the Arabs in 1947) where the Israelis were victorious, was to be left in their hands and in return the Israelis would have to surrender the Negev (originally given to them by the UN) to the Arabs. Central Palestine, according to Bernadotte's plan, was to be divided according to the boundaries laid down in the partition resolution of 29 November 1947, and the port of Haifa and the airport of Lydda (Lod) were to become free ports. Bernadotte insisted that his 130-page report should be tabled as a draft resolution at the third session of the General Assembly scheduled for 21 September 1948. But then things took a sharp turn.

On 17 September while travelling in a convoy of three UN cars in Jerusalem to an appointment with Dov Joseph, the Israeli government representative responsible for the administration of Jerusalem, Bernadotte's convoy was blocked by a jeep carrying three men, who jumped out, rushed to Bernadotte's car and shot him. The shots which

killed Bernadotte were fired by Yehoshua Cohen – he later became
Ben-Gurion's personal guard – who belonged to a Jewish group
dubbing itself Hazit Ha'Am (Fatherland Front), which was composed
of Lehi members. Although the plan to assassinate the UN mediator
was conceived in Jerusalem by Lehi members operating more or less
independently, their commander, Yehoshua Zatler, did bring the plan
before the Lehi Central Committee. As Yitzhak Shamir, a member of
this three-man committee, later recalled: 'Our opinion was asked and
we offered no opposition.'[10]

The police investigation of the murder was sluggish and rumours
were rife that Ben-Gurion's government was in no hurry to investigate
and, although deeply shocked, it regarded the murder as beneficial for
Israel as it, inevitably, slowed down international approval of the
Bernadotte plan which the government itself strongly opposed.
However, what Ben-Gurion did, and most effectively, was to exploit
the shock of the murder to clamp down on dissident groups in
Jerusalem and consolidate his government's hold over all Jewish
armed forces. More than 250 Lehi members were arrested by the
government, and the Irgun which was also operating in Jerusalem, was
forced to hand over its weapons and dissolve itself; this was the final
end of the Irgun and Lehi in Jerusalem. And it was also the end of
another separate, semi-independent organization – the Palmach.

The Palmach ('Shock Companies'), set up on 15 May 1941, was the
elite force of the Haganah and many of its men were veterans of
Wingate's SNS squads. When established during the Second World
War, the Palmach had two primary aims. First, to defend the *Yishuv*,
the pre-state Jewish community against Arab bands, and second to
defend the country against any possible invasion by Axis forces. We
should recall that at that time German Field Marshal Erwin Rommel's
divisions were already grinding towards Egypt and the British were
preparing to transfer to a defence line further north. The Palmach, so
it was envisaged, would cut German communications and employ
guerrilla tactics if the Germans invaded Palestine.

In 1942, however, a shortage of funds threatened the Palmach's
future and the left-wing movement, Ha'Kibbutz Ha'Meuchad, offered
to feed and house its people. As long as Ha'Kibbutz Ha'Meuchad was
associated with Mapai, Ben-Gurion's party, there was no real problem.
But in 1944, Mapai split and most of Ha'Kibbutz Ha'Meuchad left to
form a new party, Achdut Ha'Avodah, to which about half of the rank
and file of the Palmach belonged. The implication of this split was that

although the Palmach operated under the Haganah, Ben-Gurion had no political authority over its members. Now Ben-Gurion saw his chance to end this situation by clamping down on the Palmach. Thus, although the Palmach fought well during the war and some of the brightest military commanders of the future Israeli army, notably Yigal Allon and Yitzhak Rabin, learned their trade in this organization, it had to disband. Thus came the end, on 7 November 1948, of the Palmach National Command and then of its units.

END OF WAR AND THE EMERGENCE OF A DEMOCRACY

Fighting, negotiations of armistice agreements, a general election and the forming of a government in Israel came together in the autumn and winter of 1948 and well into 1949. Israel breached the truce when she opened fire on 15 October 1948 to implement Operation Yoav (also known as Operation Ten Plagues, a reference to the horrors that God had inflicted on the Egyptians). This was an attempt to create facts on the ground, mainly in the Negev, which Israel wished to keep because of its rich soil and access to the Red Sea, at a time when the UN Assembly was intending to open discussions on the Bernadotte Plan, which by now had become the political testament of a man who had sacrificed his life for peace in the Holy Land, and who recommended that the Negev should be given to the Arabs. Yitzhak Rabin, a leading commander in this military operation, later testified: 'It was necessary to find a pretext to open the war so that we would not be held responsible for violating the truce. . . . We decided to send a convoy of food to the area of Faluja so that the Egyptians would open fire on it and thus provide us with a pretext to renew the fighting. . . .'[11] No fools, the Egyptians refused to fall into the trap and, as Rabin later testified, 'in the end, with the aid of a random shot here, another there, we had our pretext'.[12]

The Israelis then struck and in a bold campaign, lasting nine days, smashed their way to the south, cut the Egyptian front, trapped a quarter of the Egyptian contingent force in a pocket, neutralized another and drove the rest of the expedition back to an untenable arc stretching from Gaza to Asluj. On 21 October, the Israelis seized the capital of the Negev, Beersheva, which the UN on 29 November 1947 and later also Bernadotte had allotted to the Arabs. 'The occupation of Beersheva', noted Premier Ben-Gurion in his *War Diary* on 22

October 1948, 'is most valuable . . . the debate in the UN [on giving it to the Arabs] would be altogether different now that it is occupied [by us.]'

In the mean time, in the centre of the country, and again as a response and a show of defiance towards the UN intention to discuss Bernadotte's proposal to make Jerusalem an international city, Israeli forces struck and widened the corridor connecting Jerusalem with other parts of the country. In the north, from 29 to 31 October 1948, the IDF executed Operation Hiram (after the biblical King Hiram of Tyre, the ally of David and Solomon who had sent cedars of Lebanon to build the Temple of Jerusalem) against Lebanon, occupying 14 south Lebanese villages.

It was also during this period that Israel took measures to consolidate her hold over the Arabs of Israel. We should recall that not all the Arabs who had resided in Palestine fled during the war and an estimated 156,000 of them remained within Israel's borders, clinging stubbornly to their property and lands in villages and in the five mixed towns of Acre, Jaffa, Haifa, Ramleh and Jerusalem. On 21 October 1948, Israel established a military government in Arab areas, set up 'security zones' and imposed restrictions on the movement of Arabs between towns and villages. New laws also allowed the military administration to remove permanent residents from the declared 'security zones' and transfer them elsewhere. This was soon done to several Negev Bedouin tribes and to the inhabitants of the Arab villages Sha'ab al-Birwah, Um al Faraj and Majdal, among others.

After reimposing a fresh truce, the Security Council, on 16 November 1948, passed Security Resolution 62 which called on the parties to negotiate and to work together to replace the truce by armistice agreements. Soon after, on 11 December, the UN Assembly met in Paris and passed Resolution 194 which established the Palestine Conciliation Commission (PCC) composed of representatives of the United States, France and Turkey. It was charged with assuming the functions of the UN mediator, negotiating a peace settlement between Israelis and Arabs, facilitating measures to repatriate and resettle the Palestinian refugees and formulating a plan to organize a permanent international regime in Jerusalem. The significance of UN Resolution 194 was that it effectively buried Bernadotte's Plan with its controversial territorial provisions.

It took the newly established commission some time to set itself up and, in the interim, the task of mediation between Arabs and Israelis was passed on to Bernadotte's deputy and successor, the black American Dr Ralph Bunche, who had earlier served as head of the Trusteeship Department in the UN General Secretariat. Bunche was not an impressive man at first sight, but he was determined and incredibly hardworking and he possessed an outstanding intellect, a' broad range of knowledge and experience and a sharp and most agile mind.

Before Bunche's mediation could even begin, the Israelis, in open breach of the truce, struck again, on 22 December, and inaugurated Operation Horev, which aimed at pushing Egyptian forces deeper into the Sinai peninsula. The other Arab armies sat still, while the Israelis easily broke up the Egyptian line at Auja and drove into Egypt proper in a wide flanking movement aimed at El Arish. The last vestiges of Egypt's invasion force were thrust from Israel's soil and the Egyptians sent into eastern Sinai in headlong retreat with Israeli troops in hot pursuit. A whole Egyptian brigade was left behind, trapped in a pocket surrounded by Israeli forces; among those caught there was a young major, Gamal Abdel Nasser, the future President of Egypt.

The situation in the Negev soon deteriorated into an international crisis, when Britain intervened on Egypt's side – under the terms of the 1936 Anglo-Egyptian Treaty Britain was obliged to assist Egypt in the event of attack from an outside party – losing in the process six Spitfires to Israeli Messerschmitts. The Security Council now convened and called for the immediate resumption of the truce between Israel and Egypt, and a forceful message from American President Harry Truman to Ben-Gurion persuaded the Prime Minister to withdraw his forces from the Sinai and to accept a new truce which came into effect on 7 January 1949. The next day Ben-Gurion noted in his *War Diary*: 'A wonderful day. Did the war end today?'

On 13 January 1949, under the inspired leadership of the UN mediator Bunche, armistice negotiations between Egypt and Israel commenced on the island of Rhodes. Israel was represented by two teams, one political headed by the Director General of the Foreign Ministry Walter Eytan and consisting of the office's most senior experts on Arab affairs, the other, a military team composed of high-ranking officers of the IDF, including Yitzhak Rabin, Yigael Yadin and Yehoshafat Harkabi.

General election

While these crucial talks were under way, Israel's citizens were preparing to take part in the country's first democratic elections. Because of the ongoing war the first elections to Israel's 120-member Knesset had had to be postponed and by now, with the war more or less over, elections could take place. The date was fixed for 25 January 1949, with an electoral procedure based on a system of proportional party lists.

The Israeli political party was an important element in the life of Israelis, with most of the major parties having evolved from social movements in the pre-state period. The major party divisions were partly along economic lines – socialist or capitalist, and partly along religious or secular lines. Mapai – Mifleget Po'alei Eretz Yisrael (Palestine Workers' Party) was the leading socialist political party in the pre-state period and Achdut Ha'Avodah, drawing its main support from the kibbutz movement, was another socialist labour party which had once been part of Mapai but split off in 1944 for ideological reasons. When independence came, Achdut Ha'Avodah, together with a more leftist movement dominated by the kibbutzim of Ha'Shomer Ha'Tzair, formed a single parliamentary party called Mapam – Mifleget Poalim Meucheded (United Workers' Party). Israel also had a Communist Party, Maki, which was a non-Zionist group. This party had favoured the establishment of a binational Arab–Jewish state, but it was persuaded to support Israel's independence by the favourable shift in Soviet policy in 1947; the party's main support came from the urban slums and from Israeli Arabs.

Herut (Freedom) which was established in 1948 was the main opposition party when the state was founded and most of its members were former Irgunists and their supporters. It developed from Ze'ev Jabotinsky's Revisionists, who left the World Zionist Organization in 1935 because they favoured a more militant policy towards Britain and the Arabs, and adhered to the revisionist ideology that held that there was a Jewish historic right to the whole land of Israel on both sides of the Jordan river. In economic policies, Herut opposed the socialist measures favoured by Mapai.

The Progressives (Independent Liberals) were a party established a few months before the first general election with a membership consisting mostly of professionals, academicians and a small kibbutz movement. The General Zionists were another party which had existed already during the British Mandate and drew its members from those in industry, commerce and citrus growers.

The major religious parties competing for votes were: Mizrachi; Ha'Poel Ha'Mizrachi, based on the religious labour movement; Agudat Yisrael, which was the ultra-Orthodox party; and Po'Alei

Agudat Yisrael – all were united in the United Religious Front. There were also small parties standing for election, such as the Sephardim, WIZO, the Yemenites Association, the Arabs of Nazareth and the Fighters' Party, a list which was a metamorphosis of the Lehi; all in all 21 party lists competed for the 120 Assembly seats.

These parties were familiar to the Israelis who went to elect their parliament in January 1949. Most voters had grown up with these organizations either in Zionist Congresses or in elections to the Va'ad Leumi. Some of the party names were kept in the popular consciousness by a vivid gallery of leaders. Thus, Mapai was the party of David Ben-Gurion. Achdut Ha'Avodah of Yitzhak Tabenkin who directed it from his kibbutz, himself removed from any ambitions of office. And Mapam's patriarchs were Meir Ya'ari and Ya'akov Hazen who guided their representatives behind the scenes but did not themselves have any wish to join a government. The leading Herut figure was Menachem Begin, who had commanded the Irgun in the pre-state era, and the Progressives were headed by Pinchas Rosen, a pillar of German Zionism. The religious parties were naturally inclined to hierarchical structures with the Mizrachi and Ha'Poel Ha'Mizrachi led by the respected rabbi Yehudah Fishman (subsequently Maimon) and the pragmatic Moshe Shapira; Agudat Yisrael was symbolized by the permanently gloomy eyes and flowing beard of Rabbi Yitzhak Meir Levin.

The Israeli population on the eve of the first elections to the Knesset was 782,000 and of these 500,000 (the voting age was set at 18), including 33,400 Arabs, were eligible voters. Eighty-seven per cent of them cast their votes and when the results were announced, Ben-Gurion's Mapai had won 46 of the 120 seats; Mapam including Achdut Ha'Avodah, 19 seats; the United Religious Front, 16 seats; Herut, 14 seats; the General Zionists, 7 seats; the Progressives, 5 seats; the Sephardim, 4 seats; the Communists, 4 seats; the Arabs of Nazareth, 2 seats; with one seat each to the Fighters' Party, WIZO and the Yemenites Association. Put differently, the Labour parties won 57 seats, the centre-right parties 31, and the religious parties 16, a voting profile that had existed in the pre-state community; in the new Knesset there were 117 Jews and 3 Arabs.

On 14 February 1949, the newly elected Knesset convened in Jerusalem and Yosef Shprinzak, a veteran labour leader, was chosen as Speaker of the House. Two days later, on 16 February, the Knesset elected Chaim Weizmann, the veteran Zionist, who had fought the major battles of Zionism from the Balfour Declaration in 1917 to the recognition of Israel by the United States in 1948, as the first President of Israel. Weizmann's first formal duty was to request the leader of the largest elected party Mapai, Ben-Gurion, to form a government.

Armistice agreements and fighting

On 24 February 1949, the day President Weizmann asked Ben-Gurion to form a government, an armistice agreement was signed between Israel and Egypt. It was a significant achievement, for it was the first agreement ever signed between Israel and an Arab state and it was expected that other Arab governments would follow suit in coming to similar arrangements with Israel.

Israel and Egypt agreed that the object of their agreement was to promote 'the return of permanent peace to Palestine', that fighting should be halted and a ceasefire be established and maintained until a final peace settlement had been achieved. They also agreed to exchange prisoners of war and to establish a mechanism in the form of a Mixed Armistice Commission, consisting of representatives of each government and a UN chairman to supervise the armistice and settle any disputes that might arise. The effect of the Israeli–Egyptian agreement was to freeze the military positions that existed in the Negev. Egypt remained in occupation of the Gaza–Rafah coastal strip, about 27 miles long and four miles wide where 30,000 Palestinians resided, the strategic area of El Auja was demilitarized and the Egyptian brigade encircled in Faluja was allowed to return safely to Egypt. Most of the northern Negev remained in Israel's hands.

On 5 March 1949, in spite of the ongoing talks with Transjordan and other Arab governments on armistice agreements, Israel executed Operation Uvda (Operation Fact or fait accompli). Two of her brigades, the Negev and Golani, occupied the southern Negev and the western shores of the Dead Sea, Massada and Ein Gedi before moving to Um Reshresh (Eilat) and occupying it on 10 March. Seizing Eilat not only provided Israel with an outlet to the Red Sea, but also enabled her to drive a wedge between the eastern and western Arab worlds thus preventing Egypt from having a direct land bridge to Jordan. In his *War Diary* on 11 March 1949 Ben-Gurion wrote: 'We have reached Eilat. This is perhaps the biggest event of the last months, if not of the whole war. . . .'

While Israeli troops were consolidating their hold on Eilat, Ben-Gurion presented his coalition government to the Knesset. It was made up of his own party Mapai, the United Religious Front, the Progressive

Party, Sephardi List members and the Arabs of Nazareth; the Cabinet consisted of 12 ministers, chosen from the coalition partners. Ben-Gurion became Prime Minister and he also kept the Defence Ministry; Dov Joseph, who had been governor during the siege of Jerusalem in the war, became Minister of Rationing and Supply; Golda Meir was made Minister of Labour and Social Insurance; Pinchas Rosen from the Progressives was made Minister of Justice; Moshe Sharett was appointed Foreign Minister. On 10 March, this government was approved by the Knesset.

On 23 March 1949, Lebanon was the second Arab state after Egypt to sign an armistice agreement with Israel. Israel and Lebanon agreed that the demarcation line between them should be identical with the former international boundary and that Israeli forces should withdraw from the 14 Lebanese villages they had occupied during Operation Hiram in October 1948.

Next was Transjordan. On 3 April 1949, following weeks of tough negotiations between Israeli and Transjordanian delegations at the Yellow Room of the Hôtel des Roses, and behind-the-scene secret talks between Israel and King Abdullah at the King's winter palace at Shuneh in the Jordan valley, the two countries signed an armistice agreement of 12 long articles and two detailed annexes. One of the most complicated issues in these talks was what to do about the areas evacuated by Iraqi forces.

Iraq, whose troops were stationed in heavy concentrations in the northern part of the West Bank, refused to negotiate with Israel on the grounds that it shared no border with her and that armistice accords meant an unwarranted recognition of Israel. So Iraqi forces withdrew from these areas, believing, as did many others, that they would be replaced by Jordanian troops. But Israel thought differently. She was determined to exploit the transition to gain control over more land, and in the talks on armistice agreements exerted tremendous pressure on King Abdullah to yield a strip of territory in the Wadi Ara area, halfway between Tel Aviv and Haifa, where there were 15 Arab villages with a total Arab population of 12,000. The King was not keen to give up these lands, but realizing that he was effectively on his own and wishing to avoid a clash with the Israelis in which he stood no chance, he gave way and agreed to Israel's demands. In the armistice agreement he obtained a face-saving clause to the effect that Israel reciprocated by giving Transjordan comparable lands elsewhere, though in fact no such exchanges were made.

The armistice agreement between Israel and Transjordan established a tortuous 330-mile long boundary which ran straight down the
middle of the Dead Sea to the Gulf of Aqaba, with the Jordanian port
of Aqaba and the Israeli port of Eilat, a few miles apart, separated by
the armistice line. The densely populated Arab hill country west of the
Jordan river, which was occupied by the Arab Legion during the war,
was left under Jordanian occupation and came to symbolize the demise
of Arab Palestine as envisaged by the UN in its 29 November 1947
resolution. Jerusalem remained divided between the two countries,
with East Jerusalem in Jordanian hands and its western part under
Israel's control. The Israelis were allowed free access to Mount Scopus
and to the shrines and cemeteries on the Mount of Olives.

The Syrian government was the last to enter into armistice negotiations with Israel, on 5 April 1949, and these took place in tents in the
no-man's land between Mishmar Ha'Yarden and Rosh Pina. Five days
before these talks started, the Syrian Colonel Husni Zaim, the head of
the Syrian army, seized supreme power in Damascus in a bloodless
coup. Upon taking power Zaim came out with a dramatic proposal by
offering to meet Israel's Premier Ben-Gurion so that the two leaders
could sign a peace agreement with open borders, exchange of ambassadors and commercial relationships; Zaim also agreed to receive
some 300,000 Palestinian refugees in Syria. In return, the new Syrian
leader wanted Ben-Gurion to agree that the border between the two
countries should pass along the Jordan river and in the middle of the
Sea of Galilee. It was a bold proposal but Ben-Gurion was not ready
to consider a meeting. In his diary he noted: 'The Syrians proposed a
separate peace with Israel, cooperation, and a common army. But they
want ... half of Lake Tiberias ... I told [Israeli representatives] to
inform the Syrians in clear language that first of all [there should be]
the signing of an armistice on the basis of the previous international
border, and then [we could proceed with a] discussion of peace. . . .'[13]

Historians still differ on the Zaim offer and the question often asked
is whether by refusing to meet President Zaim, Ben-Gurion missed a
unique opportunity to sign the first-ever peace treaty with an Arab
country. Even with the benefit of hindsight it is hard to answer this
question, for Zaim was an adventurer and a megalomaniac. But then,
on the other hand, Zaim clearly attempted to introduce social and
economic reforms in Syria and he regarded peace with Israel and quiet
along the border with her in a very pragmatic way, namely as a tool to
achieve his domestic reforms. What we *can* learn from this episode is

that contrary to general perception, fanned by Israeli successful propaganda, there were indeed Arab leaders, Zaim being one of them, who wished to strike peace deals with her and they were rebuffed by Israel. Zaim's offer to meet Ben-Gurion did not, in any way, distract Israelis and Syrians from continuing their efforts to reach an armistice agreement as Egypt, Lebanon and Transjordan had previously.

Peace talks at Lausanne

In the mean time, on the initiative of the Palestine Conciliation Commission (PCC), the body established on 11 December 1948 by the UN Assembly, Israelis and Arabs were called to attend a peace conference in Lausanne, Switzerland. It opened on 27 April 1949 and delegations came from Israel, Egypt, Jordan, Syria and Lebanon with another delegation representing the Arab Higher Committee. On 12 May, following shuttling back and forth between the parties, the commissioners managed to hammer out a joint protocol to which all parties agreed and in which they declared their determination to achieve 'as quickly as possible' the objectives of the General Assembly resolution of 11 December 1948, regarding the refugees, respect for their rights and the preservation of their property, as well as territorial and other questions.

But this was easier said than done, and when the parties attempted to discuss the fine details of their general statement they found themselves at an impasse. The two main bones of contention were refugees and borders. Israel, for her part, insisted that the Arab states were responsible for the Palestinian refugee problem, for it was their aggression by attacking Israel that caused this tragedy in the first place and, therefore, as Israel saw it, it was an Arab problem to be solved by Arab governments. The Arabs, on the other hand, insisted that it was Israel's responsibility to sort out the mess and insisted that all the refugees should be allowed to choose between returning to their previous homes in what used to be Palestine and receiving compensation. The other stumbling point was borders. Israel's position was that the permanent borders with her neighbours should be based on the ceasefire lines, with only minor modifications, and she flatly refused to return to the line of the 1947 partition plan. The Arabs, on the other hand, perhaps wishing to turn the clock back, insisted on reaching a deal with the Israelis on the basis of the UN resolution of 29 November 1947 which had been rejected by them in the past. The thorny issue of Jerusalem was another matter which the parties failed to resolve.

Although the Lausanne talks led nowhere, it was the fact that Israel showed herself willing to take part in this conference, that played a major role in convincing the international community to accept her, on 11 May 1949, as a full member of the UN. This was an impressive achievement for as a member of the UN Israel entered the general rhythm of international life and demonstrated that she was a viable nation.

End of war

After four months of intense negotiations and endless haggling, Israel and Syria reached an agreement which they signed on 20 July 1949 on the top of Hill 272, near Mishmar Ha'Yarden. Under its terms the Syrians were to withdraw from the lands they had occupied west of the international boundary and, in return, Israel agreed that these territories should be demilitarized. Civilians were allowed to return to their villages in these areas and a local police force, though no troops, was to maintain security.

With the signing of the armistice agreement with Syria came the official end of the first Arab–Israeli war. It was an expensive war costing Israel some $500 million in cash and 5682 in dead and 15,000 in casualties. Yet in spite of the high price of victory, when the guns went silent, Israel could congratulate herself on some remarkable achievements. For at the end of the war Israel controlled 79 per cent of what used to be Palestine, a larger area than allotted to her by the UN in November 1947, and certainly a larger one than could have been expected (see Map 3).

Israel's propaganda machine after this war shifted gear to show how little ('David') Israel ('the few') survived against the mighty ('Goliath') Arabs ('the many') and how clean a war she fought. This, however, was not quite true. Even though Israel's population at that time was some 650,000 compared with an Arab population 40 times larger, Israel had more troops on the ground than all the Arab armies put together – 29,677 Israelis compared with 23,500 Arabs at the beginning of the war, whereas towards its end the ratio became two to one in Israel's favour. So the 'few' in this war were the Arabs rather than the Israelis who were effectively the mighty 'many', as is also quite clearly demonstrated by the results of this war. Also, contrary to

Israeli propaganda of a 'clean' fighting, this was not always the case. In fact, the legend that the Israelis fought a 'clean' war has been shot to pieces by no other than Prime Minster Ben-Gurion who in his *War Diary* commented about: 'looting, raping in the occupied towns . . . [Israeli] soldiers of all the battalions looted and stole . . .'. And then '. . . in Acre a group of soldiers . . . killed a father, injured a mother . . . their daughter was raped by at least one [Israeli] soldier . . .'. And elsewhere, 'terrible incidents in Galilee [where Israeli troops] slaughtered about 70–80 [Arabs]'.[14]

The stability brought to the region by the armistice agreements between Israel and her neighbours allowed Ben-Gurion's government to turn to the main task in hand – absorption.

3

. . . .

Years of Consolidation, 1950–1966

MASS IMMIGRATION

The immediate task of the government in the post-war independence period and in the ensuing months, was to absorb the huge influx of Jewish refugees who poured copiously, in uneven bursts, into the country. First to arrive were survivors of the European Holocaust, thousands of whom had been dispersed in displaced persons' camps in Germany, Austria and Italy. By July 1949, 52 of these camps had been evacuated and their inmates transferred to Israel. Also, the camps in Cyprus to which the British authorities, while still in Palestine, had deported hundreds of illegal Jewish immigrants, were now emptied and their internees brought to Israel. At the same time some 37,260 Jews arrived from Bulgaria, 34,547 from Turkey, 7661 from Yugoslavia, 100,000 from Poland and 120,000 from Romania. Romania had, at first, declined to allow Jews to go, but relented when generous payments were transferred to its bank accounts. The American Jewish Joint Distribution Committee – The Joint – which had been founded in 1914 to assist Jews displaced during the First World War, played a crucial role in raising the necessary funds to cover the expenses of transferring Jews to Israel and bribing governments which created difficulties.

This was an unprecedented ingathering and the task of absorption was massive and almost beyond imagination, and it put an enormous pressure on the government. Clothing, shoes and furniture were scarce and there was an acute shortage of housing. While Jews who came with enough money were able to settle in the big cities, many others lacked the necessary funds and were totally dependent on the government which, in turn, settled them in abandoned houses and flats of Arab Palestinians who had fled the country during the war. Thus, Ramleh and Lydda (Lod), the two former Arab towns whose 50,000 Palestinian inhabitants had been expelled during the war, were quickly settled by Jewish immigrants and a further 1200 Jews were moved to Beisan, which was given the Hebrew name Beit Shean. The coastal Arab town of Acre absorbed hundreds of Jews, and Yibna, just south of Tel Aviv, whose 4000 Arab inhabitants had fled during the war, was repopulated with Jewish immigrants. When the reserve of Arab-abandoned accommodation was exhausted, the government settled newly arrived immigrants in hastily erected temporary transit camps until new flats could be built for them; by the end of 1949 more than 100,000 immigrants were living in these tent and tin towns. During the first 40 months of the state, 78,000 dwellings with 165,000 rooms had been completed but these were small and basic blocks of flats with neither inner doors nor bathrooms and would in later years become Israeli-style slums.

In these early days, a problem which would become acute and haunt Israel for years to come was starting to gather pace, namely communal tensions particularly between Jews of European and American origins – *Ashkenazim* as they were called, and newcomers from Asia and Africa – Orientals or eastern Jews more commonly known as *Sephardim.*

COMMUNAL PROBLEMS

Ashkenazim *vs* Sephardim

For although immigration to Eretz Yisrael during the pre-state period was mainly from western lands, after the establishment of the state growing numbers of Jews also arrived from Arab lands where their position had become perilous and nearly untenable as a result of growing nationalism reinforced by religion, the humiliating Arab defeat and the creation of Israel on the land of Palestine in 1948. The Israeli government played a crucial role in bringing these Jews to Israel, for it saw the task of gathering Jews from the four corners of the world as a most important mission, particularly now that the Jewish communities in Arab lands were in dire straits.

In what was dubbed Operation Magic Carpet, and after crossing the

Arabian desert on foot, 50,000 Jews were airlifted from Aden in 1948–50 and were brought to Israel. In the first phase of this operation, from December 1948 to March 1949, 55 flights were carried out and in the second, and larger phase of Magic Carpet, which had begun in May 1949 and continued until 24 September 1950, an additional 177 flights arrived at Lydda airport near Tel Aviv. Jews were also transferred to Israel from Iraq, in what became known as Operation Ezra and Nehemiah, which lasted from May 1950 to December 1951. This evacuation was possible following protracted talks between emissaries of Ben-Gurion's government and the Iraqi Prime Minister who was persuaded to let the Jews go only after the transfer of large sums of money into his bank account. The Near East Air Transport Company which had been involved in Operation Magic Carpet carried out the new airlift which resulted in 123,371 Iraqi Jews arriving in Israel, with some 25,000 wishing to stay behind in Iraq. It is worth mentioning that what inspired the departure of the Iraqi Jewry was not only harsh treatment by the Iraqi regime, but also a campaign of harassment carried out by Israeli agents, who tossed hand grenades near sites where Jews used to gather in order to frighten them out of Iraq and induce them to emigrate to Israel.

By now, however, the shortage of housing was so acute that the government had to resort to a new system of absorption and settlement – the *ma'abarah* (plural, *ma'abarot*) which was a transition centre designed to speed up absorption by encouraging immigrants to become independent as soon as they arrived. *Ma'abarot* were often established near existing towns or settlements where the newcomers could find jobs and fend for themselves, and such services as clinics and social services were provided on site. However, conditions in the *ma'abarot* were primitive, harsh and disheartening, with the immigrants placed in crumbling huts of wood and tin which were exposed to blazing sun in summer and were often flooded by winter rains. During the bitter winter of 1950, the situation in some of the *ma'abarot* became so critical that the army had to be used to bring in food and salvage tents and huts that had been swept away by the unceasing torrential rains. By the end of 1952, there were 113 *ma'abarot* comprising 250,000 inhabitants, the vast majority of whom were unemployed *Sephardim*.

The fact that the veteran Jewish *Ashkenazi* elite of Israel was responsible for channelling the *Sephardim* into the *ma'abarot* increased the animosity and resentment of the *Sephardim* towards the

Ashkenazim and caused much tension between these two communities. Yet growing tensions were not only the result of the coming together of the relatively affluent *Ashkenazim* who could afford to live in the big cities with the poorer – and usually with larger families – Oriental Jews forced to live in the *ma'abarah,* but it was also the outcome of an almost impossible meeting between two different worlds. On the one hand, the more educated, sophisticated, professional western Jews, and on the other a community of Jews from various Arab lands many of whom could hardly read or write. While religion by birth united these two peoples there was little else in common, not even language, for the *Sephardim* spoke Arabic whereas the *Ashkenazim* spoke Yiddish, German, Polish and other European languages. Israel, in the 1950s, was in fact a torn-up society with a clear-cut division between Oriental Jews from Arab lands feeling discriminated and being victims of apartheid, and a majority of European Jews, fearing that the presence of uneducated Oriental Jews would turn Israel into yet another Middle Eastern society. It would take years of efforts until the walls separating the *Ashkenazim* from the *Sephardim* would eventually tumble.

Arab vs Jewish Israelis

And if this was not enough then a growing rift was also starting to develop between Arab and Jewish Israelis. We should recall that although during the first Arab–Israeli War, the majority of Arab Palestinians fled Palestine, some of them remained, clinging stubbornly to their properties and lands. By now they were a minority – numbering 160,000 in 1950 which was some 20 per cent of their original number before the 1948 war – among the growing Jewish population of Israel. This remnant of what once was a vibrant Arab society was by now a beaten community which was further weakened by the Israelis who throughout the post-war period continued to suppress it by passing discriminatory legislation against it and deporting individuals and whole groups beyond Israel's borders. Thus, on 20 March 1950, the Knesset passed the Law of Acquisition of Absentees' Property, which legalized the expropriation of property belonging to Palestinians who temporarily fled their homes and villages and which was also applied to all Islamic properties. And on 2 September 1950, Israeli forces expelled some 4000 Bedouins in the demilitarized el-Auja zone into Egyptian territory, as it also did to the Arabs of Majdal (now Ashkelon), to mention two of many other cases. This Arab minority was too weak to challenge the new rulers of the land who, although promising the Arabs 'full and equal citizenship', did all they could to deny them this very right. And thus while the Arabs were formally guaranteed civil rights, in effect they became second-class citizens perceived by Israelis as a dangerous and not-to-be-trusted potential fifth column. That the Israeli Arabs were anxious to retain their separate existence, identity and culture rather than fully integrate into the emerging Israeli society further reinforced the Israeli view that they should not be trusted. And thus, they were not, for instance, invited to serve in the army which is a key advantage for success in Israel's society and without which they were precluded from some of the benefits of Israel's welfare state.

Two bodies were set up by the government to control and supervise the Arab minority living within Israel's borders. The first was the Ministry of Minorities which was established in May 1948 and was headed by Minister Bechor Shalom Shitrit. However, the liberal approach adopted by the ministry towards the Arab minority was accepted neither by Ben-Gurion nor by his influential advisers on Arab affairs and in July 1949 the ministry was abolished, leaving the task of supervising the Arabs of Israel in the hands of the Military Government. Established on 21 October 1948, the Military Government operated in areas where Arabs were concentrated and its main task was to execute governmental policies in these areas. It was a most powerful body hated by the Arabs, for it effectively controlled all spheres of their lives imposing on them severe restrictions: it banned the Arabs from leaving their villages and travel to other parts of the country without obtaining special permission; it detained suspects without trial and it also, frequently, in the name of security, closed whole areas, thus preventing Arab peasants access to their fields and plantations which was devastating for them for they were dependent on their crops for their livelihood. The Military Government also imposed curfews on whole villages and on one occasion, when the villagers of Kfar Qassem, unaware of the curfew, returned to their homes, the Israelis opened fire killing 47. The Shin Bet, the Israeli internal security service, was also active in supervising the Israeli Arab minority, seeing its main task as gathering information on suspected individuals and organizations.

Thus the government's main – though never official – line of policy in the years after the establishment of the state was to impose on the

Arab minority strict restrictions and to ensure its inferior status. Like the Jews themselves who for so many years were forced to live in ghettos, so now the Israeli Arabs were effectively living in their own ghettos surrounded by the Israelis. And like Jews in the Diaspora who were often forbidden from taking up certain jobs, so the Arabs living in Israel were not allowed to take up senior posts, for example, in the Haifa port or in telephone exchanges. It would take nearly two decades until this sheer injustice and discrimination would be relatively eased when the Military Government was abolished.

And yet in spite of the hardships and the communal tensions among Israelis, notably between *Ashkenazim* and *Sephardim* and between Arab and Jewish Israelis, the immediate years after independence were ones of growth and development, and the most familiar sound in Israel was that of hammers and building. The government, brushing aside the sheer difficulties caused by the waves of immigrants, went on to encourage even more Jews to immigrate to Israel by passing, on 5 July 1950, the Law of Return. It became one of the most important laws ever written into the state legislation and among its stipulations was: 'Every Jew has the right to immigrate into the country . . . a Jew who comes to Israel and after his arrival expresses a desire to settle there may, while in Israel, obtain an immigrant certificate. . . .' By passing this law, Israel effectively granted every Jew the right to come to Israel as an immigrant and automatically become a citizen, though the unspoken appendix was that non-Jews – Arabs and others – were unwelcome and that Israel, in the eyes of her founders, meant to be exclusively Jewish.

THE ECONOMY IN CRISIS

The absorption of so many immigrants and the need to maintain substantial armed forces – for a 'second round' with Arab armies seemed certain – put enormous pressure on the economy. What made a bad situation even worse was that agriculture, in particular the citrus sector, which had been a major source of income, was in deep crisis; compared, for example, with the years 1938–39 in which the export of citrus was more than 15 million boxes, in 1949–50 it dropped to a mere 4.2 million. It was not helpful either that from the Mandatory regime the government inherited a high cost of living and rising prices with a rate of inflation, in the first two years of the state, hovering around 50 per cent. Israel's fragile economy was threatened with collapse and resolute governmental intervention was essential if it was to survive.

Ben-Gurion's government moved to impose an austerity programme, a task which was entrusted to Dr Dov Joseph, who with Finance Minister Eliezer Kaplan, put together an economic plan aimed at reducing prices, limiting foreign imports and increasing local production in industry and agriculture. Israelis were obliged to tighten their belts, with every citizen being allowed to use only one shop to get a limited number of food items with a food ration of only a small portion of meat and two eggs a week. From restrictions on food, the government moved, in August 1950, to impose restrictions on clothes, and each citizen was given a quota of coupons to cover all purchases of items of clothing. This austerity package, 'Tzena' as it was known, had its drawbacks, including long queues for items, lack of essential foods and a serious deterioration in the quality of local production due to the lack of competition. Also, a black market flourished in which coupons were traded and luxury imported goods were sold to those who had the money. When in the winter of 1950–51 Joseph attempted to tighten the screw even further, spontaneous protest marches by workers and housewives became widespread, and with growing public discontent the minister was eventually relieved of his post. The most upsetting fact was that while the austerity programme did have a limited positive effect on the economy it was too timid to pull Israel out of her economic crisis.

The history of nations is littered with examples where problems like those endured by Israel during these early years led to the emergence of non-democratic regimes. Not in Israel though where, on 30 July 1951, Israelis went to vote in the second general election. The result was the retention of power by Mapai, the main socialist political party of the Labour movement headed by Ben-Gurion which won 45 seats in the 120-strong Knesset, a loss of only one seat since the previous election. Further to the left, Mapam secured 15 seats, a drop of 4 and the start of what was to be a steady decline. The General Zionists, fighting on a non-socialist platform, obtained 20 seats, the right-wing Herut representation dropped from 14 seats to 8, while the Communists gained 5 seats. The United Religious Front, which held 16 seats in the first Knesset, broke up into its various component parts with Agudat Yisrael, which was established in Germany in 1912, gaining 3 seats and the other religious parties between them mustering only

10 seats. The need to build a coalition government – for no party had an overall majority in the Knesset – and the existence of so many parties with such diverse demands and agendas, required lengthy negotiations before a coalition could be set up. It took Ben-Gurion's representatives 55 meetings with the different parties before a coalition could be formed, and it was not until 7 October 1951 that Ben-Gurion presented this to the Knesset and got its approval.

With the elections behind him and a coalition in place, Prime Minister Ben-Gurion could return to the main task in hand, which was to tackle the huge crisis in the economy and rescue Israel from a situation of near-bankruptcy. In February 1952, his government introduced a New Economic Policy – sales of Treasury bills and land bonds were stopped, the currency was devalued and a forced loan of 10 per cent was imposed on all bank deposits. It led to some improvements in the economy – production was rising, the balance of payments improved, inflation was held at a manageable 7 per cent a year, the import bill was reduced from $382 to $322 million and the trade deficit was cut from $337 to $278.5 million.

Assistance also came from abroad. In response to Ben-Gurion's appeals, American Jewry issued Israel Bonds which reached a yearly level of between $40 and $60 million in the 1950s and would climb even more sharply in the 1960s, and the American Congress approved a loan of $65 million to assist Israel absorb refugees. But the economy was still in a bad shape and it is, perhaps, ironic that it should be West Germany of all countries that came, or was rather dragged by the Israeli government, to the rescue and injected enough money into the economy to have a positive impact on it.

Shilumim

What Ben-Gurion's government decided to do – and this seemed so unthinkable to many Jews – was to call on the German Federal Republic to make a payment to the state of Israel and to Jewish survivors in compensation for the material losses and persecution suffered by the Jews during the Holocaust. Could Israel accept material aid from Germany only a few years after the end of the Nazi Holocaust? And would acceptance not give fresh substance to the image of the Jews as makers and manipulators of money? But Prime Minister Ben-Gurion, the driving force behind this initiative, was a practical man, and realizing the potential economic advantage of the scheme at a time when Israel was suffering a terrible economic crisis, he insisted that by now Germany was a different Germany and that she should pay compensation – *Shilumim*, in Hebrew.

As early as December 1951, Ben-Gurion's representative, Nahum Goldmann, the New York-based Chairman of the Praesidium of the Conference on Jewish Material Claims against Germany (also known as the Jewish Claims Conference), held a secret meeting with Chancellor Konrad Adenauer in London where he presented the German leader with a Jewish claim of $1.5 billion in compensation. Goldmann enquired whether the Chancellor would confirm the sum in writing as a basis for further talks; Adenauer agreed.

On Monday 7 January 1952, Ben-Gurion brought the issue before the Knesset where emotions ran high, with the leader of the opposition, Menachem Begin, leading the opposing camp to the scheme. In his address, Begin called Ben-Gurion a 'hooligan' and as he was speaking, incited protesters attacked the Knesset building and stones came through the windows into the hall. One hundred policemen were injured and the army had to be called in to restore order and prevent the crowd from storming the Knesset. In this highly charged atmosphere a vote was taken; 61 Knesset members were in favour of accepting the principle of reparations from Germany against 50 who opposed. Begin, accused of inciting the crowd and threatening the Israeli parliament and democracy, was barred from attending the Knesset for three months and he left Israel for Switzerland, only returning after six months.

On 21 March 1952, talks – conducted in English – between Israeli and German representatives opened on Dutch territory at Wassenraar's ancient ducal castle near The Hague. A few months later, on 11 September 1952, a final agreement, the Luxembourg Treaty, consisting of four separate agreements, was signed in Luxembourg. The first of these agreements between the state of Israel and the Federal Republic of Germany was the *Shilumim*, or reparations agreement, in which Bonn agreed to pay Israel goods worth DM 3 billion (approximately $750 million) over a period of 14 years. The second was an agreement between Germany and the Jewish Claims Conference in which Bonn took it upon herself to pass a law allowing the government to pay personal compensation (Restitutions) to Jews who had suffered under the Nazis. The third agreement, also between Germany and the Claims Conference, called for the payment of DM 450 million to rehabilitate victims of the Holocaust living outside Israel. The fourth and last agreement called on Israel to pay compensation for German property, most of it belonging to the Knights Templar, which Israel had confiscated.

On 22 March 1953, the Israeli government ratified the treaty and established an Inter-Ministerial Shilumim Corporation which decided to channel the German funds and materials into priority growth sectors of Israel's economy. Subsequently, substantial funds were transferred to modernize electrical generating capacity and railroads, expand ports and agricultural irrigation, exploit the southern desert's minerals and purchase a merchant marine. The capital infusion from Germany was enormous; in 1953–54 alone it provided one-quarter of the government's entire development budget.

It was partly in response to accusations that the government was trading with Jewish blood that, on 19 August 1953, the Knesset passed a law establishing a new institution in Jerusalem to enshrine and preserve the memory of the 6 million Jews annihilated by Nazi Germany and their collaborators. The new institution was called Yad Va'shem (the Holocaust Martyrs' and Heroes' Remembrance Authority) from the verse in Isaiah 'Even unto them will I give within My house and within My walls a monument and a memorial . . . I will give them an everlasting memorial, which will never be cut off' and it became a shrine for Jewish and Israeli visitors and a permanent remembrance for the tragedy that befell the Jewish people.

Substantial funds from abroad, mainly from America and Germany, an austerity economic programme, and a steep decline of immigration to a mere trickle – in the first half of 1952 the number of immigrants was one-tenth of the number in the previous year – all helped to improve the face of Israel's economy, giving it a healthier look and enabling Ben-Gurion's government to gradually remove the rigid controls on the economy thus allowing prices to seek their own level.

TENSIONS ALONG THE BORDERS

On 23 July 1952, a group of Egyptian officers which included, among others, Gamal Abd el-Nasser, deposed King Farouk in a bloodless coup. In Israel, this political change was regarded as a unique opportunity to build up better relations with Egypt and in an attempt to seize this opportunity, Prime Minister Ben-Gurion dispatched an emissary, Sheike Dan, to Yugoslavia to ask President Tito, who had good contacts with the new leaders of Egypt, to convey a message to the Free Officers to the effect that Israel was interested in forging new and better relationships. But Nasser, the strong man of the revolution, had other priorities, mainly to tackle the serious socio-economic problems of Egypt, fight poverty and social stagnation, and for him, at this time of the revolution, relations with Israel were not a top priority. As a result conditions temporarily became far quieter on the frontier between Egypt and Israel.

Very different, however, was the situation along Israel's border with Syria where tensions were running high, particularly in the demilitarized zones (DMZs). The root cause of dispute was the question of sovereignty in those areas which had been occupied by Syria in the 1948 war but were later evacuated by her and turned into DMZs under UN observation. While Syria maintained that these lands must remain under UN supervision until the conclusion of peace between the two countries, Israel, on the other hand, insisted that these lands lay within her sovereign territory – allotted to her by the UN in the partition resolution of 29 November 1947 – and that she was only precluded from introducing arms into them. When, in the summer of 1953, Israeli bulldozers appeared and started digging a canal in an attempt to divert water from the Jordan river at a point within the DMZs to irrigate the southern Negev desert, the Syrians opened fire. On this occasion, Damascus had the support of the international community and Ben-Gurion's government, under mounting international pressure especially from the United States which also suspended a grant-in-aid until Israel reconsidered, agreed, on 25 October 1953, to suspend works in the disputed area.

What, perhaps, more than anything else led to tensions and conflict between Arabs and Israelis in these early, post-1948 war days, was the presence along the borders and in neighbouring Arab lands, of thousands of Palestinians, previous inhabitants of Palestine who had left during the first Arab–Israeli War of 1948. Israel would not allow them to return and when some of them did attempt to cross back to their homes in order to resettle, pick fruit and, occasionally, steal from the Israelis, Israel resorted to a shoot-to-kill policy aimed at punishing the infiltrators and deterring others from attempting to take the same route. When occasionally Palestinian infiltrators killed Israeli civilians this led to brutal reprisals, as was the case in October 1953, when avenging the murder of a Jewish mother and her two children, Israeli troops led by Ariel Sharon, the future Prime Minister of Israel, attacked the

Jordanian village of Kibia and killed 63 Arabs at least half of whom were civilians. This action, like many others, brought worldwide condemnation on Israel who, nevertheless, stuck to this policy, often hitting back not only at the perpetrators but also at Arab governments to force them to curb Palestinian infiltration from their lands.

NEW LEADERSHIP

In the mean time, on 7 December 1953, Prime Minister and Defence Minister Ben-Gurion resigned his posts and took up residence with his wife Paula in the remote Negev kibbutz of Sde Boker. Ben-Gurion had played so great a part in founding the state and so dominated its affairs that few could imagine an Israel without him. But he had been worn down by successive political crises and felt, so he said to associates, that he could not bear any longer the psychological strain under which he had worked in the government. He therefore decided, as he put it, to leave the work 'for a year or two or more'. The Mapai's political committee wished to nominate Levy Eshkol as Ben-Gurion's successor, but with Eshkol unwilling to take on the job the choice fell on Foreign Minister Moshe Sharett.

Born in Russia in 1894, Moshe Sharett – Shertok before he Hebraized his name – arrived in Palestine in 1906. Aged 19 he travelled to Turkey to read law, then served in the Turkish army before returning to Palestine where he embarked on a long and distinguished political career. Sharett was graced with virtues rare in a politician: a passion for truth, honesty and fairness, together with a nobility of soul. Had he not chosen politics as a career, he could easily have become a poet or writer – among the writings Sharett left is his *Personal Diary*, a most valuable and often amusing massive – seven volumes containing 2128 pages covering the years 1953–57 – historical document. Sharett had deep roots in the Hebrew and Arabic cultural traditions – as a child he lived in an Arab village – and had, as one of his disciples, Abba Eban, put it, 'disrespect for anything that was shoddy, careless, untidy, imprecise or morally questionable'.[1] Sharett, though, was very different from his predecessor both in temperament and style. Whereas Ben-Gurion was impulsive, imaginative, daring, dynamic and often acted on intuition, Sharett was quiet, prudent – even timid – rational, analytical and realistic. They had gone together through many of the most testing ordeals of Jewish history and, in many ways, complemented each other.

On 25 January 1954, Sharett presented his government to the Knesset and gained its approval. But putting on Ben-Gurion's shoes was not an easy task, not least because the departing Prime Minister was determined to continue to pull the strings from his new home in the Negev. For that purpose, on the eve of his departure, Ben-Gurion installed personally loyal people in key positions. He made Shimon Peres, perhaps his most loyal lieutenant, a Director General of the Defence Ministry, appointed Moshe Dayan as Chief of Staff of the IDF, and most crucially awarded the Defence Ministry to Pinchas Lavon.

Lavon was one of the most capable members of Mapai, a handsome, complicated intellectual with a brilliant mind and a man of great probity. But with the benefit of hindsight it is clear that putting Lavon at the helm of the most sensitive of all posts – Defence – to serve under Premier Sharett, was a ghastly mistake. This was because Lavon had a very low opinion of Sharett and he was determined to pursue his independent policy without consulting, or even reporting to, the Prime Minister. 'Lavon', Chief of Staff Dayan once remarked, 'did not keep Sharett informed of army actions on the borders, and when he did submit reports, they were partial and not always accurate.'[2] Worse still, Lavon had been hitherto thought of as a dove, but no sooner had he taken over the Defence Ministry than he began to exhibit frighteningly hawkish tendencies and from being an outspoken pacifist, once in his new post, he turned into a hardline advocate of force. Thus, in a period where Palestinian infiltrators penetrated into Israel mainly to steal rather than to kill, Lavon instructed the Chief of Staff to carry out tough and brutal reprisals and to respond to the most trivial of border incidents by carrying out far-reaching retaliations. In his *Personal Diary* Prime Minister Sharett wrote: '[Lavon] constantly preach[es] acts of madness and teaches the army leaders that diabolic lesson of how to set the Middle East on fire, how to cause friction, cause bloody confrontations . . . and perform acts of despair and suicide.'[3] Lavon's irrational policies led to an odd situation where even hard-headed soldiers such as the Chief of Staff felt obliged to resist them. As Dayan put it in his memoirs, 'On more than one occasion, I had to restrain him [meaning Lavon – AB] from ordering military action which seemed unwise to me.'[4] And if this was not enough, then relations between Dayan and Prime Minister Sharett were not good either. From the very start Sharett objected to the appointment of Dayan as Israel's Chief of Staff, claiming that he was too much a 'partisan', undisciplined, reckless and lacked a sense of political responsibility. Sharett often complained that Dayan 'makes open propaganda against me as Prime Minister and as Foreign Minister', and that the Chief of Staff is the 'artist of flexible reports . . . it is a typical sign of a war impulse'.[5]

With such sour relationships between Prime Minister Sharett, Defence Minister Lavon and Chief of Staff Dayan, it is no wonder that Israel's foreign and military policies after Ben-Gurion's departure were confused. This, in turn, led to unfortunate results, most notably sabotage in Egypt in 1954 which, while causing relatively little comment at the time, was destined to rock the corridors of power in Israel for it was the opening gambit in the scandalous 'Lavon Affair'. Here is how it all started.

Sabotage in Egypt

In July 1954, Britain and Egypt initialled an agreement by which British troops would withdraw by June 1956 from bases in the Suez Canal area, which Britain maintained under a 1936 treaty with Egypt. This agreement caused much concern in Israel for if British troops were to leave, then British installations would be handed over to the Egyptian army. Even worse, the British military buffer zone would disappear, leaving Israeli and Egyptian troops facing each other. In response to this development, the IDF's Intelligence branch, which was headed by Colonel Benjamin Givly, agreed a plan which was a classic example of agent provocateur techniques aimed at forestalling, or at least postponing, British evacuation of her Egyptian garrison. The idea behind this plan was that by faking anti-British and anti-American incidents in which bombs were planted in various places in Egypt, the American and British governments, whose property was blown up, would attribute this to Egyptian instigation and conclude that the Nasserist regime was irresponsible and could not be relied upon to protect Western personnel and property in Egypt. Then, went the fatuous Israeli thinking, Britain would reconsider her decision to withdraw her forces and Washington, which was working towards a regional military alliance centring on Baghdad and Cairo and linked to the West, a project regarded in Israel as prejudicial to her security interests, would moderate her friendly relations with Egypt.[6]

Implicated in the plot was Avraham Dar, an Israeli intelligence officer, who as early as 1951 organized a network of young Zionist Jews in Egypt, whom he trained in making and installing of incendiary devices to be used in times of war.[7] Dar was now joined by another Israeli officer, Paul Frank, and the Jewish spy ring was put into action to plant incendiary devices, primitive homemade fire-bombs, in Alexandria's parcel post office, on 2 July 1954, at the American Library in Alexandria and Cairo on 14 July, and at cinemas in Cairo and Alexandria, on 23 July. The plan, however, did not pay off. The amateurish devices either failed to explode or caused only minor damage, the ring was exposed and its spies rounded up by the Egyptian police, except for Dar and Frank who managed to get away.[8]

The matter became serious when in Egypt, on 11 December 1954, the spy ring was put on trial on charges of espionage and sabotage. It was only then that Prime Minister Sharett heard of the affair which he had neither approved nor had any prior knowledge of. Upset and angry, Sharett nevertheless went on record in the Knesset, on 13 December 1954, to denounce the 'despicable slanders designed to harass the Jews in Egypt', and the regime which was conducting a show trial against 'innocent' Jews. Behind the scenes, frantic diplomatic efforts to secure the release of the Jewish prisoners failed and, on 27 January 1955, the Cairo military tribunal court published its verdict which was, at least in Israel's eyes, stunningly harsh. Two of the accused, Dr Moshe Marzuk and Shmuel Azar who led the ring, were sentenced to death and were executed by hanging, two were acquitted, and the rest received prison terms varying from seven years to life imprisonment.

It was not clear who, in Israel, had ordered this ill-conceived operation. Was it Defence Minister Lavon? He insisted that he had not. Or was it Chief of Military Intelligence Benjamin Givly? He, as he told the author of this book, had received the order to activate the ring orally from Lavon in the course of a private meeting they had, with no one else present, at the home of the Defence Minister at Ha'heshmonaim Street in Tel Aviv. In any case, following the 'security mishap', as it came to be known, and growing tensions between Defence Minister Lavon, Prime Minister Sharett and army officers, Lavon offered his resignation on 2 February 1955, and stepped down. The official explanation for the sudden resignation was 'disagreement over the structure of the Defence Ministry and the IDF' and by way of compensation Lavon was made Secretary General of the Histadrut. The Mapai elders then sent a delegation to Sde Boker to persuade Ben-Gurion to return to the Defence Ministry and work under Prime Minister Sharett. He agreed.

Although Sharett himself wished to see his predecessor back in government, the return of the strong man who by that time came to be known as the 'old man', made life harder for Sharett. Although the two, as mentioned previously, had worked together for many years, their ways began to diverge from the mid-1950s because they failed to see eye to eye on the most important issue on Israel's agenda, namely security, and the preferable way to respond to Palestinian infiltration and terrorism. Ben-Gurion championed an activist policy of severe and prompt military retaliation in respond to Palestinian infiltration. Sharett, on the other hand, advocated a more moderate policy in which each case would be considered on its merits and consideration given to what was the right time and place to react militarily, and to ensure that force was used wisely in combination with diplomacy. It was, in other words, activism (Ben-Gurion) against moderation (Sharett), two different approaches which in the days, weeks and months ahead collided.

A mere six days after returning to government, Ben-Gurion and Chief of Staff Dayan walked into Prime Minister Sharett's office, holding rolled-up maps, to demand his approval for an attack on the Egyptian garrison in Gaza. They insisted that such an assault should be made in response to the killing of a cyclist not far from Rehovot in southern Israel. Sharett, most reluctantly, approved the operation but, attempting to prevent excessive bloodshed, he insisted that no more than ten Arabs should be killed in the operation. On 28 February 1955, a military force under Ariel Sharon executed the Gaza raid by attacking the Egyptian garrison in Gaza. Complications on the ground meant that the operation was extended beyond what was first planned, leading to the killing of 38 Egyptian soldiers and two locals.[9] This was a far greater number of casualties than Prime Minister Sharett had authorized and he suspected that the raid was enlarged on purpose. Furious and stunned, he wrote to Ben-Gurion, 'I suppose, *though I am not entirely sure*, that the [increase in Arab casualties] from 10 . . . to 37 [was] an unavoidable result of the development of the battle.'[10]

Nasser was humiliated as never before and in later years claimed that the attack on Gaza led him to change his priorities from domestic to defence and turn to Moscow to supply him with arms so that he could face Israel if she attacked him again. In April 1955, Nasser concluded, ostensibly with Czechoslovakia but in reality with the Soviet Union, an arms deal under which Egypt was to receive a substantial quantity of weapons, including modern Migs and tanks.

Israel looked on with growing exasperation as the balance of power tilted in favour of Egypt, and with panic engulfing the whole nation, as hysterical politicians warned of the 'new danger', the Israelis responded by donating money to buy new weapons to redress the balance.

It would not be wrong to conclude that Israel's hasty and disproportionate attacks on her neighbour, mainly in response to Palestinian infiltration but also, at times, in the apparent absence of Arab provocation, and which reached a peak in the attack on Gaza in February 1955, increased tensions in the region and led to the arms race. In April 1955, Nasser's regime started offering open support for Palestinians in the Gaza Strip to carry out attacks on Israel.

THE POLITICIZATION OF THE HOLOCAUST

The Holocaust continued to haunt Israel. In 1955, a 72-year-old survivor of the Holocaust, named Malkiel Gruenwald, accused a fellow Hungarian Jew, Rudolph Kastner, of having made a deal with the Nazis to save his own family and 1684 other Jews, while three-quarters of a million other Hungarian Jews were deported to the death camps of Auschwitz. The story of the train that Kastner had managed to persuade the Nazis to send to Switzerland has always been controversial.

In March 1944, SS Chief Adolf Eichmann had offered a trade of 'blood for goods' under which he would spare the lives of 800,000 Jews if the Allies provided the German army with military vehicles and provisions. Rudolph Kastner, then Vice-Chairman of the Zionist Relief and Rescue Committee of Budapest, personally negotiated with Eichmann for the release of a train with Jews to Switzerland, promising that he could arrange the vehicles and provisions demanded by the Nazis to be supplied by the Allies. Kastner eventually succeeded in convincing the Nazis and a train packed with Jews, many of them either friends or relatives from Cluj, Kastner's home town, left Budapest at the end of June 1944. The train reached Switzerland in December 1944, after the passengers had been interned for a time at Bergen-Belsen.

The accusations were made in Israel when Kastner was a senior official in the Ministry of Industry and Trade, and the fact that the lawyer representing Gruenwald was a certain Shmuel Tamir, a former

Irgun member and a Herut activist, seemed to indicate that Gruenwald's accusations might be a politically motivated attempt to attack the ruling party, Mapai. There was nothing unusual about this, for Israeli society of the 1950s tended to view all issues, including the Holocaust, through a political prism, and political parties did indeed take advantage of such opportunities to promote their own political interests which inevitably led to a situation where the line of demarcation between memory and politics totally disappeared. In this case, Menachem Begin's Herut succeeded in identifying Kastner with Ben-Gurion's Mapai and levelling the accusations against Kastner with the institutions of the Labour movement. The state, in turn, brought an act of slander against Gruenwald and at the trial, which became an extraordinary court drama, Kastner argued that he had negotiated with the Nazis in order to save *all* the Jews of Hungary in return for material to be provided by the Allies to the Germans. It was the Allies, Kastner pointed out, who had refused to follow up the deal.

On 22 June 1955, the judge in the trial, Benjamin Ha'levi, issued his judgement. He acquitted Gruenwald of charges of libel and, ruling against Kastner, said that Kastner 'has sold his soul to the devil'. This harsh judgement made Kastner a hate figure in Israel – soon after the judgement was made Kastner was shot at close range by three men outside his home – and brought much criticism on the Mapai Party for not doing enough during the Holocaust to rescue Jews, and in some cases, as was the case with Kastner, it even dealt with the Nazis to save some Jews at the expense of others. The damage to the Mapai Party was substantial. In his *Personal Diary* Prime Minister Moshe Sharett wrote that the verdict was a 'blow . . . a nightmare, horrible, strangulation for the party. . .'.[11] It was indeed. And in the general election of 26 July 1955 the party went down five seats on previous elections.

But still Mapai was the victor and Ben-Gurion, who stood for the premiership instead of Sharett, was able to form a coalition government which he presented to the Knesset on 2 November 1955. Ben-Gurion kept for himself, in addition to the premiership, the Defence Ministry and offered the job of Foreign Minister to his predecessor Sharett, who after much hesitation – for by now his conflicts with Ben-Gurion had become sharper – agreed.

On the economic front things seemed brighter than before. Oil was discovered in marketable quantities in the Negev, German reparation payments were invested in the improvement of communication facilities, and the merchant marine was developing. A new harbour was opened near Haifa and work started on a pipeline to bring water from the Yarkon river to the southern Negev desert. There, between Beersheva and the Dead Sea, immigrants from Morocco established the town of Dimona, which later became the textile centre of the Negev. In the Lachish area, just opposite the Hebron Hills, a new enterprise began under which, and in an area of 125,000 acres, 45 agricultural settlements and two agricultural schools with 3000 new settlers were established. Culturally, Israel was also developing and, in 1955, the Academy of the Hebrew Language was set up to make the fullest use of biblical forms and also to coin new words where the vocabulary of the Bible was inadequate. Once more, however, security matters came to overshadow domestic affairs.

THE 1956 KADESH CAMPAIGN AND AFTER

We should recall that following Israel's attack on Gaza, in February 1955, President Nasser turned to Russia for assistance and this then led to a massive supply of modern arms from Czechoslovakia to Egypt. This transfer of arms had a strong effect on thinking in Israel, particularly on Chief of Staff Dayan who concluded that Israel should force a showdown with Egypt to destroy her new military arsenal before it could be fully absorbed and tilt the military balance in Egypt's favour. Such a strike, argued Dayan, and he exerted much pressure on Prime and Defence Minister Ben-Gurion, should also aim at relieving the blockade imposed by Nasser, in September 1955, at Sharm el-Sheikh at the southern tip of the Sinai peninsula which effectively closed Israel's sea lane from Eilat to East Africa and the Far East, thereby stifling Eilat port as well as the development of the Negev. But Ben-Gurion was still undecided and, it is often claimed, this is why he brought Dayan's proposals before the Cabinet, knowing that the ministers would reject such militant proposals. Indeed, when the matter was put to the ministers, they turned it down, deciding only that Israel should act against Egypt 'in the place and at the time that she deems appropriate'.[12] Ben-Gurion did not attempt to convince the ministers otherwise and he received a furious letter from Dayan, on 5 December 1955, stating that:

> The formula that we shall act 'in the place and at the time' we deem appropriate is a realistic formula when indeed the place and time for

such action are apparent . . . I therefore see our failure to act now, and our continued recognition of the Israel–Egyptian Armistice Agreement . . . as a *de facto* surrender . . . in my view we should undertake as soon as possible (within one month) *the capture of the Straits of Tiran.*[13]

Concurrently with his attempt to put pressure on Ben-Gurion to attack Egypt, Dayan also tried to force the hand of the government by enlarging military operations with the object of causing a highly volatile situation to deteriorate into war. He had used this deteriorating policy throughout the second half of 1955, and that his intention in doing so was to cause an all-out war with Egypt we know from such people as Gideon Rafael, an official in Israel's Foreign Ministry, who commented, on the basis of Dayan's words to officials, that the Chief of Staff wished 'to create a situation of such gravity that it would force the Arab states to take up open battle with Israel'.[14] Yisrael Beer, a senior adviser to Ben-Gurion – who was later exposed as a Soviet spy – pointed out in his memoirs that the intense military operations in the second half of 1955 were aimed only at exacerbating the situation to bring about war and that 'Dayan's only objective was to find reasons to justify the move which he had already decided to make, namely attacking the Egyptians as soon as possible'.[15]

Dayan and others in Israel who were keen to strike at Egypt had their opportunity in the wake of President Nasser's announcement, on 26 July 1956, that he had decided to nationalize the Suez Canal Company, most of whose shares were held by Britain and France. With diplomacy failing to reverse Nasser's decision and Britain and France embarking on preparations to regain control of the Canal by force, Premier Ben-Gurion allowed his Director-General of the MOD, Shimon Peres, to check, particularly with France, the possibility of Israel joining in an attack on Egypt. For although Ben-Gurion was still undecided on whether it was in Israel's interest to join France and Britain in a war against Egypt, he gradually came to believe that Israel could gain from joining the project. In his diary, on 3 September 1956, Ben-Gurion mentioned that for the most part he accepted what Chief of Staff Dayan had said to him, namely that Israel 'had to go on the offensive to entangle, deceive, surprise and break the enemy'.[16]

What, more than anything else, freed Ben-Gurion's hands was that he had succeeded, on 18 June 1956, in forcing moderate Foreign Minister Sharett to resign from office. As we mentioned previously, for many years Ben-Gurion and Sharett had worked together, but in the years after independence, their ways began to part and by the mid-1950s there was no harmony and they had become almost unable to bear the sight of each other and their clashes became more and more apparent. Now with Sharett out of the way and his successor, Golda Meir, being Ben-Gurion's loyal disciple, Ben-Gurion could more easily proceed with activist policies and even contemplate war against Egypt.

Gradually Israeli planners became involved with France and Britain in preparing for an attack on Egypt. The Israelis insisted throughout that while Israel could assist France and Britain to regain control of the Suez Canal she should, in return, be allowed to take advantage of the situation to proceed with her own goals, namely to occupy Sharm el-Sheikh and break Nasser's blockade of the Straits of Tiran, to strike at Palestinian bases in the Gaza Strip and, finally, to destroy the arsenal of weapons which Egypt had received from Czechoslovakia.

On 22 October, Prime Minister Ben-Gurion, in conditions of total secrecy, set out with a few aides including Peres and Dayan for a fateful summit in France to put the finishing touches to Israel's participation in a joint military operation with France and Britain against Nasser. By now, military plans were more or less at their final stage and the upshot of the collusion was that Israel would land forces close to the Suez Canal, thus creating a 'threat' to it whereupon France and Britain would send an ultimatum to both Israel and Egypt demanding that there should be no military movement by either side within ten miles of the Canal. Israel would accept while Egypt, so it was assumed by the planners, would almost certainly reject the ultimatum. At this point, Britain and France would intervene by invading the Suez Canal zone and regaining control of the waterway. After posing as a 'threat' to the Canal, Israel – so it was planned – would proceed with operations to achieve her own objectives. The operation was to be timed for the end of October when weather conditions would be ideal and, equally important, at a time when the election campaign in America was at its final stage which, so the planners assumed, would make it difficult for President Eisenhower to oppose Israel for fear of risking the important Jewish vote.

Talks between Israel, France and Britain at Sèvres went on for many hours. Apprehensive that Israel's cities might be attacked by Egypt and also wishing to have tangible reassurance that Israel would not be accused of initiating the war, Ben-Gurion made Israeli participation conditional on France providing air and sea cover for Israel's cities. Indeed, soon after the meeting in France, two French squadrons of 36 Mystères and 36 F-84Fs were stationed at Haifa and Lod and, in addition, a French naval squadron, including the cruiser *Georges-Leyges*, took up station off the Israeli coast.[17] Also, apprehensive that at the last moment Britain might turn her back on Israel, or even turn against her, by invoking treaty relationships with Jordan and Iraq, Ben-Gurion demanded a formal British commitment to the war plan. Both France and Britain accepted Ben-Gurion's demands. But the Israelis wished to gain even more in return for providing the pretext for war, namely French assistance to Israel in developing nuclear technology. In his memoirs, published in 1995, Shimon Peres revealed, for the first time, details about this matter:

> Before the final signing [with France and Britain to attack Egypt], I asked Ben-Gurion for a brief adjournment, during which I met Mollet and [Defence Minister] Bourges-Maunoury alone. It was here that I finalized with these two leaders an agreement for the building of a nuclear reactor at Dimona, in southern Israel . . . and the supply of natural uranium to fuel it. I put forward a series of detailed proposals and, after discussion, they accepted them.[18]

This was an enormous achievement, and the culmination of previous exhaustive talks between Peres and French officials in which Peres requested a small, 1000 kW atomic reactor for civilian purposes. Now, at Sèvres, Peres used the occasion to commit France politically to this project and he succeeded.

Eventually, the Protocol of Sèvres was signed between representatives of France, Britain and Ben-Gurion, and from Sèvres Chief of Staff Dayan cabled to his deputy, General Meir Amit, ordering him to start mobilization of armoured units immediately. On 28 October, just a day before the campaign was due to be launched, Ben-Gurion convened his Cabinet, informed ministers of the plan to attack Egypt in cooperation with France and Britain and sought and gained their approval.

On 29 October at 16:20, 16 Israeli Dakota and Nord transport aircraft escorted by fighter jets, crossed the border between Israel and Egypt and 39 minutes later dropped 395 men of Rafael Eitan's 890 paratroop battalion at Parker's Memorial just east of the Mitla Passes. This was the 'threat' to the Suez Canal envisaged in the

French–British–Israeli plan and the opening gambit of the Kadesh War – 'Kadesh' after the desert post where the Israelites had rested on their way to the Promised Land – or the Sinai Campaign as it came to be known in Israel. Around this time, another force, led by Colonel Ariel Sharon, embarked on a 190-mile journey across the Sinai to link up with Eitan's troops.

The next day, 30 October, Britain and France issued their prearranged ultimatum to Israel and Egypt. Israel accepted but Egypt, as expected, rejected, and following this refusal France and Britain began aerial bombardment of Egyptian airfields, at 7:00 p.m. on 31 October. In the mean time, the Israelis proceeded to implement their war plans. They struck hard at the Egyptian army, destroyed and confiscated much of its arms which had been provided to Egypt through the Czech–Egyptian arms deal, occupied the Sinai peninsula and relieved the blockade on the Straits of Tiran, and, finally, destroyed fedayeen bases in the Gaza Strip.

On 7 November 1956, in a victory speech before the Knesset, Ben-Gurion declared with some hyperbole that 'This was the greatest and most glorious military operation in the annals of our people, and one of the most remarkable operations in world history', and then, taking leave of his senses, he hinted that Israel would remain in the Sinai and in control of the Straits of Tiran. This was a premature announcement and Ben-Gurion himself would later say of this speech 'I was too drunk with victory.' Indeed, international pressure on Israel for an immediate withdrawal was mounting and in the UN the vote for an immediate ceasefire and full Israeli pull-out from the Sinai was 65 to 1 – Israel. There were threats as well. A report was going around Paris that the Soviets intended to 'flatten' Israel and the Soviet ambassador in Italy was making similar threats. American President Eisenhower added to the pressure by threatening that Israel's attitude would inevitably lead to measures such as the termination of all United States governmental and private aid, UN sanctions and eventual expulsion from the UN. Realizing that he had no option but to reconsider, Ben-Gurion convened his Cabinet and on 8 November, in a late-night radio broadcast, he announced that Israel would withdraw from the lands she had occupied.

On 16 March 1957, four and a half months after the Sinai Campaign began, Israeli forces withdrew from the Sinai and were replaced by UN forces which deployed in posts in the Gaza Strip, along the Egyptian–Israeli border and at Sharm el-Sheikh which commands the

Straits of Tiran. There was no formal international pledge that the Straits would remain open for Israeli ships to pass through, but Israel was led to understand that freedom of navigation through the Straits would be maintained.

Israel's first war since the War of Independence was short, decisive, low cost – 172 killed and 817 wounded – and it gave Israel a period of relative quiet along her borders, particularly with Egypt. Following this war the economic picture improved and Israel moved into a period of relative abundance. The opening of the port of Eilat through breaking Nasser's blockade of the Straits of Tiran, stimulated the development of the Negev and Eilat, and an oil pipeline was laid between Eilat and Beersheva and from there oil was transferred to the refineries in Haifa. The first flow of oil started on 14 April 1957. The opening of the Straits also provided Israel with a maritime outlet to Asia and Africa which were penetrated by Israeli advisers, scientists and technicians who brought the benefits of Israel's unique expertise in conquering an intractable soil and developing industries where none had existed before. The government made no secret of the pragmatic goals it hoped to achieve through its investment, particularly in Africa, notably the opportunity to avoid political isolation; by the 1960s, Israel was able, thanks to this support, to establish diplomatic relations with all but one of the African countries south of the Sahara.

With her borders relatively quiet Israel was for a period able to devote time and energy to carry out other projects, notably to complete the biggest drainage enterprise of the Huleh marshes in the extreme north-eastern corner of the country. This massive drainage operation created additional farmland, although it later transpired that not all the peatland was suitable for agriculture and there were hydrological and environmental repercussions which had not been taken into consideration. This project was completed in 1957.

DOMESTIC ISSUES

The riots of Wadi Salib

Not all went well, however, and after the Kadesh War Israel had to face severe socio-economic domestic problems and growing tensions between *Ashkenazim* and *Sephardim*. We should recall that Jewish immigrants poured into Israel throughout the 1950s and their numbers grew steadily from 18,000 in 1954, to 37,000 in 1955, to 56,000 in

1956 and 72,000 in 1957. While some 40,000 of these immigrants came from Poland and Hungary, the vast majority were Jews from the Maghreb, with the largest single component from Morocco. As was the case before, the *Ashkenazi* newcomers went straight to the cities while the *Sephardim* were assigned – usually by the *Ashkenazi* elite of Israel – to the most deprived neighbourhoods, notably in Haifa, and to development towns in southern Israel on the fringes of the Negev desert where unemployment reached staggering proportions. Gradually their desperation and frustration grew, reaching boiling point on 9 July 1959, when riots erupted in a slum inhabited by North African Jews in Haifa's Wadi Salib, one of the shabbier slums of the formerly Arab part of Haifa. The police intervened and shot a demonstrator which further increased the unrest following rumours that he was killed. Disturbances continued for several more days and extensive damage was caused to property – shops and cars were set on fire and there was much looting. The disturbances then spilled over to other deprived parts of Israel where *Sephardi* citizens were living. Shocked by the eruption of such violence, the government appointed a non-party committee to investigate the causes of the uprising. It issued a report in August whose bottom line was that from the moment of their arrival in Israel, the North African Jews had been exposed to a series of grave psychological shocks and found it difficult to integrate into the more settled Israeli society; but the report drew no elaborate social blueprint for the future and the growing problems and enmity between *Ashkenazim* and *Sephardim* were left unresolved and continued to haunt Israel for years to come.

The 1959 general election

On 3 November 1959 general elections were held for the fourth Knesset and Ben-Gurion's Mapai won 52 seats, more than it had ever obtained. Ben-Gurion formed a coalition which he presented to the Knesset on 16 December. New young faces who would rise to prominence in Israel's politics in the years ahead took key positions in Ben-Gurion's new administration. Abba Eban, the bright diplomat who represented Israel in the UN and the United States during Israel's birth and after was made Minister without Portfolio; Moshe Dayan, the hero of the Sinai Campaign, was made Minister of Agriculture; Shimon Peres, the architect of the collusion with the French in 1956, was made deputy Defence Minister. That these Young Turks entered government and occupied key positions, caused deep resentment among Mapai's veterans who suspected that by installing these young men in government, Ben-Gurion was attempting to bypass the old guard. There was some truth in this but Ben-Gurion was also careful to include some of Mapai's veterans, notably Golda Meir who stayed on as Foreign Minister, Levy Eshkol who carried on as Minister of Finance and Pinchas Sapir, who was made Minister of Commerce and Industry. Initially, Ben-Gurion's 1959 government promised a bold competence that would overshadow all its predecessors and hold out the prospect of a four-year term; in the event, however, this government held office little over a year.

THE LAVON AFFAIR

The reason for this was a scandal which came into the open in 1960 and the extraordinary revival of what by now became known as 'The Lavon Affair' or 'The Affair'.

Pinchas Lavon, we should recall, had resigned in 1955 from the post of Defence Minister amid accusations that he had given the order to activate a spy ring in Egypt, which attempted to direct incendiary devices at British and American targets and whose members were arrested and two of them were later executed. Now, however, Lavon demanded that Ben-Gurion clear him of the responsibility for the security mishap, a request which came in the wake of new evidence brought to Lavon's attention by an intelligence officer named Yosef Harel (in 1947 Harel had been the commander of the famous *Exodus 1947*) who told him that secret files had been tampered with and forged to make it seem as if Lavon had initiated the sabotage in Egypt. Other evidence showing that Lavon was apparently framed came to light in the course of the trial of Paul Frank in Jerusalem. Frank, we should recall, was one of the two agents who had escaped from Egypt. As it turned out, he had been a double agent and almost certainly informed the Egyptian authorities about the other plotters, explaining the speed with which the ring had been rounded up. Frank was brought to Jerusalem to stand trial and during his hearing he accused two officers of falsifying evidence in 1954 in order to place the blame for the security mishap in Egypt on the then Defence Minister Lavon. It also emerged that in previous hearings and investigations Frank had been coached and advised by people close to Military Intelligence Chief Benjamin Givly on how to testify against Lavon.

Upon Lavon's request to be rehabilitated, Ben-Gurion appointed a committee of judicial inquiry which was headed by one of the most distinguished Israeli lawyers, Supreme Court Justice Chaim Cohen – hence, the Cohen Committee. After a thorough investigation, the committee submitted its report, on 15 October, in which it concluded that the intelligence documents implicating Lavon had indeed been forged and it thereby completely exonerated Lavon from any responsibility for the security mishap. With such a dramatic conclusion, Lavon insisted that Ben-Gurion should announce, at once, that he had been vindicated. But Ben-Gurion could not clear Lavon without impugning the integrity of the military people, and this may explain why Ben-Gurion insisted that the findings of the Cohen Committee were not sufficient to clear Lavon's name and that a fuller judicial investigation was needed. Lavon felt betrayed.

There followed months of acrimony in which Ben-Gurion seemed to many of his colleagues to have become obsessed with insisting that a full inquiry alone could clear Lavon's name. The leaders of Mapai, however, fearing that a full inquiry of the sort insisted upon by Ben-Gurion might embarrass the party by revealing far too much controversial and potentially harmful material, decided, on 30 October 1960 – against Ben-Gurion's will – to appoint a seven-man ministerial commission of inquiry headed by Minister of Justice Pinchas Rosen to examine the matter and to recommend to the Cabinet their conclusions on the steps to be taken.

The Committee of Seven, as it became known, spent two months investigating the affair and presented its findings to the Cabinet on 25 December 1960. It came to the same conclusion as the previous inquiry committee, namely that former Defence Minister Lavon had not given the order to launch the bombing campaign in Egypt in 1954 and that the order and the mishap took place without Lavon's knowledge and that it had found 'reasonable grounds' for believing that 'a high-ranking officer', a reference to Intelligence Chief Benjamin Givly, had faked evidence in order to incriminate Lavon. In a vote in the Cabinet, in which Ben-Gurion abstained, the ministers who were weary of this affair and desired to remove it from the national agenda, endorsed the findings of the committee and cleared Lavon of having given the order to activate the spy ring in Egypt.

However, Ben-Gurion was a stubborn man and he insisted that the committee was not an authorized court of law, had not conducted its inquiry as a court, and had no right to issue a verdict in a conflict between two contestants and that 'ministers cannot be judges' and that only a full-scale judicial inquiry would do. Ben-Gurion insisted that the balance of Israel's democratic structure had been violated and the action of the Cabinet, without judicial authority, was a major corruption of the democratic process and of judicial integrity. On 31 January 1961, in a gesture which came to his colleagues as a bolt from the blue, but was not uncharacteristic of Ben-Gurion, the Prime Minister tendered his resignation to the President.

Attempting to placate Ben-Gurion and persuade him to return to government, the Mapai Central Committee, despite the verdict that Lavon was not to be blamed for what had happened in Egypt in 1954, decided to vote for his dismissal from his job as Secretary-General of the Histadrut. The vote on Saturday, 4 February 1961 was secret and resulted in 150 members in favour of Lavon's dismissal, 96 against and 5 abstentions. Lavon was sacrificed – cynically, hideously, brutally – to retain Ben-Gurion and he was forced, on 9 February 1961, to leave his Histadrut position amid rift and mutual accusations in the party.

Mollified at last, Ben-Gurion agreed to withdraw his resignation and form a new government, but by then his former coalition partners, Mapam and Achdut Ha'Avodah, were refusing to join his government as long as he remained the candidate for Premier. On 16 February 1961, Ben-Gurion officially informed President Yitzhak Ben-Zvi – he succeeded Chaim Weizmann who had died in 1952 – that he was unable to put together a new coalition. New general elections were called for.

These were held on 8 August 1961, and the campaign was bitter with the decisive, central issue being the moral fitness of Mapai to rule Israel. When the votes were cast, Ben-Gurion's Mapai emerged as the largest party with 42 seats in the Knesset – a loss of 5 from the previous election – and Ben-Gurion was entrusted with forming a government and was able to present a new patchwork coalition to the Knesset on 2 December 1961. Ben-Gurion stayed on as Prime Minister, but the Lavon Affair had inflicted a terrible blow on his leadership and judgement. He completely lost his high place in public esteem and confidence and he would never recover from the acrimony and animosity of this affair.

In 1961, a new influx of immigrants, which would add 194,000 Jews over a period of three years, started to arrive in Israel. Although many of these newcomers came from eastern Europe, the traditional source of Jewish immigration, the vast majority arrived from Muslim countries – Iran, North Africa and particularly from Morocco – and their arrival gradually tipped the numerical scales against the European elements in Israel's society.

GERMANY AGAIN

The trial of Adolf Eichmann

In the case of Adolf Eichmann in 1962, Israel was to use the death penalty for the first and, to date, the last time.

Eichmann was a Nazi official and SS officer, one of the active participants of the January 1942 Wannsee Conference in which the Nazi leaders mapped out their plans for the Final Solution of the Jewish question, involving the mass deportation and murder of European Jewry. After the war Eichmann escaped to Argentina where he lived under an assumed name. He was tracked down by Israeli agents who, led by Head of the Mossad Isser Harel, abducted him to Israel in May 1960. He was imprisoned and after about a year of questioning his trial opened on 11 April 1961 at Beit Ha'Am, a large public auditorium in Jerusalem. At the head of the panel of judges sat Supreme Court Justice Moshe Landau and the prosecutor was Israel's Attorney General, Gideon Hausner, a balding 46-year-old, middle-sized man, who made an eight-hour introductory address of high drama. 'As I stand before you, Judges of Israel', he said, 'I do not stand alone. With me, in this place and at this hour, stand six million accusers.' In his address, Hausner traced the course of Nazi anti-Semitism and wartime killing, and Eichmann's role, as a leading administrator of the Final Solution, in the annihilation of Jews in concentration, labour and death camps.

There was a ghoulishness about the whole long trial – the published transcript of which ran to 6000 pages – with its grisly details of testimony, with the way in which witnesses who had been through the traumatic events gave their evidence, about Eichmann himself seemingly a meticulous, soulless bureaucrat, a rather nondescript man in spectacles and always wearing a dark suit.

On 14 August 1961, after 114 sessions, the main proceedings came to an end and the court adjourned before meeting again, on 11 December, to announce the verdict. Eichmann was found guilty and condemned to death. His appeal to the Supreme Court which was heard three months later was rejected and an appeal, on 29 May 1962, for clemency to the President was also turned down. On midnight 31 May Eichmann was hanged, his body cremated and his ashes scattered in the sea outside the territorial three-mile limit.

The Eichmann trial was a significant event in the sense that not only was the criminal brought to justice but also that it was a unifying event for the Israeli nation as a whole – for Israelis of *Ashkenazi* origin and also for *Sephardim* who had not undergone the Holocaust experience. In bringing Eichmann to justice and turning the trial into a major event, the ruling party Mapai and its leader Ben-Gurion were also attempting to depoliticize the Holocaust, for we should recall that during the Kastner trial, the Holocaust had been used as a weapon by Herut and other political parties to attack Mapai and gain politically. By now, however, it seemed essential to make the Holocaust a non-political, non-party issue crossing party lines. In this the government indeed succeeded.

The German Scientists' Affair

In the year Eichmann was tried and punished, it was revealed that German scientists had been working in factories in Egypt assisting her to develop rockets adapted for use from launching pads which could be moved close to Israel's borders and strike at her centres of population. The German rocket experts also advised Nasser on ways of producing radioactive waste bombs that would have a limited fallout of radioactive material and could be used to poison food and water. Israel was indignant that President Nasser should give asylum to former Nazis – such as SS officer and propaganda official, Johannes von Leers, the Nazi security expert Leopold Gleim, among others – but even more so that former Nazi scientists should assist in developing weapons which could be used against Israel. Just how to address the problem caused division and debate among Israel's political–security leaders. On the one hand, Head of the Mossad Isser Harel, a most influential figure in Israel, held that the weapons developed in Egypt with German assistance posed a serious threat to Israel's security and any means were justified to stop these Germans from assisting Egypt. Prime Minister Ben-Gurion, on the other hand, whether out of conviction or simply because he wished to avoid a rift with Germany which might disturb the flow of compensation funds, insisted that there was no reason for alarm and that the missiles around which the storm had arisen were unusable. Quiet and behind-the-scenes diplomacy should be used to sort out the problem, Ben-Gurion insisted, and he ordered the Mossad to refrain from taking any measures against the German scientists. But Head of the Mossad Harel thought otherwise and, ignoring the Prime Minister's instructions, initiated a campaign aimed at frightening the German scientists. This included sending them bombs concealed in envelopes. When Ben-Gurion realized what was happening he was enraged and, on 25 March 1963, fired Harel, putting in his place as Head of the Mossad former General Meir Amit, who like Ben-Gurion held that the missiles posed no serious threat to Israel. It later indeed emerged that Ben-Gurion was right in his judgement. The missiles were not effective and were never used against Israel.

ENTER LEVY ESHKOL

On 16 June 1963, Ben-Gurion resigned as Prime Minister for the third and last time. He had been a powerful figure for more than a decade in the pre-state era and was a pivotal point in the lives of Israelis in the state's first 15 years. His squat figure, beetle brows, white tufts of hair, staccato speech and quick jerky manner of moving about – all gave an impression of clarity and purpose. His statements such as 'What matters is not what the *goyim* (nations of the world) say, but what the Jews do', were probably more extreme than he seriously intended, but he did manage to get across the message that Israelis have to understand the need for self-reliance and autonomous decision. However, in the early 1960s, Ben-Gurion's excessive concern – obsessiveness might be a better word – with the Lavon Affair, turned him into a lonely figure and he eventually placed himself on a road where even his close colleagues drifted away from him. Now, aged 76, he finally departed and was succeeded by Levy Eshkol.

Born in the Ukraine in 1895, Levy Shkolnik as he was known before Hebraizing his name to Eshkol, immigrated to Palestine, then part of the Ottoman Empire, at the age of 19. He worked as a labourer, a watchman and a trade union leader and was one of the pioneers who founded Deganiah B, one of the first kibbutzim to be established in Palestine. Upon the establishment of the state of Israel Eshkol was co-opted by Ben-Gurion as Director-General of the Ministry of Defence, effectively as Deputy Defence Minister. From 1949 to 1953, Eshkol was Director of the Jewish Agency's land settlement department and simultaneously, from 1950 to 1952, he held the key portfolio of Finance Minister. The huskily built, broad-featured Eshkol differed from his predecessor in attitude and temperament. Unlike Ben-Gurion who intervened in almost everything, especially in military affairs, Eshkol was far less hands-on and he was a pleasure to work with. He had a common touch and a gift for understanding what was in a simple man's mind. He was a smiling man, good natured and a superb organizer and administrator, always resourceful and ready with a humorous remark to ease tensions. Tireless in discussion, he won over his colleagues by solid and patient persuasion. There was a perception in Israel, even before Eshkol was made Prime Minister, that he found difficulty in reaching quick decisions, and whereas when Ben-Gurion was hesitating his admirers used to say that he was thinking, with Eshkol whenever he was thinking, his critics used to say that he was hesitating. But rather than hesitation Eshkol's approach reflected a different style of management which Israelis, so used to Ben-Gurion's bold and decisive, even authoritarian style, were not used to.

Entrusted to form a government by President Zalman Shazar – he succeeded Yitzhak Ben-Zvi who had died after a severe illness on 23 April 1963 – Eshkol embarked on setting up his administration. Like his predecessor, he kept the post of Defence Minister in addition to the Premiership. Golda Meir stayed on as Foreign Minister, Pinchas Sapir became Finance Minister, Zalman Aran replaced Abba Eban as Minister of Education and Culture, while Eban himself was appointed Minister without Portfolio and Deputy Prime Minister. Moshe Dayan stayed on as Minister of Agriculture and Shimon Peres remained as Deputy Defence Minister. On 24 June 1963, Eshkol presented his government to the Knesset, dubbing it 'a government of continuation'.

Although Eshkol was lucky to have a good and experienced military adviser in the person of Yitzhak Rabin, who was made Chief of Staff on 1 January 1964, it was nevertheless unfortunate for him that the coming years were dominated by security affairs, an area in which he was not considered an expert. An Arab League meeting in Cairo on January 1964 established a joint Arab command to confront Israel and gave official recognition to the Palestine Liberation Organization (PLO), whose recruits were to be drafted from among Palestinian refugees, and its dominant figure, in the coming years, was to be Abu Ammar, better known as Yasser Arafat. The PLO was soon to embark on a campaign of 'armed struggle' – 'terrorism' as the Israelis saw it – to free Palestine. And although these Palestinian attacks on Israel posed no real threat to the existence of the state, it became an unpleasant part of life in Israel.

In the domestic arena, in 1965, Eshkol consolidated his power base by negotiating a merger between his Mapai party and Achdut Ha'Avodah, the main rival for Labour support, which resulted in a left-of-centre party, the Alignment (the Alignment for the Unity of Israeli Workers). By merging the two parties, Eshkol was able both to draw nearer to the leadership of Achdut Ha'Avodah and at the same time to marginalize people close to his predecessor Ben-Gurion, who chafing at his isolation in the remote kibbutz of Sde Boker, directed a fantastically bitter vendetta against Eshkol, turning the life of his successor into hell by announcing at every opportunity that Eshkol was unfit to lead Israel. Why did he do so? Was it because he wanted to replace Eshkol as he did Sharett in 1955? We shall never know the answer, though one likely explanation is that Ben-Gurion hoped that Eshkol would agree to reopen the Lavon Affair by appointing a judicial commission, an action to which Eshkol had been opposed. Another 'sin' committed by Eshkol – at least in the eyes of Ben-Gurion – was his decision to permit the remains of Ze'ev Jabotinsky – the spiritual leader of the right in Israel – to be interred in Israel complete with a state ceremony. Ben-Gurion's bitterness culminated on 29 June 1965 when he formed a breakaway party under the name Rafi (the Israel's Workers' List). This newly established party which included such names as Shimon Peres, Moshe Dayan, Teddy Kollek, Chaim Herzog and Yitzhak Navon, had no coherent social and economic programme, and the only obviously new plank in its programme was electoral reform which, if accepted, could have swept this splinter party out of existence.

General elections for the sixth Knesset were held on 1 November 1965 and Eshkol's Alignment received 45 seats, making it by far the largest single party in the Knesset. Ben-Gurion's Rafi won a mere 8 per cent of the vote with ten Knesset seats, which was a tremendous defeat for Ben-Gurion and, effectively, the end of his political career. Begin's Herut, which just before the election had merged with the Liberal Party to form Gahal, gained 26 seats. Eshkol's government was slow to be formed and was completed only on 12 January 1966. It had a majority of 75 in the 120-member Knesset and consisted of the Alignment, Mapam, the National Religious Party (Mafdal), the Independent Liberal Party and two smaller parties. The opposition included Gahal, Ben-Gurion's Rafi and the religious Agudat Israel.

That year, Eshkol decided to abolish the Military Government in Arab areas in Israel which had been set up during the first Arab–Israeli War. This meant that the Arabs of Israel, those who remained after the 1948 war, were freer than before and were now allowed to leave their towns and villages and travel to other parts of Israel without obtaining special permission. This was a most important and brave decision on the part of Eshkol, which he undertook in spite of strong opposition from his Chief of Staff Rabin, and a decision which would lead to a marked – though far from perfect – improvement in Israeli–Arab relations within Israel itself.

Perhaps the most acute problem which needed Eshkol's full attention was the economy which was in bad shape, with the overriding problem being inflationary pressures caused by full employment, the influx of financial transfers from abroad, government conversion of foreign exchange receipts and borrowing from the banking system. The rise in labour costs also far exceeded worker productivity and the continual rise in the military burden – annual defence expenditures multiplied sixteenfold between 1952 and 1966 – did no good to the economy either. The need to tackle the economy was urgent because the crisis had had a profound effect on morale in Israel, and a growing number of Israelis, many in the liberal professions, emigrated, especially to America. In 1966, immigration was exceeded by emigration.

Eshkol now called for a moderation of growth and development and he introduced a policy of restraint which included a severe reduction in government spending, credit restrictions, a freeze of part of the German restitution payments, a freeze on wages and prices and a curb on building activity. But the price of restraint was heavy. This cut GNP growth to only 1 per cent in 1966 and resulted in widespread unemployment. Development towns in the Negev, the southern desert, were hit particularly hard with unemployment reaching a staggering 20 per cent. Ironically, it would take a fully fledged war to pull Israel out of this economic crisis.

4

....

The Six-Day War and Afterwards, 1967–1973

DESCENT TO WAR

Nineteen sixty-seven was a fateful year. War broke out in the spring and it turned out to be a milestone in the history of Israel and the Middle East. It all started in the north, where since the end of the 1948–49 war tensions had been simmering between Israel and Syria, with the three main sources of dispute being water, Syrian-sponsored Palestinian infiltration into Israel and squabbles over the demilitarized zones (DMZs) along the border between the two countries.

We should recall that in 1953 Israel was forced by the UN to abandon her plan to divert water from the Jordan river to the southern Negev desert. But still keen to develop the arid land of the Negev, Israel in 1959 embarked on an ambitious project to construct the National Water Carrier (Ha'movil Ha'artzi in Hebrew) to carry water pumped from Lake Kinneret (the Sea of Galilee) to the south, a project which was completed in 1964. The Arabs, particularly the Syrians, objected to this project and at a summit meeting held in Alexandria, from 5 to 11 September 1964, they approved a detailed plan to divert the tributaries of the Jordan river – the Hasbani and the Banias – that arose on the Arab side thus preventing their water from reaching Israel. In response, the Israelis used tanks to destroy the Syrian heavy machinery brought in to carry out the work of diverting the water, and when the Syrians moved their equipment beyond the firing range of tanks, the Israelis dispatched warplanes to continue the destruction. This war of tanks and warplanes against Syrian tractors, bulldozers and diggers reached its peak in four major border incidents which took place on 17 March 1965, 13 May 1965, 12 August 1965 and 14 July 1966. In the end the Syrians were forced to abandon work on the diversion of the Banias, while the Lebanese abandoned their half-hearted preparations for diverting the Hasbani. Water, however, continued to be a main source of dispute between Syria and Israel.

Syrian sponsorship and support for Palestinian guerrillas also kept tensions high between Israel and Syria. The Ba'ath (meaning Renaissance) regime in Syria was strongly anti-Israeli and regarded Palestinians as its pawns in the fight against the Jewish state. Thus, it not only supported Palestinian guerrillas by providing them with arms, but also allowed them to cross the international border into Israel to terrorize her citizens. Israel's strategy was to strike against the Palestinian infiltrators *and* those hosting and assisting them and this, inevitably, led to tensions with Syria.

Perhaps the main source of tension between Israel and Syria in the late 1950s and early 1960s arose from Israel's attempts to expand her hold on the DMZs. Although Israel had agreed, in 1949, that areas occupied by Syria during the first Arab–Israeli War should become DMZs, she nevertheless wished to strengthen her hold on these lands which she considered to be hers. The methods employed by Israel to expand her control in these areas were explained, in a rare interview, by Moshe Dayan, the former Chief of Staff: 'It used to go like this', Dayan explained:

> We would send a tractor to plow someplace of no value in the Demilitarized Zone knowing, in advance, that the Syrians would start shooting. If they refrained, we would instruct the tractor to keep on advancing, until the Syrians lost their temper and started shooting. Then we would start firing artillery and, later, also send our air force. . . .[1]

A major escalation and a turning point in the countdown to war took place on 7 April 1967, when an exchange of fire in the DMZ led to an air battle in which Israeli planes shot down six Syrian Migs, two of them in the skies above Damascus. The damage to Syria's national prestige was immense. Also, around this time Israeli leaders, notably Chief of Staff Yitzhak Rabin and Premier Eshkol, issued declarations which were perceived by Arabs as a plot to attack Syria and overthrow her regime. Because Egypt and Syria had a defence pact, signed on 4 November 1966, which committed each to aid the other if she should be attacked by Israel, the tensions resulting from the 7 April air battle, and what was regarded in some Arab quarters as threats by Israeli leaders to attack Damascus, also led to growing tensions between Israel and Egypt.

The spark, however, which ignited this powder keg, came from an unexpected direction – from Moscow which, on 13 May 1967, passed intelligence information to Syria and Egypt to the effect that Israel had mobilized forces on her border with Syria in preparation for an invasion of Syria. Ironically, Israel's announcement that, for economic reasons, there would be only a modest march on Independence Day, 15 May, in Jerusalem, was adduced as further evidence that most of her troops and arms had been shifted to her frontier with Syria. Israel, however, denied allegations that she was preparing an invasion of Syria and Premier Eshkol even invited the Soviet ambassador in Israel, Dmitri Chuvakhin, to tour the frontier and see for himself that no forces were mobilized; the ambassador declined the invitation.

We now know that no Israeli troops had been moved and no preparations for action had been made by Israel and the Soviet report was a lie. What is the explanation for this mysterious episode? A rare document, found by the author of this book, recording a conversation between a Soviet official and a CIA agent, shed some light on this affair. It shows that the Soviets deliberately released this false report in order to draw America, which was bogged down in the Vietnam War, into another quagmire, this time in the Middle East. 'The USSR', so said the Soviet official to the CIA agent,

> Wanted to create another trouble spot for the United States in addition to that already existing in Vietnam. The Soviet aim was to create a situation in which the US would become seriously involved economically, politically and possibly even militarily, and would suffer serious political reverses as a result of siding [with the Israelis] against the Arabs.[2]

As the false Soviet report came at a time of great tensions between Israel, Syria and Egypt, it was taken very seriously, particularly by President Nasser of Egypt, who regarded himself as the leader of the Arab world and was under growing pressure, especially from Jordanian and Saudi radio stations, to support his Arab brothers against the aggressive Israelis.

Nasser, therefore, rushed to defend Syria against what we now know was a non-existent threat, and he mobilized two armoured divisions, quite a substantial force, into the Sinai desert in an attempt to distract the Israelis and oblige them to transfer forces from the Syrian frontier to the south to meet the Egyptian threat. Nasser also dispatched his Chief of Staff, Mohammed Fawzi, to Damascus on a fact-finding mission to confirm the Soviet report and coordinate moves with the Syrians. Not surprisingly, Fawzi found nothing unusual along the Syrian–Israeli frontier and reported this to Nasser who, nonetheless, failed to recall his troops and even strengthened them.

Nasser's actions did not immediately cause alarm in Israel where Prime Minister Eshkol and his principal adviser on military affairs, Chief of Staff Rabin, decided only to monitor the situation without calling up reserves to strengthen the regular army. They had two good reasons for sticking to a policy of wait and see. First, a mobilization of reserves would cause a serious disruption of life, paralyse Israel's economy and might in itself escalate the crisis. Second, there had been a precedent to Nasser's action which had, nevertheless, not led to an all-out outbreak of war. This took place in February 1960 when, following an Israeli raid on Syria, President Nasser dispatched forces into the Sinai to distract the Israelis from continuing their attacks on Syria. After a short time Nasser dispersed the forces without ordering them to attack the Israelis. If now, thought the Israelis, Nasser was repeating the same exercise and attempting to impress on his Arab brothers that he was tough on the Israelis, who were apparently threatening Syria, then it would not lead to war and, therefore, no mobilization of forces was needed. What further strengthened the view in Israel that Nasser was bluffing was that some of his best military units were still engaged in the civil war in the Yemen and unless the troops were available at home, so it was thought in Israel, Nasser was unlikely to strike. Thus, Israel's response to the mobilization and deployment of Egyptian troops in the Sinai was relatively mild – on 15 May the IDF was placed on alert and a day later a limited mobilization of two brigades was ordered.

But things did not stop there. On 16 May, Major-General Indir Jit Rikhye, the commander of the United Nations Emergency Force (UNEF) in the Sinai and the Gaza Strip, was instructed by the Egyptian Chief of Staff General Fawzi to remove his troops from along the border between Israel and Egypt. These UN troops, we should recall, had been deployed since the end of the 1956 war along the border between Israel and Egypt and in the Gaza Strip and Sharm el-Sheikh, which controlled the Straits of Tiran. Legally, Nasser could evict these troops because they were stationed on the Egyptian side of the border and were there with Nasser's consent (Israel, after the 1956 war, refused to have UN troops on her side of the border). While it is true that these UN troops were too weak to stop any serious fighting between the parties, their presence as a buffer zone between Israelis and Egyptians was seen as a symbol of non-belligerence. And now, coming on top of the deployment of Egyptian forces in the desert, the demand for the UN troops to withdraw was seen, and rightly so, as a further escalation of the crisis. It is worth mentioning that Nasser, through his Chief of Staff, requested only a *partial* UN withdrawal, namely from along the Gaza to Eilat line though not from Gaza and Sharm el-Sheikh, but the Secretary-General of the UN, the Burmese U Thant, without even referring the matter to the Security Council, responded that he would not accept 'half measures' and that either *all* the UN forces remained in place, or *a complete* withdrawal would have to take place. The reason, as the Secretary-General explained, was that for the UNEF to carry out its assignment, it could not abandon some of its positions and remain in others. This was one of the most stupefying acts in UN history and, as it turned out, a grave error of judgement on U Thant's part because Nasser could not now, without losing face, get down from the tall tree he had climbed. And it was little wonder that the President's response, which came on 17 May, was that if a partial withdrawal of the UN troops was not possible then *all* of them should go. Which they did.

By now, with Egyptian forces deployed in the Sinai and the UN out, the situation seemed graver. To make things even worse, Arab governments began to release a stream of extreme and threatening declarations. In Damascus, on 18 May, it was announced that Syria's armed forces and militia had been brought to 'maximum preparedness', and the Syrian Minister of Defence and Air Force Commander Hafiz el-Assad declared that it is high time to launch the battle 'for the liberation of Palestine'. Jordan put her armed forces on alert and, at the same time, Iraqi forces moved towards Jordan – that is, closer to Israel – and the governments of Kuwait, Yemen and Algeria announced their readiness to dispatch troops and equipment to assist Syria and Egypt. In Israel, these developments caused much concern, raised the spectre of war and triggered a full mobilization of forces.

But there was more to follow and the crisis reached its zenith on 23 May when President Nasser declared the closure of the Straits of Tiran to Israeli shipping. 'The Aqaba Gulf consists of Egyptian territorial water', Nasser announced before pilots in the air force base of Abu Suweir. 'Under no circumstances will Egypt allow the Israeli flag to pass the Aqaba Gulf.'[3]

The Aqaba Gulf or the Straits of Tiran as the Israelis called this waterway, was perceived by Israel as a vital interest because from the port of Eilat and through these Straits, her ships sailed to the Red Sea and to the Indian Ocean. Access to the port of Eilat was vital for Israel's economy as, in the mid-1960s, it accommodated over a million tons of cargo and through it Israel exported some 30 per cent of her mineral exports. We should recall that, after the 1956 Sinai Campaign, Israel stated that reimposition of Egypt's blockade of the Straits would be regarded by her as an act of war, a *casus belli*, and now with Nasser declaring his intention to blockade the Straits the issue had become not only an economic matter but also a test of prestige for both Nasser and Israel.

It is hard to say, even with the benefit of hindsight, why Nasser escalated the situation, in particular why he closed the Straits of Tiran which he must have known was a vital interest of Israel. One explanation is that he was simply carried away, which was not unusual for him. He was intoxicated by the praise and adulation showered on his army by the Arab world the moment it marched into the desert and he conducted an exercise in brinkmanship that eventually carried him, and the Middle East as a whole, over the brink. Another possible explanation is that Nasser was encouraged by the personal vendetta of Ben-Gurion against Eshkol, in which Ben-Gurion depicted Eshkol as 'weak' and 'indecisive'. Nasser, according to this explanation, thought that he could have the fruits of victory without a fight and that even if he took such measures as blockading the Straits of Tiran, the 'weak' and 'indecisive' Eshkol would still not stand up to the challenge. Or perhaps Nasser thought that here was an opportunity to take advantage of the crisis and occupy Israel's town of Eilat and the southern tip of the Negev desert so as to secure the land bridge between Egypt and Jordan which was regarded as a vital interest of the Arab world. Whatever the explanation may be, the fact remains that Nasser's actions in particular, but also mobilization and declarations of war by King Hussein of Jordan and the government in Syria and other Arab states, caused great anxiety in Israel, and with men and material now deployed along the borders, Israel embarked on what came to be known as the Waiting Period – Hamtana in Hebrew – a sort of a phoney war.

In the period immediately after the closure of the Straits of Tiran, the Israeli High Command devised a military plan for the occupation of the Gaza Strip. The line of thought behind this strategy was that with the Strip occupied, Israel could use it as a bargaining card to compel Nasser to open the Straits of Tiran. But as the view developed that Nasser would not consider the Gaza Strip sufficiently important to trade it against the opening of the Straits, Israel's military plans were recast and envisaged a larger military action to relieve the blockade on the Straits and a thrust into the Sinai desert to engage the Egyptian army.

THE WAITING PERIOD

Diplomacy and confidence crisis

With tensions running high, Prime Minister Eshkol dispatched Foreign Minister Abba Eban to seek international support in France, England and America. In Paris, on 24 May, Eban met President Charles de Gaulle who, mistakenly thinking that Eban was seeking French support for an early Israeli strike, lashed at Eban by saying: 'Ne pas faire la guerre.' Reception in London was warmer. Prime Minister Harold Wilson pledged that Britain would join with others in an effort to open the Straits and would fully support international action to uphold the right of unrestricted passage in the Straits of Tiran. But by far the most important leg of the Foreign Minister's diplomatic mission was Washington.

While Eban was on his way to meet President Lyndon Johnson, Israeli citizens were preparing themselves for war. Basements and cellars were cleaned out for use as air-raid shelters, sandbags were filled to line the trenches dug in every garden and school yard, windows were taped and covered in black paper, car headlights were painted blue, parks in every city had been set aside for possible use as mass cemeteries, hotels were cleared of guests so that they could be used as huge emergency first-aid stations. Tel Aviv, the bustling metropolis with its cafés and bars, became a city of women and children, as all men were called up for war service. A sense of isolation and indeed fear of a coming catastrophe descended on Israel and the word 'Holocaust' was frequently used. Such was the panic that Holocaust survivors rushed to pharmacies to purchase poison tablets lest they fell into enemy's hands.

With tensions mounting and the mood in Israel becoming desperate, there was growing public pressure on Premier and Defence Minister Eshkol to allow Ben-Gurion back into the government either as Premier or Defence Minister. Ben-Gurion himself, in 1967, had already passed his eighty-first birthday and was quite out of touch with the state's affairs. But he had led Israel through previous crises, notably the 1948 and 1956 wars, and he was not only regarded as a strong and charismatic leader but also as an expert on military affairs, whereas Eshkol was more of a financial expert. The campaign to have Ben-Gurion back in government was run by the 'old man's' chief lieutenant, Shimon Peres, and by Menachem Begin, a long-time political opponent of Ben-Gurion, who showed on this occasion a measure of public spirit. In a face-to-face meeting with the Prime Minister Begin proposed that Eshkol step aside, letting Ben-Gurion take over as Premier in a government in which Eshkol himself served as Deputy Prime Minister. Alternatively, proposed Begin, Eshkol should carry on as Prime Minister and appoint Ben-Gurion as his Defence Minister. But as the relationship between Eshkol and Ben-Gurion was at a low ebb, as a result of past disagreements regarding the Lavon Affair, Eshkol bitterly opposed having his predecessor back in government. 'These two horses', Eshkol said to Begin, 'can no longer pull the same cart.'

While all this was happening, on 26 May, Foreign Minister Eban explained to President Johnson, in Washington, that Israel could not stand idly by while the Straits of Tiran were blocked and Arab armies were poised to strike within '24 hours'. That Nasser had threatened to close the Straits of Tiran was true but that the Arabs were intending on striking within '24 hours' was a lie, and this baseless statement – which Eban knew it to be – was aimed only at putting pressure on Washington and testing her resolve. Not being a fool and having his own intelligence on the situation, the President warned Eban that Israel must not be the first to open hostilities and that 'Israel will not be alone unless it decides to go alone.' The President thought, and so he told Eban, that the first priority should be to induce Nasser to end the blockade of the Straits and that this could be done but that he, the President of the United States, could not move an inch without authority from Congress. While supporting the idea of an international armada crossing through the Straits of Tiran in defiance of Nasser's statement of blockade, the President, significantly, did not take it upon himself to organize such an armada.

In the mean time, pressures were growing in Israel. On the morning of 27 May (03:00 Israeli time), the Soviet ambassador in Tel Aviv, Dmitri Chuvakhin, roused Prime Minister Eshkol to deliver a message from Prime Minister Kosygin, urging Eshkol not to take any military steps against either Syria or Egypt. Eshkol received the ambassador in his pyjamas, hence the Night of the Pyjamas, and he reassured the ambassador that Israel did not intend to open fire.[4]

On his return to Israel, Foreign Minister Eban reported to the Cabinet that the President of the United States had assured him that the US would use 'every measure' at her disposal to open the Straits to Israeli shipping. Eban's recommendation was to adhere to a policy of waiting and to give Washington a chance to sort out the crisis. The reaction of ministers was mixed: nine were in favour of accepting Eban's proposal to wait, nine, including Prime Minister Eshkol, called for immediate military action. A tie. The Cabinet then decided to wait 'another week or two' and Eshkol – who favoured an immediate strike – had the unwelcome task of taking this decision to an anxious public and impatient military commanders who wished to strike at once.

He went live on air, in the evening of 28 May, to let a nation, whose nerves were stretched to breaking point, know of the Cabinet's decision to proceed with the policy of waiting. Eshkol's speech was awaited with expectancy and throughout the country, in the desert and along Israel's other frontiers, ears were glued to the radio sets – there was no television yet in Israel. But it was a disastrous broadcast. The speech was hurriedly prepared, hastily typed and Eshkol, because of his busy schedule, had no time to look over it before being rushed to the microphone. So he faltered and stumbled over the words and his speech which came to known as the 'stumbling speech' did little to reassure the nation. For Eshkol, though, this was not yet the end of the ordeal. From the radio studio he was rushed to face his military commanders to justify the Cabinet's decision to wait. In the 'Pit', as the military headquarters in Tel Aviv is called, Eshkol – flanked by Chief of Staff Rabin and Minister of Labour Yigal Allon – invited his commanders to speak their minds. They did so without inhibition. And that night came to be known in Israel's history as the Night of the Generals. Division commanders Ariel Sharon and Yisrael Tal said to Eshkol that 'the issue is not the opening of the Straits but rather the existence of the State of Israel'. Sharon went on to say that 'now is the time for the military to move, without any more delays', and he warned Eshkol of 'a sharp escalation of casualties with each passing day of waiting'.[5] Chief of Staff Rabin, although not agreeing with the continuation of the policy of waiting, said nothing, leaving his subordinates to express their views. 'I could not as the Chief of Staff', Rabin explained to the author of this book, 'speak against the government's decision not to strike in front of the other commanders.'[6] Defending the decision of his Cabinet not to open fire – Eshkol himself, we should remember, was one of nine ministers who were in favour of a strike – the Prime Minister urged the generals to be patient since one should continue negotiations in order to exhaust all other possibilities before going to war. But rather than calming the situation, this statement heated the debate further and when a young colonel, Avraham Ayalon, interrupted the Prime Minister in an outburst of frustration, Minister of Labour Yigal Allon proposed that the discussion break for a recess.

Gradually the public began to show signs of impatience and the bolder Nasser became the more Israelis questioned Eshkol's ability to cope with the situation. On 31 May, with growing criticism and public pressure for a resolute stance, Eshkol agreed to relinquish the Defence portfolio – though remaining Prime Minister – and nominate Minister of Labour, Yigal Allon, to the post of Defence Minister. But the religious party Mafdal, then a coalition partner, wanted to see Moshe Dayan of Rafi rather than Allon as Defence Minister. The reason for that was that most members of Mafdal were moderate and they hoped that the appointment of former Chief of Staff Dayan to Defence would be a bold enough step to frighten Nasser into backing away from a confrontation. They also believed that Dayan, like his mentor Ben-Gurion, was *against* war – Ben-Gurion believed that Israel should avoid war unless she had a mutual agreement with a friendly power, i.e. the US – and his appointment, rather than that of the more belligerent Allon, would prevent war. Pressure to make Dayan Defence Minister also came from another unexpected quarter – from housewives, who held a big demonstration in Tel Aviv chanting 'we want Dayan'. Eshkol, whose sense of humour never abandoned him even in moments of deep crisis, dubbed these earnest, zealous, sober-faced ladies 'the Merry Wives of Windsor'. By then being as realistic and down-to-earth as he was, Eshkol understood that the game was up. So he set up a wall-to-wall government of National Unity which, for the first time in Israel's history included Begin's Herut party – Begin himself was appointed Minister without Portfolio – and Rafi, with its member Dayan, the victor of the Sinai Campaign, Defence Minister.

Moshe Dayan was born in 1915 in kibbutz Deganiah, northern Palestine. He joined the Haganah, the illegal Jewish underground organization in Palestine, in his teens and, in 1936, joined Orde Wingate's SNS and participated in raids against the Arabs who revolted against the British and attacked Jews. Dayan was later imprisoned by the British in Palestine, but after his release, in early 1941, he led a British reconnaissance unit into Syria, then under a pro-Nazi French regime. It was during this raid that he was severely wounded, lost his left eye and from that time the wearing of a black patch became his trademark. During Israel's 1948 War of Independence, Dayan fought against the Syrians in defence of Galilee, and later led Israeli troops to occupy the Arab towns of Ramleh and Lydda in central Palestine. He was close to the then Premier and Defence Minister Ben-Gurion who made him, in December 1953, Chief of Staff of the Israeli armed forces. In this job, Dayan proved himself to be an aggressive and imaginative soldier of rare originality of mind. It was he who drew up the plan of Israel's 1956 campaign against Egypt on the back of a cigarette packet, and when hostilities broke out, riding on a vehicle, he led his forces from the front. Two years after this successful war, in 1958, Dayan retired from the IDF and joined the Mapai Party. He was elected to the Knesset in 1959 and served as Minister of Agriculture in Ben-Gurion's government and later in Eshkol's. In 1964 he resigned to join Ben-Gurion's Rafi Party and was a member of the Knesset.

Dayan was a colourful character, admired by men and, in particular, women. He had a trait very few leaders possess, namely a strong sense of how things would develop in the future, and this often proved accurate and even prophetic. But he was also a pessimist and though an extraordinarily brave soldier, as a politician he far too often failed to fight for his opinions and backed down from his realistic views the moment he was facing an opposition. But popular trust in the one-eyed Dayan was overwhelming and his appointment to the post of Defence Minister instead of Eshkol restored confidence in the armed forces and the government.

While Israelis were celebrating the appointment of a new Defence Minister and while Dayan himself was beginning to function, in Washington another Israeli emissary was in talks with officials. After Foreign Minister Eban's report to the Cabinet of his meetings in Washington and the impression he left on ministers that the Americans intended to take resolute action to open the Straits of Tiran, a cable came from President Johnson which seemed to contradict Eban's rosy report. Eshkol felt he needed further clarification of Washington's stance and he, therefore, dispatched a special envoy, Head of the Mossad, Meir Amit, for further talks with the Americans. In Washington, Amit met officials of the intelligence community (mainly the CIA) and later Secretary of Defense Robert MacNamara. He said to MacNamara that he intended to recommend to the Cabinet the launching of a pre-emptive attack on Egypt to which the American Secretary of Defense responded by saying: 'I read you loud and clear.' This was taken by Amit to be a green, or at least, an amber light for Israel to strike.[7]

In Israel, Dayan's appointment as Defence Minister on 1 June made little difference to the battle plans which had already been completed before his appointment. Nevertheless, his guidelines to military commanders, on 2 June, were crucial in clarifying how he wanted the coming war to be run. He insisted that, if and when war broke out, the IDF should reach the Straits of Tiran and relieve the blockade imposed by Nasser.[8] For although Nasser's declaration of his closure of the Straits was for Israel the last straw and a *casus belli*, with the escalation of the crisis the blockade had turned into a peripheral issue and the main need, as the military High Command saw it, was to break the backbone of the Arab armies, especially the Egyptian army in central Sinai. In this crucial meeting Dayan also instructed his commanders *not* to occupy the Suez Canal. The line of thought behind this policy was that if Israeli forces kept their distance from the Canal then Nasser could, after the war, operate it and there would be little incentive for him to keep on fighting lest by doing so he would deter potential users from sailing through the Canal which would then result in Egypt losing important revenues. Finally, Dayan insisted that the Gaza Strip which, as he put it, 'bristled with problems', should not be occupied as that Strip had a large Palestinian population which Dayan did not wish to see joining that of Israel. The limitations and restrictions imposed by Dayan with regard to the Gaza Strip and the Suez Canal were clear and precise. As Aharon Yariv, then Director of Military Intelligence, who was present at the 2 June meeting, explained to the author of this book, 'Dayan said to the General Staff: "I give you now the instructions of the Defence Minister: First, to hit the Egyptian army; Second, not to reach the Suez Canal, and third not to enter the Gaza Strip." . . .'[9]

By this time, roughly two weeks after Nasser's first mobilization of forces in the desert, the Egyptians had seven divisions and a strength of 100,000 men in the Sinai. Syria had concentrated more than 50,000 troops along her frontier with Israel, and King Hussein had mobilized his 56,000-strong army. Libya, Iraq, Algeria and Kuwait all sent reinforcements and in the Gaza Strip Palestinians deployed weapons supplied to them mainly by Egypt. Israel, by now fully mobilized, concentrated the main bulk of her forces in the desert to face the Egyptian army. Tensions were high and war seemed imminent.

Back in Israel after his diplomatic mission to Washington, Head of the Mossad Amit reported to the Cabinet in an emergency session on Saturday 3 June. Surprisingly, however, Amit did not recommend a strike but rather proposed giving Washington another chance to take measures to sort out the crisis. But by now the newly appointed Defence Minister Dayan was determined that the circumstances required resolute action by Israel, otherwise she would lose her deterrent power, and he proposed to send the IDF into battle. Thus, ironically, Dayan, who was made Defence Minister mainly under the dovish pressure of the religious ministers of Mafdal, hoping that he would block a war, was now the driving force behind the new policy of striking at Egypt as soon as possible.

The next day, Sunday 4 June, Eshkol convened his Cabinet which approved the taking of military action. In a later, tête-à-tête meeting, Dayan and Eshkol agreed to strike on the next day.

SIX DAYS OF WAR

The attack on Egypt

We should recall that what sparked this crisis were tensions in the north, along Israel's frontier with Syria, but by now all eyes were fixed on the south where vast Israeli and Egyptian forces were facing each other. When the order came to embark on war, the Israeli air force, on 5 June 1967 at 7.45 a.m., began to implement Operation Moked. Leaving just 12 aircraft to protect Israel's skies, the striking Israeli force followed a very roundabout approach, flying via the sea and coming down from the west on airfields all across Egypt. When the Israeli warplanes were approaching their targets, the air-raid sirens began wailing through Tel Aviv and then through the entire country. On the 8 o'clock news bulletin the announcement of the IDF spokesman went, 'Air and armoured battles have been taking place since the early hours of the morning following an enemy move toward Israel.' This, of course, was an outright lie for it was Israel, rather than the enemy, which was the first to open fire.

Operation Moked succeeded beyond all expectations. Within 190 minutes the backbone of the Egyptian air force was broken – 189 aeroplanes were destroyed in the first wave of attack, mostly while still parked on their runway, and by the end of the first day of war a stunning 298 Egyptian planes lay in ruins. The air strike caught the Egyptian politico-military leadership totally by surprise, for although expecting the Israelis to attack, they did not imagine that the assault would be so massive and come from an unexpected direction.

But bombing was only one element in the Israeli strategy and, at 8.15 a.m., the ground forces were issued with the code words *Sadim Adom* (Red Sheet). Now, backed by complete air superiority, for with the Egyptian air force largely destroyed the Israeli air force was unopposed and had mastery of the sky, three Israeli divisions went into action and thrust into the Sinai desert. They engaged the enemy and then pursuing the Egyptians, who were in full flight across the desert, approached the bank of the Suez Canal. On 7 June, the Cabinet met to discuss the war in the desert and the military representative sent a note to Minister Yisrael Galili, saying: 'Concerning the Suez [Canal] . . . until now the decision has been not to reach the Suez [a reference to Dayan's instruction of 2 June not to occupy the Suez Canal – AB] . . . I propose that we do reach the Suez [Canal]. Militarily it is possible . . . I believe that this is the last possible minute for a decision in this direction.'[10] But Defence Minister Dayan stood firm and the Cabinet decided that the forces should keep their distance from the water. Later that day, Dayan told his press conference that Israel had 'achieved her political objectives . . . against Egypt . . . Israel could have taken positions on the [Suez] Canal but did not wish to do so [Israel's] quarrel has nothing to do with the Suez Canal.'[11] So insistent was Dayan on this issue, that when he felt that the forces had disobeyed him and had moved closer to the Suez Canal, he instructed Chief of Staff Rabin to stop them and pull them back, which Rabin did. But not for long. When Rabin came back to Dayan to say that there was no military logic in stopping short of the Suez Canal, Dayan gave way and allowed the forces to push on and advance all the way to the Suez Canal.[12] As one division commander in this war, Ariel Sharon, later remarked, 'Dayan had not wanted to advance to the Canal. But the army had pressured him to do it anyway out of what its field commanders regarded as tactical necessity. And he had given way.'[13] Dayan himself, suggesting that his arm was effectively twisted by the forces and that he was forced to accept a military diktat, pointed out, after the war, that he 'did not want, under any circumstances, to reach the Canal. [He] issued orders to stop some distance from it. But the army established facts on the ground and [he] had no choice.'[14]

We should also recall that in his 2 June meeting with military commanders, Dayan had ordered that the Gaza Strip should not be occupied, for it 'bristled with problems', as Dayan put it. However, on the first two days of the war, Palestinians shelled Israeli settlements from within the Gaza Strip and, in the words of then OC Southern Command, Gavish: 'To avoid heavy damage I ordered the capture of [the] Gaza [Strip].'[15] It is not clear whether or not Dayan himself allowed the forces to enter the Gaza Strip and occupy it, for after the war he bitterly complained that 'It had apparently been decided at the army level that the target would be [the] Gaza [Strip]. . . .'[16] And when, on 10 June, he met General Gavish in the desert, he was so furious that he lashed out at Gavish by threatening, as Gavish told the author of this book, that he would haul him before a military tribunal for disobeying his orders not to reach the Suez Canal and occupy the Gaza Strip.

With the benefit of hindsight it is clear that Dayan's original intention not to occupy the Suez Canal and the Gaza Strip was correct. But he failed to impose his policies on his subordinates and allowed the troops, mostly by turning a blind eye, or simply by crumbling under their pressure, to dictate Israel's policies for years to come.

In the mean time, while Israeli troops were taking positions along the Suez Canal's eastern bank, a small naval force landed and captured Sharm el-Sheikh, which controlled the Straits of Tiran, and relieved the non-existent blockade of the Straits. For although Nasser declared to the entire world his intention to impose a blockade on the Straits, and this was indeed the *casus belli* for Israel to go to war, in reality such a blockade was never imposed.

War with Jordan and attack on liberty

From the start, the Israelis, through various channels, urged King Hussein of Jordan to keep out of the battle. So why did the King make the colossal mistake of joining the war? Perhaps because he was a man of honour. He had signed a defence pact with Nasser in Cairo, on 30 May, obliging him to come to Egypt's aid should she be attacked, and when the Israelis did strike at Egypt, Hussein felt he was committed. According to King Hussein himself, he joined the battle because he had no other option, for with Palestinians making up more than half of Jordan's population, he could not stay out lest his kingdom disintegrate from within. Perhaps the King also felt that if he stayed out he would miss the boat and not enjoy the fruits of Arab victory over the Israelis. Whatever the explanation, when the messages from the Israelis reached the King he drily replied, 'Jordan is not out. Jordan is already engaged. Jordan is already involved in military activities.'[17]

Jordanian 155-mm Long Toms fired on Israeli towns and shells landed in the Tel Aviv area; at 12.25 a.m., Jordanian warplanes attacked Netanya and some time later Kfar Sirkin and Kfar Saba came under fire. In Jerusalem, the King's troops crossed the armistice line and occupied the Government House Headquarters of the UN, formerly the residence of the British High Commissioner. When attacked, Israel reacted massively. Her air force put the small Jordanian air force out of action and Israeli ground forces moved, from different directions, to occupy the West Bank. In Jerusalem, Israeli troops moved to seize Government House and link up with the Mount Scopus enclave, isolated in a DMZ within the King's own territory and guarded only by a force of 85 Israeli police.

Soon the main item on the Cabinet's agenda was Arab East Jerusalem. Should Israel occupy it? Pressure not to do so came from an unexpected quarter – from the religious Mafdal Party whose leading member, Moshe Chaim Shapiro, argued that it would be unwise to seize Jerusalem because it would become an albatross around Israel's neck, or as he put it, '[if Israel occupied Jerusalem then] rather than we own Jerusalem, Jerusalem would own us'. But with growing pressure, particularly from ministers Menachem Begin and Yigal Allon, and the feeling that here was a historical opportunity not to be missed, and with an imminent UN ceasefire a possibility, the government, at 7.00 a.m. on the morning of 7 June, instructed the IDF to seize Jerusalem.

Subsequently, Israeli forces attacked with a pincer movement in the north and the south to cut the Old City off from Jordanian reinforcements coming from the east. Later that morning, Colonel Mordechai 'Motta' Gur reported that his paratroopers had penetrated the Lions' Gate and were approaching the Dome of the Rock. By 9 June the old walled town of Jerusalem fell into Israel's hands and when it was all clear, Moshe Dayan, accompanied by Chief of Staff Rabin and OC Central Command, Uzi Narkiss, marched into Jerusalem through the

Lions' Gate. 'The IDF liberated Jerusalem', Dayan announced at the Wailing Wall, 'We have returned to our holiest places, we have returned in order not to part from them ever again.' That day the poet, Naomi Shemer, released her ballad 'Jerusalem the Golden', which soon became the anthem of this war:

> We have come back to the deep wells
> To the marketplace again.
> The trumpet sounds on the Mount of the Temple
> In the Old City.
> In the caverns of the cliff
> Glitter a thousand suns.
> We shall go down to the Dead Sea again
> By the road to Jericho.

The Chief Rabbi of the IDF, Shlomo Goren, blew the *shofar* near the Wailing Wall and seeing a unique opportunity to assert Israel's authority over Jerusalem for ever, he proposed to OC Central Command to 'put a hundred kilograms of explosives under the Mosque of Omar (according to Moslem tradition it was from this site that the Prophet Muhammad had purportedly ascended heaven) and that's it, we will get rid of it once and for all'. Narkiss rejected this offer.[18] And there were other ideas which came in the wake of the occupation of Jerusalem, notably Ben-Gurion's, to demolish the Old City walls because they had been constructed not by Jewish hands but by Ottoman sultans. While these extreme proposals were rejected out of hand, the government, nevertheless, moved ahead to do some work before the fog of war disappeared. Thus bulldozers were hastily transferred to Jerusalem and razed to the ground some 200 Palestinian houses facing the Wailing Wall, so as to create a parade ground in front of the wall and to clear space for the masses of Jews expected to come to embark on Jerusalem.

With the war in full swing an incident occurred which would dent Israeli-American relationships for years to come. This was the Israeli air and naval assault on the United States ship USS *Liberty*, which resulted in the death of 34 US men and the wounding of some 171. *Liberty,* an American spy ship, was despatched by Washington to the Middle East to monitor the progress of the battle between Israelis and Arabs and report back home. However, on 8 June, while sailing approximately 12.5 miles off the coast of the Sinai peninsula, in the vicinity of El Arish, she was attacked by the Israelis. The attack has been a matter of controversy ever since and over the years there have been speculations on whether the Israeli assault was premediated – planned and deliberate – aimed at preventing *Liberty* from following up events, particularly that Israel was massing forces in Galilee in order to seize the Golan Heights, or whether it was – as the Israelis have always claimed – 'a tragic case of misidentification'. The key to understanding what really happened on that fateful day lies in the recordings of conversations, over the radio system, between Israeli pilots – attacking the ship – and the air control tower in Tel Aviv. While these critical tapes are still kept – and for good reasons – under lock and key by the Israelis, here – published for the first time – are extracts from these recordings which shed some new light on this affair.

As the tapes clearly show, the drama begins at 13.50 with Colonel Shmuel Kislev, the Chief Air Controller in Tel Aviv, radioing to the leader of the Kursa Flight, consisting of two Mirage IIIC aircraft armed with 30 mm guns and a few air-to-air missiles: 'You've got a ship [a reference to *Liberty* – AB] in location 26.' Kislev then proceeds with his instruction: 'Now, take the Kursa Flight to there. If it's a warship – attack it.' While the Kursa Flight is on its way to locate *Liberty*, at 13:53 a question – very clearly heard over in the tapes – is aired in the control room in Tel Aviv: 'What is it? An American [ship]?'

What then follows is extraordinary and, indeed, highly suspicious, and seems to indicate a possible cover-up by the Israelis: Colonel Kislev picks up an internal phone and asks his superior – the Commander of the Air Force? The Deputy Commander of the Air Force? – 'What do you say [about the query just raised regarding to the ship's identity]?' The reply he gets is: 'I don't say.' The tone: 'I don't want to know.'

At 13:56, the leader of the Kursa Flight asks for permission to strike. Given that the possibility that the ship is American is on the cards, one could have expected a responsible military commander to instruct his pilots to investigate before dropping their bombs – to look, for example, for a flag. But no. Colonel Kislev in an impatient voice is heard over the tapes, saying: 'I have already said: if this is a warship ... to attack'. What follows is the first run on the ship and at 13:59 the leader of the Kursa Flight reports to air control: 'We have hit her very hard. Black smoke is coming out. Oil is spilling out of her into the water. *Yofi* (splendid) ... *Yotze mehaclal* (extraordinary). She is burning. She is burning.' Two minutes later, at 14:01, Kursa Flight reports again: 'OK. I have finished. I have just finished my ammunition. The ship is burning. There is an open fire on her. Very big and black smoke.'

At 14:03, Colonel Kislev instructs yet another flight – the Royal Flight, consisting of two Super Mystère jets armed with 30 mm guns and two canisters of napalm, to continue with the attack. 'You can sink her', says Kislev to the Royal Flight. Then the instructions of the leading pilot to his colleagues can be clearly heard over the tapes: 'We attack . . . go up . . . together. . . .We will come from her front . . . mind the masts . . . don't bump into the masts. . . . I will come from her left you from the right behind me.'

At 14:14 a pilot can be heard over the tapes asking: 'What state [does the ship belong to]? Kislev: 'Probably American.' Pilot: 'What?' Kislev: 'Probably American.' Nevertheless, and in spite of the positive identification of the ship as American, 12 minutes later, at 14:26, three Israeli motor torpedo boats arrive on the scene and at 14:31 attack her with five torpedoes which put *Liberty* out of action. According to the Israeli official narrative, they had tried – but failed – to warn the navy not to attack and it was only *after* the attack when a helicopter was sent in order to render assistance that the vessel 'was finally identified as a ship of the US Navy'.

The attack on Syria

War on the Golan Heights did not start until 9 June for, realizing the fate of Egypt and Jordan, the Syrians attempted to keep a low profile. In Israel, in the mean time, with both Egypt and Jordan out of action, there were growing calls, in the government, for a strike against Syria. Defence Minister Dayan objected. He said that, if Israel struck, the Soviets might intervene on Syria's side. Indeed, after the war evidence came to light showing that the Russians had made preparations to attack military objectives in Israel should Israel open fire against Syria. Dayan also felt that if Israel occupied the Golan Heights, Israelis would later find it difficult to give the land back to the Syrians and this would become an obstacle to reaching a final peace with Syria. Dayan was a lonely voice against an attack but he was, nevertheless, the Defence Minister of, by now, a victorious army and the ministers had to give way. So the Cabinet decided merely to wait and not to strike at the Syrians. But then – as usual – Dayan shrank from his realistic policies and he gave way by allowing Israeli forces, early on the morning of 9 June, to attack and occupy the Golan Heights. He later justified his change of mind by saying that fresh intelligence information, derived from a cable from President Nasser to the Syrian President Nur el-Din Attasi, intercepted by the Mossad early on the morning of 9 June, had shown that even if attacked Syria would probably not stand up and fight and this was why he eventually decided to unleash the Israeli forces. With the green light given to attack, Israeli forces struck hard at the Syrians and moved ahead to occupy the Golan Heights in spite of UN pressure and increasing tensions between Washington and Moscow – the latter threatening to 'take any measures to stop Israel including military'. With the Golan Heights in Israeli hands the war ended.

THE NEW SOCIETY

The stunning victory in the war had a strong impact on all spheres of Israel's life and society. The speed of the operation staggered the Israelis, whose immediate reaction to the victory was euphoria and jubilation as a spontaneous expression of relief that Israel had gained a decisive victory with relatively few casualties; the number of killed was 777. In six days the fighting was over and, by then, Israeli troops were stationed less than 31 miles from Amman, 38 miles from Damascus and 69 from Cairo. Occupation of the Sinai desert and the Gaza Strip, the Golan Heights and the West Bank provided Israel's cities with a buffer zone and dramatically reduced the danger of extinction by a surprise Arab attack (see Map 4). Israelis, after this war, believed that they were more secure than at any time in their history. Furthermore, victory had a special historical meaning because of the capture of territories central to the religious past: the old town of Jerusalem with the Western Wall, and Judaea and Samaria (the West Bank) which was part of biblical Eretz Yisrael and where such sites as Machpela were situated. For Israel's religious community, the occupation of these lands established the relationships between 'People, God and Promised Land', reawakening in them a strong sense of their Jewish identity.

Victory also had a dramatic impact on Israel's economy. The deep recession witnessed early in the year disappeared almost overnight and Israel even enjoyed a small economic boom. Financial contributions cascaded in from Jews in North and South America, from western Europe, South Africa and elsewhere and Jews purchased tens of millions of dollars of State of Israel Bonds; in the six months following the war Israel received an unprecedented $600 million in such contributions. Unemployment which was considerable before the war was mopped up and within a short period of time Israel's foreign exchange reserves increased by an unparalleled 75 per cent. The port of Eilat was reopened and more even than before turned into one of the most important centres of communications to and from Israel. A land bridge from Eilat to Ashdod was built and East African and Asian cargo ships could now unload on to trucks at Eilat, transport the goods to the port of Ashdod and reload them on ships destined for Mediterranean ports; soon this land bridge was operating at a rate of 900 tons a month. In addition, the capture, during the war, of the Sinai oil wells of Abu Rudeis saved Israel some $60 million in hard currency expenditures (by 1970) and relieved Israel from worries about oil shortages.

Tourism was booming. In 1967 alone 328,000 visitors arrived in Israel, in 1968 some 432,000 came and in 1970 the number of tourists reached 650,000. The money spent by tourists, nearly $100 million in 1968 alone, was reinvested and led to a boom in new hotel construction as well as in other related tourist services. And with production rising by 10 per cent, exports by 17 per cent and capital investments by 25 per cent a year, a wave of prosperity engulfed Israel and there was a dramatic rise in the standard of living unprecedented in Israel's history.

No less important was the effect of the war in narrowing the gaps between the various segments of Israeli society. Hitherto, the *Ashkenazi* Israelis felt entitled to better treatment and privileges by virtue of their sacrifices before and immediately after the establishment of the state of Israel. On the other hand, the Oriental Jews – the *Sephardim* – most of whom joined later felt discriminated and marginalized by the *Ashkenazim*. But after the war in which the Oriental Jews performed their duty and proved themselves brave and devoted soldiers, even the *Ashkenazim* had to concede that the Oriental Israelis had earned an equal right of property in Israel. But then, while the important role they played in winning the war made the *Sephardim* feel better and led to a sheer improvement of their status in society, it also – quite dramatically – increased their expectations of further radical changes in their position in society.

The effect of war on relations between Arab and Jewish Israelis worked in two different directions. On the one hand, the Arab Israelis, who were considered a potential fifth column before the war, did not take any action during the war against the Israelis and thus demonstrated that they could be trusted and the dismantling of military rule which had taken place just before the war was justified. After the war there was an improvement in relationships between Arab and Jewish Israelis and more Arab Israelis were drawn into the Israeli market and the orbit of relative affluence. But this trend was offset when, with contact being restored between the Israeli Arabs and their brethren in the occupied territories, some of Israel's Arabs were drawn into the Palestinian guerrilla and resistance movements which emerged after the war.

But whereas the war helped to narrow the gaps between *Ashkenazim* and *Sephardim* and also, to a certain degree, between Arab and Jewish Israelis, it also sowed the seeds of division among Israelis with regard to the question of what to do with the occupied territories. Shortly after the war, the Land of Israel Movement was formed, initially by leading members of Mapai and Achdut Ha'Avodah, who were joined by elements from the right and from the National Religious Party and they called for retention of the occupied territories for the sake of security as well as for religious and historical reasons. On the other side of the spectrum, mostly from leftist parties, were those Israelis who feared that the burden of holding on to the occupied territories would erode the society from within and leave Israel with a growing Arab population who, once emerged from the shock of defeat, would become a major security and, in particular, demographic risk to Israel. For were Israel to annex the Gaza Strip, the percentage of Arabs – including the Arabs of Israel – would rise to 24 per cent and were it to annex the West Bank in addition to the Gaza Strip, the Arabs would attain 35 per cent of the population, which would, so those who wished to return the land argued, jeopardize the Jewish character of the state. This debate regarding the fate of the occupied land would become the major issue dividing Israeli society in the years ahead.

SNAIL'S PACE DIPLOMACY

But in the immediate aftermath of the war and before the fate of the occupied territories even turned into a public debate, the government attempted to act decisively and return most of the occupied land to its original owners. The reason for that was that the Eshkol government was apprehensive that the international community would pressurize it to withdraw from *all* the occupied lands, as it had done after the 1956 war, and it therefore wished to take the initiative and dictate the agenda. It thus offered a dramatic proposal for peace with Egypt and Syria which was enshrined in a governmental decision of 19 June 1967, which was then relayed to the American administration by Israel's Foreign Minister Eban to pass on to the Arabs. In the following rare report, written down by American Secretary of State Dean Rusk, Israel's offer is summarized:

> Secretary [of State] and [UN] Ambassador [Arthur] Goldberg received Israeli Foreign Minister Eban ... 7:15 P.M. June 21 [1967]. Hour's conversation. Eban stated Israeli inter-ministerial committee had come to some tentative conclusions which he would like to discuss with secretary but not others. . .
>
> **Egypt–Israel.** Israelis wanted peace treaty on basis [of] present international frontiers. From Egypt, Israel wanted only security, no territory ... important thing is that there must be treaty which committed Egyptians. Israelis unwilling to accept another understanding on basis of assumptions.
>
> **Israel–Syria.** Israelis would like peace treaty on the basis of the international frontiers with some understanding that Syrian hills overlooking Israeli territory would be demilitarized ... Eban concluded that Israel was offering both Egypt and Syria complete withdrawal to international frontiers. These terms not ungenerous.
>
> **Gaza.** Eban noted that Egypt had never claimed Gaza. Israel would make every effort on behalf of Gaza population.
>
> **West Bank of Jordan.** Eban said Israeli thinking 'less crystallized'.[19]

Israel's thinking was 'less crystallized' with regard to the West Bank because she was reluctant to give it up. These lands were regarded by Jews as part of biblical Eretz Yisrael and there was strong opposition, even within the non-religious ruling party itself, to returning this 'liberated' land to Arab hands. But there was also a strategic justification for not wanting to give up the occupied West Bank and that was that it turned Israel's 'narrow waist' into something wider. Before seizing the West Bank Israel's width at some parts measured scarcely nine miles from the Jordan bulge to the Mediterranean, and by clinging to the occupied territories west of the Jordan river Israel made it more difficult for a potential Arab invading force coming from the east to cut it in two. Yet although no specific offer was made with regard to the West Bank, it was around this time that the so-called Allon Plan was conceived by Deputy Prime Minister Yigal Allon and was submitted to the Cabinet for discussion on 26 July 1967.

The Allon Plan called for the retention of a strip of land, six to nine miles wide along the Jordan river, most of the Judaean desert along the Dead Sea, and a substantial area around greater Jerusalem, including the Latrun salient. In these territories, especially on the barren hills along the river Jordan, so envisaged Allon, permanent Jewish settlements would be built as strategic bulwarks against a potential Arab attack from the east. Jerusalem would be retained as Israel's unified capital, and the Gaza Strip with its 250,000 Palestinians, mostly refugees of previous wars, would remain under Israel's control, the Strip being linked to the West Bank by a highway. The single remaining enclave, that of Samaria, populated by some 400,000 Arabs, would be granted independence in close political economic and military liaison with Israel and would be connected to Jordan by means of a wide corridor around Jericho. As part of this plan, Allon also envisaged the resettling of hundred of thousands of Palestinian refugees in northern Sinai near El Arish, while other Palestinians might be settled in the independent enclave of Samaria, or be encouraged to emigrate to Canada, Australia, New Zealand or Brazil. The Cabinet neither adopted nor rejected the Allon Plan, but it gradually became the blueprint for successive Labour government policies in the occupied territories.

In the mean time, on 28 August, an Arab summit was held in Khartoum, the capital of Sudan, the first meeting of Arab leaders since their defeat in the war. It adopted three noes: 'No peace, no recognition and no negotiations with Israel', a tragic decision which played into the hands of those in Israel who did not wish to give up any occupied land, enabling them to argue that the Arabs were intransigent, did not wish to make peace with Israel and, therefore, there was no reason why Israel should return any occupied land to them. Not much later, on 30 October, Eshkol's government took a crucial decision which stated that agreements with Egypt and Syria must give Israel secured borders; this effectively spelled the death of the previous moderate and compromising decision of 19 June 1967.

In the UN General Assembly, in the autumn of 1967, Israel won a diplomatic victory when the Assembly demanded neither an Israeli withdrawal nor compensation, but instead decided to refer the dispute between Israel and the Arabs, regarding the occupied lands, to the Security Council. Subsequently, the Security Council met in October and November 1967 and after lengthy discussions adopted, on 22 November 1967, Resolution 242. This was sponsored by Britain and adopted unanimously. It spoke of the inadmissibility of the acquisition of territory by war and the need to work for a 'just and lasting peace' within 'secure and recognized boundaries' based on withdrawal of Israeli armed forces 'from territories occupied in the recent conflict' (note the lack of 'the' before 'territories'). Rejected by some Arab states, notably Syria and the Palestinians, the latter complaining that there was no recognition of their rights other than as refugees, interpreted by those that accepted it, including Israel, to suit their preconditions, 242 became more an expression of a stalemate than a means of a resolution. An integral part of 242 was the appointment of a special envoy, the Swedish ambassador to Moscow Dr Gunnar Jarring, to meet with the parties and assist them to promote agreement and achieve a peaceful settlement in accordance with the provisions and principles of Resolution 242.

The slow pace of the diplomacy and the absence of a meaningful breakthrough in the Jarring mission led to a growing sense in Israel that she had time on her side and that the status quo in the occupied territories would remain unchanged for the foreseeable future. Gradually, some Israelis took direct action on the ground to settle the occupied lands. Notable was the case, on 4 April 1968, of a group of religious Jews who, without governmental consent, established the foundations for the future city of Kiryat Arba and a Jewish neighbourhood in the heart of Hebron. The government might still have taken a strong line but there seemed to be considerable popular support for a return to Hebron – it was abandoned after the 1929 disturbances – and, within the Cabinet itself, minister Yigal Allon was particularly active in persuading colleagues to let the settlers stay. They stayed, as did many other illegal settlers in illegal settlements which popped up on the barren hills of the disputed West Bank. It was here, on the West Bank in the post-1967 war, that religious Zionism began to demonstrate self-confidence impelled by a messianic vision that the Jewish occupation of the land of Israel was a decisive step on the road to redemption, whereas secular Zionism was in general retreat.

ENTER GOLDA MEIR

On 26 February 1969, Prime Minister Levi Eshkol died and was succeeded, on 7 March, by Golda Meir, the first woman ever to become Prime Minister of Israel. Born in 1898 in Kiev, Golda Meyerson, as she was then known, was brought up in Milwaukee after her family had emigrated from Russia to America. In 1921, she arrived in Palestine on the wretched *SS Pocahontas*, settled there and became involved in the *Yishuv's* politics. Just before the declaration of independence Golda Meir, dressed in Arab dress, travelled to Transjordan to try to persuade King Abdullah not to join other Arab governments in invading the Jewish state. She failed. Later during the war which followed, Meir played a leading role in raising much needed funds for buying arms. Her extraordinary speech to a Jewish group in Chicago led to an equally extraordinary fund-raising effort by American Jewry in support of Israel and Meir returned home with $50 million. She was later chosen as Israel's first envoy to Moscow, promoted to Minister of Labour in Ben-Gurion's governments and when Foreign Minister Sharett was pushed out of office by Ben-Gurion, just before the 1956 Sinai Campaign, she was chosen to succeed him. Now aged 71, in poor health and exhausted by public service and politics, Meir was recalled from retirement to lead the country and save her party from a damaging succession struggle between Moshe Dayan and Yigal Allon. She doubted her own physical capacity when she reluctantly took office and said she would remain no more than a few months.

Golda – as she was commonly known – was stout and striking with her hair always knotted at the back and with eyes that perpetually reflected an inner sadness. She was emotional and tough at the same time and already, before becoming Prime Minister of Israel, she was among the most admired women in the world. She was, though, very different from her predecessor. While Eshkol was a man of compromise and flexibility, Meir was dogmatic and intransigent. Whereas Eshkol was a 'moderate' – which after the 1967 war became known as a 'dove' – Meir, a disciple of Ben-Gurion, was an 'activist' – a 'hawk' in post-1967 terminology. And while Eshkol was truly a democrat who would listen to various opinions and points of view before making a decision, Meir was less so and she established her small 'Kitchen Cabinet' – the Kitchen of Golda, as it was commonly known – of close ministers, who settled things between themselves and then presented the Cabinet with a virtual fait accompli.

Perhaps the most complicated problem which Meir inherited from Eshkol and which she and her Defence Minister Dayan had to tackle and give priority to, was a bloody war along the Suez Canal. It came to be known as the War of Attrition.

WAR OF ATTRITION

After the June 1967 war Israeli troops deployed within a stone's throw on the eastern bank of the Suez Canal and Nasser – humiliated by his defeat – could take war to them. He had sufficient arms to wage a new war for, although much of Egypt's war material had been destroyed or captured by the Israelis, the Soviets after the 1967 war moved swiftly to refill Egypt's arsenal.

Clashes between Israeli and Egyptian forces across the Suez Canal started as far back as 21 October 1967, when an Egyptian destroyer torpedoed and sank the Israeli destroyer *Eilat* in international waters off Port Said; 47 sailors were killed. Israel retaliated by shelling Egyptian oil refineries close to the city of Suez and setting alight the adjoining oil storage tanks, thus causing the evacuation of tens of thousands of civilians from Suez City and Ismailia. The next year, between 8 September and 26 October, clashes along the Suez Canal intensified and developed into a massive artillery duel. Israel, not used to a long-drawn-out static confrontation, attempted to keep the initiative and, in addition to returning artillery fire and using her air force in support of the troops, retaliated by dispatching ground forces to operate across the Canal. But, recognizing the advantages of imposing a 'war of bloodshed' on the close-knit Israeli society, President Nasser was determined to proceed with the war and strike at the Israelis, in the hope that, broken in spirit as well as in body, the Israelis would eventually withdraw from the Canal zone.

In an attempt to reduce the number of casualties the Israeli General Staff decided – not without a fierce internal debate – to construct a defence line along the Suez Canal in order to provide troops with cover and protect them from Egyptian fire.[20] But the newly established line of defence – the Bar-Lev line as it came to be known after the brain behind it Chief of Staff Bar-Lev – played into Egyptian hands providing them with a static target to aim their guns at. Thus, in March 1969, after a relatively calm period, the Egyptians resumed the war and carried out massive barrages of the Bar-Lev line, which rose to a crescendo between 8 and 10 March. Israel returned fire and sent troops into Egyptian territory but to no avail – the fighting continued with undiminished fury, leading to increasing numbers of Israeli casualties and to growing uneasiness in Israel.

On 28 October 1969, in the shadow of the continuing war along the Canal, a general election was held in Israel. Meir's Labour Party which merged with Mapam to form the Alignment (Ma'arach in Hebrew), won 56 seats of the 120 in the Knesset, compared with 63 seats won by its component parts in 1965. Begin's Gahal won 26 seats, the National Religious Party 12 and the Independent Liberal Party 4. As the leader of the largest party Meir was asked by the President to form a new coalition government.

In the mean time, on 9 December 1969, the American administration, which by now was led by Richard Nixon with Henry Kissinger as his National Security Adviser and William Rogers as his Secretary of State, came up with a new peace plan – the so-called Rogers Plan. At its heart was UN resolution 242 and it envisaged Israel's return, with only minor modifications, to the international border, a solution to the Palestinian refugee problem, and retention of a united Jerusalem but with her eastern part no longer annexed to Israel. On 15 December, in her speech to the Knesset to present her new wall-to-wall National Unity government Prime Minister Meir launched a savage attack on the Rogers Plan and, on 22 December, her Cabinet finally rejected it, saying that Israel's security and peace would be in grave danger if the American proposals were to be accepted.

In the absence of a diplomatic solution, war along the Suez Canal continued and in a further attempt to stop it the government resorted to a massive air bombardment of Egyptian positions. First came Operation Boxer, the air bombardment of Egyptian positions along the Suez Canal, which was successful in, temporarily, silencing Egyptian fire. But with the Egyptians recovering and resuming attacks on the Bar-Lev line, the government next decided to allow an escalation of air attacks through the adoption of the strategy of air force deep penetration. The line of thought behind this new strategy was that by extending the bombing campaign deep into Egypt, Israel would force Nasser to shift troops and equipment from the Suez Canal zone to protect other parts of Egypt and this, in turn, would relieve pressure on Israeli troops in the Bar-Lev line.

The IAF began to execute the new strategy on 7 January 1970 and in this massive campaign, which went on until 18 April 1970, it flew

3300 sorties and dropped 8000 tons of munitions both along the Canal and deep in Egypt. It was a devastating bombing campaign which not only hurt the Egyptian army but also led to the evacuation of some half a million civilians who moved from the Suez Canal zone to other parts of Egypt to escape the ferocity of the onslaught. At first, it seemed as if Israel's new strategy was paying off. For, as the Israelis rightly predicted, the Egyptian High Command was forced to transfer resources from the Suez Canal zone to protect Egypt's underbelly which, in turn, relieved some of the pressure on the Bar-Lev line and subsequently led to a decline in the number of Israeli casualties. Early optimism was dashed, however, as international criticism of Israel grew and was intensified when some of the victims turned out to be innocent civilians rather than Egyptian military personnel. International outcry and condemnation reached a peak following the mistaken bombing by an Israeli Phantom of a factory, on 13 February 1970, which killed 70 civilians and then the bombing by mistake, on 9 April 1970, of a school in which 30 children were killed.

But, perhaps, more worrying for the Israelis was that their massive bombing campaign led to a growing Soviet intervention in the conflict. In January, when Israel started executing her new strategy, President Nasser flew to Moscow where he demanded, and received, sophisticated weapons, including SAM-3 anti-aircraft missiles and Mig-21s. Not only did Moscow supply these sophisticated weapon systems, but it also operated some of them herself and took a direct part in fighting the Israeli bombers. In a rare interview, the Russian Popov Konstantin Ilych, who was involved in shooting down five Israeli Phantoms in Egypt and was given the award of Hero of the Soviet Union, recalled:

We arrived in Egypt in March 1970. We came into port at night. At 23.00 we discharged the ship. During the night we painted Egyptian logos and numbers on our machines and we changed into civilian clothes. The next day we were already in our positions. . . . We received an order to get ready to fight. The first [Israeli] Phantom was shot down by Captain Mamelyuk . . . [then] the Israelis started a massive operation and my group shot down 5 Phantoms.[21]

And with growing Soviet intervention in this war, the Israelis decided to de-escalate the situation for, as Defence Minister Dayan put it: 'Now that the Russians are there I would prefer to wait and see what we can and ought to do . . . we must be very wary about taking offensive action, lest this lead us into encounters with Soviet pilots.'[22]

Military operations in Egypt were taking place against a growing public revulsion of the continuing war and its high number of casualties. A new school of poets and writers, seeing in war only horror and suffering, came out with new works in which they expressed their contempt for war and suffering. The 'Queen of the Bath', a satirical show attacking 'joy' over war and the 'cult of fatalities' was, perhaps, the most outspoken piece of Israeli anti-war literature during this period. It was an expression of the tiredness of Israelis with wars and sacrifice and a novelty in a society which, until the 1967 war, had shown itself willing to sacrifice without a second thought or protest.

In the mean time, Dr Nahum Goldmann, President of the World Zionist Organization, informed Prime Minister Meir, on 24 March 1970, about contacts he had had and an invitation which was issued to him to visit Egypt and meet President Nasser to talk peace. Meir, who had a very low opinion of Goldmann, refused to follow up the invitation, arguing that with Goldmann 'the line between reality and imagination is always blurred'. While this response killed the initiative, the story was leaked to the press, on 5 April, and caused a stir. Furious students, on the eve of being recruited to service in the IDF, sent an open letter to Meir to complain about the missed opportunity and to say that they did not know if they would be able to do what they had to do in the army.

Under growing pressure, at home and abroad, the government began to show more flexibility and was more receptive to the American initiative of 19 June 1970 which was known as the Second Rogers Plan. This called for a 90-day ceasefire along the Suez Canal, a military freeze of the situation on both banks of the Canal and the resumption of the Jarring peace mission. Towards the end of July Egypt accepted the plan and, on 31 July, the government of Israel voted 17 against 6, to accept this American initiative. As a result, on 7 August 1970, a three-month ceasefire came into force and indirect talks between Israel and Egypt were resumed.

But there was a political price to be paid for this, for accepting the Second Rogers Plan implied the open acceptance of UN resolution 242 which Begin's Gahal Party, part of the coalition government, opposed. Now insisting that acceptance of the Rogers Plan was the beginning of a major unconditional retreat from the ceasefire lines, Begin resigned from the coalition thus bringing an end to the government of National

Unity. However, the Jarring mission, part of the Rogers Plan, had hardly left the ground when it was shot down almost immediately by Egypt which breached the ceasefire agreement. According to this agreement, the situation along the Canal had to be frozen – no movement of either troops or military equipment was allowed. But on the day the ceasefire came into effect, the Egyptians, in cooperation with the Russians, established and moved forward some 28 SAM-2 and 14 SAM-3 batteries. Israel responded, at the beginning of September 1970, by suspending her participation in the Jarring talks until the situation, which had prevailed on the eve of the signing of the ceasefire agreement, was restored.

GOLDA AND ANWAR EL-SADAT

That month Egypt's President Nasser died and was replaced by his deputy Anwar el-Sadat. The succession of Sadat to power opened a new era in Israel's relations with Egypt. For while Nasser, who had lost the Sinai in 1967, demonstrated, except in his invitation to Nahum Goldmann of March 1970, little appetite for talks with Israel, his successor Sadat showed himself, from the start, willing to negotiate in order to get back Egypt's lost land. Almost immediately upon his succession to power, Sadat accepted proposals put forward to him by the UN mediator, Dr Jarring, to discuss peace with Israel and with Meir's acceptance indirect talks were resumed at the beginning of January 1971. Not much later, on 4 February 1971, Sadat announced to the Egyptian Parliament that 'If Israel withdrew her forces in Sinai to the [Mitla and Gidi] Passes' (which is about 48 kilometres east of the Suez Canal), then

> I would be willing to reopen the Suez Canal; to have my forces cross to the East Bank [of the Suez Canal] . . . to make a solemn, official declaration of a ceasefire by six, rather than three, months; to restore diplomatic relations with the United States; and sign a peace agreement with Israel through the efforts of Dr Jarring, the representative of the secretary general of the UN.[23]

To no avail. Prime Minister Meir was determined not to yield an inch for less than a full peace. This she believed was the only safe method of doing business with the Arabs and anyway, there was no reason to hurry, for as she once put it, 'we have never had it so good'. Meir even failed to listen to people around her, notably to Defence Minister Moshe Dayan, who suggested pulling back a little way from Suez so that the Egyptians could then resume navigation and rehabilitate their canal zone cities which, in turn, would reduce their appetite to fight in a war. In Sadat's – and Dayan's – offer for an Israeli withdrawal, Meir saw the beginning of the return of Israel to the old boundaries without the equivalent of peace treaty. She thus rejected, in a speech to the Knesset, Sadat's bold initiative.

On 8 February, the Swedish diplomat Dr Jarring suggested that Israel and Egypt give prior commitments to accepting his peace plan which, in a nutshell, demanded a commitment from Sadat to enter into a peace agreement with Israel and from Meir an undertaking to withdraw from Egypt to the former international border. On 15 February 1971, Sadat agreed in principle to Jarring's proposals demanding, however, a specific commitment from Israel to withdraw from the Sinai and the Gaza Strip, a commitment to settle the Palestinian refugee problem and a commitment to agree to the establishment of a UN force to maintain the peace. Israel's reply to Jarring's proposal came on 26 February and was that Israel will not withdraw to the pre-5 June 1967 lines. This killed the Jarring mission.

Sadat's offer to open a dialogue with the Israelis was taken more seriously by American President Richard Nixon who, in the summer of 1971, sent Under Secretary of State Joseph Sisco – a highly qualified professional and a skilful diplomat – to the Middle East to try and break the impasse by convincing Prime Minister Meir to agree to a certain limited withdrawal from the Suez Canal. Soon, however, Sisco returned to Washington empty-handed and downhearted and, as he later recalled, 'After two days of in-depth discussions, it was clear we weren't making much progress . . . the reaction of the Prime Minister was a negative one. . . .'[24] Disappointed by the failure of diplomacy and aghast at Israel's unilateral steps, such as her building of a modern airport in the Sinai and a town with deep-water port on the shore of the Sinai, Sadat declared that 1971 would be the 'year of decision'. What that meant was far from clear and, anyway, no one in the Arab world or in Israel took him seriously.

However, Sadat kept trying to open a dialogue with the Israelis. In an attempt to impress on the United States that he was serious and to hint that the key for such a dialogue lay in Washington, rather than in Moscow, Sadat took a bold step and, on 18 July 1972, expelled from

Egypt some 15,000 Soviet advisers who had arrived there following his predecessor's visit to Moscow in January 1970. But even this did not bring Washington to pressurize Israel to accept withdrawal. Israel, after all, was at that time a strategic asset for the United States in the Middle East and Washington would not challenge Meir's insistence on not yielding an inch of land for less than a full recognition and acceptance of Israel by the Arabs. So the stalemate continued, and, in the mean time, Israel was involved in a bloody war against Palestinians in the Gaza Strip and abroad.

TERRORISM, IMMIGRATION AND RIOTS

When in 1967 Israel seized the Gaza Strip, the Palestinian population there numbered about 400,000, about half of them were refugees or descendants of refugees who had fled Israel during the 1948 war. Following the June 1967 war, many of these Palestinians found daily jobs in Israel and the markets of the Gaza Strip as well as those of the West Bank, opened to Israeli products. However, the Palestinian leadership, realizing that coexistence with Israel would inevitably sideline the Palestinian problem, attempted to turn the inhabitants of the occupied territories against the Israelis. As a result, starting in 1968, the Gaza Strip was hit by a wave of brutalization, torture and murder directed by Palestinians against fellow Palestinians aimed at frightening them away from any ties with Israel. This campaign, however, did not in any way distract the Palestinian leadership from continuing its fight against the main enemy – Israel – and under such people as Yasser Arafat and George Habash, secret cells were set up, which carried out 'missions' against the Israelis. At the beginning of 1971, Defence Minister Dayan instructed OC Southern Command, Ariel Sharon, to sort out the problem and stop the Palestinian violence in the Gaza Strip. Subsequently, in a seven-month-long brutal campaign, starting in July 1971, Israeli troops, supervised by Sharon, killed 104 Palestinians, arrested and deported others and ended Palestinian resistance in the Gaza Strip and quietened the area.

International terrorism was also rife in the early 1970s. Conducted by Palestinians and their supporters, it was aimed at attracting world attention to the plight of the Palestinians and forcing the hand of the Israeli government in releasing Palestinians held in her prisons. On 8 May 1972, Palestinians, belonging to Black September, took over a

Sabena aeroplane flight number 571 en route from Brussels to Tel Aviv, landed it in Israel and demanded the release of 317 Palestinian prisoners. The government, refusing to give up to this demand, instructed the army, on the morning of 9 May, to free the people on board. Led by a young officer named Ehud Barak, the future Prime Minister of Israel, a commando team stormed the aircraft and released the passengers. Not long after this event, on 30 May, three Japanese gunmen, members of the radical Red Brigade, armed with machine guns, hand-grenades and working for the PLO, opened fire in the arrival hall at Lod airport, killing 27 passengers. Palestinian terrorism reached a peak on 5 September 1972, when 11 athletes, members of the Israeli team participating in the Olympic Games in Munich, were taken prisoners by a Palestinian group and were later killed in a botched German operation to rescue them. Israel soon hit back. A special unit led by Ehud Barak, himself dressed as a woman, assassinated three Beirut-based PLO leaders responsible for the killing in Munich. This was only one raid among many to punish those Israel held responsible for the Munich killing. A vicious circle of tit for tat had developed.

Yet, in spite of international terrorism, tensions along the Suez Canal and on Israel's frontiers with her other Arab neighbours, and the sporadic violence in the occupied territories, Jewish immigrants poured into Israel. The influx had steadily declined in the pre-1967 war years to an annual figure of 18,000 by June 1967, but in the years 1968–73 250,000 newcomers arrived in Israel. These were mainly Russian and American Jewish immigrants, the latter encouraged by a growing solidarity with Israel, the feeling that quality of life in America was deteriorating coupled with the growing recession that visited the US at a time when Israel's economy, as a result of the war, was booming. The arrival of these immigrants to Israel helped sustain the post-1967 mini economic boom and thus in 1971, GDP grew by a massive 11.1 per cent and in 1972 it went up to 12.6 per cent. But it also caused social tensions and seemed to reverse the trend of improved relations between *Ashkenazim* and *Sephardim* in Israel. As said, the important role played by the *Sephardim* during the 1967 war narrowed the gap between them and the *Ashkenazim* in Israel but also dramatically raised expectations by the *Sephardim* for quick change in their conditions – for better housing, education and jobs. But that the government was in the early 1970s diverting funds to help absorb new immigrants frustrated the *Sephardim* who felt that investing in the newcomers came at their own expense. Impatient with the slow progress of improvement in their conditions and upset at the allocation of funds to the newly arrived immigrants, the *Sephardim* took to the streets. They were led by a new protest group calling itself the Black Panthers whose members came from one of Jerusalem's poorest neighbourhoods – Musrara. They demonstrated and rioted and drew attention to the problems of low education and poverty among the *Sephardim*. But unlike the riots in Wadi Salib in 1959, violence now was not a major element in the protest and instead, the Black Panthers initiated symbolic activities, such as stealing bottles of milk from rich neighbourhoods and distributing them in poorer areas. They also showed themselves capable of realizing the importance of penetrating to the centre of the political process and soon their representatives entered the Knesset.

But still, the post-1967 war years were dominated by foreign and security affairs – all other problems lost their urgency or were trivial in comparison. The people in charge of these matters were, first and foremost, Golda Meir and Moshe Dayan. She – proud and stubborn to the point of being unable to adapt to changing circumstances, he – imaginative and creative. The people of Israel were confident that as long as these two were in charge, no evil would befall them. They were soon to be proved wrong as these two – Dayan and Meir – led them into war.

5

Yom Kippur War and the Death of Labour, 1973–1977

SADAT PREPARES WAR

In the winter of 1973 Egypt's President Anwar el-Sadat gave diplomacy another chance by dispatching his National Security Adviser, Hafiz Ismail, to talks in Washington. Ismail met President Richard Nixon in the White House on 23 February 1973 and he then held three secret meetings with Kissinger on 24–25 February. Kissinger later recalled: 'Hafiz Ismail wanted Israel to return to the 1967 borders, in return for which Egypt would be willing to make peace – a big step because no Arab state had ever before flatly said they would make peace.' But then Kissinger was not altogether convinced that Egypt's offer was genuine and he was still questioning Sadat's motives and intentions. In a later interview Kissinger frankly admitted: 'I thought of Sadat as a character out of Aida. I didn't take him seriously. He kept making grandiloquent statements but never acted on them. . . . Frankly, I thought he was bluffing.'[1] Back in Cairo, Ismail reported to Sadat on his meetings in Washington and according to the then Chief of Staff of the Egyptian army, Saad el-Shazly, Ismail reported that Kissinger had said to him: 'I cannot deal with your problem unless it became a crisis', which, according to el-Shazly, was regarded by Sadat as a sign that: 'Kissinger was encouraging him to go to war. That war was the only option.'[2]

Sadat was disappointed. His overtures failed to impress Israel's Prime Minister Meir, who rejected them and even went on to adopt the so-called Galili Plan designed to invest much money in the occupied territories, including the occupied north-eastern Sinai, adjacent to

139

Rafah, where Israel planned to build an industrial estate. Sadat also felt that he had failed to impress Washington with his sincerity about opening a dialogue with Israel and he was upset by *détente*, the improvement in US–USSR relations during the early 1970s, which he regarded as prejudicial to Egypt's interests for it was unlikely, as Sadat saw it, that the superpowers would embark on a major initiative in the Middle East in case this had a negative effect on their improved relations. Closer to home, in the Arab world and particularly in Egypt, Sadat became a laughing stock as his repeated promises that the 'year of decision' was just round the corner did not materialize and with the passage of time came to be regarded as empty words. Gradually, Sadat came to the conclusion that, as Kissinger had said, his only remaining option was to create a crisis, which would then bring intervention from the superpowers and subsequently lead to the opening of a dialogue with Israel. And it was against this background that Sadat directed his military commanders to prepare for a *limited war* against Israel. This, it is worth mentioning, was in itself a startling turnabout and a radical departure from previous policies for, previously, Egypt had clung stubbornly to a policy of a total, all-out war against Israel to recover *all* the territory lost in 1967. Why did Sadat, so drastically, change Egypt's policy from a *total* to *limited* war? Here is the explanation.

After the June 1967 war, President Sadat's predecessor, Nasser, concluded that for Egypt to be able to embark on an all-out war against Israel to liberate *all* the land she had lost in the war, two preconditions must be first fulfilled. The first, that Egypt would have Scud missiles so she could threaten Israel's centres of population. The second, that the Egyptian air force would have advanced long-range warplanes to enable it to penetrate deep into Israel and strike at airports, communication centres and other strategic installations. Indeed, on his visit to Moscow on 22 January 1970, Sadat's predecessor Nasser, according to Chief of Staff Mohamed Fawzi who had accompanied him, 'repeated his demand for [long-range] fighter-bombers because the range of our bombers does not enable us to reach deep into Israel'.[3] Sadat, like his predecessor, also recognized that without these weapons – Scuds and long-range warplanes – he would not be able to liberate Egypt's occupied lands. He referred to this matter in a secret letter he sent to President Leonid Brezhnev on 30 August 1972 in which he said: 'I mentioned in our frequent discussions that we needed a *retaliation weapon* which would deter the enemy . . . because of his knowledge that we would then be able to retaliate in kind and attack his inland positions. *It was obvious, and still is, that, deprived of such a retalia-tion weapon, we would remain incapable of taking any kind of military action. . . .*'[4] The 'retaliatory weapons' to which Sadat was referring in this were Scud missiles but, in the same letter, he complained of the 'embargo you have imposed on us for the last five years, in regard to "retaliation weapons . . ." '. That the Soviet embargo on Sadat also included long-range warplanes, which Egypt so desperately needed if she was to embark on a total war to liberate the whole of the Sinai, we know from a recent testimony of Pavel Akopov, a Soviet diplomat who was present at meetings in which the supply of weapons to Egypt were discussed. According to Akopov: 'I was present at negotiations [regarding the supply of weapons to Egypt] with Nasser and after-wards the same issues were raised by Sadat all the time . . . Sadat was always putting the question of supplying him with this sort of arma-ments which we could not give them: say aircraft that could fly from Cairo to Tel Aviv, and he was always asking for them so that he could bomb Tel Aviv. . . .'[5] Moscow, it should be mentioned, refused to supply Egypt with advanced fighter-bombers and with 'retaliatory weapons', because it was clear to her, as it was to Sadat, that with these weapons in hand, Egypt would be in a position to strike at Israel and this, in the early 1970s, was not in Moscow's interest because of her improved relationships with Washington.

And here lies the explanation of Sadat's decision to abandon Egypt's traditional aim of a total war to liberate the whole of the Sinai and concentrate, instead, on the more limited aim of liberating only part of the Sinai. His realization that Moscow was unlikely to provide him with long-range warplanes and Scuds, seen by his predecessor and by himself as preconditions to a successful campaign against Israel, led Sadat to conclude that he should try to achieve a more limited goal and hope that a limited but punishing strike against Israel would allow him to break the political impasse and get his land back through polit-ical negotiations. As Egyptian General Mohamed Abdel Ghani Gamassy put it: 'The idea of a limited war came from the fact that we did not have enough equipment to go into a general war, the Soviets would not give us enough arms.'[6]

On the basis of Sadat's instructions, the Egyptian High Command began drawing up plans for a limited war against Israel and it also embarked on frequent false mobilizations of forces to deceive the Israelis. Twenty-two mobilizations would take place between 1972 and 1973, with the attack on Israel being finally launched on the twenty-third. Syria, keen to recover the Golan Heights she had lost in 1967, joined with Egypt in preparations for a surprise attack on Israel. Coordination between the two countries was carried out through the 'Higher Council' of Egyptian and Syrian Generals which was set up for that purpose.

ISRAEL STUMBLES INTO THE TRAP

A double agent

That Israel stumbled into this trap and failed to prepare herself for war on two fronts and mobilize her reserve forces in time to deter or if necessary to face an Egyptian–Syrian assault was, contrary to general knowledge, mainly due to a colossal failure of the Mossad. To understand how this happened we should go back to the days after the June 1967 war.

About two years after that war, a young Egyptian showed up at the doorstep of Israel's embassy in London and asked to work for the Mossad. This was an odd and an unusual way of volunteering for the organization and, not surprisingly, the Mossad's representative at the embassy sent the visitor away. But the Egyptian insisted and before turning on his heels he left his details, promising to return, which he did a few days later. By then the Mossad had already checked the identity of the uninvited visitor, realizing, to its utter shock and disbelief, that the young Egyptian – in his mid-twenties – was not only a senior Egyptian official, but also a very close family member of President Nasser. In fact, he was so much liked by the President that Nasser made him join his Presidential Staff and, in addition, appointed him a roving ambassador undertaking missions throughout the world on the President's behalf. A charming young man, Nasser's relative was brilliant at showing that he was close to the throne and he was also brimming with new original ideas and initiatives. With a budget approved by the President, he collected files on key figures in the Arab world, especially in Kuwait and Saudi Arabia, where he established strong contacts. By the late 1960s, he had become a rising star among President Nasser's close associates. No wonder, thus, that the Mossad had no hesitation in immediately recruiting the young Egyptian who became, perhaps, the most senior spy it ever recruited.

If the Mossad was apprehensive that the death of Nasser, in September 1970, would interfere with the work of its Egyptian spy it was soon reassured. As it turned out, the death of Nasser was an advantage to the young Egyptian – and consequently for the Mossad – for an unsure and fledgling Sadat was desperate to surround himself with key people and Nasser's relative was definitely one of those the new President wanted to see around him. Under Sadat, the young Egyptian blossomed and was appointed to various key posts, including Minister Without Portfolio and Secretary for Information of the President; soon he became Sadat's henchman and confidant.

Only a few people in Israel knew the identity of the Mossad's top Egyptian agent and because he was so close to the throne he was not only paid handsomely (£100,000 per meeting with his Mossad handler), but his reports were read, exactly as he provided them without changing so much as a comma, by the top political–military establishment of Israel: by the Prime Minister, the Defence Minister, the Head of the Mossad and the Director of Military Intelligence. They, in order not to utter the name of their top spy dubbed him, and used to refer to him, as 'The Doctor', or otherwise, Ha'mehutan, meaning the Son-in-Law.

The Son-in-Law turned over crucial information to the Mossad which, when cross-examined and compared with data from other sources and agencies, was found to be authentic, reliable and correct. One of the most important documents ever handed over by the Son-in-Law to his Mossad contact was the transcript of a conversation President Nasser had in Moscow, on 22 January 1970, when he, as we have already shown, 'repeated his demand for [long-range] fighter-bombers because the range of our bombers does not enable to reach deep into Israel'. Another crucial document which the Egyptian spy turned over to the Mossad was the secret message from President Sadat to President Leonid Brezhnev, on 30 August 1972, in which Sadat, as we have already shown, asked for 'a retaliation weapon' (meaning Scuds) adding that 'it was obvious, and still is, that, deprived of such a retaliation weapon, we would remain incapable of taking any kind of military action [against Israel] . . .'.[7] Not only did the Son-in-Law hand over these two (and other) documents, but he also explained to his Mossad contact that for both Nasser and Sadat having long-range fighter-bombers and Scud missiles was a *precondition* for embarking on war and that without these weapons at her disposal Egypt would *not* attack Israel.

On the basis of this dramatic written and verbal information Israel's post-1967 war strategy was recast. It became known as 'the

Conception', and in a nutshell it said that Egypt would embark on a war against Israel only *after* it had obtained advanced fighter-bombers and Scuds. Since they believed that without these resources Egypt would *not* attack, the Israelis started monitoring Egyptian airfields to see if these weapon systems had arrived in Egypt for if they had, then after a period of training and assimilation and, if by then the Sinai was still in Israel's hands, Egypt would be ready, militarily, for an attack and would most likely make one.

What the Israelis, however, failed to realize was that the Son-in-Law, whom they considered to be their top spy in Egypt and whose reports were regarded as essential reading for Israel's top politico-military leadership, including the Prime Minister and the Defence Minister, was in fact, a double agent also working for President Sadat.[8] And while the documents he handed over and his explanations that Egypt would not strike without fighter-bombers and Scuds was indeed true at the time, this policy was later abandoned by Sadat who, as shown, came to the conclusion that Moscow was unlikely to provide him with these crucial weapons and that his best option was to embark on a limited, rather than a total, war against Israel. Clearly, the top Mossad agent knew about Sadat's new policy for he was his right-hand man and clearly fully in his confidence, but he failed to notify the Israelis of the change. This had very grave consequences for Israel for she continued to believe in 'the Conception', namely that Egypt would not strike without her preconditions being met.

Furthermore, the Son-in-Law also gradually embarked on a calculated campaign of misinformation. He had warned the Israelis of an imminent war in 1972 which never happened. He repeated this warning in the spring of 1973 and this time he created great difficulties for the Israelis after telling his Mossad handler that Sadat would strike at Israel on 15 May. In response to this warning, the IDF High Command drew up a plan, code named Blue-White, which was aimed at speeding up military purchases and crystallizing preparations for war. There were differing views within the Israeli military establishment regarding Israel's most appropriate response to the agent's warning. Director of Military Intelligence, Eli Zeira, insisted that the probability of war was remote and that he considered that Egypt would not strike. But Zeira was overruled by Chief of Staff David Elazar and Defence Minister Dayan, who decided that what the Son-in-Law said about an imminent attack was probably true and that the warning should be taken seriously even though it contradicted this spy's own previous information, namely that Egypt would not attack without having long-range warplanes and Scuds. Thus, on 19 April Blue-White was implemented. But the Egyptian attack failed to materialize and, on 12 August 1973, the forces were dispersed – this was just seven weeks before the Yom Kippur War. This vain mobilization cost Israel no less than $45 million and caused many to complain that the government had needlessly wasted taxpayers' money.

We now know that Sadat did not intend to attack Israel in April–May 1973 and that the false alarm was part of the Son-in-Law's misinformation campaign. Sadat later wrote: 'I had no intention of starting a war in May.'[9] In fact, it was only on 22–23 August 1973 that a final decision regarding the date of an attack on Israel was made in Alexandria and, therefore, the top Mossad agent could not have known earlier than that of 15 May or any other possible date as D-day for war. The only conclusion is that he was simply lying to the Mossad.

It is fairly clear then, that the Son-in-Law, the double agent, played a crucial part in the Egyptian deception plan since what he said was taken very seriously indeed by the decisions-makers in Israel. Hypnotized by their top Egyptian spy the Israelis, however, failed to realize two crucial things. First, that the information provided by the Son-in-Law that Egypt would *not* strike at Israel before obtaining Scud missiles and advanced fighter-bombers ('the Conception') was no longer valid in the spring of 1973 and, therefore, it was mistaken to base Israel's strategy on it, for war was to be expected even *without* the fulfilment of the Egyptian preconditions. Secondly, that the Son-in-Law, whom the Mossad considered to be its best agent in the Arab world was, in fact, hiding crucial information while, on the other hand, feeding the Mossad with false information regarding Egyptian intentions, as he had blatantly done late in 1972 and, particularly, in April–May 1973 when his false warning caused a massive, and un-necessary, mobilization in Israel. This latter major call-up was unfortunate for Israel; for it evoked such criticism that when, later that year, war was imminent and the need to mobilize the reserves was urgent, the Israeli political–military leadership hesitated, apprehensive that it was, yet again, a false alarm.

A tale of a Libyan aeroplane

Until now there has been no published explanation of how the Son-in-Law managed to mislead the Mossad, which at the time was, perhaps, the world's best intelligence agency. The answers to this had first to do with a colossal *operational* failure of the Mossad. It is an accepted practice of intelligence services to ensure that handlers of spies are changed and rotated frequently, in order that handler and spy do not become too close which might, in turn, reduce the alertness of the handler and his ability to supervise efficiently the performance of the spy he is in charge of. With the Son-in-Law things were different. He insisted that the Mossad should *not* change his handler and this resulted in a situation where, for many years, he had the same supervisor who, by becoming too close to the charming Egyptian spy, failed to maintain the good supervision which would have enabled him to find out in time that the spy he was handling was, in fact, a double agent.

Another explanation for the stunning success of the Son-in-Law in misleading the Mossad, particularly and most critically, in the period just before the outbreak of the October 1973 war, has to do with an event which, at the time, seemed irrelevant but in hindsight was crucial in enabling the Egyptian spy to deceive the Mossad.

It all started on 21 February 1973, when a Libyan Boeing 727 flight number 414 en route from Libya to Cairo was caught in a storm and started heading towards Israel. The Israelis, suspecting that the plane was on its way to attack the Dimona research reactor – there had been intelligence warnings that such an attack was planned by terrorist groups – dispatched two Phantoms which, failing to intercept it, shot the plane down. As it later emerged, the pilot of the Libyan aircraft had made a navigation error and this led to the tragic event in which 108 innocent passengers, including the former Libyan Foreign Minister, Saleh Bou Yassir, perished.

Colonel Muammar Qaddafi of Libya was furious and demanded that Egypt, whom he blamed for its inefficiency and inability to guide the airliner to a safe landing, retaliate swiftly against Israel. President Sadat attempted to calm the Colonel down by saying that he was preparing his forces for a decisive battle against Israel, which would be suitable revenge for the Libyan plane, as well as for many other Arab humiliations and it was unwise to be distracted from the main battle by secondary incidents. Any premature action, argued Sadat, might spoil the war and even be counterproductive with the occupied lands remaining in Israel's hands. Qaddafi remained unconvinced and vowed to take his revenge. On 2 April 1973, Sadat travelled in person to Tripoli in a last-ditch attempt to persuade Qaddafi to refrain from attacking the Israelis. But to no avail. Israel, Qaddafi said to Sadat, must understand that 'Libya is not an easy prey.' By now realizing that the Libyan Colonel was adamant, Sadat asked him: 'What sort of action do you have in mind?' to which Qaddafi replied: 'I want to blow up an *El Al* plane', and he added, 'A tooth for a tooth and an eye for an eye.'[10] At this point Sadat surprised Qaddafi by saying: 'We will do our best to help you.' Sadat then appointed – none other than – the Son-in-Law, his right-hand man and the top agent of the Mossad in Egypt, to liaise with Qaddafi and draw up the delicate operation to hit an Israeli plane. Although Sadat strongly opposed any premature military action which could thwart his own planning for an all-out war against the Israelis in case his attempts to regain his occupied lands through diplomacy failed, it was nevertheless important for him to remain on good terms with the Libyan Colonel.

Together with Qaddafi's man, Major Hawny, the Son-in-Law planned an operation to take place in Rome where, as past experience showed, the authorities were soft on caught terrorists and where Israeli planes were relatively unprotected. The Son-in-Law planned that a team of five Palestinians, to be picked by Colonel Qaddafi, would approach the international airport of Rome from sea or by foot and from a distance of between 800 and 1000 metres hit an Israeli aeroplane with a portable missile as it took off. With his plan approved by Sadat and Qaddafi, the Son-in-Law obtained the missile from the Egyptian arsenal on behalf of the presidential office. He then packed it in two boxes – one of these was $6 \times 2 \times 5$ feet – which he then dispatched on Egypt Air to Italy as 'carpets' with his wife – who was not aware of the contents – as a courier. In Rome, his wife passed the two 'carpets' to Egyptian personnel who put them in a waiting mini truck before transferring them to the Egyptian Arts Academy in Rome. In Cairo, in the mean time, upon receiving the message from his wife that the packages had arrived safely, the Son-in-Law boarded a flight to Rome, where he personally delivered the missile to a Libyan agent to transfer to the commandos. From this moment, however, things started going terribly wrong.

Just after midnight of 5 September 1973, Italian military intelligence, escorted by police, arrived in a house at the village of Ostia, three miles away from Italy's international airport Fiumicino, climbed to the second floor and knocked on the door of flat number 12. When a young man of Arab appearance opened the door, they pushed him aside, stormed in, and after a short search found and confiscated the

missile which the Son-in-Law and his wife had successfully smuggled
from Egypt to Italy. A few hours later, the rest of the Palestinian team
which had arrived in Italy to carry out the operation against an El Al
aircraft, were arrested at the small Atlas hotel in central Rome. This
put an end to Qaddafi's attempt to ravenge the shooting-down of the
Libyan airliner.

When the Italians came to confiscate the missile and arrest the
Palestinian commandos, they were equipped with accurate information as to the location of the missile and the hotel where the
Palestinians were lodging. This crucial information was passed to
them by the Mossad. But who tipped off the Mossad? The answer,
never previously published, is that it was the Son-in-Law – Sadat's
right-hand man, Mossad's agent, the chief planner of the operation
against the Israelis – who tipped off the Mossad. By doing so he
achieved three things: firstly, he prevented a terrorist attack on an
Israeli airliner at a critical time when Sadat was putting the finishing
touches on his long-awaited war against Israel – it would start four
weeks later. Secondly, by helping Qaddafi in this operation but sabo-
taging it behind his back, the Son-in-Law enabled Sadat to remain on
good terms with the Libyan Colonel. Thirdly, and perhaps most importantly, by tipping off the Mossad and probably saving Israeli lives, the
Son-in-Law enhanced his own reputation for reliability within the
Mossad which, in turn, enabled him, as we shall soon see, to embark
on the final stage of deceiving the Israelis and land his final blow.

In the mean time, on 25 September 1973, King Hussein of Jordan
flew to Israel, met Prime Minister Meir in the Midrasha, the headquarters of the Mossad in Herzelia, just north of Tel Aviv, and warned
her of an imminent attack by Egypt and Syria. This is what he said to
her (it is brought here verbatim):

King Hussein: From a very very sensitive source in Syria, that we
have had information from in the past and passed it on, in terms of
preparations and plans, actually all the units that were meant to be
in training and were prepared to take part in this Syrian action are
now, as of the last two days or so, in position of pre-attack. That
meant to be part of the plan, except for one minor modification –
the 3rd division is meant also to cater for any possible Israeli movement through Jordan on their flank. That includes their aircraft,
their missiles and everything else, that is out on the front at this
stage. Now this had all come under the guise of training but in

accordance with the information we had previously, these are the pre-jump positions and all the units are now in these positions. Whether it means anything or not, nobody knows. But I have my doubts. However, one cannot be sure. One must take those as facts.

Golda Meir: 'Is it conceivable that the Syrians would start something without full cooperation with the Egyptians?'

Hussein: 'I don't think so. I think they would cooperate.'[11]

This was an extraordinary event – the King of Jordan, whose country was officially at war with Israel, flew to the enemy to warn them of an imminent invasion by his Arab brothers. As the conversation between Meir and the King was secretly filmed and taped by the Mossad, Defence Minister Dayan also received the transcript which was in English, and which he passed over to the Chief of Staff who, on the next day 26 September, discussed the matter with his colleagues. As extracts from this discussion between Dayan and the High Command are now available, it is shocking to realize that the Israelis simply failed to understand what the King was saying to the Prime Minister. For while, as the above original extract shows, his warning was that '[Egypt *and* Syria] would cooperate [in their attack]', Chief of Staff Elazar said in the meeting that: 'It is unknown if [Syrian preparations to open fire] are in cooperation with the Egyptians.' He also said – disregarding the fact that according to the transcript the King's was a clear warning of a *joint* Egyptian–Syrian attack – that 'There could be nothing more idiotic for Syria than to attack on its own.' Dayan, like Elazar, also failed to understand what the King was saying and commented that the Syrians 'will find it difficult to go to war without Egypt'.[12] The end result was that the crucial warning – just ten days before the war – was not heeded. No reserves were mobilized to deter the assembling Syrians and Egyptians.

But perhaps the main reason why the warning of the King was not taken seriously by the Israelis, was again – new, fresh and critical – information received from the Son-in-Law which seemed to indicate that any danger of war was far away. On 28 September, that is just three days after Hussein's warning to Israel of a planned attack on her by Egypt and Syria, the Son-in-Law accompanied his boss Anwar Sadat in a visit to Saudi Arabia, where he joined the President in a meeting with the Saudi King. Only three – the President, the King and the Son-in-Law – took part in this meeting in which Sadat informed

King Feisal that Egypt was intending to strike at Israel. After this meeting, the Son-in-Law contacted his Mossad handler to say that Sadat had decided *to postpone* the war. Now given that the Son-in-Law was present in the meeting between Sadat and King Feisal, his report to the Mossad of a postponement of war was an outright lie and a convincing proof that he was deceiving the Israelis. However, the Mossad put more trust in the Son-in-Law than it did in King Hussein, because only a few weeks earlier this Egyptian spy had 'proved' his credibility by issuing a critical warning to the Mossad of the planned terrorist attack against the El Al aeroplane in Rome in the wake of which the terrorists were arrested and the attack forestalled.

In the mean time in Egypt and Syria final preparations were under way for the planned attack on Israel. In Egypt mobilization was announced in the last week of September, but to lull suspicion and to camouflage its intention, the Egyptian High Command ordered, on 4 October, the demobilization of 20,000 men of the September intake. Also instructions to officers desiring to leave during the exercise to go on the Umra, the small pilgrimage to Mecca, were announced in *Al Ahram*. In Syria, to lull Israel's suspicion, the new Minister of Information, George Saddeqni, announced that on the week of 6 October, President Assad would be visiting the distant provinces of Deir Al-Zour and Hasaka. While all this was happening, representatives of the two armies met in Syria and fixed 6 October at 2 p.m. as the date and hour of opening fire.[13]

On Friday, 5 October at 11.30 a.m., Prime Minister Golda Meir convened her Cabinet to discuss the deteriorating situation. By now it was clear that huge Egyptian and Syrian armies were massing along the borders and information was being received that Soviet advisers were leaving both Egypt and Syria. In this critical meeting, the Chief of Staff and Director of Military Intelligence described the situation on the fronts but judged that an attack was not likely, and the assumption was that if war were imminent there would be further indications and intelligence reports to this effect. The Cabinet decided to entrust the Prime Minister with the authority to mobilize the reserves if this should be necessary the next day (next meeting of the Cabinet was scheduled for Sunday). Had mobilization already been ordered on Friday – for Israel's doctrine of warfare demanded mobilization in face of such a concentration of enemy troops along the borders – history might have taken a different turning, but this was not to be the case. It seems that those present at this crucial Friday meeting – just a day before war broke out – believed, wrongly as we shall see, that Israel's regular army together with the air force could delay the advance of an invasion until the arrival of the reserves. At the same time they greatly underestimated the enemy's strength and determination. What also deterred the Israeli ministers from ordering all-out mobilization was a fear that an increase in the fighting forces might be seen as a threat which could accelerate the danger of war and even lead to a clash of arms. Fresh in everybody's mind was the false mobilization of April–May 1973 – triggered, as we should recall, by false information from the Son-in-Law – which cost Israel a fortune and led to much criticism. Was this yet another false alert, ministers asked themselves on this Friday? Last, but not least, there was the 'reassurance' given to the Mossad by the Son-in-Law, that, as discussed above, he had been present at a meeting in which Sadat told the King of Saudi Arabia of his decision to postpone his war with Israel.

INVASION

The Arab strike came on the next day, Saturday, 6 October, which was Yom Kippur, the most sacred day in the Jewish calendar. Just before 2 p.m., 222 warplanes took off from seven Egyptian airfields and flew low on bombing missions against Israeli military targets in the Sinai; the opening gambit of the Egyptians was similar to that of the Israelis in 1967 – a massive air strike. Soon after, Egyptian guns opened a tremendous bombardment along the entire Suez Canal and in the first minute of this barrage 10,500 shells landed on Israeli positions, a rate of 175 shells per second. In the mean time, 60 warplanes took off from several air bases in Syria to bomb Israeli targets on the Golan Heights and guns opened a fierce and intense barrage to soften up Israeli positions.

While this was happening, ministers and military personnel were in emergency session in the Tel Aviv office of Prime Minister Meir waiting for the war to start. A final confirmation that war would break out was given in person to the Head of the Mossad, Zvika Zamir, by the Son-in-Law. The Son-in-Law and Head of the Mossad met on the night of 5 October in a flat in London, at the request of the Egyptian spy who insisted on seeing Zamir in person. At this crucial meeting for which he was late, leaving Head of the Mossad to wait for him nervously, the Son-in-Law said that war would break out on Saturday 6 October at 6 p.m. This warning, the Son-in-Law must have known, was much too short a notice for the Israelis, who had to call up and mobilize their reserves to the fronts. But even now the Egyptian spy was clearly misleading the Mossad, for rather than at 6 p.m., as he was telling Zamir, the war would start four hours earlier, at 2 p.m.

Mobilization of reserves started at around 10 a.m. but only after an acrimonious argument between Defence Minister Dayan and Chief of Staff Elazar. Dayan favoured a limited mobilization of the air force and two army divisions, one to the north, the other to the south, which could, so he wrongly believed, together with the air force, hold up the attackers. Chief of Staff Elazar, on the other hand, insisted on full mobilization so he could undertake an immediate counter-attack; Elazar was offensive-minded but for this he urgently needed a massive concentration of forces. As the two failed to agree the matter was brought to the Prime Minister and she, with minimal military knowledge, opted for Chief of Staff Elazar's proposal and ordered a full, all-out mobilization of reserves. But precious time had been lost. From the final confirmation given to the Head of the Mossad by the Son-in-Law in London that war would break out – it was passed by Zamir to Israel at 4 a.m., 6 October – to the actual starting of war at 2 p.m., there remained ten hours of which about five had been spent on endless arguments between Dayan and Elazar, regarding how many troops should be mobilized. In the mean time none were mobilized until Prime Minister Meir made the final decision.

At 2.05 p.m., while the meeting at Meir's office was still under way, the Defence Minister's aide-de-camp walked in and passed a note to Dayan informing him of the Arab strike which by then had swung into action. Five Egyptian divisions – the three northern divisions constituting the 2nd army and the two southern divisions making up the 3rd – crossed the Suez Canal and built connecting bridgeheads to create a continuous front. Every 15 minutes a wave of troops crossed and, by 3.15 p.m., the Egyptian army had already put 20 infantry battalions – 800 officers and 13,500 men, complete with portable and hand-dragged support weapons – into the desert. From 5.30 p.m, the Egyptians started landing commando forces, carrying portable anti-tank weapons, deep into the Sinai in an attempt to prevent Israeli reserves from reaching the front line at the Suez Canal.

Confronting this massive five-division invasion were no more than 10 Israeli infantry platoons, 12 artillery batteries (52 cannons), 290 tanks, 2 ground-to-air missiles (Hoks), and 6 anti-aircraft batteries. This very thin shield, a mere 450–500 troops, was deployed in 16 strongholds and 4 observation places. The reason why there were so few troops along the frontier and that only about half of the Bar-Lev line positions were manned, was that Ariel Sharon, OC Southern Command until a few weeks before the war, did not believe in the concept of the Bar-Lev line, but failing to persuade his superiors that Israel's strategy should be mobile and a line of defence would crumble in war – in which he was to prove right – he found a way round it by retaining the line but shutting down 16 out of its 30 strongholds.[14] The catastrophic result was that the fortifications were too far apart to give each other effective fire-support and, by now, the Egyptian troops after crossing the Canal, could move easily into the desert through the wide gaps between the fortifications. The few Israeli troops in the Bar-Lev line found themselves in dire straits and could do little to stem the Egyptian troops who surged across the Canal like a tidal wave. The Bar-Lev line gave out, crumbled and the strongpoints fell. What made matters worse was that Shmuel Gonen – he was made OC Southern Command on 15 July 1973 succeeding Ariel Sharon – having been told, on the basis of information received from the Son-in-Law that war would start at 6 p.m., decided to deploy at the last minute so that the Egyptians could not gain a clear picture of his forces layout and could not alter their plans accordingly. When the war started earlier than expected this proved to be a catastrophic error.

The movement of reserves to the front was crucial but it all took time and, to make matters even worse, the air force failed, because of the horrific damage it suffered from the efficient Egyptian and Syrian missile systems, to provide support to the forces on the ground and stop the enemy. In the first hours of war not only did the Bar-Lev line crumble, but with it the whole Israeli belief – or wishful thinking – that the regular army supported by the air force could hold up any potential Arab invasion. In the north, following their successful air strike, Syrian armoured forces – a first wave of 500 tanks and a later addition of 300 – crashed through the lines along the entire front and penetrated into the Golan Heights. So overwhelming and massive was this assault that Israeli forces on the Golan Heights, though greater than the usual standard force on the Heights (an air battle on 13 September had resulted in a partial mobilization of Israeli forces), still failed, in the opening phase, to stem the Syrian thrust which was seriously threatening the Jordan river.[15]

FIGHTING BACK

Golan Heights

Because Israeli settlements were so close to the border with Syria and there were few obstacles to halt the Syrians from moving deeper into the Golan Heights, the Israelis had to give priority to this front. On the night of 6 October, the General Staff dispatched a further division to reinforce the two already on the Golan Heights; but the situation remained serious. To relieve pressure on the front, Chief of Staff Elazar asked for political permission to bomb Syrian cities. This was granted and the air force, on 9 October, struck at the Syrian Defence Ministry and the Air Force Headquarters in Damascus, as well as at targets in Homs. What, however, provided almost a miraculous reprieve and was a stroke of luck for the Israelis, was that on that day, the Syrians ran out of ground-to-air missiles and the air force made the most of this situation. As Defence Minister Dayan later remarked in his memoirs: 'That night, 9 October, I found the mood had changed ... there was a feeling that on that day they had passed the rock-bottom point and that the momentum of the Syrian attack had been broken. The enemy forces had begun to retreat.'[16] Two days later, on 11 October, the Israelis struck at the 40th Jordanian tank brigade, which was dispatched by King Hussein to assist the Syrians – it lost 27 killed and 50 wounded and 14 of its tanks were disabled beyond repair – and then turned on the Iraqi forces, which had also been sent to assist the Syrians. They hit them hard, drove back the entire Syrian–Jordanian–Iraqi assault and retook the Golan Heights. 'At the end of the first week of war', noted Defence Minister Dayan in his memoirs, 'the Syrians ... were on the defensive, and the campaign was being fought on their soil.'[17] By then the Israelis recovered all the ground they had lost and a bit more into the bargain.

War in the desert

In the Sinai, on 8 October, roughly two days after the massive Egyptian invasion, and without waiting to concentrate, the Israelis opened a major offensive aimed at throwing the Egyptian war machine out of gear and wiping out the forces that had crossed the Suez Canal before they were properly established on its eastern bank. But it ran into failure and the Israelis paid a heavy price in casualties and material for this abortive effort. Soon, however, the scales tilted against the Egyptians. They had enjoyed, when war started, the advantage of surprise and preponderant superiority of forces, but by now the Israelis were approaching the full tide of their mobilized strength, they had recovered their balance, were regrouping, switching forces from the Golan Heights, where the Syrians had been virtually knocked out of the war on 11 October, and were ready to hit back. The coming Israeli success, though, arose not so much from superior insight or strategy, as because of the miscalculations and shortsightedness of the Egyptians. As already mentioned, Sadat had originally directed his generals to plan a limited war against Israel and the Egyptian military plan did indeed reflect this directive in that it was aimed only at achieving very limited goals – to cross the Suez Canal, penetrate no more than a few miles into the desert, obtain a lodgement and defend it while remaining under the safe cover of the SAM missile system. But in an attempt to follow up their initial success and under intense pressure from Damascus to keep on fighting in order to pin down the Israelis and relieve pressure on Syria, the Egyptian High Command, with Sadat's consent, decided to alter the original limited war plans and push deeper into the desert. This was, perhaps, their biggest mistake in this war for away from their missile umbrella, the Egyptians tanks and troops were exposed to the Israeli air force. As they moved deeper into the desert, on 14 October, the advancing Egyptians, brutally harassed by Israeli warplanes and hit by superior dug-in Israeli tanks, were thrown back leaving flaming tanks behind them. Now the tables turned. The Israelis moved into the offensive and under the command of General Sharon penetrated through an undefended gap between the Egyptian 2nd and 3rd armies, and successfully crossed the Suez Canal. By 20 October, the Israelis had secured three bridges across the Suez Canal which enabled them to transfer growing numbers of troops and tanks on to the western bank of the Canal.

On Monday, 22 October, a ceasefire was announced (expressed in UN Resolution 338), which came into force at 6.52 p.m. But on 23 October, determined to improve their bargaining position, the Israelis breached the ceasefire and launched a concerted assault by four armoured brigades. They encircled the 3rd Egyptian army in the southern part of the Suez Canal and the town of Suez and continued south to reach Adabia on the coast some ten miles below Suez. By 24 October, the 3rd Egyptian army – two reinforced divisions, about 45,000 men and 250 tanks – was completely cut off and that evening, after Soviet threats and growing American pressure, Israel agreed to a second ceasefire. It declined, however, to return to the previous lines of 22 October.

POST-WAR – SOCIETY AND DIPLOMACY

Given the awful opening conditions on 6 October and that Israel was caught off guard and totally unprepared for war on two fronts, she had gained a stunning military victory. Indeed, when the guns fell silent, Israeli troops were stationed within 63 miles of Cairo and 28 miles of Damascus. But the price of victory was high: 2687 men died and 7251 were wounded and the cost of the war exceeded $7 billion in lost equipment, fall in production and lost exports. The war also had emotional, psychological and political repercussions. It shattered complacency, eroded the sense of confidence and plunged the nation into one of its most serious crises; Israel after this war was in the throes of prolonged trauma. Reserve soldiers who fought in the war and saw at first hand the shortcomings of the military-politico leadership, were unwilling to forgive or forget and upon returning home from the fronts they started, almost spontaneously, a protest movement which sought a thorough investigation into how Israel was caught off guard and had been so unprepared. The leadership was criticized as never before with the sharpest darts aimed at Defence Minister Dayan, who turned from a war hero into a villain and met with outbursts of implacable hostility wherever he went. As the national temper mounted and the anti-government protest grew by the day, Prime Minister Meir announced, in early November 1973, the appointment of a judicial commission of inquiry to be headed by the President of the Supreme Court, Justice Shimon Agranat, to investigate the initial decisions of military and politicians concerning intelligence received before the war, and the IDF's general state of preparedness at that time.

In the mean time, American Secretary of State Henry Kissinger embarked on shuttle diplomacy in an attempt to summon an international peace conference in Geneva where the implementation of Resolution 242 would be discussed. He partly succeeded. On 21 December 1973, a conference sponsored by the United States and the Soviet Union opened at Geneva's Palais des Nations to which Israel, Egypt and Jordan, but not the Syrians and the PLO, sent delegations. It was not a successful conference and it was adjourned within a single day amidst a farrago of mutual recrimination. But, nevertheless, an instrument called the Geneva Peace Conference mechanism through which future negotiations were to take place was established,.and it was also decided that the next diplomatic move should concentrate on achieving a disengagement of Israeli and Egyptian forces to reduce friction and prevent the renewal of war.

Israel, in the mean time, was preparing herself for a general election which had originally been scheduled for 31 October 1973 but had to be postponed because of the war. The election campaign was fierce and, naturally, revolved around the issue of who was responsible for the Yom Kippur fiasco. All other issues were pushed aside as the Labour leaders sought to justify their actions and called for a mandate to continue with the post-war diplomacy. The odds were that Labour would lose its political hegemony, but by portraying itself as the only political force that could lead Israel towards the coveted peace with the Arabs, it succeeded in persuading a shattered and war-weary Israeli public to vote for it. Thus, in the 31 December 1973 elections, the Labour Alignment emerged as the largest party wining 51 seats, 5 seats down on the last elections, while the main opposition, the Likud Bloc, a merger between Gahal and two smaller right-wing parties, obtained 39 seats.

On 18 January 1974, an agreement was signed by the Chiefs of Staff of Israel and Egypt. Under its terms, Israel was required to withdraw from the areas she occupied west of the Suez Canal while a 19-square-mile area east of the Canal was split into three zones. One in which Egyptian forces – no more than 7000 soldiers, 30 tanks and 36 artillery pieces – remained, a middle buffer zone controlled by the UN and an eastern zone in which Israel kept the same number of forces as Egypt did in its zone. The last clause of this agreement said that it was not a final peace treaty, but the first step towards peace.

THE AGRANAT REPORT

On 10 March 1974, Meir presented her new government to the Knesset which granted it a vote of confidence. While there were new faces, notably former generals Yitzhak Rabin and Aharon Yariv, Meir nevertheless kept Moshe Dayan as her Defence Minister. As it turned out, this was a mistake, for Moshe Dayan, the god whose feet turned out to be made of clay, was held by the public as the chief responsible for the Yom Kippur debacle and he attracted growing criticism which, inevitably, reflected on the government as well. The public clamour rose to a crescendo on 1 April 1974, with the publication of the interim report of the Agranat Inquiry Commission, set up by Meir in November 1973 to investigate the 'blunder' – the failures before and at the initial phases of the Yom Kippur War. The interim report exonerated Meir and Dayan and laid the blame for the shortcomings squarely on the military people, mainly on Chief of Staff David 'Dado' Elazar and the Director of Military Intelligence Eli Zeira. But if the government thought that the report would allay public discontent, then the exact opposite proved to be the case. For the Israelis simply refused to accept the verdict of the commission and wanted to see the heads of the politicians roll as well.

By now old, ill, exhausted by the war and public life and abandoned even by her own party members, Prime Minister Meir gave up. On 10 April 1974, in the course of an acrimonious debate in the Labour Party Knesset faction, she announced her resignation as Prime Minister. 'I have reached the end of the road', she said, and she then added, 'I cannot bear this burden any longer.'[18] Nobody asked her to stay and her short-lived government fell.

On this dramatic day another drama took place in Israel. A group of Palestinians, belonging to George Habash's Popular Front, entered the northern town of Kiryat Shmona and killed 18 Israelis, 8 of them young children. This did nothing to lift the national mood which was anyway at a low ebb.

Twelve days after Meir's resignation, on Monday 22 April 1974, the Party Central Committee set out to select its candidate for the office of Prime Minister. Two contenders ran: Yitzhak Rabin, the Chief of Staff during the Six-Day War, and Shimon Peres, who was the candidate of the party's Rafi (right) wing, and at that time Minister of Information. After much soul searching, the party elders, led by Pinchas Sapir, the strong man and kingmaker of the Labour Party who had himself declined an offer to assume the premiership and succeed Meir, threw their weight behind Rabin, who defeated Peres with a majority of 44 (298 to 254).

On 15 May, another vicious terrorist attack shook Israel to the core. Three Palestinians of the Hawatma group seized a school in Israel's northern town of Ma'alot, took 100 children hostages and demanded the release of Palestinian prisoners. Meir, still a caretaker Prime Minister, instructed the military to use force to release the hostages. The army stormed the building but the price was high, 22 children were killed in the course of the operation.

On Friday 31 May 1974, on the eve of her leaving office, Meir presided over the signing of a disengagement of forces between Israel and Syria. This followed tough and exhausting indirect negotiations between the two countries, brokered by the American Secretary of State, Henry Kissinger. Under the terms of this agreement, Israel was required to withdraw from Syrian territory seized during the war, and the Golan Heights was divided into three zones – Israeli, Syrian and a UN buffer zone in which the town of Quneitra, taken by Israel during that war, was included. With the signing of the Israeli–Syrian disengagement agreement came the official end of the October 1973 Yom Kippur War.

ENTER YITZHAK RABIN

On 3 June 1974, Yitzhak Rabin presented his government to the Knesset and got its approval. It was largely a new government in that Meir and Dayan had left, and out of the government's 19 ministers only 7 had served in the previous administration. Yigal Allon remained Deputy Prime Minister and Foreign Minister, and Shimon Peres, Rabin's arch rival, was made Defence Minister as a conciliatory gesture to Labour's right wing.

The new Prime Minister of Israel, Yitzhak Rabin, was a native 'Sabra' who was born in Jerusalem in 1922. He grew up in a social-ist–Zionist family and after studying at the Kadoorie Agricultural College joined the Haganah, the Jewish underground organization in British Mandatory Palestine. During the 1948 Arab–Israeli War, Rabin served in the Palmach, the striking force of the Haganah, and took part in operations to relieve the Arab blockade on Jerusalem; he also fought in the centre of the country and, in different stages of the war, partici-pated in military operations against the Egyptian army. Aged 26, Lt-Col. Rabin was entrusted, along with three other colleagues, with negotiating a post-war armistice with Egypt, in 1949. Then, for the next two decades, the military remained his chief domain. Rabin's finest hour came in June 1967, when he oversaw Israel's decisive victory over the Arabs in six days of war. Rumours, however, that he had suffered some sort of nervous collapse on the eve of the war, haunted him for many years and were used by his opponents to discredit him. On 1 January 1968, Rabin retired from the military and, for the next five years, served as Israel's ambassador in Washington, where he established vital ties with US politicians and leaders of the powerful US Jewish community. The post of ambassador groomed Rabin for political life and, fortuitously, meant that he was out of Israel during the Yom Kippur War. Thus, while other Labour figures, notably Prime Minister Meir and Defence Minister Dayan, were blamed for not foreseeing a war, Rabin had clean hands and he was wholly untainted by any connection with the disastrous failures of this war. Rabin was elected as a Labour MK in December 1973, became Minister of Labour in April 1974, and then, following Meir's resignation and after successfully beating off Peres, became Prime Minister of Israel.

Rebuilding the IDF and tackling the economy

Perhaps the most urgent task facing Rabin was to rebuild the IDF. Lessons from the war had to be drawn and implemented, equipment had to be replaced and, no less important, the right balance had to be struck between the need to return to some sort of normality, mainly through the releasing of reserves to civilian life and, at the same time, the need to be prepared for the possibility of a renewal of war. Together with his Defence Minister Peres, Rabin gave top priority to a three-year rebuilding programme for the IDF and ordered an immediate study of the country's defence needs.

The other major task facing Rabin – hardly compatible with the need to rebuild the IDF – was to tackle the economy which was in terribly bad shape. The war had been ruinously expensive and the massive increase in defence spending, which in the post-war period grew to a staggering 40 per cent of the entire national budget, had had an enormously negative impact on the economy. Worse still, after years with growth in the region of 10 per cent annually, in the four years after the war, growth fell to less than 3 per cent a year. In addition, the trade deficit increased dramatically and inflation, in 1974, reached a record level of 56 per cent with the prices of most goods rocketing and resulting in an overwhelming burden on the citizens, with the poorer segments of society, mainly the *Sephardim*, being hit particularly hard. On 9 November 1974, Rabin took his first major step towards bringing the economy under control by announcing a 43 per cent devaluation of the Israeli pound; this was the start of a prolonged programme of devaluations. He banned the import of cars and luxury items for a six-month period and attempted to persuade Israelis that with 300,000 of Israel's 1.1 million labour force employed in public service they had to shift manpower to production to raise the level of exports.

To worsen the already depressed national mood, terrorism raised its ugly head again and hit hard both in Israel and abroad. In November 1974, a group of Palestinians entered the town of Beit Shean, killed 4 Israelis and wounded 20. In December, a Palestinian threw a hand grenade into a cinema in Tel Aviv injuring 51. In March 1975, Palestinians took hostages at the Savoy Hotel in Tel Aviv and held them for two days before troops intervened. Then in July 1975, a bomb in Zion Square in Jerusalem killed 13 and injured 65.

The Sinai II Agreement and settlements

On 4 September 1975, following months of negotiations between Israel and Egypt through the mediation of Secretary of State Henry Kissinger, Israel and Egypt signed the Sinai II agreement. It envisaged the withdrawal of Israeli forces for some 18 miles into the Sinai, which was also to include a withdrawal from the Sinai oilfields and the two strategic passes in the Sinai peninsula, the Mitla and the Gidi, captured by Israel in 1967. It was agreed that Egyptian forces should occupy less than four miles of the evacuated territory, while the rest of the terrain should be manned by a UN contingent in a wide buffer zone. Electronic monitoring stations in and near the Mitla and Gidi passes and looking into Egyptian territory were to be operated by Israelis, and Egyptian observers were to operate devices looking into areas controlled by Israel. While Rabin failed to win a public pledge from President Sadat of non-belligerency, it was nevertheless agreed that the parties would avoid 'resorting to the threat or use of force or military blockade against each other'.

Through separate letters exchanged between Prime Minister Rabin, Secretary of State Kissinger and President Gerald Ford, the Americans agreed to provide Israel with substantial quantities of the latest weapon systems, to meet Israel's oil needs over a five-year period (if those supplies were not available elsewhere) and, in the event of a major threat to Israel's security, to consult promptly with her to see what support, diplomatic or otherwise the US could lend to Israel. This commitment was strengthened by an American pledge not to recognize the PLO, unless it accepted UN Resolution 242 and refrained from terrorism, and to veto punitive measures against Israel in the UN

Security Council. Thus the Sinai II agreement not only reduced friction between Israel and Egypt and decreased the probability of a renewed war but it also established closer ties between Israel and the United States.

But not all went well for Israel on the international arena. On 10 November 1975, the UN General Assembly was asked to condemn Zionism as 'racism' and when the vote was taken 75 states voted for with only 35 opposing the resolution. Israel was shocked and dismayed.

On the domestic front, apart from the economy, Rabin had to deal with the growing influence of religious groups attempting to establish more settlements on the disputed West Bank. A test case for the government was Eilon Moreh, near the ancient city of Sebastia, where settlers, without governmental approval, went on to build a new settlement. Rabin instructed the military to remove the settlers by force and this was done no fewer than seven times. But then, in December 1975, Defence Minister Shimon Peres gave permission to move the settlers 'temporarily' into a military camp at Kaddum and soon afterwards they were moved to another site, Mount Kabir, from where they were never again forced to withdraw. The impetus given to the settlers by the government's compromise was enormous, and for the government itself it was a fateful turning point for it proved to everyone that it was not strong enough to enforce the law.

Operation Entebbe

The post-Yom Kippur War was a gloomy period in Israel's history but what did bring a gleam of light during these days was a brilliant – though in a historical perspective insignificant – military operation. It came in the wake of the hijacking, on Sunday, 27 June 1976, of an Air France passenger airliner carrying passengers from Tel Aviv to Paris. The Palestinian hijackers instructed the pilot to fly the plane first to Casablanca, where it spent the night, and the next morning to Khartoum and from there to Entebbe Airport near Kampala, the capital of Uganda, some 2500 miles from Israel. The Israeli and Jewish hostages were confined in an old, unused terminal and the hijackers demanded that Israel's government release 53 Palestinians imprisoned in five countries. The Palestinians gave an ultimatum of 48 hours within which the released Palestinians were to be brought to Entebbe, otherwise, the plane would be blown up; under pressure the deadline was extended by 72 hours, until 11.00 on 4 July.

The Rabin government was determined not to give in to the hijack-ers' demands lest similar terrorist operations should force the hand of the government again in the future. All options, diplomatic and mili-tary, were considered and on 3 July the government gave the go-ahead for a military operation to rescue the captives.

Four Israeli Hercules transport planes and a Boeing 707 command plane took off and flew mainly along the East African coast in the direction of Entebbe. There, the leading Hercules dovetailed behind a British cargo flight and landed without arousing suspicion in the tower. While the aircraft was still taxiing, an advance paratroop unit jumped out and placed mobile landing lights for the other three transport planes. The rest of the landing party disembarked with a Mercedes automobile and two Land Rovers that precisely resembled President Amin's usual entourage. The Israelis drove towards the old terminal building, killed a Ugandan guard and burst into the terminal, where the hostages were confined. The four Palestinians stationed there were promptly gunned down and the Israelis killed another two before bundling the hostages out of the hall and into the evacuation planes. Fifty-seven minutes after the initial landing, the first Hercules took off loaded with freed hostages and 42 minutes later, the fourth and last aircraft departed; all planes landed in Nairobi for refuelling before proceeding to Israel. During the operation, one Israeli officer, Lt-Col. Yonathan (Yoni) Netanyahu, was killed by a bullet in the back. Another hostage, an aged Israeli woman, who was in the hospital at Kampala at the time of the raid, was subsequently murdered by vindic-tive Ugandan soldiers.

The rescue operation and release of the passengers cheered up the nation and, for a few days, lessened the depression and tension of a tight post-war period. But it did not really change anything and, in fact, it led to ever-growing tensions in the government, where Prime Minister Rabin and his Defence Minister Peres were locked in battle over credit for the successful rescue operation. While Rabin claimed that Peres's role in the affair was marginal at best, Peres attempted to take the credit for himself by hinting that Rabin had hesitated to adopt the military option.

The fall of Rabin

The Rabin government did not survive for long and it was a very triv-ial incident which eventually brought it down. On a Friday afternoon in December 1976, the first F-15 fighter-bombers bought in the United States were scheduled to arrive in Israel. The purchase of these modern, state-of-the-art warplanes, was considered a considerable achievement for the government and this is why Prime Minister Rabin arranged a welcome ceremony complete with government leaders and military men. But the planes were to land less than an hour before the onset of the Sabbath in Jerusalem and by holding the ceremony so close to the Sabbath the state, in effect, was forcing its own leaders to violate a basic Jewish precept, namely not to travel on the Sabbath. Indeed, when the warplanes were slightly late and the ceremony ran into the Sabbath and the holy day was violated, this aroused anger among the religious parties, one of which, Po'alei Agudat Yisrael, with two seats in the Knesset, brought a no-confidence motion against the government. When the vote was taken, the National Religious Party (Mafdal), the second largest partner in the Labour coalition and torn between its loyalty to the coalition government of which it was a partner and its religious beliefs, decided to abstain. Livid – for he expected full support by the coalition partner Mafdal – Rabin retaliated by removing this party's ministers from the government, thus leaving his shaky government backed by only 57 votes, 4 less than the 61 needed for a majority in the 120-member body. Then on 21 December 1976 Rabin resigned, calling an early general election to take place on 17 May 1977.

With elections looming Rabin was challenged for the party leadership by his arch-rival Shimon Peres. The contest between the two was fierce and at the Labour Party convention, where the matter was put to the vote, on 23 February 1977, Rabin beat Peres by the narrowest of margins, 1445 to 1404, with 16 abstentions. Then, only three weeks after his re-election as party leader, Rabin suffered a terrible blow, when an article in the *Ha'aretz* newspaper, on 15 March 1977, disclosed that his wife Leah had maintained a bank account in Washington, DC, which, at that time, was forbidden by Israel's currency laws. Before long the plot thickened when it emerged that Rabin was himself a joint signatory to the account. When the Attorney General, Aharon Barak, informed Rabin that he intended to place his wife on trial – Rabin himself would get the benefit of the doubt that he had been ignorant about the account – Rabin decided to resign from the race for the premiership. He tended his resignation on 7 April 1977 and, two weeks later, on 21 April, a special meeting of the party Central Committee confirmed Shimon Peres's candidacy for the premiership in Rabin's place.

ENTER SHIMON PERES

Shimon Peres was an old hand in Israel's politics. His political career began while working with David Ben-Gurion, the first Prime Minister of Israel, who made the 29-year-old Peres Director General of the Defence Ministry. Peres had played an important role in fostering Israeli–French relations and a most critical role in coordinating with the French in the 1956 Sinai Campaign. It was in the course of his negotiations with the French on Israel's participation in this campaign, that Peres was able to commit France politically to providing Israel with a nuclear reactor. A few years later, in 1965, when Ben-Gurion resigned from Mapai to set up Rafi, Peres was one of the first to join him, and on the eve of the 1967 Six-Day War, he was the leading mover in efforts to replace Prime Minister Eshkol, first with Ben-Gurion and then with Dayan. He also proposed – but this was rejected – to deter the Arabs from attacking Israel by taking out of the basement Israel's secret weapon – the atomic bomb.

Shimon Peres was one of the most inspirational Israeli statesmen of the twentieth century – dynamic, imaginative, creative, with a lively and fertile mind brimming endlessly with ideas – a sort of political wizard always able to conjure problems out of existence and steer the political system in daring new directions. But he had fatal flaws. He was possibly too clever and he aroused, if not among foreigners then at least among Israelis, every feeling except trust and in all his greatest acts there always seemed an element of self-seeking. In the eyes of many Israelis, Peres was a tricky, manipulative, unprincipled and unreliable politician, who always repaid loyalty with disloyalty, and that Rabin, who knew Peres well, showed his distaste for him and, famously, said of Peres that he was an 'indefatigable intriguer' did little to boost Peres's credibility.

In the election campaign, Peres – leading the Labour-dominated 'Alignment' comprised a reunited Labour Party (the old Mapai, Achdut Ha'Aabodah and Rafi) in alliance with the leftist Mapam – had to fight for votes against Menachem Begin who headed the Likud bloc, a confederation representing Begin's Herut Party, the much smaller Liberal Party and tinier factions, such as the State List and La'am. While Peres's Labour Alignment was seen as the party of the establishment, well-to-do veterans, mostly of European origin, Likud championed the demands of the recent immigrants from the Arab lands and Russia, the residents of the city slums and neglected development towns. Peres's was an uphill battle, for the party he had just inherited was clearly in poor shape, not only was it blamed for the Yom Kippur War fiasco, but its position was undermined by a series of financial scandals, with one disgraceful revelation following another. There were bankruptcies, jail sentences and suicides among the party's leading members.

To make matters even worse, Peres was challenged not only on the right, that is by the Likud, but also on the centre where, the renowned archaeologist and former general, Yigael Yadin, stood at the head of a new political party, the Democratic Movement for Change, or Dash, as it was known. This new party had its origins in the protest demonstrations of the post-Yom Kippur War and among its leading members were former army generals and intellectuals. It offered its moderate centrist followers – mostly educated, upper-middle-class Israelis of European origin – the opportunity to cast a protest vote against both Labour and Likud. Modernization was one of the main platforms of Dash, which also favoured electoral reform, with constituency districts replacing the anachronistic party lists and oligarchical party central committees. It also called for decentralizing government power and establishing a Ministry of Welfare to focus all the authority needed for social reform and ensure far greater government effort on behalf of the dispossessed and the outsiders in society.

Elections and the death of Labour

On 17 May 1977, the elections were held and proved a landmark in Israel's history. Begin's Likud won a stunning victory by winning 43 seats, in comparison with a mere 32 seats for Labour, which accounted to a disappearance of a third of its strength. Labour's crushing defeat largely resulted from the success of the Dash Party, which at its first appearance in a national election won a stunning 15 seats and took enough votes away from Labour to make Likud Israel's largest party; as much as two-thirds of Dash's votes came from voters who had supported Labour in 1973. What further helped Likud to win the elections was the massive shift away from Labour of the *Sephardim*. In the 1950s, *Sepharadic* Jews tended to vote for Labour, for after all it was the party of government and it provided them with food and shelter. Even as late as 1969, and in spite of growing resentment of the *Sephardim* towards the government, the Labour movement still received 55 per cent of the *Sephardim* vote. But in 1973, the figure dropped to 38 per cent and in the 1977 election it went down to 32 per cent. The shift away from Labour – so much associated with the *Ashkenazim* – was an expression of the frustration of the *Sephardim* who in spite of an absolute rise in their real income still felt discriminated against in relations to the *Ashkenzim* whose per capita consumption remained 65 per cent higher than that among the *Sephardim*. Thus the combination of the shift of the *Ashkenazim* away from Labour to Dash and of the *Sephardim* to Likud resulted in the collapse of Labour.

The emergence of the Likud as the party of government for the first time in the 29 years of Israel's existence and the defeat of Labour was more than a mere change of government. It was – a revolution Israeli style. After 1977 Israeli politics would never be the same again.

6

. . . .

Begin's Years, 1977–1983

BUILDING A COALITION

The emergence of ultra-Orthodox power

In the election the Likud gained 43 seats and together with Ariel Sharon's Shlomzion which joined it it had 45 seats in the 120-member-Knesset – still short of the necessary 61 majority. Thus, like other elected Prime Ministers before him, Begin had to embark on lengthy and intricate negotiations to persuade potential partners to join his coalition. Yigael Yadin's Dash Party with its 15 seats was a potential partner and Begin tried hard to persuade it to join. To no avail. Dash insisted on radical changes to the electoral system, namely to have constituency elections instead of the party list system, and it also imposed such demands on the future government's foreign policy that Begin felt he could not accept. Dash would join the coalition later in October without, however, a Likud promise on any of the above issues, though with Yadin becoming Deputy Prime Minister and his party being awarded the ministries of Communication, Labour, Justice and Transport.

But for the time being, with Dash insisting on her demands and Begin unwilling to budge, the Prime Minister had to turn to the religious parties, calling on the National Religious Party, the Mafdal, which won 12 seats in the election, and on the non-Zionist ultra-Orthodox Agudat Yisrael with its 4 seats, to join his coalition. Mafdal – traditionally the ally of Labour governments and a constant junior partner in its coalitions – agreed to join the Likud's coalition but extracted a heavy price from Begin, namely three ministerial posts, including Education and Culture which, so Mafdal hoped, could help her mould the secular Israeli society in a way more tuned with Mafdal's religious beliefs.

Unlike Mafdal, Agudat Yisrael, 'the Aguda', as it was known, did not request any ministerial posts but, nevertheless, its demands in return for joining the coalition were harsh. This ultra-Orthodox party had always, except during the first three years of the state, kept away from participating in Israel's coalition governments. But now – seizing its bargaining strength and realizing that here was an opportunity to extract concessions in matters close to the hearts of the religious community it was representing – Agudat Yisrael decided to enter into negotiations with the Likud on joining its coalition.

In the tough talks which followed, Agudat Yisrael insisted that Yeshiva students should be allowed to carry on with their studies and instead of joining the IDF at the age of 18, as all Israeli citizens do, they should be allowed to defer the date of conscription for many years which, practically, meant a very short – if at all – service in the army. This demand was accepted by Begin with the implication that from a quota of 800 Yeshiva students being allowed to defer their conscription before 1977, the numbers went up dramatically. The Aguda also insisted that girls should have the right to declare that their religious ways of life are not compatible with military service and upon making such a statement should be exempt from military service. This demand was also accepted by the Likud which was, again, a break from previous practice. For under Labour governments Orthodox girls had been allowed to claim exemption from military service, providing they appeared before a special panel, underwent a thorough investigation of their traditionalist bona fides and if exempt had to contribute an equivalent period of national service in the civilian sector. Now, however, with Begin's consent, girls wishing to be exempt from military service were only obliged to make a token appearance before a military review committee which was to act as a mere rubber stamp for their exemption; as a result from 21 per cent in 1976, the number of girls exempted from military service rose to·32 per cent in 1980. Agudat Yisrael also insisted – and Begin agreed – for Shlomo Lorentz of the Aguda to head the Finance Committee of the Knesset, which meant that the ultra-Orthodox party obtained a huge influence on the ways funds were allocated in Israel. It also demanded – and the Likud agreed – to ground El Al flights on Sabbaths, change Israel's liberal abortion law, among other demands. Of the 43 clauses of the coalition agreement, fully 30 dealt with religious matters which shows just how many concessions the religious parties were able to extract in return for their joining the coalition. In hindsight we can say that 1977 was a turning point in Israel's history not only in that the Likud defeated Labour for the first time in three decades, but also in that following this election a new power emerged in Israel's politics whose influence would steadily grow in future years – the ultra-Orthodox.

In a political coup Begin made Moshe Dayan, once a bastion of the Labour movement but relegated to the political wilderness following the 1973 Yom Kippur War debacle, his Foreign Minister. This was a clever tactical move, for Begin knew perfectly well that his own image abroad was negative and by having Dayan in his government he could demonstrate that his was a serious and responsible administration. To his associates Begin said that world leaders 'will respect Dayan' and 'accept him everywhere in the world'. As for Dayan, who defected from Labour proclaiming himself 'an independent', he knew that a prominent post in government could effectively cleanse him of the Yom Kippur stain and restore his reputation. He, therefore, accepted Begin's offer after the Prime Minister gave him an undertaking not to annex the occupied territories unilaterally – as Dayan suspected Begin might do – as long as Israel was negotiating peace with the Arabs. Former general Ariel Sharon who wished to become Defence Minister – a request which was rejected by the Liberals, a faction within the Likud – was made Minister of Agriculture and head of the Ministerial Committee responsible for settlements. Simcha Ehrlich, chairman of the Liberal Party, was made Finance Minister and the prestigious post of Defence was awarded to Ezer Weizman, who had coordinated the right wing's effort in the election campaign and was credited with the victory of the Likud.

On 20 June 1977, Begin introduced his new government and in his speech to the Knesset he declared that he would fight corruption and inflation, reduce the tax burden, raise Israel's GNP through encouragement of investment and reverse bureaucratic interference in the market. Begin also made it clear that while he was keen to work towards peace with Israel's enemies, he was also, at the same time, determined to settle Jews in all parts of biblical Eretz Israel, namely the West Bank, or Judaea and Samaria as he often referred to these occupied lands. After a seven-and-a-half hour debate in the Knesset Begin won a 63–53 vote of confidence in his new government. The former terrorist was now the top man in Israel's politics.

FIRST STEPS TO PEACE

Crucial meetings in Romania and Morocco

Soon after, on 25 August 1977, Begin travelled to Bucharest where he met Romania's President Nicolae Ceauşescu, the only Communist leader to retain diplomatic relations with Israel after the 1967 war. In a rare interview Begin later told how, 'Ceauşescu spoke of the need to make peace', and how Begin asked him to persuade President Sadat, of whom Ceauşescu was a personal friend, to visit Israel. 'You are on good terms with him', Begin told Ceauşescu, 'perhaps you could tell him that I'm willing to meet him.'[1]

Begin also sent signals to Sadat through the Americans to whom he submitted the so-called Rosen Document – after the Foreign Ministry's legal adviser who wrote it – of 46 points, detailing Israel's proposals for peace with Egypt. This document was delivered by the Americans to Sadat on 10 September 1977 and it was followed by a handwritten personal letter, with a wax seal, from the American President to Sadat, in which Jimmy Carter urged the Egyptian President to test Begin's sincerity for peace by taking a bold states-manlike move to help overcome the hurdles on the path to the Geneva Conference, the mechanism which Carter still saw as the preferred vehicle to advance peace between Israelis and Arabs.

Perhaps the strongest indication sent by the new elected Prime Minister of Israel to Sadat that he was eager to make peace with Egypt, was his approval of a meeting between his Foreign Minister Dayan and Egypt's Deputy Prime Minister Hassan el-Tohami, in Rabat, Morocco. Only a few people in Israel, Egypt and Morocco knew of this meeting which was arranged in great secrecy, took place on 16 September and its protocol – substantial extracts from which are in Appendix 1 – is published here for the first time.[2] This rare document is significant for it demonstrates that, contrary to common belief, no promise was made a priori by Foreign Minister Dayan to Sadat, through el-Tohami, that Israel would return the Sinai to Egypt. Therefore, the claim that, apparently, Sadat's decision to accelerate peace talks with Israel was made with the full knowledge that the Sinai was already in his pocket, is baseless and, as Prime Minister Begin later explained, 'none of us promised Sadat anything in advance'.[3] Also, this document shows that both Israel and Egypt preferred to deal directly with each other rather than using American or Russian mediation.

Just three days after his secret meeting with el-Tohami in Morocco, Foreign Minister Dayan travelled to America to meet President Carter and his Secretary of State Cyrus Vance in order to explore ways of breaking the impasse between Israelis and Arabs. In Washington, Dayan was confronted by an American President – Carter of course knew nothing of Dayan's talks with el-Tohami in Morocco – who insisted that Israel was taking 'a very adamant stand' and that the Arab side appears to be 'more flexible' and that Israel should show flexibility by accepting a Palestinian 'entity' on the West Bank, dismantle Jewish settlements and take part in the Geneva Conference, the mechanism created by former Secretary of State Henry Kissinger after the 1973 war. Dayan politely rebuffed the President's demands.

Historic visit to Jerusalem

A month or so after Begin's visit to Romania, President Sadat met the Romanian leader in Bucharest. 'You have already seen Begin', Sadat said to his host, 'Tell me. First, in your view, does he want peace? And, secondly, is he strong [enough to deliver]?' Ceauşescu answered both questions in the affirmative which greatly encouraged Sadat.[4] Sadat was also encouraged by the outcome of the secret meeting el-Tohami had with Foreign Minister Dayan in Morocco, for he understood from his emissary – although this was not in fact the case – that Dayan's message in this secret meeting was that Israel was willing to withdraw from the Sinai.[5] And with these positive signals and a previous personal request from American President Carter to take 'a bold statesmanlike move', Sadat decided to take the bull by the horns. On Wednesday, 9 November he faced the Egyptian Parliament and declared that he was willing to go to the ends of the earth for peace, 'even to the Knesset itself'. This dramatic announcement – not taken seriously at first – soon sent shock waves throughout Egypt, where Foreign Minister Ismail Fahmy resigned in protest, in Washington, which was, as has been said, still hooked on the Geneva Conference as the preferable mechanism to promote peace in the Middle East, and also, of course, in Israel. With the ball now firmly in his court Prime Minister Begin was quick to respond by, first, issuing a verbal invitation to Sadat to come to Jerusalem, and five days later by issuing a formal invitation through the US embassies in Tel Aviv and Cairo.

But there was deep confusion in Israel. Chief of Staff Mordechai Gur, on 15 November, said in an interview to the daily *Yediot Aharonot* that, 'Sadat should know that if his intention is another deception, in the style of the Yom Kippur war, then we are aware of it. We know that the Egyptian army is preparing itself for war against Israel . . . in spite of Sadat's declaration that he intends to come to Jerusalem.'[6] Others in Israel warned of the potential danger that instead of Sadat descending it might be, in fact, a terrorist group which, upon landing in Israel, would storm out of the aeroplane and gun down the top Israeli leadership waiting for Sadat on the tarmac.

But none of this in fact happened. Instead, on Saturday 19 November 1977, only ten days after Sadat's dramatic 'ready-to-go-to-the-ends-of-the-earth' speech to the Egyptian Parliament and only four days after Begin's formal invitation for Sadat to come to Jerusalem, an Egyptian airliner touched down at Ben-Gurion International Airport near Tel Aviv and out of it descended Egypt's President Sadat. Bedecked with Egyptian and Israeli flags, he moved through a reception line of Israeli dignitaries, shaking hands with Prime Minister Begin and President Ephraim Katzir, the Israeli Cabinet, the Chief Rabbis, Ariel Sharon, who led the Israeli counter-attack across the Suez Canal in 1973, Moshe Dayan and many people such as former Prime Minister Golda Meir whom Sadat had never met but instantly recognized.

It was in Jerusalem, a little while later, that Egyptians and Israelis discovered that the whole historic visit was built, in fact, on a misunderstanding. This emerged when Sadat remarked that Egypt had received a message through el-Tohami, following his secret meeting with Dayan in Morocco, to the effect that Israel was ready to withdraw from all of the Sinai. Begin instantly interrupted by saying, 'Mr President, we did not say that', and Dayan added that in his meeting with el-Tohami he had made it clear – as shown in the protocol of their meeting in Appendix 1 of this book – that his role was only to report back to Begin and that he promised nothing to the Egyptian emissary. But Sadat insisted: 'Tohami said you were ready to withdraw', to which Dayan replied, 'Mr President, I did not say that', and a little while later, 'If Tohami said we were prepared to withdraw then he is a liar.'[7]

The following day after attending an early morning prayer at the Al-Aqsa mosque in Jerusalem and visiting Yad Va'shem, the Holocaust Memorial, Sadat arrived at the Knesset to address it. 'I come to you today on solid ground to shape a new life and to establish peace', he said to the packed hall, and he went on to present his agenda for peace:

I have not come here for a separate agreement between Egypt and Israel. . . . I have not come to you to seek a partial peace. . . . For this would mean that we are merely delaying the ignition of the fuse. . . . I have come to you so that together we should build a durable peace . . . in all sincerity I tell you we welcome you among us with full security and safety. This in itself is a tremendous turning point . . . today I tell you, and I declare it to the whole world, that we accept to live with you in permanent peace based on justice. We do not want to encircle you or be encircled ourselves by destructive missiles ready for launching, nor by the shells of grudges and hatreds. . . . Today, through my visit to you, I ask you why don't we stretch out our hands with faith and sincerity . . . peace cannot be worth its name unless it is based on justice and not on the occupation of the land of others. . . . I tell you you have to give up once and for all the dreams of conquest and give up the belief that force is the best method for dealing with the Arabs . . . our land does not yield itself to bargaining, it is not even open to argument. . . . We cannot accept any attempt to take away or accept to seek one inch of it nor can we accept the principle of debating or bargaining over it. . . . Complete withdrawal from the Arab territories occupied after 1967 is a logical and undisputed fact. . . . As for the Palestinian cause – nobody could deny that it is the crux of the entire problem . . . there can be no peace without the Palestinians. . . . Here I tell you . . . that it is no use to refrain from recognizing the Palestinian people and their right to statehood as their right of return.

It was a speech which contained all the elements Israelis feared – a call for a total withdrawal from all the occupied lands taken in 1967, statehood for the Palestinians and their right of return – and so harsh were Sadat's words thought to be by the Israelis, that while the President was still on the podium delivering his speech, Defence Minister Weizman passed a note to the Prime Minister, saying: 'We should be prepared for war.'

On 21 November, 43 hours after landing in Israel, Sadat departed for Cairo. His trip to Jerusalem was among the most dramatic events of modern history and a momentous event in Israel's history. For the first time in 30 years of bloody conflict and five all-out wars, the head of an Arab state, in fact the largest and strongest of all Arab states, stretched out his hand for peace and recognition. True, this visit was no more than a symbolic gesture but it, nevertheless, broke the psychological barrier and promised to be a catalyst for more substantial negotiations.

At Marakesh, Morocco, on 2 December 1977, Foreign Minister Dayan and Egypt's Deputy Prime Minister el-Tohami met again to see how their countries could build on Sadat's visit and proceed with the peace process. Reading from a handwritten document, el-Tohami emphasized that the forthcoming negotiations must deal not only with Egyptian–Israeli relations, but also with the Palestinian issue. Dayan, in turn, handed el-Tohami a handwritten piece of paper containing his 'idea' – rather than a 'proposal' – of how he believed Israel and Egypt should proceed and what, in general, were the compromises Israel was willing to make. It envisaged an Israeli withdrawal from the Sinai, but with the Jewish settlements and airfields remaining in Israel's hands; Sinai east of the Gidi and Mittla passes to be demilitarized and these areas to be patrolled by joint Israeli–Egyptian patrols until the year 2000; Sharm el-Sheikh, in control of the Straits of Tiran, the important lane for ships heading to and from Israel's port of Eilat, to remain under UN supervision. While the word 'autonomy' for the Palestinians was never mentioned in Dayan's unofficial paper, the notion of 'self-rule' for the Palestinians was mentioned. There was also a reference to the Golan Heights, seized by Israel from Syria in 1967, but el-Tohami simply tore out the bit of the paper where the Golan Heights was mentioned and handed it back to Dayan – a clear indication that Egypt did not intend to deal with the Syrian issue.

On 25 December 1977, a summit meeting took place in Ismailia between Prime Minister Begin and President Sadat. The going was tough. The decisive stumbling block was Sadat's insistence on the establishment of a Palestinian state in the occupied lands of the West Bank and the Gaza Strip, an idea which was rejected out of hand by Begin. Indeed, the joint statement summarizing the unsuccessful summit and read by the host Sadat clearly demonstrated the gulf between the parties on this issue. It went: 'The delegations ... discussed the Palestinian problem. The view of Egypt is that in the West Bank and Gaza there should be established a Palestinian state. The Israeli view is that the Arab Palestinians living in Judaea, Samaria and the Gaza Strip should enjoy self government.'[8] Perhaps the single success of the Ismailia summit was the setting up of two working committees; one political, to be led by the foreign ministers of Egypt and Israel, and a military committee, to be led by the defence ministers of the two countries. This arrangement ensured that, in spite of the crisis caused by the disagreement on the Palestinian issue, contacts between Israel and Egypt would continue. For Prime Minister Begin it also solved the headache of having to deal with Defence Minister Weizman and Foreign Minister Dayan who, although related to each other, were in outright competition and each complained that Begin favoured the other.

On 16 January 1978, the first meeting of the political committee was held in the Hilton Hotel in Jerusalem and proved to be yet another setback on the road to peace between Israel and Egypt. The delegates failed to agree even on the agenda for talks and the situation turned into a crisis when, in the official banquet that evening, Prime Minister Begin turned to the Egyptian Foreign Minister and, in what was seen as a condescending manner, said, 'The Foreign Minister of Egypt was still very young when the Holocaust was inflicted on the Jews by the Nazis.' Then raising his voice Begin concluded his speech by saying, '*No*. I declare in my loudest voice. *No* to withdrawal to the 1967 lines, *no* to self determination for the terrorists.' These harsh words went down very badly, offending Foreign Minister Kamel and, even more so, President Sadat who subsequently summoned his delegation back home.

Deadlock, which in the winter of 1977–78 was the main feature of Israeli–Egyptian relations, was exacerbated by what seemed in Egypt, the Arab world and Washington, as Israel's provocative policy of settlement in the disputed land. For the Begin government was determined to turn the West Bank into a settled land so as to pre-empt any future attempt to return it to Arabs' hands, and it also built settlements in the Sinai in order to use these later as a trade-off for air bases which Israel insisted on keeping. Upon learning that the Sinai Committee, a small Cabinet group led by Foreign Minister Dayan and Agriculture Minister Sharon, approved a plan to establish settlements in the Sinai and that it was channelling substantial funds for this project, President Sadat exploded with rage. Yet, it was not only Sadat who was upset by the government's hardline approach, but also segments of the Israeli population who were so elated by Sadat's historic visit but so disappointed with the lack of subsequent progress in the peace process that they were determined to pressurize the government and spur it to pursue the road for peace. Thus came into being the Peace Now movement.

THE HOME FRONT

The Peace Now movement

The movement was sparked by a well-publicized letter which was signed by 350 reserve officers and sent to Prime Minister Begin. The so-called 'officers' letter' stated that: 'A government that prefers the establishment of the State of Israel in the borders of a Greater Israel (namely, including the occupied territories of the West Bank and the Gaza Strip) above the establishment of peace through good neighbourly relations, instills in us many doubts . . .' and it went on to say, 'A government that prefers the establishment of settlements . . . to the elimination of the historical quarrel [with the Arabs] and the establishment of normal relations . . . awaken in us doubts about the justice of our cause . . .' and then 'A government policy that will encourage the continuation of control over . . . one million Arabs may damage the democratic, Jewish character of the state and make it difficult for us to identify with the state of Israel.' While the Prime Minister himself was less than impressed with the letter – though he did later meet with representatives of those who wrote it – it did strike a chord among many Israelis, mainly of the left, and it led to the birth of Shalom Achshav – Peace Now, an extra-parliamentary movement guided by three main principles. Firstly, an opposition to any policy involving perpetuating Israeli rule over the Arab inhabitants living on the occupied West Bank and the Gaza Strip. Secondly, Israel's future borders should be based on security considerations rather than on the location of Jewish settlements. Thirdly, Israel should be ready to make territorial concessions for the sake of peace.

With growing numbers of Israelis joining the movement, Peace Now opened branches throughout Israel, organized big demonstrations to persuade the government to make concessions – mainly territorial – for the sake of peace and its representatives also met Palestinian and Arab leaders. Although Peace Now became an influential force of moderation in Israel in the late 1970s, particularly in the period after Sadat's visit to Jerusalem and before the signing of peace treaty with Egypt, its success in mobilizing the Israelis would reach a peak later in the early 1980s.

A Sephardi *President*

In April 1978, on the initiative of Prime Minister Begin, and for the first time in Israel's history, a President of *Sephardi* origin was elected. For 30 years this post had been held by people of *Ashkenazi* origins: Chaim Weizmann from 1948 to 1952; Yitzhak Ben-Zvi from 1952 to 1963; Zalman Shazar from 1963 to 1973 and Ephraim Katzir from 1973 to 1978. While the job of President in Israel was never an influential one – Chaim Weizmann is remembered as saying that the most he was allowed to do as the President of Israel was 'to poke my nose in my handkerchief' – symbolically it was nevertheless a most important job. And Begin believed that by bringing to the Knesset a candidate of *Sephardi* origin and gaining the necessary support for him to be elected he could boost the status of the *Sephardim* in Israel and repay them for helping to elevate him from an opposition leader to Prime Minister.

To be sure, the idea of appointing a candidate of *Sephardi* origin to the post of President in Israel was already raised in 1973 when following the death of President Zalman Shazar Yitzhak Navon was made a candidate. Navon came from a respected *Sephardic* family of Jerusalem where he grew up and was educated. He later studied Arabic and Hebrew literature, Islamic culture and pedagogy and he was a teacher. During Israel's War of Independence he served in the Haganah and in the 1950s he worked with both David Ben-Gurion and Moshe Sharett. In 1965, he joined Ben-Gurion and others – Shimon Peres, Moshe Dayan, Teddy Kollek, among others – who broke away from Mapai and helped establish Rafi and he later was elected to the Knesset and served as a minister in Israel's governments.

But when the candidacy of Navon was put forward in 1973, then Prime Minister Golda Meir objected – for political rather than ethnic reasons. By nature Meir could never forget or forgive, and she was adamant that Navon should be punished for his sin of being disloyal to Mapai and joining Ben-Gurion in establishing the breakaway Rafi. Eventually Navon's candidacy was dropped and instead Ephraim Katzir, a renowned scientist – of *Ashkenazi* origin – was chosen to the post. At that time many in Israel, particularly the *Sephardim*, felt that Meir's opposition to Navon's candidacy was an act of anti-*Sephardi* discrimination, and this not only did little to improve relations between *Sephardim* and *Ashkenazim* in Israel but it also reinforced the view that Labour was anti-*Sephardi* and arrogant, which in turn encouraged many *Sephardim* to vote for the Likud in the 1977 election. Now, some five years later, Prime Minister Begin proposed that Navon – although politically closer to Labour than to Likud – should be the candidate for the Presidentship. But Begin encountered strong opposition from the Liberals, a faction of Likud, for they insisted that one of them – Elimelech Rimlat – should be appointed to the post. Adamant, however, about the importance of electing a *Sephardi* as President, Begin pressed ahead and eventually, after much political manoeuvring,

Navon, supported by 86 votes in the Knesset, was elected and as Israel's fifth President he became the first President of *Sephardi* origin to hold this post.

The economy

We should recall that in the election campaign Begin pledged to give priority to the economy – to fight inflation, root out corruption, reduce the tax burden and the cost of living and raise Israel's GNP. Since Begin made Simcha Ehrlich of the Liberals – representing free enterprise – his Finance Minister, many expected changes that would affect the sectoral balance and introduce market forces and deregulation. Indeed, as early as October 1977, Ehrlich came up with a 'New Economic Policy' which seemed to indicate new direction in Israel's economy. One of the pillars of this new economic programme was the selling of state-owned enterprises. While controlling these companies – prominent in energy production, banking, mineral extraction, water development, among others – enabled the government to make quick profits by trading in their shares, these enterprises lacked efficient workforces and bureaucracy was rife. But then while many in Israel praised Ehrlich's attempt to dispose of these inefficient state-owned companies, in reality very little was sold, for the problems which led the government to try and sell these companies in the first place were the same that deterred potential buyers from purchasing them.

Another component of Finance Minister Ehrlich's 'New Economic Policy' was the liberalization of the foreign exchange, and what he attempted was to liquidate the nation's currency speculation by allowing supply and demand to play freely in the market. But while by doing so the government, which approved the plan, was able to pull the rug from under the thriving black market in dollars, this new policy of liberalization of foreign exchange also led to growing windfall profits to Israelis who had foreign exchange, mainly people who were the recipients of restitution payments from Germany. The implications of this were mainly social for it did much to widen the gap between the rich – mainly *Ashkenazim* – and the poor, mainly of *Sephardic* origins living in slums or in developed towns in the Negev. Worse still, by allowing free convertibility, Finance Minister Ehrlich unwittingly encouraged excessive exchange of American dollar loans into shekels which, in turn, fuelled inflation which the government was keen to lower. Efforts to nationalize health care so as to remove Israel's single largest medical programme from the Histadrut and attempts by the government to cut taxes failed as well; in fact, taxes remained as high under Likud as under Labour.

Why did the government's 'New Economic Policy' fail to materialize? Perhaps because Prime Minister Begin was impatient with economic and other domestic matters and was too preoccupied with foreign affairs. Also, the entrenched bureaucracy supported the old ways and there were strong interest groups, notably the Histadrut, the trade union representing workers and an important employer and controlled by Labour, which opposed any changes that could potentially have a negative effect on the workers. Another explanation for the failure to introduce changes in Israel's economy was that Likud itself believed in the social tenets promulgated by Labour, and as it came to power mainly to represent the low-income strata it felt that it could not, for example, cut subsidies and take other measures which would undermine the support of those who brought it to power in the first place. The Liberals who held the Finance Ministry and who were keen to transform and liberalize the economy and cut the budget did not have enough power within the Likud to introduce major changes. Soaring oil prices, growing defence expenditures, government initiatives such as the extension of free tuition to all four years of high school and Project Renewal, a major effort to eradicate slums, also had their negative effect on the budget, as did the building of new settlements in the occupied territories which swallowed huge amounts of money every year.

Gush Emunim and the building of settlements

Indeed, neither growing pressures on the budget, nor strong opposition in Israel by Peace Now and from abroad would deter the government from proceeding with its programme of settlement building in the occupied territories. For settling these lands and turning it into an integral part of Israel itself was one of the most important *raisons d'être* of the Likud government.

To be sure, settlements have been established in the Sinai and on the occupied West Bank land also under Labour governments. But Labour, with its secular outlook, adopted a pragmatic approach and its chief consideration of how many and where to build new settlements has always been – security. Thus, new towns were often built along the Jordan river – seen as a strategic asset never to be returned to Arab hands – and far from densely populated Arab areas. With Likud, however, things were much different and the main consideration regarding the number and the location of new settlements was ideology rather than pragmatism. The Prime Minister himself was a great believer in the right of Jews to settle in all parts of biblical Eretz Yisrael and it was notable that on the very day he was charged by the President with forming a new government, he paid a visit to Rabbi Zvi Kook, the spiritual leader of the Gush Emunim movement, which was the main source of settlers.

Gush Emunim (meaning the Bloc of the Faithful) was born in 1974 and since then came to represent the new Israeli settler. Convinced that the Jewish people had historic rights over Judaea and Samaria – the West Bank – and that by settling this historic homeland the Jews would come nearer salvation, this movement was determined to accelerate the pace of settling these lands. By 1977, Gush Emunim had already established 12 settlements on the occupied land and now, with Likud in power, the movement was given a tremendous boost. Indeed, the new Prime Minister did not even try to hide his sympathy for Gush Emunim and he let them understand that he was fully behind them. We should recall the incident under the Rabin Labour government where an illegal settlement – Eilon Moreh – was established near the ancient city of Sebastia by Jewish settlers who were later removed by the government into a military camp at Kaddum. Now, Begin paid a visit to Kaddum, promising its settlers that 'there will be many more Eilon Morehs'. His government then accorded full legal status to Kaddum and to Ofra, another settlement in Samaria, and to Ma'aleh Adumin on the Jerusalem–Jericho road and then moved on to approve the Gush Emunim's plan to establish 60 new settlements on the West Bank. From troublemakers under Labour the settlers of Gush Emunim were transformed under Likud into a mainstream movement.

In settling the occupied lands the Likud government was aiming at weakening Arab hold on this land and tilt the demographic balance in favour of Israel. Thus, rather than establish settlements away from Arab towns and villages, as did Labour, the Likud encouraged the building of new villages close to areas of extensive Arab habitation and then went on to impose a string of restrictions on the Arabs to prevent them from developing agriculture and industry. Hence, Arab land was confiscated, ostensibly for security purposes, and severe restrictions were imposed on the use of water by Arabs. Backed by the government, Gush Emunim set up its settlements each comprising a few dozen families and based on private initiative and partial cooperation. Residents who did not wish to work in agriculture were allowed to travel to Israel proper to seek jobs. So aggressive was Likud's settling programme and so keen was Gush Emunim on carrying out this policy that in 1977–78 alone, 24 new settlements were established; by 1993, there will be some 136 settlements in the occupied territories with 116,000 settlers.

Terrorism and Operation Litani

Terrorism hit Israel hard during this period. Most notable was the attack, on 11 March 1978, by nine Palestinians on two buses just north of Tel Aviv in the course of which 28 Israeli passengers perished, 78 were wounded and the 9 hijackers were all killed by Israeli security forces. Israel's reaction to terrorism has traditionally been harsh, but this time it was harsher than ever. Four days after the terrorist attack, on 14 March, the government dispatched Israeli forces into Lebanon to carry out Operation Litani. Directed against the PLO and its infrastructure in southern Lebanon – after the PLO was driven out of Jordan in September 1970 (Black September) the confrontation between Israel and the PLO shifted to Lebanon – it was the biggest military operation the IDF had undertaken since the 1973 Yom Kippur War. The Israelis hit hard at the PLO, which it held responsible for the terrorist attack on the Israeli buses and which it wanted to deter from carrying out more such attacks, destroyed much of its infrastructure and captured arms and documents.

The international community regarded the Israeli military operation as excessive, which in a way it was, and on 19 March 1978 the UN Security Council adopted Resolution 425 by a vote of 12 to 0, calling on Israel to withdraw from Lebanon. On 20 March the Council adopted Resolution 426 entrusting a UN force, UNIFIL, to deploy in southern Lebanon and monitor the activities of the Palestinian guerrillas. On 30 June, in the face of growing international criticism, Israel agreed to pull her forces out of Lebanon except for a 'security zone'. But neither Operation Litani, nor even the presence of UNIFIL, prevented the PLO from re-establishing itself in southern Lebanon, and often there were incidents in which the PLO and the Israelis exchanged fire. Lebanon would continue to be a sore problem for Israel.

CAMP DAVID AND AFTER

The absence of meaningful contacts between Israel and Egypt, particularly after the dramatic visit of President Sadat to Jerusalem, continued to cause concern to President Carter who, in the summer of 1978, gave his Secretary of State Vance the mission of bringing together the foreign ministers of Israel and Egypt, on neutral ground, to see if enough desire for peace remained on which to build. This led, in July, to a summit meeting between Dayan and Egypt's Foreign Minister Muhammad Ibrahim Kamel in the presence of Vance in Leeds Castle in England. The summit, however, proved to be yet another failure. As before, the decisive stumbling block was Egypt's demand for a tighter linkage between an Israeli–Egyptian settlement and a solution to the Palestinian problem, as well as Egypt's insistence that all Jewish settlements and airfields in the Sinai should be evacuated. With the failure of the Leeds summit, President Sadat became even more frustrated and, on 27 July, he instructed the Israeli members of the military committee, which had been set up at the Ismailia summit and was meeting in Egypt, to leave Cairo and return to Israel. And by now, with the momentum of Sadat's dramatic visit to Jerusalem all but gone and attempts to revive talks having all but failed, and fearing that Sadat, as he had several times hinted, might precipitate a conflict, President Carter decided to take a bold step and bring Begin and Sadat to a marathon summit meeting, assuming that once the two leaders came together neither would be able to walk out without losing political face. The formal invitations for this summit which was to take place at Camp David, the presidential retreat in Maryland, and to open on 5 September 1978 were delivered personally to Premier Begin and President Sadat by Secretary of State Vance. They both accepted.

Begin, at the head of a small delegation which included, among others, Foreign Minister Dayan and Defence Minister Weizman, arrived at Camp David determined to push for an agreement with Egypt on general principles (DOP), which might serve as a basis for future meetings, where the specifics and remaining differences could be sorted out by the ministers of foreign affairs and defence. What Begin wished was to deal with the Sinai, keep the West Bank and, as far as possible, steer clear of the Palestinian issue. Unlike Begin, President Sadat came to Camp David determined to produce a firm framework for a permanent peace and to tackle *all* specific issues while still at Camp David. He wanted the Sinai back with unequivocal sovereignty over all of it and a solution to the Palestinian problem.

On 6 September, the day after the arrival of the delegations at Camp David, President Carter brought Sadat and Begin together for a first face-to-face meeting, with no aides present, to explore their differences. It did not pay off. Sadat, who opened, presented a very aggressive and ridiculously harsh proposal which incorporated all the time-worn Arab demands and charges against Israel. Reading from a 12-page document, he listed Egypt's demands among which were full Israeli withdrawal from the Sinai, removal of Jewish settlements from the Sinai, withdrawal from airfields, withdrawal from East Jerusalem, right of return to Palestinian refugees to what used to be Palestine, or alternatively compensation to them and a demand that Israel pay reparations for the use of the occupied lands.

In a follow-up meeting on the next day (third day of the summit, 7 September), Begin responded to Sadat's proposal by rejecting it out of hand. 'This smacks of a victorious state dictating peace to the defeated', Begin said to Sadat, and added 'this document is not a proper basis for negotiations'. Tempers ran high. 'Premier Begin', Sadat shouted, 'Security [to Israel] – yes. Land – no!' President Carter later wrote in his diary: 'I thought Sadat would explode.'[9] Following this unsuccessful meeting Carter concluded that Begin and Sadat could not interact constructively on a personal level and from then on he tried, as much as he could, to keep the two apart.

But it was more than a lack of chemistry between Sadat and Begin, for the hurdles which blocked talks before, mainly the fate of Jewish settlements and airfields in the Sinai desert and the Palestinian problem, continued to haunt the parties even in Camp David. On 10 September, which was day six of the summit, and following repeated failures by Israelis and Egyptians to bridge their differences, President Carter and his team submitted their own draft for peace and repeatedly amended it in the following days as talks proceeded. But crises continued to bog down the summit. Friday, 15 September was a particularly dramatic day when it seemed as if the summit would have to adjourn without an agreement being reached. What precipitated this crisis was an unsuccessful face-to-face meeting between Dayan and Sadat in which the Israeli Foreign Minister made it clear to Sadat that Israel would not abandon her settlements in the Sinai. This statement upset Sadat so much that he decided to leave Camp David and return to Egypt. Unaware of this crisis, Secretary of State Vance had gone to discuss a matter with Sadat only to find the President packing his bags. Vance rushed back to Carter looking ashen and shaken and as Carter later recalled: 'His face was white, and he announced, "Sadat is leaving. He and his aides are already packed. He asked me to order him a helicopter!"'[10] Intervening in the crisis, President Carter persuaded Sadat to stay and went on to warn Prime Minister Begin that should the Israeli leader not demonstrate more flexibility and if no agreement were reached by the next day then Carter would adjourn the summit and put the onus for its collapse on Israel.

Gradually, Sadat and Begin moved closer and narrowed the gulf between their demands. Sadat agreed to a weaker linkage between an agreement with Israel regarding the Sinai and a deal on the West Bank and Gaza. Begin, after Carter took it upon Washington to finance the building of two new airfields for Israel in the Negev, softened his position by agreeing to give up the airfields in the Sinai. A momentous breakthrough came when Begin softened his position on the issue of Israeli settlements in the Sinai. As National Adviser Brezezinski later recalled: 'After a protracted and heated argument, in which Begin shouted "ultimatum", "excessive demands", and "political suicide", Begin finally agreed to leave it to the Knesset to decide on the fate of Jewish settlements and he also agreed to remove the requirements of party loyalty and let each member of the Knesset vote as an individual on this issue.'[11] Leaving the Knesset to decide on the issue was, from Begin's point of view, a clever way to sidestep the problem and not go down in history as the first Prime Minister to agree to the evacuation of Jewish settlements. Begin's dramatic climbdown followed a critical intervention by the hawkish Minister of Agriculture, Ariel Sharon, who talked with Begin over the phone and assured the Prime Minister that abandoning Jewish settlements would not jeopardize Israel's security. This intervention is often regarded as support from Sharon to Begin at a critical moment but, as it later emerged, this was not the way Begin saw it and, in fact, he was furious with Sharon's intervention. As Begin put it: 'He (Sharon) phoned me and said it was possible to agree on the settlement issue. It was an open line, and clearly everything said in the conversation was recorded. It wasn't good that he telephoned on an open line.' And elsewhere: 'Whatever was said in the conversation was written down. No doubt that the Americans heard what he said in the open line.'[12] Begin, in other words, felt that by calling him on an open line Sharon, in fact, had twisted his arm and weakened his argument that the settlements were needed for Israel's security.

But when it came to the issue of Jerusalem, another stumbling block on which the parties failed to agree, Begin refused to budge. This hurdle was eventually overcome by covering the issue in separate letters from Sadat and Begin to Carter in which each leader expressed his view with regard to Jerusalem. In his letter, Begin referred to a law passed by the Knesset on 28 June 1967 giving the government power to apply Israeli law, jurisdiction and administration to any part of Eretz Yisrael. 'On the basis of this law', Begin's letter went, 'the government of Israel decreed in July 1967 that Jerusalem is one city indivisible, the capital of the state of Israel.' Sadat, in his letter to President Carter, said that Arab Jerusalem is an integral part of the West Bank. Resorting to the exchange of letters meant that the parties agreed not to agree and the status quo on Jerusalem remained unchanged.

With all matters sorted out, Sadat and Begin signed the Camp David Accords in Washington, on Sunday, 17 September 1978. In fact, two separate documents were signed. One, entitled 'A Framework for Peace in the Middle East', and a second 'A Framework for the Conclusion of a Peace Treaty between Israel and Egypt'. The first foresaw peace between Israel and all Arab states but focused on the West Bank and Gaza. It envisaged three stages of negotiations: in the first, Egypt, Israel and Jordan would lay the ground rules for electing a self-governing authority in the occupied territories and define the authority's roles. In the second stage, after the self-governing authority was established and functioning, a transitional five-year period would begin and Israel would dismantle her military government in the territories and withdraw her troops to specific security locations. In the third stage and not later than a year after the onset of the transitional period, discussions would be launched between Israel, Egypt, Jordan and elected representatives of Palestinians living in the West Bank and Gaza to determine the final status of the territories. Thereafter, a separate committee of Israelis, Jordanians and elected West Bank and Gaza Palestinians, would negotiate a formal peace treaty between Israel and Jordan.

The second document signed at Camp David was much more specific and, for both Israelis and Egyptians, more important. 'A Framework for the Conclusion of a Peace Treaty between Israel and Egypt' dealt with the future of the Sinai and arrangements for concluding peace between Israel and Egypt within three months. It defined all aspects of withdrawal from the Sinai, military arrangements in the peninsula, freedom of navigation in the Gulf of Suez and the Suez Canal and normalization of relations between Israel and Egypt.

The Camp David summit lasted 13 days and proved to be the most difficult and least pleasant stage in the Egypt–Israel peace negotiations. The agreements reached at this summit were a remarkable success for two bold leaders, Begin and Sadat, but also for President Carter whose determination, mastery of enormous detail, effective mediation skills and perseverance, in sometimes angry and always complex negotiations, were superb.

One aspect, almost totally ignored in the vast literature on the Camp David talks, is the attempts to bring in other Arab states so that the summit would result in more than a separate deal between Egypt and Israel. These attempts – all of which failed – were carried out mainly by the Americans but also by the man we have already mentioned in previous chapters and whom we dubbed the Son-in-Law.

The Son-in-Law, we should recall, was a relative of President Nasser and Sadat's right-hand man and also an agent of the Mossad – in fact, a double agent who worked for both Egypt and Israel. Now, when the meeting at Camp David was under way, he was working hard to bring together President Sadat and King Hussein so that the King would join the peace process. While it is clear that it was in the interests of both Israel and Egypt for other Arab states to join the process, it is far from clear who, in fact, asked the Son-in-Law to assist in bringing in other Arab governments. Though he had been Sadat's right-hand man and a senior minister in Egypt's governments, by now his relations with Sadat were at a low ebb and, in fact, it was around the time of the summit at Camp David that he was stripped by Sadat of his diplomatic passport. This brings us to the other possibility which is that it was, in fact, Israel which used the services of the Son-in-Law and his good contacts with Arab leaders to enlarge the number of Arab states joining the peace accords. In any case, he failed in his mission and the treaty remained one between Israel and Egypt.

On 25 September 1978, Prime Minister Begin brought the Camp David Accords before the Knesset which was called from recess, and when the vote was taken, after 17 hours of debate, 84 members gave their approval, 19 including the Speaker of the Knesset and a future Prime Minister Yitzhak Shamir objected and 17 abstained. With this ratification by the Knesset, Israelis, Egyptians and Americans gathered in Washington's Blair House, on 12 October 1978, to work out the

details of the peace treaty – the exact language outlining the new relationship between Israel and Egypt and the schedule for Israel's withdrawal from the Sinai. Early optimism that this meeting would soon be
completed were dashed when the negotiators ran into trouble. There
was an argument about how to make it clear that the old
Egyptian–Arab mutual defence agreements did not take precedence
over the new treaty with Israel, and some controversy about how soon
Israel should make her first withdrawal and whether Sadat would then
be willing to exchange ambassadors. There was also a disagreement on
the issue of Israel's insistence on her right to continue building Jewish
settlements in the West Bank and Gaza and the linkage between an
Egypt–Israel settlement and the West Bank/Gaza negotiations. For
although at Camp David Sadat acquiesced to Begin's vaguer formulas
with regard to the linkage between the two issues, the Egyptians now
insisted on a tighter link and while talks were still under way, Egypt's
Acting Foreign Minister Boutros-Boutros Ghali, on 3 November,
declared that Egypt would insist on a definite timetable for Palestinian
autonomy before committing herself to a formal peace treaty with
Israel. In the middle of November 1978 the Blair House talks reached
a standstill and then completely broke down. By December, there was
a total stalemate with the three-month deadline for completion of the
treaty fast approaching. With American intervention the only way out
of the deadlock, Secretary of State Vance embarked, on 11 December,
on a frenetic week commuting between Jerusalem and Cairo. It was to
no avail – the stalemate continued and when Vance returned to
Washington 'his mood was one of disappointment and bitterness at
Begin's tactics'.[13]

On 1 March 1979, President Carter received Begin in Washington
and in four days of talks was able to extract from the Prime Minister
approval for several new proposals. With this small triumph, Carter
embarked on five days of shuttle diplomacy between Jerusalem and
Cairo and succeeded, on 13 March, in finding formulas which satisfied
both Begin and Sadat and enabled the parties to put the finishing
touches to the agreement. Begin then put it before the Knesset. The
debate lasted 27 hours and when a vote was taken on the final agreement, 95 members raised their hands to approve, 18 voted against, 2
abstained and 3 declared that they were not participating in the vote.

On 26 March 1979, Israelis and Egyptians gathered in Washington
for the official signing of the peace treaty, but even now the parties,
particularly the Israelis, continued to haggle. Prime Minister Begin, in

a rather unusual move, requested a private meeting with the President to which the President's National Security Adviser was also invited. According to Brezezinski:

> Begin told the President that he had a personal request to make, namely that Carter, as a gesture of friendship for Mrs. Begin, forgive Israel the outstanding debt on the massive $3 billion aid that the United States was extending to Israel. Begin repeated the phrase 'as a gesture for Mrs. Begin' several times. Carter, who on financial matters was a bit of a miser, looked at first quite stunned, and then, turning to me, he burst out laughing.

With these and other last-minute hurdles out of the way, the signing ceremony, attended by 1400 guests, took place on the north lawn of the White House where, witnessed by President Carter, Begin and Sadat signed their historic peace treaty and shook hands. On the night of the signing in Washington there was a big party. National Security Adviser Zbigniew Brezezinski later wrote:

> In a huge tent in the garden of the White House we celebrated the peace treaty. It was a remarkable evening. Not only was there joy, but a sense of real reconciliation. I sat at the table with the Weizmans and the [Muhammad] Alis and Kissinger. Weizman had his son with him. Badly wounded during one of the conflicts with the Egyptians, to some extent he has been permanently scarred. Yet he was there, partaking of this event, mixing with Sadat's children. Weizman was especially moved when he told me that Sadat had embraced his son, and I could sense that the parents were deeply touched when their son and Sadat's son shook hands and embraced.[14]

Withdrawals and resignations

Israel started immediate preparations to return land to Egypt but this led to growing desperation among those on Israel's right who opposed the return of occupied land, and in October 1979, right-wing elements joined forces and formed themselves into a separate party, Tehiyah (Revival), whose principal platform was the abrogation of the Camp David Accords and the peace treaty. Also, and for quite different reasons, Foreign Minister Dayan, on 23 October 1979 – by then ill with cancer – resigned in protest against what he regarded as the Prime Minister's attempts to drag his feet and sabotage efforts to conclude arrangements to allow the Palestinians the autonomy agreed at Camp David. Dayan had good reasons to believe that the Prime Minister was putting the autonomy question on the back-burner, for the person Begin put in charge of these sensitive talks, Interior Minister Yosef Burg, was, to put it mildly, less than enthusiastic to come to any agreement which would result in Israel giving up lands which he, as a religious man, believed to be biblical Eretz Yisrael. Also, the government continued to confiscate Arab lands for 'security reasons' and then proceeded to build new settlements on these lands which was regarded by Dayan as nothing but an attempt to make the autonomy talks fail.

Although showing little enthusiasm to honour his promises with regard to the West Bank and Gaza, Begin was determined to keep his word and the letter of Israel's agreements with Egypt regarding the Sinai. Thus, on 15 November 1979, the monastery of Saint Catherine was returned to Egypt and on 25 November Israel withdrew her forces from the oilfields in Alma.

In the mean time, the settler movement, sensing that there was a government in Jerusalem which was sympathetic to its cause, did not hesitate to exploit the situation. At the end of 1979, a group of settlers, led by Rabbi Moshe Levinger, slipped into the Hadassa clinic, one of the centres of Jewish life in Hebron before the Arab riots of 1929, and refused to move from there. The government not only let them stay but granted them legal status and protection; the next year saw the largest increase in settlements in the occupied lands for 30 years with 38 new settlements set up.

On 26 May 1980, Defence Minister Ezer Weizman followed in the steps of Dayan and resigned from the government. The official reason was disagreements with the Prime Minister over cuts to the defence budget, but in reality, it was rather, as with Dayan's decision to resign from the government, Weizman's disillusionment over what he regarded as Begin's deliberate foot-dragging over implementation of Palestinian autonomy agreed at Camp David and the increase in funds allocated for Jewish settlements in the occupied territories. Weizman hoped that the Deputy Prime Minister and leader of Dash would resign as well, which would bring down the government, but this did not happen. Weizman's resignation was significant because coming on top of the departure of Moshe Dayan, his departure meant that the government became much more radical, right-wing and aggressive than

before. Foreign affairs were now left in the hands of Dayan's successor the hawkish Shamir who had opposed the Camp David Accords
and voted against them in the Knesset, and defence matters were
looked after by Begin himself – he still objected to have Ariel Sharon
as his Defence Minister – with the aggressive, hawkish no-nonsense
Chief of Staff Rafael Eitan, as his chief adviser on military affairs.

On 30 July 1980, Begin moved to consolidate Israel's control over
Jerusalem by securing the passage through the Knesset of a Basic Law
of Jerusalem. Throughout the years, it should be mentioned, Israeli
leaders had declared Jerusalem to be the eternal capital of Israel, but
they stopped short of enshrining this position in law. Begin, however,
being a legalist by nature, wished to formalize Israel's control over
Jerusalem and insisted that her position vis-à-vis Jerusalem should be
enshrined in a law. Passed by the Knesset, the 'Law of Jerusalem' laid
down that Jerusalem would never be divided, that it would be the seat
of all the national institutions, some of which still remained in Tel
Aviv, that access to the holy places should be guaranteed to members
of all religions, and that the city should take priority in the national
development budget.

'TAMUZ 1'

Nineteen eighty-one saw a steep escalation in tension between Israel
and Iraq over Baghdad's attempts to develop nuclear capability.

As early as 1976 Iraq had signed an agreement with France for a
research reactor with an output of 40 MW which was known in France
as Osiraq and in Iraq as 'Tamuz 1'. Israeli experts predicted that Iraq
would be capable of detonating an initial 'nuclear device' within nine
years and soon afterwards of producing bombs deliverable by aircraft
or ground-to-ground missiles. In the summer of 1978, Prime Minister
Begin discussed the matter with his ministers some of whom, notably
Minister of Agriculture Ariel Sharon, proposed to regard the development or attainment of nuclear weapons by Arab states, in this case Iraq,
as a *casus belli* and to take measures, including military ones, to
prevent them from achieving a nuclear capability. The idea of using
military force against the Iraqi reactor was rejected at that time and,
instead, Begin gave instructions that an attempt be made to find a
diplomatic solution to the problem by exerting pressure, particularly
on France, which provided Iraq with her nuclear reactor and was

Baghdad's main supplier of enriched uranium, the essential material for the development of nuclear capability. Subsequently, Foreign Minister Shamir raised the issue with French chargé d'affaires, Jean-Pierre Chauvet, and demanded that under no circumstances should military-grade fuels be placed at Iraq's disposal. Chauvet, attempting to reassure Shamir, insisted that it would be sheer madness for Saddam Hussein, President of Iraq, to drop an atomic bomb on Israel because by doing so he would also harm thousands of Arabs. This reassurance failed, however, to satisfy Israel which decided that, parallel to diplomatic pressures, other steps should also be taken to stop, or at least delay, the development of nuclear capability by Iraq.

In April 1979, saboteurs – according to some reports Israeli agents – broke into a warehouse near Toulon in France and blew up the casings for Iraq's first scheduled Osiraq reactor, components that had been scheduled for shipping within the week. This action, however, only delayed this supply to Iraq and new casings were delivered in the autumn of that year. Then, in June 1979, the first instalment of enriched uranium reached Iraq and the estimates in Israel were that after three more shipments, Iraq would be able to irradiate enough fuel from her Osiraq reactor to produce weapon-grade plutonium. A year later, in June 1980, Professor Yahia el-Meshed, the physicist who directed Iraq's nuclear research programme, was murdered in his hotel room in Paris – according to some reports – by Israeli agents. A glimmer of hope that the Iraqis would stop operating their nuclear reactor came during the Iraq–Iran War when Iran struck at the Iraqi reactor; but the damage was minimal and the operation of the reactor was soon resumed.

With the international community failing to stop Iraq, Begin summoned, on 14 October 1980, a group of ministers to discuss the growing danger to Israel and what measures Israel should take to stop Iraq from developing the bomb. But there was considerable difference of opinion among the ministers, and it was decided only that the final decision on whether military action should be taken would have to be made by the whole government. About two weeks later, on 28 October, Begin summoned the government to a secret meeting to discuss the matter and this is how he summarized the discussion:

A big clock is ticking over our heads. Somewhere on the banks of the Euphrates and Tigris people are sitting and planning to exterminate us, they prepare the weapons ... every passing day brings them closer to their goal. We have to ask ourselves, what is the implication of a state like Iraq producing nuclear weapons? The implication is that, the life of every man, woman and child in Israel is endangered. Within five years, maybe within only three, the Iraqis could possess two or three atomic bombs, each with the capability of the bomb dropped on Hiroshima. Saddam Hussein is a ruthless dictator . . . he would not hesitate to use weapons of mass-destruction against us . . . if Iraq held atomic weapons one of two things would happen, either we would have to surrender to their demands, or we would be in danger of annihilation . . . the only way to delay operation of the reactor is by a military raid.[15]

A vote was taken in which ten ministers supported Begin's proposal to bomb the Iraqi nuclear reactor against six ministers who still objected. A few months later, with reports of continuing work on the Iraqi reactor and since Begin understood that once the reactor became operational an attack on it could not take place because this might disseminate a lethal radioactive cloud over Baghdad, 10 May 1981 was set as the date for an air strike on the reactor. But at the last moment, with Israeli pilots were sitting in their cockpits ready to take off, Begin called off the operation. The reason for this was a 'personal and highly confidential' handwritten letter he had received from the leader of the opposition in which Peres urged Begin not to bomb the Iraqi reactor. 'Israel', so Peres warned Begin, 'would be like a thorn in the wilderness [if she struck at Iraq]. I add my voice to those who advise you not to act.' Did Peres want the operation called off because he felt that a successful raid would boost Begin's prestige and help him win the general election which was imminent? We shall probably never know the answer to this question. At any rate, whether it was because Begin wished to rethink, or simply felt that this leak – Peres was not supposed to know about the operation – might endanger the pilots, he decided to postpone the attack. But not for long.

On Sunday, 7 June 1981, at 4.00 p.m., eight Israeli F-16s and a smaller escorting umbrella of fighter planes were dispatched to destroy Iraq's nuclear reactor. Taking off from the Etzion air base in the Negev, the planes had extra fuel tanks and special bomb racks that carried two 2000-pound MK-84 iron bombs. Flying in a tightly bunched formation to project the radar signature of a large commercial aircraft, and with the setting sun behind them, the Israelis flew east across the Gulf of Aqaba and along the northern width of Saudi Arabia close to the border with Jordan, approaching Iraq at a low altitude to avoid detection. The first bombs, fired at the concrete and lead protective dome of the Iraqi reactor, were fitted with delayed action fuses to allow penetration into the dome before explosion. The next bombs struck only moments later and finding the holes in the dome destroyed the reactor inside. It was a remarkable military feat.

Opposition leader Peres was right about one thing: Israel was, indeed, for a time, isolated by the international community and condemned for her attack on Iraq. American President Ronald Reagan first condoned, then criticized the attack both in official statements and in his support of a UN Security Council resolution of condemnation. A scheduled shipment of F-16 aircraft was postponed and Israel's violation of Saudi airspace strengthened Riyadh's appeal for effective radar protection, that is AWACS planes, from the United States. But with the benefit of hindsight, there can be little doubt that had it not been for Begin's decision to order the destruction of that installation, the Gulf War that broke out ten years later might well have had a far grimmer outcome than it did.

A SECOND LIKUD GOVERNMENT

While the successful air raid on the Iraqi nuclear reactor increased government prestige at a critical time just before the general election, it was mainly the government's economic strategy which seemed to promise a second term in office for Likud. Begin's Finance Minister, as of January 1981, Yoram Aridor, whose two prudent predecessors, Simcha Ehrlich and Yigal Horowitz, were forced to resign after failing to cope with Israel's ailing economy – inflation in 1979 went up to 116 per cent and in 1980 to 133 per cent – presided in the months just before the general election over a shameless squandering of the state's fiscal resources in order to bribe votes. He slashed taxes and import duties on a wide range of consumer goods, and simultaneously, pumped the nation's modest dollar and Common Market currency reserves into Israel's banking system, thereby artificially shoring up the value of the Israeli shekel. Ignoring warnings of economic suicide, Aridor presided over a period in which Israelis invaded the shops to purchase imported commercial items in what turned out to be an orgy of buying. Colour television sets – in February 1981 the public purchased 50,000 sets – cars, air conditioners; everything the public could desire was suddenly 30, even 40 per cent, cheaper than before.

The election campaign was fierce. Begin's Likud emphasized its success in foreign policies and promised to continue its economic policies and accelerate the building of settlements in the disputed occupied territories. Labour, led by Peres, called for a new direction in Israel's foreign policy and an effort to ease the international isolation brought about by such acts as the passing of the Jerusalem Law (1980) and the bombing of Iraq (1981). Above all Peres's Labour called for greater fiscal responsibility.

One casualty of the coming elections was the Democratic Movement for Change – Dash. Having joined Begin's coalition a few months after the establishment of the first Likud government, amid high expectations of being a catalyst for political change and also curbing settlements, it had been ignored by Begin and suffered internal divisions. One by one the Dash Cabinet ministers drifted away from their earlier idealism and, on 2 April 1981, the party voted to disband. Thus came to an end a brave political experiment, the creation of a third force of political moderation in Israel emphasizing domestic and social affairs.

Israelis went to the polls on 30 June 1981 and when the vote was cast the results were another success for Likud and a bitter disappointment for Labour. No longer facing the challenge of Dash, Labour won 47 seats, a gain of 15 – the exact number of seats won by Dash in 1977. Even after this impressive comeback it was, nevertheless, still behind Begin's Likud which won 48 seats, a gain of 3 on the previous election. The results of the 1981 election proved beyond any doubt that a new era in Israel's politics was well under way and that the previous 1977 election did not represent an aberration but rather the end of Labour dominance in Israel's politics. It also became clear that the right's political consolidation was rooted in ethnicity – of those 375,000 new Likud voters over 60 per cent came from Oriental communities.

Mafdal, the religious party, suffered a terrible blow in the election when the number of its seats was cut by 50 per cent to six seats – it lost voters to Likud, to the new Tehiyah Party which gained three seats in the Knesset and to the Movement for Tradition in Israel (Tami), which was led by a previous Mafdal minister, Aharon Abuhatzeira, and which gained three Knesset seats. Dayan's venture to establish a centrist Telem group achieved only his own election and the Independent Liberals failed to elect a single candidate.

As the leader of the largest party, Begin was invited by President Yitzhak Navon to form a new government and, as before, he had to conduct tough negotiations with the religious parties which continued to extract a high price for their joining the coalition. Among other things, Agudat Yisrael insisted that a new law should be passed through the Knesset – it happened soon after this election – to ensure that 'sociological considerations', for example economic hardship, could not be acceptable, as it was until now, for abortions performed in public hospitals.

Begin presented his government to the Knesset on 6 August 1981 where he gained the support of 61 against 58. It was quite a radical government in comparison to Begin's previous administration. Gone were moderates such as Dayan, Weizman and Yadin and very influential positions were given to hawkish characters such as Yitzhak Shamir and, crucially, to former General Ariel Sharon whom Begin made his Defence Minister. Begin appointed Sharon to this sensitive job in spite of fierce opposition by colleagues and friends, believing that Sharon was the right person to deal with the final return of land to Egypt, due to take place in 1982, and the removal of Jewish settlements from the Sinai. Sharon, after all, was the champion of the settlers and he could, so Begin believed, remove them without too much of a problem and public protest. In that Begin was proved to be right – for when the time came to return the remaining land of the Sinai to Egypt, Sharon sent in bulldozers to flatten the town of Yamit and he dispatched troops to evacuate the settlers who staged a last-minute stand against returning the land. It was, indeed, much to Sharon's credit that the return of the remaining parts of the Sinai to Egypt was completed successfully.

WAR IN LEBANON

Sharon was too ambitious to see his task as merely removing settlers from the Sinai and his thoughts and aspirations were elsewhere – in Lebanon. Since 24 July 1981 there had been a ceasefire between Israel and the PLO and it was holding relatively well. But this failed to satisfy Sharon who detected two principal problems in Lebanon which, as he saw it, could not be solved by the existence of a ceasefire. The first of these problems was the presence of the PLO in this country and its build-up of armed forces. Sharon believed that it was important to weaken the PLO in Lebanon, not only in order to reduce a growing military threat to Israel, but also because the weakening of Yasser Arafat in Lebanon, as Sharon and some others in Likud believed, would inevitably weaken the PLO in the West Bank and Gaza which, in turn, would make it easier for Israel to tighten her grip on these territories and foster an alternative moderate Palestinian leadership. The second problem which Sharon detected in Lebanon was the presence of Syrian troops and their anti-aircraft missile system in eastern Lebanon, in the Beka'a, which hindered the free movement of the Israeli air force in the skies of Lebanon. Sharon perceived the presence and growing influence of Syria in Lebanon to be prejudicial to Israel, among other reasons, because a Syrian military deployment in Lebanon meant that should war break out between Israel and Syria, Israeli troops would find it difficult to use Lebanon as a corridor, a back door, to attack Syria from the west. Given this background, it is not surprising that from his first day in the Defence Minister's office Sharon devoted much time and energy to planning a major campaign in Lebanon to eliminate Arafat's PLO and hit the Syrians. A feature of the preparations for this campaign was the attainment of closer working relations with Bashir Gemayel, the rising star in Lebanese politics, who controlled the Maronite Christians and their Phalange forces.

Sharon, it is worth mentioning, was by no means the first Israeli leader to work with the Maronites in the Lebanon and give them support. Assistance had already started under previous Labour governments, reaching a peak during the civil war in Lebanon in the mid-1970s. Throughout the years, two competing schools of thought had dominated Israel's policies towards the Maronites in Lebanon. One, which was held mainly by Israel's Military Intelligence Services, maintained that the Christian Maronites should not be trusted and they should not be given support. The other school of thought, led mainly by the Mossad, Israel secret's service, saw positive benefits from working with the Maronites because such cooperation could provide Israel with a window into the Arab world. During his years in office Prime Minister Begin supported the latter school of thought, although his motives were very different from Mossad's. Begin regarded the Maronites in Lebanon as a persecuted minority group, like the Jews themselves, and believed it was Israel's moral duty to protect them against those wishing to wipe them out, mainly the Muslim world. Thus, it was that Mossad's instrumental view of the Maronites and the Prime Minister's moral line combined during Begin's years in power to produce ever-growing cooperation with the Maronite Christians which reached an unprecedented peak during Sharon's tenure as Defence Minister.

Sharon, as was said, wished to strike at the PLO *and* the Syrians in Lebanon. But he was shrewd enough to understand that his colleagues in government would not approve an attack on the Syrians in Lebanon for fear that a clash there might get out of hand and lead to an all-out war with Syria on the Golan Heights. Therefore, in his presentations of a potential military operation in Lebanon, Sharon played down the danger of an armed confrontation with the Syrians in Lebanon and insisted that the intention of a future military operation was only to hit at the PLO in Lebanon and to avoid any confrontation with the Syrians.

Sharon also presented his plans for Lebanon to the American administration which though critical of the bombing of the Iraqi reactor was, under Ronald Reagan, closer to Israel than the previous administration had been. Sharon travelled in person to Washington where, on 25 May 1982, he saw the American Secretary of State Alexander Haig. They had a face-to-face meeting in the State Department in the course of which Haig, perhaps inadvertently, effectively gave Sharon a green light to operate in Lebanon. Haig seemed to approve of Israeli action there pending an 'internationally recognized provocation', though he qualified his approval by adding that any Israeli reaction to such a provocation must be, as he put it, 'proportionate to that provocation'. Sharon could not have wished for clearer approval from Israel's most dependable ally and, indeed, 'the international provocation' which Sharon was waiting for was provided not much later by an incident in London.

There, on 3 June 1982, Israel's ambassador was shot and seriously wounded by Palestinian gunmen. In response, the Cabinet which was called by Prime Minister Begin to an emergency session decided to dispatch warplanes to bomb PLO targets in and around Beirut. In deciding to strike at the PLO, Begin's Cabinet brushed aside the fact, already known at the time, that those who had carried out the attempt on the life of the Israeli ambassador belonged to a breakaway group commanded by Abu Nidal, a man who was a sworn enemy of the PLO and its leader Arafat.

Following Israel's air strike, the PLO responded by shelling Israeli settlements in Galilee, which, added to the attempt on the life of the ambassador in London, seemed to provide Israel with the 'internationally recognized provocation' required by Washington for Israel to operate in Lebanon. On Saturday, 5 June 1982, Begin summoned his Cabinet to approve Resolution 676, which authorized a military invasion into Lebanon. The resolution read:

(a) The IDF is entrusted with the mission of freeing all the Galilee settlements from the range of fire of terrorists, their Headquarters and bases concentrated in Lebanon. (b) The operation is called 'Peace for Galilee'. (c) During the implementation of the decision the Syrian army should not be attacked unless it attacks our forces. (d) The State of Israel continues to strive to sign a peace treaty with independent Lebanon, while maintaining its territorial integrity.[16]

It emerges from testimonies and memoirs of ministers that when approving Operation Peace for Galilee they understood that it should be a limited operation which would last between 24 and 48 hours, and that forces would move into a depth of approximately 28 miles north of Israel's border. Beirut, the capital of Lebanon, would be left, as Defence Minister Sharon told his fellow ministers, 'out of the picture'. Things were soon to turn out very differently.

Given a green light from the Cabinet, the IDF therefore advanced across the border to invade Lebanon. Along Lebanon's coastal road, and joined by forces landing from sea, Israeli tanks and troops rolled northwards to link up with Bashir Gamayel's Maronite Christian Phalange in the outskirts of Beirut which, according to Sharon's assurances, was to be 'out of the picture'. In Lebanon's eastern sector, a substantial force under the overall command of General Avigdor Ben-Gal, a veteran and hero of the Yom Kippur War, advanced northwards under the nose of the Syrians in the direction of the Beirut–Damascus road in a move which threatened to cut off the Syrians in Beirut from those in eastern Lebanon. This aggressive move compelled the Syrians to fight back and by doing so they, unknowingly, gave Sharon on a silver plate the opportunity he was waiting for, namely 'to return fire' and exploit the opportunity to strike at the Syrian missile system in Lebanon. Indeed, when Israeli forces, bogged down in a place called Zahalate, needed air support, Sharon approached the Cabinet and warned ministers that unless the Syrian missile system in the Beka'a valley was destroyed, the Israeli air force would not be able to provide support to the ground forces and that this would mean the loss of life. Such an argument left ministers with a terrible dilemma – on the one hand they wished to reduce the number of Israeli casualties, but on the other they were eager to avoid a clash with the Syrians which might escalate into an all-out war on the Golan Heights. A long discussion ensued about the merits of an air operation against the Syrian missile system and when the old, wise and experienced Minister of Interior, Dr Yosef Burg, agreed to support this air raid, Sharon knew that he had won over the Cabinet. He passed a note to Amos Amir, Deputy Commander of the Air Force, who was present at the meeting awaiting its decision. 'Amos', it went, 'I ride horses and I know that when you jump over obstacles the highest obstacle is the most difficult. Minister Burg has been the highest obstacle and we have overcome it ... Arik.'[17] Subsequently, the Cabinet approved the air operation which was delivered on the afternoon of 9 June by 96 F-15 and F-16 aircraft. It was a most efficient strike and within two and a half hours the Israeli planes had knocked out 17 of 19 Syrian batteries in eastern Lebanon and severely damaged the remaining two, which were also knocked out in a renewed attack on the next day. In the course of this assault, the Syrian air force intervened, losing 96 Migs without any cost to the Israelis. This was a sensational triumph for the Israeli air force which can only be compared with its success in the morning of 5 June 1967 when it destroyed almost the entire Egyptian air force on the ground. Following this massive air strike, Israeli forces on the ground embarked on an all-out assault against the 1st and 3rd Syrian Armoured Divisions, attacking them along the entire line particularly east and west of Lake Karoun (see Map 5).

The war with the Syrians was short and decisive and ended when a ceasefire was introduced on 11 June. Events in Beirut were more complex with Israeli forces, not wanting to enter the capital, having to carry out a long siege in an attempt to pressurize Arafat's PLO into leaving Lebanon. Upon Sharon's orders Beirut was shelled and troops crept forward to tighten the noose around Palestinian quarters and forces. With salvo after salvo of artillery shells landing on Beirut, which combined with bombing reduced the city to ruins, the Lebanese government felt it had to expel Arafat to end the destruction. It, therefore, insisted that Arafat leave Beirut and he agreed. Then, in the weeks of August and September 1982, with the active intervention and mediation of Washington, 15,000 PLO and other Palestinian guerrillas withdrew from Beirut and dispersed in Arab countries. Syrian forces also pulled out from Beirut.

Sabra, Shatilla and Peace Now

The expulsion of the PLO and the Syrians was only part of Sharon's overall strategy and with Arafat out of the way, Sharon also wished to see the Maronite leader, Bashir Gemayel, elected President of Lebanon so that he could sign a peace treaty with Israel. In August, backed by Israeli bayonets, a lot of cash and helicopters which had flown members of the Lebanese Parliament to Beirut to vote, Gemayel was elected President but was assassinated before he could take office in September. This was a devastating blow for Sharon who, both in the period before the war and throughout it, had invested hugely in Gemayel. There was still worse to follow for, after the assassination of Gemayel, Israel's allies, the Maronite militiamen led by Elie Hubeike, entered Palestinian camps at Sabra and Shatilla with Israeli permission, and brutally killed hundreds of innocent Palestinians and Shia Lebanese in a revenge for the assassination of their leader Gemayel.

Even before this massacre of Palestinians at Sabra and Shatilla Israelis, appalled by the growing number of Israeli casualties in the 'operation' which all of a sudden turned to 'war', began to show their impatience with the adventure in Lebanon. Public revulsion grew even further when, as the going became tough, Sharon's own colleagues in government attempted to distance themselves from a war which they had approved. Now, the Peace Now movement, which played a crucial role and led many demonstrations after Sadat's visit to Israel and before Camp David, began mobilizing the Israeli public. Under its lead, on 25 September 1982, the largest demonstration in Israel's history took place in Tel Aviv where more than 400,000 Israelis gathered to protest against the war and to demand that the government set up a judicial commission of inquiry to determine the degree of Israel's responsibility for the massacre at Sabra and Shatilla. Under this massive public pressure and with President Yitzhak Navon threatening to resign, Prime Minister Begin was forced to agree to such an investigation.

In the mean time, the government was hoping to conclude an agreement with the new President of Lebanon, Amin Gemayel, who succeeded his assassinated brother. At the beginning of December 1982 Sharon announced that he had already reached an agreement on a framework for peace with Lebanon and detailed negotiations between Israel and Lebanon, with US presence, opened in Khalde on 28 December. But before these talks could be concluded Israel was rocked by the publication of the Kahan Commission report into the events of Sabra and Shatilla.

Published on 7 February 1983, it concluded that the Israeli army bore indirect responsibility for the massacre by the Maronites in the Palestinian refugee camps of Sabra and Shatilla. It recommended that Defence Minister Sharon be removed from office, for disregarding the danger of acts of revenge by the Maronites against the population in the refugee camps in the wake of the assassination of the Maronite leader Bashir Gemayel. It also recommended that the term of office of the Chief of Staff not be extended and that the Director of Military Intelligence be removed from office. As for Prime Minister Begin, the commission concluded that he was not fully alert to developments on the ground and criticized him for unjustifiable 'indifference' and 'for not having evinced during or after the Cabinet session any interest in the Phalangists' actions in the camps'.

The report caused much tension both within the government where Sharon, who had no friends and did not deserve to have any, was isolated as never before and within society as a whole. During a Peace Now demonstration in Jerusalem, which called on Begin to implement the Kahan report, a hand grenade was tossed into the crowd and one of the Peace Now demonstrators, Emil Grunzweig, was killed. The Cabinet, now under even greater pressure, adopted the report in full and Sharon, the architect of the war in Lebanon, was kicked out of office and was replaced by Israel's former ambassador in the US, Moshe Arens.

Israel's invasion into Lebanon marked a new era in the attitude of Israelis to war. If between 1948 and 1967 the Israelis had shown an unconditional willingness to serve and sacrifice, and if after 1967 in spite of growing criticism and dissension Israelis were still willing to take up arms and rally behind their leadership in war, then in 1982, for the first time in Israel's history, solidarity seemed to break down while war was still being waged. Israelis not only criticized the war, but some also took a stand by refusing to fight in Lebanon. In Lebanon not only did men perish, but there perished also the zest and idealism with which Israelis had marched into earlier battles.

An agreement between Israel and Lebanon was signed on 17 May 1983 after the shuttle diplomacy of US Secretary of State George Shultz. It officially ended the state of war between the two countries, gave Israel a security buffer zone in southern Lebanon, and called for withdrawal of Israeli and Syrian troops from Lebanon. This agreement, however, was not worth the paper on which it was written for it ignored Syria's interests in Lebanon. Damascus, not surprisingly, announced that it would not be bound by it and thus this agreement collapsed hardly a day after it was signed; it would later be abrogated by the Lebanese government as well. With or without an agreement, the IDF planned a redeployment in Lebanon south of the Awali river so as not to be involved in the growing intercommunal strife in the areas it held.

Begin resigns

On 28 August 1983, the day the redeployment of Israeli forces was due to start, Prime Minister Begin said at a Cabinet meeting 'I cannot go on' and, on 15 September, he formally submitted his resignation to the President of Israel. Begin never explained his motives and it was thought that his poor health – he suffered bouts of deep depression – and failing physical powers together with the death of his wife to whom he was very close, were the main reasons for his resignation. But perhaps closer to the truth is the explanation given by the writer Yizhar Smilansky, who published on 31 August 1983 a poem in the *Davar* paper under the title 'Why did Begin Resign?'

> Because night after night
> When wearied he went to bed
> He found his bedroom full
> brimming with ghosts
> Five hundred ghosts – even more
> Standing mute before him
> Nothing said
> Filling his sleeping chamber
> Leaving him sleepless
> Standing mute before him:
> You!

Begin left the stage after 2276 turbulent days at the helm leaving a compromised legacy. Perhaps his greatest achievement was the peace he negotiated and signed with President Sadat of Egypt, an achievement for which he received, on 10 December 1979, the Nobel Prize for Peace. But this achievement was overshadowed by the war in Lebanon. True, the obloquy for this bloody disaster is often attached to the architect of this war, Ariel Sharon, but Begin was at the helm and he bore the ultimate political responsibility for this sad chapter in Israel's history. And, in any case, Sharon could not have got his way without Begin's full backing. Another legacy of Begin's years, the massive settling of the West Bank, is a controversial policy whose merits are still hard to assess. Elsewhere, on the home front, Begin failed to carry out the largest part of his 1977 and 1981 domestic promises and he presided over years of failed economy, soaring inflation and a growing gulf between rich and poor.

7

The Road to Peace, 1983–1991

ENTER YITZHAK SHAMIR

Begin never concerned himself with the future leadership and so had never groomed anyone to succeed him. When he suddenly left the stage there was no natural successor to pick up the baton. Soon, however, two candidates emerged to claim the vacant place – Deputy Prime Minister David Levy and Foreign Minister Yitzhak Shamir.

Levy was born in 1937 in Morocco, one of 12 children of a carpenter. He emigrated to Israel in 1956 and settled in Beit Shean, a shanty town in the Jordan valley where he worked as a construction worker. He was gradually sucked into local and then national politics, and his meteoric rise to power in Likud was due not only to his talents – he was energetic, articulate and had sharp political instincts – but also to the fact that Likud, in its attempts to attract voters of *Sephardic* origins, was eager to recruit to its ranks authentic *Sephardic* politicians such as David Levy. When Menachem Begin won the 1977 elections he made Levy Minister of Immigrant Absorption and after the Likud 1981 victory, Levy could add to the list the title of Deputy Prime Minister. But David Levy had too many detractors who belittled him for his vanity, considered him a lightweight and made tasteless jokes about him.

The other candidate, Shamir, was born Yitzhak Yezernitzky in 1915 in the small Polish town of Rujenoy, whose population of 5000 had some 3500 Jews. Aged 20, Shamir emigrated to Palestine which was then under British Mandate. This was fortunate for him since most of his family, including his parents and his sister, who had remained in Europe, perished in the death camps. In Palestine, young Yitzhak worked as a building worker and then as a bookkeeper, but he was never far from the *Yishuv*'s politics and in 1939 he took the oath of allegiance to the Irgun and joined as a full member. A year later, when the Irgun split, Shamir joined Avraham Stern ('Yair') in the Lehi and after the British gunned Stern down in 1942 Shamir became one of the troika of Lehi's Central Committee and one of the most wanted Jews in British-ruled Palestine. Arrested by the British in mid-August 1946, he was put on the cockpit floor of a British Halifax bomber bound for Africa from where a little time later he escaped with a group of other Jewish prisoners. Via Paris Shamir arrived in Israel just six days after its establishment in 1948. He continued to be active in the Lehi until the organization was disbanded by Prime Minister Ben-Gurion following the assassination, in September 1948, of the UN mediator, Count Folke Bernadotte. Shamir later joined the Mossad, Israel's secret service, and served for ten years in a senior capacity in Europe. Retiring from the Mossad, he joined, in 1970, Begin's Herut Party and was elected to the Knesset on behalf of Herut in 1973. After Likud's victory in 1977, Begin gave Shamir the proffered crumb by making him Speaker of the Knesset and, in 1980, following the resignation of Moshe Dayan from the Foreign Ministry, Shamir succeeded him. Shamir had always had strong opinions. He was a staunch believer in the right of Jews to settle all parts of biblical Eretz Yisrael and consequently was a strong opponent of returning land to the Arabs and had voted against the Camp David Agreements. The Kahan Commission which investigated Israel's responsibility for the massacre of Palestinians in the refugee camps of Sabra and Shatilla in 1982, criticized Shamir for his indifference to the events.

On 1 September 1983, the Herut Central Committee convened to choose one of these men as Likud's leader and Begin's successor. When the vote was counted Shamir emerged as the victor by beating Levy 436 to 302.

Diminutive, stocky, muscular, brush-moustached, with a pair of hard grey eyes, a man of few words, the new leader of Likud, Yitzhak Shamir, was a suspicious man who trusted hardly anyone, least of all Arabs. 'The Arabs are the same Arabs', he once remarked, and 'the sea is the same sea', by which he meant that the ultimate goal of Arabs was to drive the Jews into the sea. Shamir had a lot in common with his predecessor. They were both born in Poland, about the same age, both disciples of Ze'ev Jabotinsky, brought up to be proud of their Jewish heritage and with many of their attitudes permanently affected by the Holocaust. But the differences in their personalities and style were no less striking. Begin was much concerned with form, courtly gestures and ceremonies and, like an actor, drew strength – even inspiration – from the approving roar of a crowd. Shamir was almost the opposite.

Economic turmoil

Upon his selection, Shamir embarked on the business of forming a coalition government and by the time he presented it to the Knesset, on 10 October 1983, he was already deeply involved in the first serious crisis of his government – the economy. It had become apparent from late September, following reports that the government was unable to secure further international loans, that drastic restrictions would soon be imposed on foreign currency transactions and that a major devaluation of the shekel was imminent. As a hedge against these anticipated government measures, the public early in October began selling off large quantities of its blue-chip bank shares – whose value had been artificially and unconscionably sustained by the banks themselves over the years as lure for inflation-proof investment – to raise money for an apparently safer investment in dollars. Encountering this growing wave of selling and frantic to maintain their inflated share values on the Stock Exchange, the commercial banks started importing dollars from their subsidiaries abroad. But with the public's appetite for dollars insatiable, the banks soon exhausted their hard currency reserves and, panicking, turned to the government for help. On 9 October, trading in bank shares was suspended on the Tel Aviv Stock Exchange and this emergency measure was followed by an all-night Cabinet meeting – it was, in fact, the first meeting of Shamir's new government. Early the next morning the Treasury announced a 23 per cent devaluation of the shekel and a 50 per cent increase in the price of subsidized goods. But the crisis was not yet over. For with the publication in a daily newspaper, on 13 October, that the Treasury was planning a dollarization of the Israeli economy to bring stability by pegging the shekel to the American dollar, the public intensified its already wild rush to the dollar. Opposition to the dollarization plan, the brainchild of Finance Minister Yoram Aridor who himself was a chief contributor to the catastrophic economic situation, was fierce from the start. For the implication of such a strategy would be that Israel could no longer print money to pay for her debts, and instead she would have to introduce substantial cuts in the budget with the results being the lowering of standards of living in Israel and growing unemployment. With the public in a panic, pressure mounted on Prime Minister Shamir to drop the dollarization idea altogether and at once. Shamir called an emergency meeting of his Cabinet and then just a few minutes before the opening of this meeting, Finance Minister Yoram Aridor announced his resignation. Subsequently, Shamir made Yigal Cohen-Orgad, a critic of Aridor's economic policies, particularly the dollarization scheme, his Finance Minister and went public to calm the nation by announcing that the dollarization scheme was dropped. A few days later, on 20 October 1983, with the run on the dollar easing, the Stock Exchange was reopened for limited activity, and when trading in bank shares resumed these shares swiftly lost an additional 35 per cent of their nominal value and the Treasury, which by now took over from the banks, was forced to pump some $150 million into the Stock Exchange to block an even steeper decline. In an additional effort to restore stability, Shamir's government barred Israelis from purchasing more than $3000 in foreign currency for travel abroad and introduced a wide range of new taxes. This crisis in the economy which also entailed a dramatic drop in Israel's currency reserves below the $3 billion danger line and a 207 per cent inflation by the end of 1983 eroded support for the Likud and the popularity of the government plummeted.

WORKING TOGETHER

The Government of National Unity

Normally Israelis go to the polls once every four years and the next elections were due to be held in November 1985. Instead, elections were brought forward by 16 months following the decision of the Movement for Tradition in Israel (Tami), a three-man ethnic coalition faction, to defect from the government after several disagreements over social and economic policies. It then joined forces with Labour to dissolve the Knesset and bring about new elections which were set for 23 July 1984.

The election campaign complete with high-powered public relations gimmicks and US-style televised debate between the leader of the opposition Peres and Prime Minister Shamir was, on the whole, fairly tranquil, lacking the confrontations which had characterized previous election campaigns. Peres and his team concentrated on Likud's record of mismanagement and economic failures, while

Shamir and his team stuck to themes that had succeeded in earlier campaigns, portraying Labour as a party of the privileged *Ashkenazim*, of corruption and a party willing to return Jewish land to Arab hands.

The result of the elections was a victory of Peres's Alignment – it won 44 seats out of the total of 120 Knesset seats (3 seats down on the 1981 elections), while Shamir's Likud won 41 seats (7 less than in 1981). Twenty-six lists, 13 of them entirely new, registered for the elections. Of these, a relative newcomer, the Orthodox Shas which spoke in the name of the *Sephardi* Jews and was one of several that, like Tami, combined ethnicity with religion, won four seats, which was the beginning of a stunning rise in power and influence in Israel's politics. One anomaly of these elections, though, was the election of the Kach (Thus) Party. It was headed by Meir Kahane, an American-born Jew and a rabbi of the Brooklyn Yeshiva, who in the 1960s organized in America the Jewish Defence League and 12 years later, in 1972, moved his base of operation to Israel. He then founded his truculent Kach Party, which was anti-Arab in both word and aspiration and called for the compulsory transfer of the Arabs of Israel and of the West Bank. While in the previous 1981 elections Kahane had failed in his bid for the Knesset, this time round, he managed to gain 25,000 or so votes needed to obtain him a seat in the Knesset. This would, a year or two later, bring the Knesset to pass legislation banning political parties from participating in Knesset elections if found to be undemocratic or racist; Kahane himself would meet with violent death when he was assassinated on one of his visits to the United States.

As leader of the party which gained the majority of seats in the Knesset, Peres was entrusted by President Chaim Herzog with forming a government. However, he was unable to put a coalition together and when this task was passed over to Shamir he was no more successful than Peres had been. It was an odd situation, but then the vote in the 1984 elections was so close as to be virtually a tie with 60 seats gained by the Labour bloc and 60 by the Likud bloc. The only way forward, thus, was for Likud and Labour, the two main elements in Israel's politics, to establish a grand coalition and work together.

A series of meetings followed between the leaders of the Likud and Labour, Shamir and Peres, in a luxurious suite at the King David Hotel in Jerusalem to try and form a wall-to-wall government of National Unity. Of these talks Peres later wrote: 'We would negotiate without let-up . . . I did not realize how difficult that pledge was to prove. Yitzhak Shamir is blessed with inexhaustible reserves of patience and equally rich stocks of stubbornness. He is capable of sitting for hours, saying little and committing himself to nothing . . . I spoke at length; Shamir's salient contributions were long silences. . . .'[1] In the end – after 39 days of negotiations – a deal was struck and the two leaders were able to patch together a coalition government based on the sharing of power and a rotating premiership. Shimon Peres became Prime Minister, with the outgoing Premier Shamir as his deputy and Foreign Minister. Under the rotation agreement which was an integral part of the formation of the National Unity government, Shamir would succeed Peres as Prime Minister after 25 months. Defence went to Labour's Yitzhak Rabin and he was to serve throughout the entire life of the government under both Peres and Shamir. It was a big government of 25 ministers – 12 went to the Labour block and 12 to the Likud block and one to Mafdal – 6 without portfolio, and it had the support of 97 Knesset members. In order for this very large government to be able to function properly, it was agreed to form an inner Cabinet consisting of five members from Labour and five from Likud, which meant in practice that each of the two big parties in the government had a veto over the policy proposals of the other. The agenda of this new government, as agreed between Peres and Shamir, was to end Israel's presence in Lebanon, to tackle the ailing economy, to attempt to come to a peace agreement with Jordan and to consolidate the peace treaty with Egypt. With regard to the building of settlements in the occupied territories – always at the top of Likud's agenda but not of Labour's – a compromise was reached by which no more than five or six new settlements should be established during the first year of the coalition government.

Peres entered the Prime Minister's office full of energy and hope, determined to make the most of his time as Prime Minister. He immediately instructed Defence Minister Rabin to produce and present to the inner Cabinet a detailed plan for a phased withdrawal from Lebanon, where Israeli forces had been bogged down since the 1982 Lebanon war, and with the critical cooperation of Likud's Ministers David Levy and Gideon Pat, which meant that the Likud component of the inner Cabinet could not veto the plan, succeeded, on 14 January 1985, in securing the Cabinet's endorsement for a withdrawal from most parts of Lebanon. This was then carried out in stages between February and June. In the first phase Israel strengthened its proxy, the Christian Lebanese militia in southern Lebanon, the so-called South Lebanese Army (SLA) under General Antoine Lahad. In the next phase, Israeli forces pulled back to an interim position south of the Zaharani river, before withdrawing again to a narrow security zone, three to four miles deep, along Israel's border with Lebanon. With this phase successfully completed, the bulk of troops could return to their bases inside Israel, leaving relatively small forces behind to patrol the self-declared security zone.

Second only to the Lebanon morass on Prime Minister Peres's agenda was the state of the economy which he was determined to stabilize and then to regenerate growth. This was no easy task given that during Likud's seven years in power Israel's foreign currency debt had nearly doubled, the annual trade deficit reached $5.5 billion and the annual inflation rate exceeded 400 per cent. Likud had indeed mismanaged the economy, especially during the years when Yoram Aridor was Finance Minister, but the disastrous state of the economy was not all self-inflicted. The high price of oil, agricultural depression caused by world recession and low demand for several of Israel's most profitable winter fruits and vegetables as well as growing competition in the European Common Market, had had a negative impact on Israel's economy. Soaring defence costs and the building of settlements in the occupied territories, which cost some $1.5 billion a year in public funds and conceivably an additional $1 billion in private investment, added to the economic difficulties, as did the fact that Israel's economy was service-oriented with the productive branches overshadowed by the commercial, financial and communal sectors. At the same time, and as if the economy was not in such dire straits, the nation – living in a fool's paradise – appeared to be awash with affluence.

Working closely with his Minister of Finance, Yitzhak Modai, Peres produced an emergency economic programme which was undertaken in July 1985. Wages (with the full support of the Histadrut), prices and the exchange rate – after a 25 per cent devaluation of the shekel – were all frozen. There was strong opposition to this plan mainly by Likud minister David Levy, an authentic representative of the *Sephardim*, the poorer segment of Israeli society. But Levy failed to establish a large enough ministerial opposition to the economic plan which was then accepted and approved by a large majority in the government. The tough measures proved to be so successful that within a year inflation, the main economic problem, was brought down to a manageable 20 per cent.

Peres was an efficient and successful Prime Minister. His popularity ratings topped 80 per cent and there was broad public appreciation of what he had been able to achieve in the short time allotted to him. So successful was he that some of his associates advised him not to rotate the premiership with Shamir but rather to end the National Unity government, hold elections, win and lead Israel to a better future. But, acknowledging that breaching his agreement with Shamir might inflict a devastating blow on his shaky reputation and reliability, always doubted by many in Israel, Peres decided to go ahead with the rotation.

The London Agreement

On 21 October 1986 Peres and Shamir rotated – Peres became Foreign Minister and Shamir Prime Minister. While Shamir's peace policy, so far as he had one, was to buy time and his immediate object was to keep his record clean, Peres, as Foreign Minister, had lost none of his energy and he was determined, after taking Israel out of Lebanon and stabilizing the economy, to accomplish the next item on the National Unity government's agenda, namely to come to a peace agreement with Jordan and other Arab states. He and King Hussein of Jordan had a common friend in Lord Mishcon – Victor Mishcon – the London solicitor, and Peres asked him to set up a meeting with the King. At Mishcon's house in central London, on Saturday, 11 April 1987, Peres with his aide and political Director-General of the Foreign Ministry, Yossi Beilin and Efraim Halevi from the Mossad – representing the Prime Minister and keeping an eye on the often too enthusiastic Peres – met the King. They held discussions for over seven hours and succeeded in producing a written agreement which came to be known as the London Agreement. It was a shrewd document containing an imaginative formula which in itself was an acrobatic manoeuvre to avoid potential minefields. It gave the parties – Arabs and Israelis – what they wanted and paved the way for them to come together and discuss the real matters and issues separating them. As Peres later explained,

> We agreed that an international conference should be convened to launch the [peace] process, but should not itself impose solutions. In practice, we agreed that the conference should assemble once, and that every subsequent session would require the prior consent of all the parties. We agreed, too, that there should be a unified Jordanian–Palestinian delegation which would not include members of the PLO. Finally, we agreed that following the opening

session the actual negotiating would be done in bilateral, face-to-face groups, with Israelis and their Arab adversaries sitting opposite each other to talk peace.[2]

In other words, the King and Peres found a middle way between the Arab demand to conduct peace talks in the framework of an international conference – hence the idea of having an international conference to launch the process, and Israel's to talk bilaterally with the Arabs – hence the idea that after the opening session the actual negotiations be done in bilateral, face-to-face groups. And because neither Jordan nor Israel wanted to see the PLO at the negotiating table, they simply stated in the London Agreement that only parties accepting UN Resolutions 242 and 338 – and the PLO rejected these resolutions – could take part in peace talks. But at the same time the King–Peres formula allowed Palestinian participation by having a local Palestinian representative in a joint Jordanian–Palestinian delegation. In addition, knowing that only Washington had the clout to offer such a bold formula to the parties, the King and Peres agreed to ask Washington to 'present' the London Agreement to the parties – Israel and the Arabs. While a date was put on the agreement, the document itself was not signed for whereas the King was in a position to sign it, Peres himself was not. After all he was no more than a Foreign Minister in a government of National Unity and he still had the daunting task of selling the London Agreement to a suspicious, sceptic, right-wing Prime Minister.

In the mean time, however, Peres dispatched his aide, Yossi Beilin, to Helsinki to present the London Agreement to American Secretary of State George Shultz, who was on a visit there and to ask, as agreed with the King, that the US would present the agreement to the parties. While Shultz was enthusiastic about the agreement, he saw difficulties. As he put it in his memoirs, 'the Foreign Minister of Israel's Government of National Unity [Shimon Peres] was asking me to sell to Israel's Prime Minister [Shamir], the head of a rival party, the substance of an agreement made with a foreign head of state . . . Peres was . . . wanting me to collaborate with him. . . .'[3]

Peres himself saw Shamir after the weekly Sunday Cabinet session to tell him about the agreement with King Hussein. But the meeting did not go well and Shamir was unwilling to accept the London Agreement. The reasons for this were both personal and substantive. On a personal level Shamir felt that Peres was acting behind his back and he was furious when Peres declined to leave a copy of the document with him because, as Peres put it, if he did so then the document might be leaked to the press from the Prime Minister's office. Shamir felt that as the Prime Minister he should be allowed *to read* rather than *to be read* such a crucial document before taking a final decision.[4] On a more substantive level, Shamir disliked the formula because he was vehemently opposed to an international conference in which the Great Powers and the regional protagonists would take part, believing that in such a forum Israel would feel isolated or victimized and that such a conference would impose a solution which, given the likely composition of the conference and the known positions of most of its participants, would probably be unacceptable to Israel. It did not matter to Shamir that the international conference as agreed in the London Agreement would be only the opening phase of the negotiations between Israelis and Arabs. For Shamir, as he put it to the author of this book, *any* sort of international conference was like 'a pig in the temple'.

Determined to kill this document, Shamir dispatched one of his lieutenants, former ambassador Moshe Arens, who had good contacts with the American Secretary of State, to explain Shamir's reservations to George Shultz. Meeting with Shultz on 24 April, Shamir's emissary explained to the Secretary of State that should he decide to present the London Agreement to the parties, this would be considered by Prime Minister Shamir as a crass interference in Israel's internal affairs.[5] Shultz assured Arens that he would not present the document to the parties.

Extremely disappointed, Foreign Minister Peres, nevertheless, decided to present the agreement to the inner Cabinet which he did on 6 May 1986. The result – not surprisingly – was that the five ministers of Likud spoke against the agreement, while the five ministers of Labour were in favour. A tie. And not wanting the agreement to be rejected by the Cabinet – for a tie meant a rejection – Peres decided to withdraw the document and not to call for a vote. This was the official death of the London Agreement.

But the stalemate could not continue for long and as Peres later put it: 'We all paid a heavy price for the destruction of my milestone agreement with King Hussein. Hundreds of people, Palestinians and Israelis, paid with their lives: within months the Palestinian *intifada* broke out in the West Bank and Gaza, resulting in years of violence and bloodshed.'[6]

INTIFADA

The *intifada*, the uprising of the Palestinian Arabs, was triggered, though it was not caused, by a car crash in which four Palestinians were killed on Tuesday 8 December 1987. At first this incident failed to attract attention, but soon rumours spread throughout the Gaza Strip that the crash in which an Israeli vehicle hit a Palestinian car has been deliberate – the revenge by an Israeli for the killing of his brother a few days earlier in Gaza. On the following day, 9 December, hundreds of mourners returning from the funerals of the victims of the car crash, turned on Israeli troops stationed in the Gaza Strip's largest and poorest refugee camp, Jabalya, pelting them with stones. This, we now know, was the beginning of the *intifada*.

At first, the Israeli military and political establishment failed to acknowledge the real nature of the disturbances which were still confined to the Gaza Strip. They thought, and on the face of it there was no reason for them to think otherwise, that this was no more than a flare up of unrest not radically different from previous periods of disorder. The Israelis also believed, wrongly as it turned out, that the disturbances were initiated by Iran or the PLO. But rather than instigated externally the riots were started by local Palestinians – mostly descendants from the refugees of previous wars between Israel and the Arabs. These had been living in appalling, disgraceful, harsh and insanitary conditions in the Gaza Strip. Frustration gripped them, particularly the younger generation of Palestinians many of whom were employed on intermittent piecework inside Israel where high standards of living were a daily reminder of their own subservient status and appalling situation.

The day after the funerals at Jabalya, the Palestinians in the Gaza Strip blocked roads with rocks, tyres, broken furniture and steel sewage pipes. They also stoned Israeli troops. Unlike the events of the previous day which had been spontaneous, this time the disturbances were preplanned by the local leadership. From Jabalya the demonstrations and riots spread like wildfire to other refugee camps – to Khan Yunis, al Bourej, Nuseirat and Ma'azi and then to Rafah. They then reached the more secular and affluent West Bank – Balata, Kalandia and other villages and towns.

The Israeli use of force seemed the only remedy – a delusive hope as they would soon realize. The IDF – trained to fight against regular armies – was ill prepared and had no ready-made answer to civil resistance in which its tanks, warplanes, rockets and artillery lost all significance against the primitive weapons – mainly stones – used by the rebels. Riot gear, rather than tanks and aircraft, was the crying need. The troops needed shields and helmets, clubs and tear gas all of which were in short supply. This was an unfortunate deficiency since civil disturbance was to be the IDF's lot in the following days. Reacting to calls for reinforcement, the Israeli High Command poured forces into the occupied territories and within three days the number of troops patrolling the troubled areas was three times as great as in normal times.

The *intifada* hit Israeli society like a bolt out of the blue, causing sharp divisions. The first line of division was drawn between Jewish Israelis and the 700,000 Arab Israelis living within Israel itself (the so-called Green Line). We should recall that although most Arabs left Palestine during 1947–49 there was still in Israel, on the eve of the *intifada,* a community of Arabs making up about 17 per cent of Israel's total population. Throughout the years these Arab Israelis had become part of society – like Jewish Israelis they held identity cards, spoke Hebrew, studied and worked in Israel. But with their fellow Palestinians to whom they were linked by history and blood revolting in the occupied territories, and the Israelis resorting to what seemed to be an excessive use of force to put down the uprising, the Arabs of Israel found it increasingly difficult to remain aloof. On 17 December, just a week into the disturbances, they held a general strike and rallies in support of the Palestinians in the occupied territories. They also sent food and medicine and donated blood. In doing so, the Arabs of Israel showed themselves to be more Palestinian than Israeli and for the Jewish Israelis this was a shocking realization. Yet, to a large extent, the support lent by Israeli Arabs to the Palestinians in the occupied territories reflected their own resentment against the position to which they had been relegated in Israeli society. For though equal in theory the Israeli Arabs were in practice second-class citizens – the incomes of more than 40 per cent of Arab households were below the poverty line and Jewish families were favoured over their Arab fellow citizens when it came to social and other benefits.

On 19 December 1987, the riots spread to Jerusalem, where scenes previously seen on the streets of the Gaza Strip and the West Bank of barricades, burning tyres, Palestinian flags and stone-throwing, were repeated. Israel's strategy in Jerusalem was a systematic campaign of harassment aimed at putting intense pressure on the Palestinians to quell the riots. Troops stopped and searched Arab cars, checked the condition of windscreen wipers and seat belts or made sure that the driver and passengers had paid their taxes. Furthermore, a new rule prohibited Muslims from outside the city from praying at the Haram al-Sharif, the noble sanctuary where the Dome of the Rock and the Al-Aqsa Mosque had stood for almost 1500 years; everyone entering a mosque in Jerusalem was checked. But even these harsh measures in Jerusalem, and in other parts of the occupied territories, failed to stop the disturbances and the Palestinian uprising continued unabated.

The first few weeks of the *intifada*, from 9 to 31 December 1987, were chaotic and violent. Figures show that in this short period of time, 22 Palestinians were killed by Israeli gunfire, 5 of them children aged between 13 and 16. In addition, some 320 were injured, two-thirds of them aged between 17 and 21. The high toll among children was the result of their taking an active part in the demonstrations, but also because the practice used by Israeli troops to shoot at the legs of the demonstrators in order not to kill them was lethal for small children because of their height. On the Israeli side, 56 soldiers and 30 civilians were injured by stones and bottles. In this single month of disturbances there were 1412 separate incidents of demonstrations, stoning, tyre-burning, blocking roads and raising barricades. While, in general, the Palestinians refrained from using guns in order not to provide the Israelis with the pretext to unleash their mighty military force, there were at least 109 firebombs thrown in addition to 12 instances of arson and 3 grenade attacks.

In the mean time, after recovering from their initial shock, the Israelis in mid-January 1988 deployed two divisional commands on the West Bank and a third in the Gaza Strip; the number of men patrolling Palestinian areas rose to such an extent that there was a shortage of equipment and it was necessary to open up emergency warehouses and distribute equipment usually reserved for all-out wars with Arab regular armies. In Israel itself, the public was appalled by stories, filtering in from the occupied territories, of violence and atrocities. On 23 January 1988, between 80,000 and 100,000 Israelis gathered in Tel Aviv to denounce and demonstrate against Israel's policies in the occupied territories. Peace Now, the movement which had spearheaded the demonstrations against the Lebanon War in 1982, was now becoming a vocal voice against Israel's tactics in the occupied territories.

In February 1988, a new militant fundamentalist group which was an offshoot of the Muslim Brotherhood joined the *intifada*. It was called the 'Islamic Resistance Movement' (Harakat al-Muqawama al-Islami), that is Hamas from the Arabic acronym whose literal meaning is 'courage' or 'zeal'. Hamas was set up by Sheikh Ahmad Yassin and six other leaders of the Muslim Brotherhood in the occupied territories. The emergence of this fundamentalist group to power and influence on the West Bank and, particularly in the Gaza Strip, was partly the result of Israel's folly and short-sighted policy which attempted, in the years before the uprising, to play the fundamentalists off against the PLO in order to counterbalance and weaken the latter for it regarded Hamas as less wicked than the PLO.

Unable to beat the Palestinians in the occupied territories, Israel opted to strike at the PLO in Tunis, which was by now, through its Chief of Staff, Abu Jihad (Kahlid al Wazir), fully involved in organizing and directing the Palestinian uprising. On 15 April 1988, a special commando unit given approval by the Labour–Likud inner Cabinet landed in Tunis and assassinated Abu Jihad before the very eyes of his wife and little daughter. Later, in July and September 1988, the Israelis struck at Hamas, arrested 120 activists and liquidated its command. But neither the killing of Abu Jihad nor the raid on Hamas spelt the end of the *intifada;* the PLO continued to be involved in organizing and directing it and Hamas recovered from the blow inflicted on it and re-embarked on anti-Israeli activities as part of the *intifada.*

To quell the growing resistance and put an end to the uprising the Israelis resorted to various – sometimes ruthless – methods ranging from cutting off telephone lines and electricity, to placing extended curfews on villages, towns and whole cities. On the West Bank localized curfews were imposed, while in the Gaza Strip broader curfews were used. During 1988, no fewer than 1600 curfew orders were issued, 118 of them for five days or more; all in all some 60 per cent of the Palestinian population experienced life under curfew. The Israelis also uprooted trees and occasionally whole orchards to deny the Palestinians the hiding places from where they could strike at Israeli troops. According to Palestinian figures, during 1988 the Israelis uprooted more than 25,000 olive and fruit trees. By now the dynamiting of houses, which before the outbreak of the *intifada* was considered an extreme measure to be used only against Palestinians who had committed serious offences, became a common means of punishment. Thus, whereas before the outbreak of the *intifada* demolishing a house had required the special approval of the Defence Minister, with the uprising in full swing, it was now left to the discretion of an area commander. And figures indicate that it was used frequently: in 1987, the number of Arab houses demolished was 103 and in 1988 it went up to a staggering 423.[7] Deportations, another draconian measure, were also used to quell the disturbances, as well as the closure of schools and universities. Legal procedures to facilitate mass arrests of Palestinian rioters were revised and new detention facilities were built in Ketziot, southern Israel and Daharieh near Hebron; about 50,000 Palestinians were arrested during the first 18 months of the *intifada*, of whom more than 12,000 were held in administrative detention for periods of varying length. One out of every 80 Palestinian adults in the occupied territories was imprisoned by administrative order, while one out of every 40 had spent more than 24 hours in detention for taking part in the uprising.

Another measure used by the Israelis to put down the uprising was economic punishment, such as banning Palestinian villagers from selling their harvest in market towns, which in conjunction with other economic punishments, hit the Palestinians hard; in 1988 their standard of living, which was low anyway, fell by as much as 30 or 40 per cent. All to no avail – the uprising went on.

On 1 November 1988 amid chaos in the occupied territories, Israelis went to the polls and the *intifada*, quite obviously, dominated the election campaign. Likud politicians castigated and condemned Labour for its 'softness' on the uprising and for its willingness to return Jewish lands to Arab hands. Some in the Likud, notably Minister Ariel Sharon, blamed Labour for causing the *intifada* and claimed that had the Likud been fully in charge, namely not had Labour as a partner in the coalition, the uprising could have been 'ended in a week'. The leader of the opposition, Peres, reversed the argument, accusing Likud's desire for territorial aggrandizement and the continued call by several of its militants for annexation as having exacerbated an already explosive situation in the occupied territories.

The election was a close-run thing and although Likud's representation in the Knesset fell from 41 to 40 seats, it nevertheless emerged as the single largest party. Labour received 39 seats, a fall from its previous 44. Fifteen parties received enough votes to gain Knesset seats. On the extreme right there were three parties: Tehiya, which was headed by Professor Yuval Ne'eman and won three seats; Tsomet (Junction), a breakaway group from Tehiya which was led by former Chief of Staff Rafael Eitan and which gained two seats; and Moledet (Motherland), a new party formed in 1988 and headed by the former

General Re'havam Ze'evi which advocated the mass expulsion of Palestinians and won two seats. On the extreme left, the New Communist List won four seats and the Progressive List a single seat; the religious parties did well and were able to increase their representation from 12 to 18 seats in the 120-member Knesset. The Orthodox who had three parties gained a stunning 13 seats in the Knesset.

The business of coalition building began in earnest when President Chaim Herzog called on Shamir, as the leader of the largest party, to form a new government. Under the mathematics of coalition building Shamir could, by bringing in the religious parties and other small right-wing parties, piece together an adequate majority, 65 seats, to form a government without Labour. In the event, however, he opted again for a National Unity government with Labour, because building a government without Labour meant having between five and seven small religious and right-wing parties as part of a shaky coalition. But while in the previous broad-spectrum government with Labour there had been rotation of the premiership, this time Shamir was to remain in his post for the whole duration of the government.

On 22 December 1988, Shamir became Prime Minister for the third time. He left the Defence Ministry in Rabin's hands and proposed that Peres should become his deputy and Minister of Finance to which Peres agreed. Moshe Arens was appointed Foreign Minister, David Levy Minister of Housing and Ariel Sharon was made Minister for Trade and Industry. It was a large government of 26 ministers and it was the first time in Israel's history that Labour served in a government under another party. National Unity completed, no effective opposition remained.

Meanwhile, the war in the territories continued with undiminished fury. A year of uprising, from December 1987 to December 1988, proved to be both violent and lethal. Three hundred and eleven Palestinians were killed, 44 of them children aged between 13 and 16, and 9 children under the age of 9. In addition, 15 Palestinian civilians were killed by Israeli civilians, 6 Israeli civilians killed by Palestinian civilians and 4 Israeli security force personnel were killed by Palestinian civilians. A staggering total of 526 Palestinian houses were demolished during this period.

The use of live ammunition against stone-throwers who were mostly young children was disastrous for Israel from a public relations point of view and, in 1989, rubber bullets were introduced. These proved to be ineffective and so were replaced by plastic bullets which turned out to be more lethal than expected and so were in turn replaced by rubber bullets with steel centres. Troops were also provided with light, easy-to-handle clubs – manufactured by Arab employees from the Gaza Strip – strong enough not to break even when inflicting the heaviest of blows. Like the British Raj which came to depend on *lathis* – the sticks which beat down resisting Indians – so the Israelis came to be dependent on the club. At a meeting with troops in Ramallah, Defence Minister Rabin said: 'Gentlemen, start using your hands, or clubs and simply beat the demonstrators in order to restore order.'[8] This became known as Rabin's 'break their bones policy' and it is a testimony to how frustrated the troops had been that they took what Rabin said to them so literally that the blows they inflicted on the Palestinians left many of them permanently disabled.

How did two years of *intifada* affect Israel? The economic or material consequences were marginal. Few Israelis were displaced from their work, there were no serious shortages of commodities and no major price increases. There was a shortage of Arab labour in some areas, mainly construction, but ways were found to compensate for this mainly through the importation of foreign employees. The army leadership lost much of the high regard with which it had been held and found itself under attack from both flanks, accused of too much laxity by some and of brutality by others. Politically there was a shift of voters to the right and the cleavage between left and right in Israel deepened.

Although the *intifada* turned out to be the most dominant event affecting Israel's life in the late 1980s, there had been other events, notably a dramatic surge in Jewish immigration to Israel, mainly from the USSR and Ethiopia, which also affected Israeli life.

IMMIGRATION AND DEATH OF THE COALITION

The Ethiopian Aliyah

The story of how the Ethiopian Jews – known as Falasha, meaning 'gone into exile' – survived for so many centuries in exile clinging stubbornly to their Jewish tradition and how, finally, they came to Israel is fascinating. Because much of the history of these people is passed orally from generation to generation we may never know for sure their origins, although four main theories exist. First, that they are the lost Israelite tribe of Dan; second, that they are the descendants of

Menelik I, son of King Solomon and the Queen of Sheba; third, that they are the descendants of Jews who fled Israel for Egypt after the destruction of the First Temple in 586 BCE and settled in Ethiopia; and finally, that they are the descendants of Ethiopian Christians and pagans who converted to Judaism centuries ago. Although the Falasha had the Torah, the entire body of traditional Jewish teaching, they never acquired the Oral Law of the Talmud or the medieval commentaries that shaped modern Judaism, and thus they went on to develop their own customs.

Throughout the years there has been a fierce debate, particularly among different religious Jewish authorities, with regard to the authenticity of the Jewishness of the Falasha. This debate goes back to the early sixteenth century when Egypt's Chief Rabbi David Ben Solomon Ibn Abi Zimra, responding to a question regarding the Jewishness of these people, declared that the Falasha were indeed Jews. In 1908, the chief rabbis of 45 countries recognized the Falasha as fellow Jews. Then in 1972, Chief Sephardic Rabbi of Israel, Ovadia Yosef, declared that he had come to the conclusion that 'Falasha are Jews' and in 1975 the Ashkenazi Chief Rabbi of Israel, Shlomo Goren, told the Falasha 'You are our brothers, you are our blood. You are true Jews.' Later that same year the Israeli Inter-ministerial Commission officially recognized the Falasha as Jews under Israel's Law of Return which became the basis for Israeli governments to attempt to bring this community to Israel.

Before 1977 only a few Falasha came to Israel, but when Begin came to power his government came to an arrangement with Colonel Mengistu Haile Mariam, President of Ethiopia, in utmost secrecy, whereby Israel would airlift military supplies to Ethiopia and, in return, the Ethiopian government would allow the planes to return to Israel with Jewish Ethiopians on board. The scheme began well and soon 121 Ethiopian Jews arrived in Israel. But then when details of the arms component of the deal were leaked to the press, Israelis protested against arming the Ethiopian regime and the arrangement was brought to an immediate halt. Later, in 1980, some 209 Ethiopian Jews arrived in Israel followed, in 1981, by 956 and a year later by 891. This was taking place against worsening conditions of the Ethiopian Jews who, in the early 1980s, were forbidden by the Ethiopian government from practising Judaism and teaching Hebrew. Some members of the community were even imprisoned on charges of being 'Zionist spies'. Then, with famine gripping Ethiopia and the Ethiopian government turning to the West for famine relief, Israel asked Washington to condition any help to the Ethiopian government on its allowing the Jewish community living in Ethiopia to emigrate to Israel. Desperate for foreign aid the Ethiopian government agreed, and subsequently Israeli emissaries flew to Ethiopia and under their guidance the Ethiopian Jews – mainly men and the young who were fit and strong enough – made their way on foot across the border from Ethiopia into the Sudan from where they were to be airlifted to Israel. By 1984, as many as 10,000 Ethiopian Jews were gathered in refugee camps in the Sudan waiting to be taken to Israel, and from November 1984 to January 1985, a secret 45-day massive airlift, which came to be known as Operation Moses, resulted in 8000 of these Jews arriving in Israel. But an article published on 6 December 1984 in the *Washington Jewish Week* and full-page advertisements placed by the United Jewish Appeal, led to growing Arab pressure on the Sudanese government not to allow Jews using the Sudan to go to Israel. This then put an abrupt end to the operation and led to some several hundred Ethiopian Jews being stranded in the Sudan. With the help of the American Central Intelligence Agency (CIA), the Israeli government was able to arrange for one more airlift, dubbed Operation Joshua, which brought the stranded Jews to Israel. But with almost two-thirds of the community – comprised almost entirely of women, young children and the sick who could not walk the long distance to Sudan – still in Ethiopia, the Israeli government continued to look for ways to bring in the remaining Ethiopian Jews to Israel.

In the mean time, in Israel, the absorption of the Ethiopians was bumpy, to say the least. When the Ethiopian Jews arrived in Israel they were placed in mobile home encampments where they spent many months learning Hebrew and getting used to Israel. They were then given a sum of money and were referred to live in selected disadvantaged towns – Afula, Kirayt Gat, Ashkelon, Kirat Malachi, Netivot, Ofakim and other development towns. But their absorption in these places was an uphill battle mainly because they were in a state of shock and disorientation, being thrown into a Western advanced Israeli society which was nothing like the relatively primitive life they left behind. What made a bad situation even worse was the fact that the Ethiopian community in Israel was leaderless, for the *keses* – the Ethiopian rabbis and important pillars of this community – were persistently humiliated by the Orthodox Rabbinate, Israel's governing religious authority, which refused to recognize them as rabbis and prohibited them from officiating at religious ceremonies and properly lead their disoriented community. So traumatic was this torn community which suffered anxiety and separation that many of the newcomers committed suicide, something unheard of in Ethiopia. Worse still, some religious quarters in Israel again raised the issue of the Jewishness of the Ethiopian Jews and there were calls to force the Ethiopians to go through the process of *Giyur* – a conversion to Judaism. It did not help either that racism raised its ugly head with Israelis calling the Ethiopian Jews 'Kushim' or 'Shehorim' – meaning blacks – and journalists in leading Israeli newspapers went so far as to declare that the Falasha are 'infested with disease' particularly HIV. Gradually, mainly thorough their service in the IDF, the younger generation of Ethiopians became more integrated into Israeli society, learned the language and became part of the labour market.

The Russian Aliyah

But it was the disintegrating Soviet Union, rather than Ethiopia, which became a major source of Jewish immigration to Israel. Although in the 1970s the number of Jews allowed to leave the Soviet Union was relatively low, in 1986 their number rose to almost 6000 and in the following years the numbers grew steadily. But the problem, from Israel's point of view, was that many of these Jews preferred to go to America rather than to Israel, and thus while in 1987, for instance, 8155 Jews left the Soviet Union only 2072 of them arrived in Israel, and in 1988 out of 18,961 Jews leaving the Soviet Union only 2173 came to Israel, while in 1989 out of the staggering number of 71,000 Jews who were given exit visas from the USSR only 12,117 landed in Israel. This caused much concern in Israel for, after all, Israel's *raison d'être* had always been the 'ingathering of exiles' on the land of Israel. The Israeli government took the unusual step of exerting pressure on the American administration to close its gates to Jewish immigration from Russia and urged it not to grant refugee status to Russian Jews and, instead, send them to Israel where they would be received not as refugees but as citizens. But such a policy went against the grain of the American principles of liberty and the right to choose one's own future, and Israel's pressure was rebuffed. Gradually, however, with the growing influx of Russian Jews to America, American policy began to shift – for it cost Washington a fortune to absorb the growing tide of immigrants from Russia – to one which required Jews wishing to immigrate to the United States to obtain a visa from the United States Embassy in Moscow rather than be allowed to use an Israeli exit visa. A quota was also introduced to limit Jewish immigration to America. This was first set at 24,500 a year and then raised by President George Bush to 50,000. For Israel, this change of policy came just in time, for in 1990 the restrictions on Jews leaving the USSR were swept away resulting in a staggering 185,227 Jews arriving in Israel; within six years nearly 700,000 Jews would emigrate from Russia to Israel making Russian Jews the country's largest national group.

In previous immigrations to Israel, the government used to absorb new Jewish immigrants in centres in which the newcomers were housed for several months before leaving to fend for themselves and fully integrate into Israeli society. But by now, and particularly with the Russian immigrants who unlike the Ethiopian immigrants were able to fend for themselves, the absorption process was revised and the old method of absorption centres was replaced by a policy of 'direct absorption'. Thus, the Russian immigrants were granted a lump sum of money to allow them survive in their initial period in Israel, and upon arrival in the country they were, almost immediately, sent out to the market – the work and housing – to fend for themselves.

The wave of immigration coming to Israel from Russia in the late 1980s and early 1990s was not only large but also of a very good quality, with the majority of the adult immigrants being graduates of universities and technological institutes; the proportion of immigrants with higher education was four times larger than that of the Jewish population of Israel. Not surprisingly, the influence of these people on all spheres of Israeli society was enormous. For with many of them qualified as musicians the number of orchestras and chamber ensembles grew dramatically. Schools of drama were flooded by Russian actors, directors and choreographers. Universities and hi-tech institutions were able to absorb highly qualified engineers and technicians.

Not all went well. For the arrival of so many professionals in the relatively small Israeli market led to growing unemployment and a situation where only 30 per cent of the newcomers were employed in their fields of expertise, 19 per cent became unemployed – women's unemployment rate was twice as high as that of men – and many had to go through training programmes to adjust to the Israeli market. Social tensions between the newcomers and the veteran Israelis were also rife. For the government not only granted the Russian immigrants a cash handout, but it also provided them with an absorption basket grant which allowed them preferential treatment in house purchasing, tax breaks, reduction on customs duties and unemployment benefits. Veteran Israelis – and indeed Arab Israelis – of the poorer segments of society felt that they were discriminated against in comparison with the new Russian immigrants and questioned the government's absorbing policy. What further fuelled social tensions were rumours that – as was the case with the Ethiopian Jews – as many as 30 per cent of the Russian newcomers were not at all Jewish. Also, that among these people there were many single-parent families – a familiar phenomenon in the Soviet Union but not in Israel – did nothing to allay resentment towards the new immigrants and growing accusations that they came over to exploit Israel's welfare system.

Although the Russian immigrants were gradually able to integrate into Israeli society, full integration was a slow, and in the initial years, an incomplete process. For the fact that the Russian newcomers used to live around the same areas enabled them to live parallel but separate lives with the Russian subculture – radio, TV and a score of newspapers and journals – helping them to form a kind of exile enclave inside Israel.

Peres's 'bad smelling manoeuvre'

In the mean time, there was little unity inside the government of National Unity that had been formed in December 1988 as the cleavage between its Likud and Labour components grew deeper. Shamir, with the support of his Likud followers, planned a substantial increase in the building of Jewish settlements in the occupied territories, upsetting not only Arabs and Palestinians but also his Labour partners in the government. Insisting that the Prime Minister was not pursing peace with sufficient vigour, Peres decided at the beginning of March 1990 to end Labour's partnership in the government of National Unity. Rabin, who held the Defence portfolio, warned Peres that any attempt to break away from the government would play into Likud's hands and he went so far as to call Peres's attempts to dissolve the government 'a bad smelling manoeuvre'. But Peres, determined to break away from the political stranglehold of Likud, and perhaps also to secure for himself a more senior post in a future government, negotiated with the religious parties which seemed eager to support him in bringing down the government and then joining a Labour-led coalition. On 13 March

1990, Shamir said to the Cabinet: 'Mr Peres asked to bring about dissolution of the Unity Government and undermined its existence by unjustly charging that this Government is not trying to advance the peace process – its principal task; this leaves me no choice but to terminate his service with this government.'[9] This precipitated the collective resignation of the Labour ministers from Shamir's government and just two days later Labour led a motion of no confidence in the government which was carried by 60 votes against 55. This was the death of the government of National Unity.

But Peres's manoeuvre did not altogether work out and, as often happens in politics, it all, in the end, went terribly wrong for him and for Labour. For although Peres believed that the religious parties were already in his pocket and would join him in forming a Labour-led coalition government, they abandoned him at the last moment. Thus while successful in toppling the government Peres failed to establish an alternative coalition, and when this task was then given to Shamir he was able with the support of religious parties and two small secular ultra-nationalist parties, Tehiyah and Tsomet, to form a Likud-led government. On 11 June 1990, watched from the opposition benches by Labour, Shamir presented his new government which had the support of 62 Knesset members against 57. He put immigration absorption at top of his agenda, but also repeated the right's old pledges to build new settlements in Judaea and Samaria and broaden existing ones.

WAR AND IMMIGRATION

Missiles on Israeli cities

Within weeks of becoming Prime Minister for the fourth time, Shamir was faced with a momentous challenge. It came from Iraq which, on 2 August 1990, invaded neighbouring Kuwait, occupied it and declared it 'the nineteenth province of Iraq'. In response, at America's behest, the UN Security Council passed a string of 12 resolutions calling on Iraq to withdraw her troops from Kuwait. With Saddam Hussein, President of Iraq, failing to comply, President George Bush ordered American troops into the region and working closely with the UN, began to assemble a coalition of member states. In Israel, in the mean time, the air force was put on high alert in case Saddam Hussein should turn on Israel.

Saddam's response to the mounting pressure on him was cunning. On 12 August, he proposed a comprehensive solution to 'all issues of occupation . . . in the entire region'. He proposed the immediate and unconditional withdrawal of Israel from the occupied Arab territories of Palestine, Syria and Lebanon, as well as the withdrawal of Syria from Lebanon, and that of Iran from parts of Iraq which were still in dispute. Only after all these outstanding issues had been settled would 'the formulation of provisions relating to the situation in Kuwait' be discussed, 'taking into consideration the historic rights of Iraq to this territory and the choice of the Kuwaiti people'.[10] Publicly, the US – it was the most active member of the UN-led opposition to Saddam – declined to acknowledge any linkage between an Iraqi withdrawal from Kuwait and any other issue, but it soon became apparent to Secretary of State James Baker, who was attempting to persuade Arab governments to join the American-led coalition, that without acknowledging a linkage between the demand for an Iraqi and an Israeli withdrawal, key Arab members would be reluctant to join the anti-Saddam coalition. It was important, for instance, to have Syria, the apostle of Arab radicalism, in the coalition, but then President Assad of Syria, although on bad terms with Iraq's Saddam Hussein, was loath to give comfort to Israel, and he insisted that the linkage which had been introduced by Saddam should be recognized and addressed before Syria joined the coalition.

Indeed, there seemed to be no escape from acknowledging a linkage between the two cases if Arab countries were to join with Western ones in a massive coalition against Saddam, and in his speech to the General Assembly, on 2 October 1990, after calling again for an unconditional Iraqi withdrawal from Kuwait, President Bush announced that such a withdrawal would pave the way for Iraq and Kuwait to settle their differences permanently, for the Gulf states to build new arrangements for stability and for all the states and peoples of the region to settle the conflict that divided the Arabs from Israel.

Perhaps the strongest US recognition of a linkage between the Iraqi and Israeli cases came on 23 November 1990, when President Bush, on his way back from a Thanksgiving Day meeting with his troops in Saudi Arabia, stopped off in Geneva to meet Syria's President Assad. And it was there and then that President Bush committed himself to give serious attention to the Arab–Israeli conflict once Kuwait was liberated. 'Once we are done dealing with Saddam,' Bush said to President Assad, 'once we are done liberating Kuwait, you have my word that the United States will turn to the peace process, and will turn to it in a determined fair way.'[11] The linkage had been firmly established and acknowledged and American diplomacy scored a remarkable achievement when Assad of Syria finally joined the anti-Iraq coalition.

On 29 November 1990, the UN Security Council passed Resolution 678 which set a 15 January 1991 deadline for Iraq to withdraw its troops from Kuwait unconditionally. Should, according to this resolution, Saddam not leave Kuwait by that time, member states would be authorized to use 'all necessary means' to restore international peace and security in the area. When he failed to comply, the coalition struck on the night of 16 January by massively bombarding Iraq from the air. Desert Storm was under way.

Saddam's response to this air strike came on the night of 18 January when he launched Scuds at Israeli cities; five missiles landed on Tel Aviv and three on Haifa. His rationale was that by provoking Israel he might be able to bring down the American-led coalition, because should Israel hit back, as had always been the case when she was attacked, then Arab members would find it difficult to continue fighting, effectively, shoulder to shoulder with Israel against an Arab state.

When the Israeli Cabinet met in an emergency session to discuss how to proceed following the landing of missiles on Israel's cities, ministers and military personnel were sharply divided. While the Chief of the Air Force pressed for an immediate counter-attack, the Chief of Staff and his deputy argued that Israel should show self-restraint, sit tight and let the American-led coalition use its massive firepower to crush Iraq. And while seven of the ministers, notably Ariel Sharon but also Defence Minister Moshe Arens, insisted on taking an aggressive line and inflicting a massive retaliation on Iraq, seven others opposed and it was Prime Minister Shamir who in the end tipped the balance by siding with those resisting military retaliation. It is indeed remarkable, given that the Israeli Cabinet included such hardliners as Sharon, Arens and indeed Shamir, and that throughout her history Israel had always retaliated when attacked, that the decision was made not to hit back and, instead, to stay out of the war in spite of the Iraqi provocation.[12] Forty Scud missiles landed on Israel during the war, of which 26 hit the Tel Aviv area; 6 hit Haifa, 5 landed on the West Bank and 3 fell in the southern desert of Israel. As a direct result of these attacks one Israeli was killed and 230 were wounded, one critically. In Tel Aviv, 3991 apartments were hit, 87 were destroyed and 869 were badly

damaged. A total of 1647 people were evacuated to hotels. In the Tel
Aviv suburb of Ramat Gan, 3742 apartments were hit, 105 destroyed,
600 badly damaged and 100 public buildings and business structures
hit. A total of 1047 residents were evacuated to hotels. All in all,
though the damage inflicted on Israel was negligible, the psychological impact was enormous. The rear all of a sudden became the front
line and there was also fear in case Saddam would also use gas against
Israeli cities. As a precaution, gas masks were issued to all civilians
who duly carried them in cardboard cases for the entire duration of the
war.

Operation Solomon

Tension and war in the Middle East and the landing of Scud missiles
on Israel did nothing to stop Jewish immigration into the country. In
the very year of the war, 1991, 147,839 new immigrants arrived from
Russia to settle in Israel. This coincided with the resumption of immigration from Ethiopia, where famine and civil war became a powerful
catalyst for Ethiopian Jews to emigrate. A moment of truth came in
early 1991 when Eritrean and Tigrean rebels opened a concerted attack
on Mengistu forces, forcing him to flee his country in early May. And
with the rebels claiming control of the capital, Addis Ababa, the
Shamir government gave the go-ahead to Operation Solomon to rescue
the remaining Ethiopian Jewish community and bringing it to Israel.

Starting on Friday 24 May 1991 and continuing non-stop for 36
hours, a total of 34 El Al jumbo jets and Hercules C-130s – seats
removed to accommodate the maximum number of people – airlifted
14,324 Ethiopian Jews from Ethiopia to Israel. It was a successful
operation which brought the vast majority of the Ethiopian community
which for generations lived in exile. By the year 2000 there were in
Israel some 50,000 Ethiopian Jews – a remarkable achievement of
Likud governments.

THE ROAD TO PEACE

It is ironic that, perhaps, it was the unlawful and aggressive actions of
Iraq's President Saddam Hussein that proved the major factor in bring-
ing about a breakthrough in peace talks between Israel, the Arabs and
Palestinians. We should recall that just before the war President Bush

promised Arab leaders, notably President Assad of Syria, that should they join the coalition against Iraq, Washington would later turn its attention to sorting out the Arab–Israeli conflict. Now, with the victory over Iraq, President Bush was determined to honour his promise and on 6 October 1991 in his message to Congress he declared: 'We must do all that we can to close the gap between Israel and the Arab states, and between the Israelis and the Palestinians.'[13] Then, to turn words into reality, Bush dispatched his Secretary of State James Baker – a skilled persuader and a renowned arm twister – to the region to try and bring Arabs, Israelis and Palestinians to the negotiating table to sort out their differences.

Baker's was not an easy task. Apart from the strong characters he had to deal with, notably President Assad of Syria and Prime Minister Shamir of Israel, there seemed to be almost unbridgeable gaps between the parties, not only on issues of substance, but also on procedural matters regarding the format of talks. The Israelis insisted that peace talks with Arabs and Palestinians should be conducted face to face and not in the framework of an ongoing international conference in which they feared they would be isolated, victimized, outmanoeuvred and as a result the losers. They also objected to full participation of the UN and the European Community which they believed were overwhelmingly pro-Arab; and they would not sit at the same table with the PLO. The Arabs, for exactly the opposite reasons and because they did not see the US as impartial, wished to meet the Israelis in an ongoing international conference where the European Community and the UN would take an active part, and they also – less so Jordan – wished to see the PLO taking an active part in the discussions.

James Baker's strategy was to give Arabs and Israelis what they needed, and to square the circle he suggested an international gathering (an Arab demand) of the regional states involved in the Arab–Israeli conflict in an opening session, which would then break into small groups in which Israelis and Arabs would conduct direct face-to-face talks (an Israeli demand). To overcome Israel's objection to the PLO's participation Baker suggested having Palestinian representatives from the occupied territories, who distanced themselves from the PLO, as part of a Jordanian delegation. Also to answer Arab demands, without at the same time upsetting the Israelis, Baker proposed having the Europeans and the UN as observers only.

It took Baker eight tours to Middle Eastern capitals before he managed, with skill and persistence, to cajole, coax and persuade the parties to take part in a peace conference to be based on the above procedures which were not very different, it is worth mentioning, from the procedure agreed between Peres and King Hussein back in 1986 (the London Agreement) and which foundered on Premier Shamir's objections at that time. But now with the United States at the height of its prestige following the victory over Iraq, no one, not even stubborn Shamir, could reject the invitation to come to a peace conference in Madrid.

THE MADRID PEACE CONFERENCE

The conference opened, under the auspices of America and Russia, on 30 October 1991, in the magnificent Hall of Columns, where President Bush spoke of peace, treaties, diplomatic relations between Israelis and Arabs and territorial compromise. It was planned as a conference of Foreign Ministers, but Prime Minister Shamir felt that he should personally represent Israel, and his 45-minute speech which he delivered on the first day of the Conference was a *tour d'horizon* of past, present and future. Of the past Shamir said, among other things:

> We are the only people who have lived in the Land of Israel without interruption for nearly 4,000 years. . . . We are the only people except for a short crusader kingdom, who have had an independent sovereignty in this land. We are the only people for whom Jerusalem has been a capital. . . . No nation has expressed its bond with its land with as much intensity and consistency as we have.

Of the present, Shamir said:

> I appeal to the Arab leaders . . . show us and the world that you accept Israel's existence. Demonstrate your readiness to accept Israel as a permanent entity of reconciliation . . . In most Arab countries the opposite seems to be true: the only differences are over ways to push Israel into a defenceless position and . . . to destruction.

And as to the future, Shamir said:

> We know our partners to the negotiations will make territorial demands on Israel. But as examination of the conflict's long history

makes clear, its nature is not territorial. It raged well before Israel acquired Judaea, Samaria, Gaza and Golan . . . there was no hint of recognition of Israel before that war in 1967 when the territories in question were not under Israeli control.[14]

The two other speakers of the day were the head of the Palestinian delegation, Haider Abd al-Shafi from Gaza, and the Syrian Foreign Minister, Farouk Al Shara. The Palestinian called for partition of the land, an end to the building of Jewish settlements, the right of the Palestinians to self-determination, and for Palestinian Jerusalem, 'the capital of our homeland and future state'. The Syrian Foreign Minster called on Israel to withdraw from the occupied Golan Heights, the West Bank, the Gaza Strip and southern Lebanon and called Jewish settlements on Arab land illegal.

The next day of the conference, which was set aside for rebuttals and for Secretary of State Baker's closing statement, was more dramatic. Given the podium, Prime Minister Shamir delivered a savage attack on Syria. He said that the claim of the Syrian representative that Syria was a model of freedom and of the protection of human rights 'stretched incredulity to infinite proportions' and he added that the ancient Jewish community of Syria had been exposed to 'cruel oppression, torture and discrimination of the worst kind'. Shamir's speech evoked a sharp response from the Syrian Foreign Minister, who said to the conference, 'Let me show you an old picture of Shamir when he was 32', and describing Shamir as a 'terrorist' he held up a British photograph of the Prime Minister as a 'wanted man'.

Yet in spite of the sour atmosphere the Madrid Conference was the biggest breakthrough in Arab–Israeli relations since President Sadat's historic visit to Israel on 19 November 1977. It succeeded in establishing a two-track mechanism for future negotiations between Israelis, Arabs and Palestinians. The first, a multilateral track in which Israel, regional Arab states and other states outside the region could join in discussions about five key Middle Eastern problems: water, environment, arms control, refugees and economic development. The second framework – a bilateral track, envisaged direct talks in Washington between Israel and each of her main adversaries – Syria, Lebanon, Jordan and the Palestinians, the latter two united in a joint Jordanian–Palestinian delegation.

Soon after the Madrid Conference, on 10 December 1991, bilateral talks between Israelis, Syrians and Lebanese began and eight days

later, on 18 December, talks opened between Israelis, Jordanians and
Palestinians. Then, on 28 January 1992, multilateral talks began in
Moscow and lasted for two days. However, there was little progress
and no significant breakthroughs in either track. It was evident that in
spite of a good atmosphere in the bilateral talks between Israel and
Lebanon, the Lebanese delegation would not settle with Israel without
conferring with, and getting approval from, Damascus. And there was
also no reason to assume that Damascus would confirm a
Lebanese–Israeli accord without Syria first getting back the Golan
Heights which the Shamir government was reluctant to return.
Similarly, in spite of a good atmosphere and progress in talks between
Israel and Jordan, it became evident that the Jordanians would not sign
an agreement until Israel and the Palestinians had first sorted out their
differences. Talks with the Palestinians, however, were so bogged
down that the parties even failed to agree on an agenda and, failing
even to enter the same room, they resorted to sending memoranda to
each other and conducting 'corridor diplomacy'. Part of the problem
was that the Israelis were reluctant to give up any ground to the
Palestinians, for Prime Minister Shamir's intention, as he later put it,
was to 'conduct negotiations on autonomy [for the Palestinians] for ten
years, and in the meantime we would have reached a total of half a
million people in Judaea and Samaria', which would make it almost
impossible, as Shamir saw it, to negotiate the area.[15] The Palestinians,
in turn, also failed to show flexibility and would not move from their
tough traditional positions. Indeed, if the Israelis hoped that by insisting on having local Palestinians rather than the PLO at the negotiating
table they would face a more moderate leadership, then they were
proved wrong. At the negotiating sessions, Dr Haider Abd al-Shafi
from Gaza, Hanan Ashrawi from Ramallah – she was the spokes-
woman for the Palestinian delegation – and others were uncompromising, lacked imagination and insisted on discussing the most
sensitive issues, most notably the status of Jerusalem and the right of
return for Palestinians, before even turning to the other less emotive
issues. Also, highly dependent on the PLO leadership – with whom
Israel refused to talk – the 'local' Palestinian delegation after meeting
the Israelis in Washington would travel to Tunis to discuss their next
moves and receive instructions from Abu Mazen, the PLO official
charged with coordinating the Palestinian side of the Washington talks.
There was an insoluble deadlock in Washington since neither side
would consider terms tolerable to the other.

In Israel, in the mean time, Shamir's hold on power was weakening. His decision to join the peace process in Madrid led to the withdrawal from his coalition of three right-wing parties which eroded support in the Knesset from 66 to a mere 59. His hand forced, Shamir called for an early election to take place on 23 June 1992. A new leadership in Israel, soon to come to power, would give the peace process a new, bold and fresh momentum.

8

....

Peace and War, 1992 to Present

The most momentous issue dominating Israel's life throughout the 1990s and well into the new millennium has been the peace process. A succession of Prime Ministers, from Yitzhak Rabin, through Shimon Peres, Benyamin Netanyahu, Ehud Barak and Ariel Sharon, put all matters – economic, social and others – on the back-burner and subordinated every other aim to that of securing peace deals with Arabs and Palestinians. They were all – in their different styles and ways – competent Prime Ministers, but having to negotiate on sensitive issues, such as the return of the Golan Heights, Jerusalem, refugees, and to grapple with outbreaks of violence which became inextricably linked to the peace process did much to undermine their position, so that they all survived for a relatively short time in office.

ENTER YITZHAK RABIN

Perhaps the most significant breakthrough in the peace process after the 1991 Madrid Conference occurred during Yitzhak Rabin's tenure as Prime Minister. Rabin came to power in the 1992 general election in which the Israeli electorate delivered a stunning rebuff to Shamir's policies of territorial expansion and opted instead for Rabin's policies of territorial compromise; in this election Shamir's Likud seats in the Knesset fell from 40 to 32, whereas Rabin's Labour rose from 39 to 44. While Rabin's political persona had not essentially changed since his first term as Prime Minister in the mid-1970s – he still combined toughness, pragmatism, impatience and dedication to Israel's security – he was nevertheless more mature and experienced and he was determined to make up for lost time.

236

Rabin's first task after being elected was to form a coalition government, for although his Labour Party had won a convincing victory it, nevertheless, did not command an absolute majority in the 120-seat-Knesset. Incorporating into his coalition two ill-suited political bedfellows – the Meretz grouping, secular and left wing which won 12 Knesset seats in the election, and Shas, the ultra-Orthodox *Sephardi* Party, which won 6 seats – Rabin, on 13 July 1992, presented his government to the Knesset for approval. Recognizing the importance of 'hands on' control of the military machine in times of fateful decisions, Rabin decided to keep the Defence Minister portfolio for himself. And, bowing to party pressure, he made his arch-rival Shimon Peres his Foreign Minister but not, however, before clipping Peres's wings by insisting that the important bilateral peace talks between Israel and the Arabs in Washington should remain under Rabin's own control, while Peres should be allowed supervision only over the less significant multilateral talks where water, the environment and such other issues were discussed. Rabin was determined to deliver on promises he made on the eve of the election to strike a peace deal with Palestinians 'within six to nine months of taking office', and to tackle head-on the Syrian and Jordanian issues. But when in office he soon found out that this was easier said than done.

Talks in Washington and Oslo

For although in Washington where, as agreed at the Madrid Conference, bilateral talks between Israelis, Arabs and Palestinians were indeed taking place, the going was tough and negotiations were all but bogged down. There was worse to follow. Retaliating for the kidnapping and murder of an Israeli soldier by Palestinians, the government decided, on 17 December 1992, to expel 415 Islamic fundamentalists from the occupied territories to Lebanon. This, however, badly misfired when the Palestinian and all other Arab delegations walked out of the Washington talks in a dramatic protest until 'all 415 deportees were returned home'. While the talks were now effectively suspended, no one, not even Prime Minister Rabin, knew that a secret, unofficial channel was already operating between Israelis and the PLO. It would soon transform Palestinian–Israeli relations.

It opened in London where Abu Ala'a, a PLO official, and an Israeli academic by the name of Yair Hirschfeld got together on 4 December 1992. Their meeting took place on the advice of Hanan Ashrawi, a member of the Palestinian delegation to the Washington talks, who knowing both Hirschfeld and Abu Ala'a, suggested that they should meet to exchange views on the Israeli–Palestinian conflict. In London on this fateful day another player came into the picture. He was Terje Rod Larsen, a Norwegian socialist and the future UN envoy to the Middle East, who like Ashrawi knew the two men and told the Israeli professor that if, after meeting Abu Ala'a, they decided to continue their talks then arrangements could be made for them to meet in Norway. Hirschfeld and Abu Ala'a met at the Cavendish Hotel near Piccadilly Circus in London where they discussed ways in which they could assist in breaking the stalemate in the Washington talks. They both agreed that it was essential to meet away from media attention where there was no temptation to play to the gallery. Conversation was general and following another night meeting they parted with a commitment to meet again.

Back in Tunis, where the headquarters of the PLO had been based since its expulsion from Lebanon in 1982, Abu Ala'a reported to Arafat and to Abu Mazen (Mahmoud Abbas), who was the coordinator of the Washington talks. In his report, Abu Ala'a mentioned that Professor Hirschfeld had told him that he had good contacts with Yossi Beilin, deputy to Israel's Foreign Minister Peres. Arafat and Abu Mazen saw no objection to continuing the meetings between Abu Ala'a and the Israeli professor. As Abu Mazen later explained, 'there were no risks in it for us. If the dialogue proved fruitful we would have achieved something we were after, and if it turned out to be just small talk with an academic this could not hurt us.'[1] In Israel, in the mean time, Professor Hirschfeld reported to Deputy Foreign Minister Beilin who encouraged him to continue the talks with Abu Ala'a.

The next secret meeting was facilitated by Terje Larsen, the Norwegian who, on the eve of Hirschfeld's first meeting with Abu Ala'a in London, had offered to help by arranging, if asked to do so, future talks in Norway. This meeting took place on 21 January 1993 in the small town of Sarpsborg, some 50 miles south of Oslo, and participants on the Israeli side were Professor Hirschfeld and a former student of his, Ron Pundak, and on the Palestinian side Abu Ala'a and two other PLO colleagues. Perhaps the main characteristic of this meeting was the feeling that well-meaning men were buoyed by a desire to talk sense and not to score points as had often been the case in the now suspended Washington talks. And because previous talks between Israelis and Palestinians had often broken down because of disagreements about the past, Abu Ala'a proposed to focus on future relationships. Hirschfeld, for his part, agreed and went on to propose that they should concentrate on Gaza first and see how this place could be handed over to the Palestinians so that they could rule themselves.

The idea of 'Gaza first' was not new. It had first been raised by Israel's Foreign Minister Peres with Osama el-Baz, President Hosni Mubarak's top political aide, and later with Foreign Minister Amru Musa and Mubarak himself. Peres had asked the Egyptians to see if Arafat would be interested in a deal on Gaza as the opening gambit for further talks.[2] But Arafat had rejected the idea out of hand, suspecting that the Israelis were attempting to give him the riddled-with-problems Gaza while holding on to the West Bank and Jerusalem. Now, at this first meeting in Norway, the PLO representative, Abu Ala'a, did not reject the idea of starting with Gaza first, but he raised the possibility of discussing the future of Jerusalem as well. Hirschfeld disagreed. He said that any attempt to tackle a sensitive issue such as Jerusalem, which Israel claimed to be her eternal capital, would wreck talks at an early stage and he insisted that in this early stage they should stick to Gaza.[3] In this Hirschfeld represented a general feeling in Israel regarding Jerusalem and the Gaza Strip – asked if they would be willing to discuss the status of Jerusalem in peace talks, 83 per cent of Israeli Jews said 'No.' Asked about handling over the Gaza Strip to the Palestinians, a massive 84 per cent answered 'Yes.'[4] All in all, this first meeting between Israelis and PLO representatives in Norway went reasonably well and after two more days of talks the participants returned home. Hirschfeld and Pundak reported to Deputy Foreign Minister Beilin and Abu Ala'a to Arafat and to Abu Mazen.

The unofficial talks in Norway continued throughout early 1993 and gradually became more focused, the aim being to try and produce a Declaration of Principles (DOP) as a framework for a future Palestinian–Israeli agreement. So good was progress in Norway that in February 1993 Deputy Foreign Minister Beilin, who was constantly updated by Hirschfeld and Pundak, decided it was time to report to Foreign Minister Peres who up to this point had been totally unaware of this secret channel. Peres, in his turn, informed Prime Minister Rabin, on 9 February 1993, and proposed that, given that the Washington channel was shut down, Israel should concentrate on the Norway channel. Rabin did not want talks in Oslo – he wanted Washington. First, because negotiations in Washington followed the conditions set in the Madrid Conference which the opposition Likud had approved and could not now dismiss. Second, in the Washington talks the PLO was excluded, at least in appearance, while in Oslo Israelis were talking directly with the PLO which was emphatically not recognized by Israel as representative of the Palestinians. But in Peres's proposal Rabin saw an opportunity. He could make continuation of the Oslo talks conditional on the resumption of talks in Washington, using Oslo as a lever to persuade Arafat to send his team, which had walked out of the Washington talks following the expulsion of the 415 Palestinians to Lebanon, back to the negotiating table. So rather than rejecting Peres's proposal, Rabin said, 'I will go along with the Oslo talks as long as they are running parallel to the Washington talks.'[5] It worked. Rabin's request was passed on by Hirschfeld to Abu Ala'a in Norway and by Abu Ala'a to Arafat in Tunis and, keen to give momentum to the Oslo negotiations, Arafat met his Washington team in Amman and sent them back to America to negotiate. They grudgingly agreed and with the resumption, after four and a half months of suspension, of the Washington talks on 27 April 1993, meetings in Oslo also resumed three days later. And while negotiations in Washington between the official Israeli delegation and Palestinians from the occupied territories returned to the old pattern of stalemate, talks in Oslo between the unofficial Israeli team and the PLO continued to progress towards a DOP.

By now, however, Arafat insisted that Israel should upgrade her Oslo team, for he felt that while his team was composed of senior PLO officials, notably Abu Ala'a, on the Israeli side there were two academics whose positions did not necessarily represent the views of the Israeli government. Arafat's demand to upgrade was passed by Abu Ala'a to Hirschfeld in Oslo and by him to Foreign Minister Peres who, on 14 May 1993, discussed the matter with Prime Minister Rabin. Peres, who by now recognized that unlike the stalled Washington talks negotiations in Oslo were progressing well, suggested that he – Peres – should himself travel to Norway to take charge of these secret talks.[6] But Rabin objected because he felt that this would commit the government which was entirely unaware of the Oslo secret link to the PLO. Instead they agreed that Uri Savir, the Director General of the Foreign Ministry, should represent Israel in Oslo. This deserves mention as being both remarkable and ironic. Remarkable, because for the first time ever an Israeli official was appointed to conduct direct talks with the much demonized PLO, and ironic, because although Israel was now officially talking to the organization she still did not recognize the PLO as the representative of the Palestinian people.

On 20 May 1993, Savir arrived in Oslo. By then, after five rounds of talks, the parties already had a draft of a general framework for peace, a DOP, consisting of 14 articles and appendices including 'Guidance for the preparation of a Marshall Plan for the region.' Here is how things looked at the time of Savir's arrival in Oslo: the aim of talks between Israeli and Palestinian negotiators, according to the draft agreement, was 'to reach an agreement to establish the Palestinian Interim Self-Government Authority . . . for a transitional period leading to a permanent settlement . . .'. The draft agreement then went on to say that in order that the Palestinian people in the occupied territories may be able to govern themselves according to democratic principles, 'Direct, free and general political elections will be held.' A transitional period was defined which 'will not exceed five years', dating from the signing of the DOP and to be followed by permanent status negotiations to begin 'as soon as possible but not later than the beginning of the third year of the interim period between the Government of Israel and the Palestinian people's representatives'. By the end of the second year of the transitional period, Israeli troops will fully withdraw from the Gaza Strip and a trusteeship will be established in this area.

However, as Arafat rightly suspected, the Israeli academics represented themselves rather than the Israeli government, so that with the coming of Savir he laid down new rules for the continuation of the talks. In his first meeting with Abu Ala'a and his team Savir read from a written speech and his first point related to Jerusalem. He said that Jerusalem would not be discussed and it should not be on the agenda of talks because Israel regarded it as her own eternal capital. Instead, Savir proposed, as had Hirschfeld and Pundak before him, that talks should focus on the Gaza Strip as the first place to be transferred to the Palestinians for self-rule. Savir's next point was that, 'No matter what happened between us in the future there should be no obligatory international arbitration, everything should be resolved through direct Israeli–Palestinian negotiations.' This was a traditional stance reflecting Israel's mistrust of the international community as a fair and even-handed arbitrator. Savir's last point was about security. 'Throughout these negotiations', he read, 'Israel will insist on reliable security arrangements.'[7]

The response to these preconditions came from the PLO in Tunis on the next day and was passed on to Savir by Abu Ala'a. He said that

Arafat agreed to all of Israel's demands: Jerusalem would not be on the agenda at this stage, there would be no international arbitration and the focus of talks would be on the Gaza Strip. But Abu Ala'a added that Arafat had asked to have something else in addition to the Gaza Strip, namely some land on the West Bank, in the area of Jericho.

The idea of adding Jericho, the sleepiest West Bank town, to a deal at the centre of which would be the Gaza Strip was not new. On 16 November 1992, Foreign Minister Peres had already raised this with Egypt's President Mubarak, asking him, as he did with his previous 'Gaza first' idea, to pass it on to Arafat for consideration. Peres believed, and he was proved to be right, that a foothold on the West Bank would be an irresistible incentive for the Palestinians to engage in talks and a solid reassurance for Arafat that the Israelis were not bluffing him by handing the problematic Gaza Strip over to him and sticking to the rest.

Back in Israel, Savir reported to Peres and Rabin the result of his meetings in Oslo. The PLO representatives, he said, seemed serious and he recommended proceeding with negotiations in Oslo and adding a lawyer to the Israeli team. Rabin and Peres agreed and the choice fell on Yoel Singer, a Washington-based Israeli lawyer who in the 1970s served in the IDF's legal department and had worked on Israel's disengagement agreements with Egypt and Syria and on the Camp David Accords. But when Singer, who flew to Israel for meetings with Rabin and Peres, saw the draft prepared in Oslo he called it 'an unbaked cake'.[8] In particular, he criticized the centrepiece of the agreement – a trusteeship in Gaza to follow the Israeli withdrawal – because it would bring in the international community which Israel had always wanted to keep out. Singer also insisted that Israel should recognize the PLO. First, because sooner or later it would come out that Israel was holding secret talks with the PLO and, second, by recognizing the PLO Israel would have someone to hold responsible if the Palestinians did not keep the agreement. Rabin and Peres thought that recognizing the PLO was premature and felt that the Israeli public was not yet ready for such a move, but they decided to dispatch Singer to Oslo to turn the 'unbaked cake' into a 'baked' one.

On 13 June 1993, Singer walked into his first meeting with the Palestinians – this was round seven of the Oslo talks. He then – on the basis of the already agreed DOP – confronted Abu Ala'a and his team with more than 40 hard-hitting questions about how they interpreted the document. The questions rained down upon the Palestinian team and Singer meticulously wrote down their answers for later study. In the following meeting in Oslo, on 27 June, Singer suggested to Abu Ala'a that they 'preserve the suggested structure of the Declaration of Principles', but add 'agreed minutes to the Declaration of Principles that form part of the agreement', and make 'some changes in light of the questions and answers [of the previous meeting]'.[9] The Palestinians had to agree and Singer's amendments, which he incorporated into the original draft agreement and submitted to the PLO in Oslo on 6 July (round nine), caused a major crisis in the talks for they substantially transformed the previous agreement. 'It seemed', wrote later Abu Mazen who with Arafat supervised the Oslo talks from Tunis, that 'Singer had come with the aim of returning to point zero.'[10] Furious, the Palestinians hit back. On 11 July they submitted their own amendments to the agreement which by now included such demands as replacing throughout the document the words 'Palestinian team' with the 'PLO', to have Palestinian control of the crossing points to Jericho and Gaza from Jordan and Egypt respectively, to have a corridor linking Gaza and the West Bank and instead of Palestinian control over Jericho to have control over 'the area of Jericho'.

However, in spite of this crisis, talks in Norway continued and a revised DOP document emerged which reflected the changing positions of Israelis and Palestinians and the dropping, with the consent of both sides, of the idea of having a trusteeship in Gaza. All in all, the situation after round eleven of 25–26 July was that a DOP existed and the Israeli and PLO teams in Oslo were able to identify no more than seven points of disagreement which prevented them from reaching and signing a final agreement.

We should pause here, to turn from the unfinished talks between Israel and the PLO to the Israeli–Syrian peace talks. For in Prime Minister Rabin's mind, concluding the agreement with the Palestinians depended very much upon progress on the Syrian track. From the start Rabin wished to settle with the Syrians first, for he held that the differences between Israel and Syria were less complicated to deal with than were the issues dividing Israelis and Palestinians. He also believed that, tactically, an agreement with President Assad of Syria would severely weaken the position of Arafat and make him more cooperative. But Assad of Syria was a hard nut to crack.

Talks with Syria

Peace talks with Syria started in 1991 following the Madrid Conference. At that time Israel was represented by Prime Minister

Shamir's lieutenant, Yossi Ben-Aharon, and Syria by the veteran negotiator, Muwafiq el Allaf. These two nationalists spent much time arguing about the past and when occasionally they ventured into the future they could find hardly any common ground. Allaf insisted that the formula for peace should be based on a full Israeli withdrawal from the occupied Golan Heights on the basis of UN Resolution 242, as interpreted by Syria, while Ben-Aharon maintained that rather than being based on an Israeli withdrawal, future relationships between the two countries should be based on a 'Peace for Peace' formula. As for UN Resolution 242, which according to Israeli interpretation required Israel to *partially* withdraw from occupied territories, Ben-Aharon insisted that this had already been done when Israel pulled out of the Sinai. It was a position of deadlock and stalemate.

When in 1992 Rabin came to power he replaced Ben-Aharon with Professor Itamar Rabinovich, a scholar from Tel Aviv University whom Rabin knew and trusted. On 24 August 1992, Rabinovich walked into his first meeting with his Syrian counterpart and read from a written speech which he had agreed with Prime Minister Rabin back in Israel. What Rabinovich had to say greatly encouraged the Syrians, for he made it clear that the Rabin government was ready, in principle, to withdraw from the Golan Heights in return for peace. This was considered such a breakthrough that at a further meeting, on 31 August, the Syrians brought a working paper and offered it to the Israelis as a basis for further negotiations.

Entitled a Draft Declaration of Principles, it was prepared in Damascus between May and August 1992 and was an agenda for talks with Rabin's new government. It consisted of four pages. The first three outlined a comprehensive peace plan between Israel and her Arab neighbours – for Syria had always been the champion of a, so-called, 'comprehensive peace' in which all Arab states shared a common front in making peace with Israel – and the rest of the document dealt with Israeli–Syrian relations. This document in its entirety is published for the first time in Appendix 2 of this book, but the following are its two most important articles:[11]

5(a). Machinery of Implementation:
Total Israeli withdrawal from the Syrian Golan occupied in 1967; the evacuation and dismantling of all the settlements which have been established on the occupied Syrian territory since that date in

contradiction to the Geneva Conventions, the principles of international law and UN resolutions.

7. Security Arrangements and Guarantees:

... the two parties declare their disposition to undertake and accept the necessary measures to guarantee their security in a parallel and reciprocal manner, including the possibility of establishing on both sides and on equal footing demilitarized zones or zones with reduced armaments, and to obtain from the Security Council, from particular states or from both, security guarantees without any prejudice to the sovereignty of any party nor to the principle of equal rights for both.

In other words, Article 5(a) expressed the Syrian demand that Israel withdrew *totally* from *all* of the Golan Heights, while Article 7 was the price Damascus was willing to pay in terms of security arrangements should Israel indeed return the occupied land to Syrian hands. While this Draft Declaration of Principles was a breakthrough in the sense that it provided the negotiators with something tangible to focus their minds on, a sort of a cognitive map, it was also what more than anything else bogged the talks down. The reason for that was procedural in nature and came down to the question of where to start. While the Israelis insisted on starting discussions with Article 7, for they were keen to ensure that before offering a withdrawal from the strategic Golan Heights they knew what specific security arrangements were offered to them in return, the Syrians, on the other hand, insisted on dealing first with 5(a), for they wished to ensure that *before* going into the nature of security and peace with Israel, they got all the Golan Heights back. Thus all the negotiations from August 1992 till August 1993 were spent on the question of which article should be discussed first, and as Walid Moualem, a member of the Syrian delegation, later recalled, 'it was a vicious circle'.[12]

On 3 August 1993, in an attempt to break the deadlock and inject some momentum into the Syrian–Israeli dialogue, America's Secretary of State, Warren Christopher, travelled to Jerusalem for a meeting with Prime Minister Rabin. What was significant about this meeting was that Rabin came up with a dramatic offer. He said to Christopher that while in Damascus Christopher should ask President Assad, and Rabin emphasized that this was a hypothetical question, that should Assad be satisfied on what he was after, namely an Israeli withdrawal from the

Golan Heights, would he be willing to make peace with Israel?[13] When Christopher asked Rabin what this would mean with regard to Israel's negotiations with the Palestinians, Rabin answered that should Assad respond favourably and an Israeli–Syrian deal be made, then this would be supplemented by a small Palestinian deal. But, said Rabin, should Assad's response be disappointing then there would be a major Israeli–Palestinian agreement.

We should recall that at this time, August 1993, talks between representatives of the Israeli government and the PLO in Oslo had reached a critical stage with, apart from seven points of disagreement, all other issues settled and agreed in a written draft. Rabin was now trying to decide whether to go the extra mile in Oslo and clinch a deal with Arafat or make a bid for the Syrian option and, if this could be achieved, sign with Assad first which, as we have explained, was his preference. Secretary of State Christopher left for Damascus knowing that he had been given a significant mandate by Rabin. 'This was a very important message to me', Christopher told the author of this book, 'because it meant that I could talk about [an Israeli withdrawal] from the entire Golan Heights.'[14]

In Damascus, on 4 August, Christopher met President Assad and back in Israel on the next day he reported to Rabin. Assad, as Christopher explained to the Prime Minister, showed himself willing to make peace with Israel. But then in Christopher's detailed report it emerged that the President's response to Rabin's offer was a 'yes, but . . .'. Rabin wished the withdrawal from the Golan Heights to be spread over five years, first so he would have enough time to remove the Israeli settlements and, second and perhaps more importantly, so he would have a trial period for Syria to prove her good faith. Assad's response was that he was willing to give Rabin no more than six months to complete the withdrawal. Rabin had asked for 'adequate security arrangements' to which Assad had agreed, but on the basis of 'equality' on both sides of the border which Rabin felt he could not accept for he would then have to remove Israel's troops from substantial parts of the frontier region of Galilee. Assad also opposed the normalization of Israeli–Syrian relations before Israel had made a significant withdrawal of her troops from the Golan. 'Rabin', according to Secretary of State Christopher, 'was very disappointed in the specifics. He was disappointed that Assad had not been more forthcoming, had not shown appreciation for Rabin's willingness to consider full withdrawal.' After this lukewarm response Rabin decided to put the Syrian option on hold and return to the PLO in Oslo.

Concluding the Oslo Agreements

It was Foreign Minister Peres, whom initially Rabin had wished to keep away from the bilateral talks, who was now tasked by the Prime Minister with tackling the remaining unresolved issues between Israel and the PLO. Peres had a pre-scheduled trip to Sweden and Norway and he invited Yoel Singer who, after joining the talks in Norway in June 1993 became their prime mover to come with him. From Stockholm Peres invited the Norwegian facilitator Terje Larsen to join him and from Israel Peres's deputy Beilin arranged for Norwegian Foreign Minister Johan Joergen Holst, who was on a visit to Iceland, also to join Peres in Sweden. Peres's idea was to negotiate the last remaining obstacles with the PLO Tunis leadership over the telephone. But because Israel did not recognize the PLO the negotiations would be through a third party – the Norwegian Foreign Minister.

On 17 August 1993, at 10 p.m., Terje Larsen contacted Arafat in Tunis and the final phase of the Oslo talks got under way – over the phone. Perhaps the most complicated stumbling point discussed that night related to Article V, paragraph 3 of the draft Oslo agreement. It dealt with the question of what issues should be covered in the final status negotiations. While the Israelis did not want any mention of these issues – some of them Israel did not want to discuss at all – the Palestinian side had insisted that they should be specified in the signed DOP. Arafat would not yield on this matter and in the end he won the argument and the critical clause read: 'It is understood that these [final status] negotiations shall cover remaining issues including: Jerusalem, refugees, settlements, security arrangements, borders, relations and cooperation with other neighbours, and other issues of common interest.'[15] Another complicated matter with which Peres and the PLO had to grapple over the phone related to Annex II, paragraph 4 of the proposed Oslo agreement. This concerned control of the crossing-points into Gaza and Jericho respectively from Egypt and Jordan. The Israelis, in the Oslo talks, had refused to discuss the matter, arguing that control of the crossing-points to the Palestinian areas was part of the external security for which they would continue to be responsible. Moreover, as control of border crossing-points was an attribute of sovereignty, it would not be proper for an interim Palestinian authority, enjoying self-rule only, to assume such control. The Palestinians insisted on finding a compromise wording and an ambiguous, though acceptable, formula was agreed over the phone and this part of the

DOP read: 'The above agreement will include arrangements for coordination between both parties regarding passages: a. Gaza–Egypt; and b. Jericho–Jordan.'[16] And there were other issues discussed over the phone in this final push of the Oslo talks which lasted seven hours. The telephone bill, as Foreign Minister Peres later explained, 'was paid by the Swedish government'.[17] On the next evening, 19 August, a modest ceremony took place in Norway where the Director General of Israel's Foreign Office Uri Savir, who played such a critical role in the Oslo talks, and Abu Ala'a, the chief PLO negotiator, initialled the agreement.

Since such a momentous deal needed an American endorsement, Peres now suggested to Prime Minister Rabin that Rabin himself travel to America to notify President Clinton of the breakthrough and receive his blessing. But Rabin delegated this task to Peres, who together with Norwegian Foreign Minister Holst and a few other advisers, met Warren Christopher and Denis Ross, the special Middle East peace coordinator, at the Point Magu Marine Base in California on 27 August 1993 and told them of the Israeli–Palestinian deal. Startled though they were by the breakthrough of which they knew so little – for the Israelis had kept the talks secret from the Americans – Christopher and Ross, after a short telephone call to Clinton, gave their blessing to the deal and accepted Peres's request to host the signing ceremony in the White House.

Something was still missing – recognition of the PLO. Even though the deal had been made between the Israeli government and the PLO in Oslo, the Israelis still failed to give the PLO formal recognition as representative of the Palestinian people. On 9 September 1993, through the offices of Norway's Foreign Minister Holst, Yasser Arafat sent a letter to Prime Minister Rabin confirming that the PLO was committed to the peace process and renouncing the use of terrorism and other acts of violence. Those articles of the Palestinian Covenant denying Israel's right to exist, wrote Arafat to Rabin, are inoperative and no longer valid. In a short, laconic letter Rabin replied: 'Mr Chairman, In response to your letter of September 9, 1993, I wish to confirm to you that, in the light of the PLO commitments included in your letter, the Government of Israel has decided to recognize the PLO as the representative of the Palestinian people and commence negotiations with the PLO within the Middle East peace process.'[18] This was remarkable, for hitherto Arafat had been treated as a terrorist or a joke and either interpretation ruled out any thought of doing business with him. But now he was a recognized statesman.

Having formally recognized each other the Israeli government and the PLO could publicly sign an agreement. This was done in Washington on 13 September 1993 and Rabin and Arafat were the main signatories on the very desk that had been used at Camp David for the signing of the Begin–Sadat agreement in 1978. In his speech Rabin said:

We are destined to live together, on the same soil in the same land. We, the soldiers who have returned from battle stained with blood, we who have seen our relatives and friends killed before our eyes, we who have attended their funerals and cannot look into the eyes of parents and orphans, we who have come from a land where parents bury their children, we who have fought against you, the Palestinians – we say to you today in a loud and clear voice: Enough of blood and tears. Enough. We harbour no hatred towards you. We have no desire for revenge. We, like you, are people who want to build a home, plant a tree, love, live side by side with you – in dignity, in empathy, as human beings, as free men. We are today giving peace a chance and saying to you: Enough. Let's pray that a day will come when we all will say: Farewell to arms.[19]

The efforts that had gone into the Oslo Agreement had resulted in no more than a DOP, an agenda, and now, after the Washington signing, it was necessary to transform this framework through further negotiations into an action plan. The first item to be negotiated was the withdrawal of Israeli troops from the Gaza Strip and Jericho and the handing over of these territories to Arafat and the Palestinians so they could rule themselves. Talks to achieve this started immediately after the Washington signing and were carried out by two committees, one chaired by Foreign Minister Peres and Mahmoud Abbas, and the other consisting of experts who met in the Egyptian resort of Taba.

In the mean time, however, those opposed to the peace process were showing their hands. On 25 February 1994, a Jewish settler, Baruch Goldstein, opened fire inside the main mosque in Hebron, the site of the Tomb of the Patriarchs venerated by Jews and Muslims alike, killing 29 Arab worshippers. On 6 April, a Hamas suicide bomber killed eight Israelis in Afula, apparently as a revenge for the Hebron killing and seven days later another Hamas bomber, explosives strapped to his body, detonated himself on a bus in Hadera killing six Israelis. These killings delayed but failed to stop Israeli–Palestinian talks to implement the Oslo Agreement and, on 4 May 1994, Prime Minister Rabin and Palestinian leader Arafat signed, in Egypt, the Cairo Agreement. It envisaged three stages of transfer of power and land from Israel to the Palestinians. In the first stage, responsibility for education, culture, health, social welfare and taxation was to be transferred from Israel's civil administration to the Palestinian National Authority. In the second stage, Israel was to redeploy her forces from Palestinian populated areas, and in the third stage, elections were to take place on the West Bank and the Gaza Strip for a new Palestinian Authority. Implementation then ensued. On 25 May 1994, Israeli troops folded their flags and withdrew from the Gaza Strip and Jericho and Palestinian policemen moved into these areas. On 1 July 1994 Yasser Arafat arrived in Gaza and took control of Palestinian affairs. The former 'terrorist' was now Chairman of the Palestinian Authority.

Peace with Jordan

On 14 September 1993, that is a day after the signing of the Israeli-Palestinian DOP in Washington, Israel and Jordan signed the Israeli–Jordanian Common Agenda. It constituted the blueprint for their future peace treaty and pinpointed the matters to be discussed between the parties, namely security, water, refugees, borders and territorial matters.

On 19 May 1994, Prime Minister Rabin and King Hussein met secretly in London to draft the outlines of their peace treaty, and following this meeting, Israeli and Jordanian teams began working in earnest on the details of a general framework for peace and on the envisaged 15 bilateral agreements to be signed as part of it. About two months later, on 25 July, King Hussein and Prime Minister Rabin signed, on the White House lawn, the Washington Declaration. It was not yet a fully fledged peace agreement, but another step towards it. In this, Israel and Jordan publicly declared that the state of belligerency between them was terminated, vowed to seek a just, lasting and comprehensive peace and to take measures towards normalization of relations. In the Hashemiyya Palace, just outside Amman, on 16 October, Prime Minister Rabin met again with King Hussein for a working session to sort out the remaining issues before a full peace agreement could be signed. Over maps the Prime Minister and King went through the needed border modifications and agreed that land which Israel had occupied at the end of the 1948 war should be handed

over to Jordanian sovereignty and that Israeli farmers, who had culti-
vated this land for many years now, would remain in possession of it
as lessees. At four in the morning on 17 October, Rabin and the King
finished delineating the border and while they retired to snatch some
sleep, their teams hammered out the last remaining details. Four hours
later they initialled the agreements and on 26 October, the final
Israel–Jordan peace treaty was signed. With the ratification of this
peace agreement full diplomatic relations were established between
Israel and Jordan on 27 November.

Oslo II and Rabin's assassination

On 22 January 1995, the hands of those opposed to peace hit again
when a Hamas suicide bomber blew himself up in a busy bus station
at Beit Lid, killing 29 Israeli soldiers and a civilian. Shocking as this
was, it failed, however, to stop talks between Israelis and Palestinians
on extending the Palestinian autonomy in Gaza and Jericho to larger
parts of the West Bank. This proved to be an uphill battle because
while in the Gaza Strip there had been only a dozen or so Jewish settlements, on the West Bank there were some 140, many of them close to
areas which were to be transferred to the Palestinians. A further
complication was that the West Bank included Hebron, after Jerusalem
the most sacred town for the Jews and also an important holy site for
Muslims, where 400 Jews lived alongside an overwhelmingly Arab
population.

In complicated, crisis-ridden negotiations Israeli and Palestinian
teams hammered out a deal to divide the West Bank into three areas.
One, where there were Palestinian-populated areas, to come under full
Palestinian control, a second area, where there were Israeli settlements
and military sites, to come under Israeli control and a third area in
which the Palestinian police would be responsible for public order and
Israel would have overriding responsibility for security.[20] By mid-
August 1995, in the Israeli Red Sea resort of Eilat, hundreds of Israelis
and Palestinians were working out the details of this deal, and in ten
intensive days in September Foreign Minister Peres and Chairman
Arafat took personal charge of these talks to sort out together the most
complicated and remaining issues, notably Hebron. They succeeded.
On 28 September 1995, a hefty 410-page Oslo II Agreement, which
also included eight maps, was signed in Washington by Rabin and
Arafat in the presence of President Clinton, Egypt's President

Mubarak and King Hussein of Jordan (see Map 6). On 5 and 6 October 1995 the Knesset debated Oslo II and when the vote was cast the agreement was passed with a narrow margin of 61 to 59. In the following weeks and months, Israeli troops withdrew from six major West Bank cities – though not from Hebron – and from hundreds of Arab villages all of which were transferred to Yasser Arafat's control.

But there were elements in Israel vehemently opposing the return of land to Arab hands, and unable to kill the peace process they decided to kill the messenger. One of them, a right-wing zealot, Yigal Amir of the religious Bar-Ilan University, shot the Prime Minister in a rally in Tel Aviv on 4 November 1995. This murder shocked the nation to the core and increased suspicions and tension between right and left, religious and non-religious in society. Rabin was buried on Mount Herzl in Jerusalem, and it was a manifestation of just how much Israel's relations with her Arab neighbours had improved that at his funeral eulogies were said by Arab leaders such as Jordan's King Hussein and President Mubarak of Egypt.

Peres was now the Prime Minister and while he was determined to proceed with the implementation of Oslo II, he was also keen to give a new momentum to the Israeli–Syrian talks. He knew little of what had already been achieved on the Israeli–Syrian track for this was Rabin's pet project and the former Prime Minister had kept his cards close to his chest. It was only on the day of Rabin's funeral that Peres learnt from President Clinton, at their meeting in the King David Hotel in Jerusalem, of the state of Israeli–Syrian talks and of the pledge of his predecessor to return the Golan Heights to Syria for a real peace. Understandably, Peres was hurt by Rabin's conduct, but he nevertheless went out of his way to reassure President Clinton that he would honour Rabin's previous commitments. At a later meeting, on 19 November 1995, in Jerusalem with Dennis Ross, the special Middle East peace coordinator, Peres handed over a letter written in his own hand for him to deliver to President Assad. 'It was a letter of goodwill in which I expressed my willingness to negotiate with honour and with equality', Peres explained to the author of this book. Peres also invited Assad, through Ross, to meet him in a summit so that together they could inject new momentum into their peace talks. Of Peres's personal letter, Assad said that 'it is a good letter' and to the proposed summit he said yes in principle, but went short of agreeing to fix a date, which was effectively a no. Thus while Israeli–Syrian peace talks were resumed in Maryland on 27 December 1995, at the level of officials, progress was slow.

In the mean time in Israel, Prime Minister Peres decided to bring forward the general election due for November 1996. This was a sensible decision. By bringing forward the election Peres could exploit the mood of the moment – sympathy to Labour in the wake of Rabin's assassination – before it disappeared. Also, Peres felt that a future deal with Syria and movement towards discussions of the final status of the territories with Arafat, would require tough decisions and that a renewed mandate from the public was necessary, particularly since he had not been elected to the job but had rather succeeded the assassinated Rabin. Thus on 11 February 1996, Peres announced his decision to advance the date of the election to May 1996.

But when it came to winning general elections the cards always seemed to be stacked against Peres, and within a few weeks of announcing an election day Peres lost his massive lead in the polls. Support slipped away in the wake of a renewed bombing campaign by Hamas, the Palestinian Islamist group, which left scores of Israelis dead and wounded. It was, in a way, a self-inflicted reverse, for the Hamas bombing campaign came as revenge for the assassination by Israel, on 5 January 1996, of Yahya Ayyash, the so-called Engineer, who had personally masterminded several previous Hamas attacks on Israel. Thus, on 25 February 1996, a bomb in Jerusalem killed 24 Israelis, and on the same day a woman was killed by a bomb in Ashekelon; 24 hours later, again in Jerusalem, a bomb went off in a bus killing 18. Then a bomb exploded in a bus in the centre of Tel Aviv, killing and injuring many Israelis. Coming at a critical time just before the general election these terrorist attacks were devastating for Peres. On 13 March 1996, in an attempt to shore up the Peres government and the peace process, a summit in support of the peace process was held in Sharm el-Sheikh in which representatives from 27 countries took part, including Arab states.

And then it was Hezbullah's turn. From southern Lebanon this Shia Lebanese movement opened fire on Israeli settlements, sending Israelis in Galilee into basements. Peres, keen not to seem soft on the eve of a general election, instructed the IDF to hit back which it did by unleashing, on 11 April 1996, a massive military operation – Grapes of Wrath. But on 18 April a human error resulted in the bombing of a civilian shelter where 105 Lebanese were hiding in the UN base in Qana. It was not, of course, Peres's fault that shells went astray and he could not have anticipated such a tragedy, but the result was a terrible blow to his prestige both in Israel and abroad. And instead, as Peres had hoped when he approved the military operation in the first place, of emerging as a tough guy, he appeared incapable of effectively supervising military operations. To make matters even worse, the opposition Likud, now led by Benyamin Netanyahu, smelled blood and when an American-sponsored ceasefire was signed, on 27 April, it condemned Peres for having caved in to outside pressure and abandoned Israel's interests. With four weeks to go to the general election Peres was trailing Benyamin Netanyahu badly in the polls.

ENTER BENJAMIN NETANYAHU

Voting took place on 29 May 1996 and following a constitutional change made in the previous Knesset Israelis were asked to cast two votes, one for the Prime Minister, the other for a political party. The result was a Labour victory: it gained 34 seats against 32 for the Likud. But in the separate vote for Prime Minister, Benyamin Netanyahu won by a razor-thin margin 1,501,023 votes as against 1,471,566 for Peres.

The new Prime Minister, known as 'Bibi', was only 46 when he was elected to the top job in Israeli politics. He was born in Jerusalem, but had spent most of his childhood in America where his father was a university professor. Benyamin grew up in the shadow of his eldest brother, Yonathan – who had been killed in the daring Entebbe rescue operation. When young Benyamin was due to enlist in the IDF he returned to Israel and joined Sayeret Matkal, perhaps the best special unit of the IDF. After six years of service, he retired from the military, studied in the United States and then went into business, first in America and later in Israel. Netanyahu was always a political animal and he was gradually sucked into politics, first as a diplomat and later as a party politician. From 1982 to 1984, he was Deputy Chief of Mission to the United States and from 1984 to 1988 he served as Israel's ambassador to the UN where he excelled himself. He was first elected to the Knesset in 1988 and then embarked on a meteoric rise in the Likud. Aged 39, Netanyahu was made Deputy Foreign Minister and during the 1991 Gulf War he was Israel's principal spokesman, and later that year served as a member of Israel's delegation to the Madrid Peace Conference. By 1992 Netanyahu had become Deputy Minister in the Prime Minister's office and, in 1993, following Premier Shamir's resignation of the Likud Party leadership, Netanyahu won the resulting poll.

Netanyahu was often dubbed the 'magician', for although lacking intellectual vigour he was still a master of the sound bites and combined communication skills with youth and good looks. The gist of his world view was that true peace with the Arabs would only come when they realized that Israel was a 'wall'. Netanyahu had always condemned the Oslo Agreement and by the latter half of 1995 he was leading large protest rallies against it.

Upon his election as Prime Minister, Netanyahu patched together a coalition government by bringing together religious parties, by now a leading force in Israel's politics with 19 seats between them, the new right-wing Russian immigrant party, Yisrael Be'aliya, which was headed by Nathan Sharansky and had secured 7 seats, and the Third Way Party which was led by a defector from Labour, Avigdor Kahalani, and which opposed a withdrawal from the Golan Heights. On 18 June, Netanyahu presented his new government to the Knesset and got its approval.

For Netanyahu to deal with Arafat was a bitter pill to swallow, and while immediately after his victory he called Arab leaders such as Hosni Mubarak of Egypt and King Hussein of Jordan, he could not bring himself to pick up the phone and talk to Arafat. But there was no way of avoiding a face-to-face meeting and this took place on 4 September 1996 at the Erez Checkpoint. It was arranged by Terje Larsen, the Norwegian facilitator who played such a pivotal role in the Oslo talks and who, upon requests from the Prime Minister's office, hauled a large table to the meeting room so that when shaking hands the two leaders would be at arm's length.[21] It was a formal and stiff meeting and did little to warm Palestinian–Israeli relations which appeared to have run steadily downhill following Netanyahu's coming to power. Soon after the summit there was a major outbreak of violence.

This took place when, encouraged by the Mayor of Jerusalem Ehud Olmert, Netanyahu, on 24 September 1996, ordered the opening of an exit to the northern end of an ancient tunnel that ran under the Old City adjacent to the Temple Mount and, close to the holy Al-Aqsa Mosque in the Old City of Jerusalem. It was a provocative move – Jerusalem was still under dispute between Israelis and Palestinians – coming at a sensitive time and such was the Palestinian frustration that they resorted to violence. In three days of clashes 15 Israeli soldiers and 80 Palestinians were killed and many were injured on both sides. External mediation was urgently needed to stop the bloodshed, and intervening in this crisis President Clinton summoned Netanyahu and Arafat to the White House where it was agreed to bring things again under control and stop the violence. But this affair in Jerusalem left deep scars on both sides and killed what little trust existed between Israelis and Palestinians and when this was so necessary for tackling the compli-cated problems which still lay ahead.

Hebron and Har Homa

Hebron was unfinished business. For even though an agreement entail-ing an Israeli withdrawal from most of Hebron had already been agreed and signed by the previous Labour government, it still had not been implemented. The Israelis justified this on the ground of contin-uing Palestinian violence. Hebron was thus on Prime Minister Netanyahu's plate when he came to power, and in spite of public pledges to honour agreements signed by previous governments, he was, nevertheless, determined to revise the Hebron Agreement. Arafat objected but had not much choice, and in three and a half months of tough negotiations a revised agreement emerged on the following lines: The largest part of Hebron, designated as area H-1, with 100,000 Palestinian residents, was to be transferred to the control of Arafat's Palestinian Authority which would be responsible for both security and civil related matters in this area. The second area, designated as area H-2, with 20,000 Palestinians and including the 400 Jewish resi-dents of Hebron, was to enjoy a unique status in that Israel would retain responsibility for security and public order and for all other matters related to the Israeli residents, while the Palestinian Authority would be responsible for civil matters relating to the Palestinian popu-lation residing in this area. A complex partition plan was devised with confrontation lines in the centre of Hebron.

Perhaps the most significant contribution of Netanyahu to the Hebron Agreement was a 'Note for the Record' upon which he insisted. In this, his government and the Palestinian Authority reaf-firmed their commitments to peace on the basis of reciprocity. The Israelis, for their part, undertook to continue redeployment of forces, to release Palestinian prisoners and to start permanent status negotia-tions within two months of the implementation of the Hebron Agreement, while the Palestinian Authority committed itself to complete the process of revising the Palestinian National Charter in a way which would abolish its anti-Israeli clauses, to strengthen security cooperation with Israel, to prevent incitement and hostile propaganda, to combat 'systematically and effectively' terrorist organizations, to prosecute and punish terrorists and to confiscate illegal firearms, among other understandings.[22]

On 15 January 1997, Netanyahu brought the Hebron Agreement before his government and in spite of strong opposition, particularly from Ministers Ariel Sharon and Benjamin Begin – the latter eventually resigned in protest – managed to get it passed. The agreement was then debated by the Knesset which also approved it with 87 in favour against 17 objectors and 15 abstentions.

Revising the Hebron Agreement, adding to it the 'Note for the Record' and passing it in the face of strong opposition through government and Knesset, was no mean achievement for Netanyahu. But this victory was soon cancelled out by the Prime Minister's policies on settlements and, in particular, his government's decision of 28 February 1997 to build in Har Homa (known to Arabs as Jabal Abu Ghneim) 6500 housing units. Har Homa was a tract of land in south-west Jerusalem, and the rationale behind the government's decision to build a Jewish settlement there was that this would create a physical barrier preventing the merging of Bethlehem with the East Jerusalem neighbourhoods. But this land was still under dispute between Israelis and Palestinians and the government's decision to build there upset the Palestinians. What was worse, the Israeli–Palestinian dispute concerning Har Homa, which continued for many weeks and caught the headlines both in Israel and abroad, came at a time when the Netanyahu government had decided that the next Israeli withdrawal, featured in previous agreements with the Palestinians, would be restricted to no more than 2 per cent of West Bank land, far less than the Palestinians had expected.

With tensions running high, Palestinian–Israeli relations at a low ebb and the peace process on the verge of breaking down, a Hamas suicide bomber blew himself up on 30 July 1997 in Jerusalem killing 14 and injuring 160. Blaming Arafat for not adhering to the 'Note for the Record' part of the Hebron Agreement which committed the Palestinian leader to curbing terrorist attacks, Netanyahu went on to announce that implementation of the Oslo II Accords would be frozen. He also instructed the army to tighten security and he pushed through government a secret decision to give the Mossad the go-ahead to assassinate a Hamas leader residing in Jordan, Khaled Mashal – a botched attempt at which a few months later would shake Israeli–Jordanian relations to the core.

The Lauder secret channel

Like Prime Ministers before him, Netanyahu wished to reach an agreement with Syria before clinching any substantial deal with Arafat. The reasons for that were both personal and practical – on a personal level Netanyahu simply could not stand Arafat, and on a more practical level the Prime Minister believed that a deal with President Assad of Syria would increase his leverage on Arafat.

In an attempt to engage the Syrians in a dialogue Netanyahu dispatched the Head of the Mossad, Danny Yatom, to try and enter into discussions with the Syrian ambassador to the United States, Walid Moualem, who, in the past, had headed the Syrian delegation in talks with Labour governments. This came to nothing. Later, on 16 May 1997, at a meeting in the King David Hotel in Jerusalem with Dennis Ross, the American special Middle East peace coordinator, Netanyahu asked Ross to travel to Damascus and deliver a message to President Assad the gist of which was that Netanyahu was keen to open secret negotiations to arrive at a basic understanding on the fundamental issues separating Israel and Syria. But Assad, who was no fool, immediately realized that what Netanyahu was proposing were, at best, empty words and he rejected the offer.

In the following year, however, through a secret channel, some progress was indeed made towards a peace deal with Syria. At the centre of this secret channel was an American millionaire and businessman, Ronald Lauder, who in the summer of 1998 and with the assistance of George Nader, a Lebanese residing in Washington who had good contacts in Syria, shuttled in a private jet between Damascus and Jerusalem. He was carrying a document – Treaty of Peace between Israel and Syria – which he devised with Netanyahu and repeatedly amended as indirect negotiations progressed between the Prime Minister and President Assad of Syria. The introduction to the Treaty of Peace between Israel and Syria, 29 August 1998, read: 'Israel and Syria have decided to establish peace between them. The peace will be based on the principles of security, equality, respect for the sovereignty, territorial integrity and political independence of both.' Clause 2 was perhaps the most significant part of this document for it expressed the depth of withdrawal from the Golan Heights which Prime Minister Netanyahu was willing to consider should Assad offer him a full peace. It went: 'Israel will withdraw from the Syrian lands taken in 1967 in accordance with Security Council Resolutions 242 and 338, which establish the right of all states to secure and recognized borders and the "land for peace" formula, to a commonly agreed border *based on the international line of 1923. . . .*'[23]

But soon President Assad – the seasoned, experienced and stubborn negotiator – realized that there was not much in Netanyahu's formula. For the Israeli Prime Minister offered a withdrawal to a line 'based' on the international line of 1923 which meant that Netanyahu was not even offering a full withdrawal to this border line. And even more importantly, Assad had never accepted the international border of 1923, but had always insisted on an Israeli withdrawal to the lines which had existed on the eve of the June 1967 war. The difference between the two lines is significant. The international border line of 1923 ran east of the Sea of Galilee and at its closest to the water line, in the north-eastern part of the lake, it was still 10 metres east of it which denied the Syrians access to the water of the lake, while the border line which had existed on the eve of June 1967 and which was created following the illegal grabbing of land by the Syrians in the years prior to 1967 – Israel did the same thing – ran, in some parts, *on* the water line and gave Syria direct access to the water of the Sea of Galilee. For President Assad recovering all the lost lands was a matter of honour, dignity and access to precious water, but for Netanyahu the thought of the Syrians dipping their toes in the Sea of Galilee, the water reservoir which provided some 40 per cent of Israel's water supply, was unthinkable. Deadlock. And after ten shuttles between Jerusalem and Damascus the Lauder secret channel collapsed.

The Wye Memorandum

In the spring of 1998 American diplomacy, led mainly by Dennis Ross, attempted to persuade Prime Minister Netanyahu to withdraw from a further 13 per cent of the West Bank as part of the implementation of the Interim Agreement of 28 September 1995, namely the Oslo II Agreement. Netanyahu, however, rejected this demand, agreeing only to consider a 10 per cent withdrawal. To square the circle a new formula was devised, based on the idea of 'green areas' or 'nature reserves'. The gist of this was that Israel would withdraw from 13 per cent of land of which 10 per cent would be transferred to the Palestinians and in the remaining 3 per cent, to be called 'green areas' or 'nature reserves', the Palestinians would not be allowed to build and Israel would have responsibility for security. With such a formula

Netanyahu could still argue that he did not give up 13 per cent of West Bank land and, at the same time, the US could tell the Palestinians that they had got their 13 per cent. But there were other matters to discuss before an Israeli withdrawal could become a reality, and to clinch the deal President Clinton invited Netanyahu and Arafat to talks at Wye Plantation where he wished to conduct Camp David-style negotiations until an agreement was reached. Netanyahu was not enthusiastic, but like another Likud Prime Minister, Shamir, who was dragged to the Madrid Conference, so now Netanyahu felt that he could not say no to an invitation of the President of the United States. So he acquiesced.

The summit opened on 14 October 1998 and, on 23 October 1998, after nine and a half days of tough negotiations, the Wye River Memorandum was signed. As previously agreed, Israel was to relinquish 13 per cent of the land of which 10 per cent was to be turned over to Palestinian control and the rest was to become nature reserves. In return, Netanyahu insisted, and Arafat committed himself to this, that the latter take measures to prevent acts of terrorism, crimes and hostilities against Israel, and make known his policy of 'zero tolerance for terror and violence'. Arafat also committed himself to apprehending individuals suspected of perpetrating acts of violence and terror for purposes of further investigation, and to punishing all persons involved in acts of violence and terror. Netanyahu demanded, and it was accepted by Arafat at Wye, that the Palestinian side should establish 'a systematic programme for the collection and appropriate handling of all illegal items', and that the numbers in the Palestinian Police should be reduced from 36,000 to 30,000. Arafat also agreed to reaffirm the letter he sent to President Clinton, of 22 January 1988, concerning the nullification of those Palestinian National Charter provisions that were inconsistent with the new relationships between the sides. According to the Wye Memorandum, permanent status negotiations were to resume on an accelerated basis so that agreement could be achieved by 4 May 1999.

In spite of early optimism that the Wye Memorandum would result in a new momentum for peace this did not happen. The main reason for this was that Arafat failed to stick to commitments he made at Wye Plantation and he went so far as to make it clear his intention to unilaterally declare, and not as part of an agreement with Israel, a Palestinian state. In response, on 20 December 1998, Netanyahu summoned his government and a decision was made to halt the implementation of the Wye Memorandum until Arafat declared that he would not declare a state, would halt all violence, would collect weapons and would fulfil the other obligations to which he committed himself at the Wye Plantation summit. Israeli–Palestinian relations went downhill. By now the Israeli public had lost all hope and although much blame for the failure of the peace process was directed against Arafat, Netanyahu himself also came under severe criticism in Israel and abroad. And with support for the government in the Knesset dwindling and his own position becoming untenable, Netanyahu announced that he would bring forward the general election.

ENTER EHUD BARAK

The election was held on 17 May 1999 and Ehud Barak, at the head of One Israel, a merger of Labour with two smaller parties, Memad and Gesher, won a landslide victory over Netanyahu and became Israel's tenth Prime Minister.

Barak was born Ehud Brog in 1942 in kibbutz Mishmar Ha'Sharon, Palestine, where he grew up. Aged 18, he joined the IDF and was recruited to the mysterious commando unit, Sayeret Matkal, where he distinguished himself and eventually became its commander. He personally led his commandos in daring operations, notably the rescue, on 8 May 1972, of more than 100 passengers from a Sabena airliner which was hijacked by Palestinians and landed in an airport near Tel Aviv. Later, on 10 April 1973, dressed as a woman complete with blonde wig and impressive false breasts, Barak led his commandos on a raid into the heart of Beirut to revenge the killing of 11 Israeli athletes in September 1972 at the Munich Olympic Games. A distinguished soldier, Barak won rapid promotion within the ranks of the IDF, and by the time the *intifada* in the occupied territories broke out in 1987 he was already deputy Chief of Staff. It was Barak, who from a Boeing 707 supervised the assassination of Abu Jihad, number two to Yasser Arafat and at that time controlling the *intifada*. On 1 April 1991, Barak was made Chief of Staff of the IDF and after almost four years in this job he retired on 1 January 1995 as the most decorated soldier in the Israeli army.

On 16 July 1995, following the statutory lapse of time needed before a military officer could enter politics, Barak joined the Labour Party and on the following day entered Rabin's Cabinet as Minister of the Interior. The assassination of Prime Minister Rabin dramatically accelerated Barak's rise. He became Foreign Minister in the new Prime Minister Peres's Cabinet and in 1997 challenged Peres for leadership of the Labour Party. In a bitter hard-fought contest Barak defeated Peres, took his place as leader of Labour and won the 1999 election. A collector of old clocks – which may account for his obsession with imposing deadlines left and right – Barak was a man of high intelligence and fighting spirit. But he was a bad party man who surrounded himself with people loyal to him from his military days and rarely turned to the party for support or advice.

From his first day in office, Barak made his priority clear: making peace with Arabs and Palestinians. But he also emphasized – as he did in the election campaign – his intention to introduce a 'social justice programme', which came to be known in Israel as Barak's 'social revolution', of which a centrepiece was the disentanglement of religion from politics in Israel. This idea came in response to the outcry of secular Israelis against the growing influence of religious parties and institutions and their turning of Israel, as many non-religious Israelis saw it, from a secular to a non-tolerant Jewish state. It was, though, clear to Barak that his secular programme will have to wait in order that he could fully concentrate on the main task in hand, the making of peace.

Immediately after forming a coalition government, Barak embarked on his peace mission, meeting with the relevant world leaders – Hosni Mubarak in Alexandria on 9 July, Yasser Arafat in the Erez Crossing on 11 July and King Abdullah of Jordan in Aqaba on 13 July. In Washington, on 14 July 1999, Barak met President Clinton and in a five-hour meeting (Clinton: 'I could have listened to him for the whole night') explained his peace plans to the President. Barak said that he was keen to move ahead with the peace process on both the Palestinian and Syrian tracks – although he sounded more enthusiastic when mentioning the latter – and he went out of his way to emphasize that peace deals with Arabs and Palestinians should be concluded while Clinton was still in office. The reason was that any newly elected American President would be unlikely to be able to devote much time and energy to Middle Eastern affairs during his initial period in office. Perhaps Barak also thought that none of the new contenders to the White House were likely to be as friendly to Israel as was Clinton. In a press conference to conclude his first visit as Prime Minister to the United States, Barak praised President Clinton and said – although he was advised by Clinton not to do so lest he should be proved to be wrong – that 15 months would be a desirable time frame in which to achieve peace with the Palestinians, peace with the Syrians and a with-drawal of Israeli troops from Lebanon, which had been one of Barak's pledges in his election campaign.

It was during the Washington visit that Barak and Syria's President Hafiz el-Assad started trading public compliments, sending a stream of astonishingly warm messages unprecedented between leaders of these two hostile nations. Barak praised Assad for having created a 'strong, independent, self-confident Syria', and added that, 'Syria is of great importance for the stability of the Middle East'. Assad, in his turn, hailed Barak as a 'strong and sincere man', who 'wants to make peace with Syria and who operates according to a well-planned strategy'.[24] But even these extraordinary exchanges failed to break the deadlock and bring the parties to the same table. Assad still insisted that talks with Israel should be resumed 'at the point at which they stopped in 1996', and that Barak should publicly honour Rabin's promise that Israel withdraw to the lines of 4 June 1967, and that Barak should spell out his willingness to surrender *all* of the Golan Heights down to the shores of the Sea of Galilee, allowing Syria direct access to the water. Barak, although knowing that Rabin and later Peres had promised Assad through the Americans that if Israel's demands were met she would withdraw from all of the Golan Heights, insisted that other matters, notably good security arrangements and normalization of relationships, should be discussed first. Barak clearly wanted to see progress on the Syrian track for, like his mentor Rabin before him and other prime ministers, he always believed that the 'Syria first' option took precedence over the more complicated Palestinian option where the issues were so large, complex and invested with such symbolism as to almost defy resolution.[25] A deal with Syria also entailed peace with Lebanon and guaranteed control by Damascus of Hezbullah, the radical Shiite Muslim guerrillas in south Lebanon, which could enable Barak to achieve yet another goal, namely withdrawal of Israeli troops from Lebanon. But then, with the Syrian track still stalled in spite of the encouraging exchanges of positive statements between Assad and Barak, the Israeli Prime Minister – somehow disappointed – was forced, like previous prime ministers, to turn to Arafat.

Talks with the Palestinians

Like Netanyahu before him who spoke from both sides of his mouth – promising to honour agreements signed with the Palestinians by previous

governments but then insisting on revising them as he had done with
the Hebron Agreement, so did Barak. He undertook to honour the Wye
Memorandum which was brokered by President Clinton and signed by
Netanyahu with Arafat in 1998, but then insisted on the need to change
it. Why? Because Barak had misgivings about Israel's phased territorial concessions which he regarded as squandering political capital. He
was apprehensive that by the time Israel came to negotiate with the
Palestinians over the most complicated and sensitive issues, notably
the future of Jerusalem, refugees and borders, she would not have
enough bargaining power, namely territory, to extract concessions
from the Palestinians. So by revising the Wye Memorandum Barak
wished to ensure that while the principles of the hardest issues were
being negotiated, Israel would still essentially control 60 per cent of
West Bank land. While Arafat loathed having to reopen the Wye
Memorandum, with Barak holding the tangible assets, namely the
land, and Arafat himself able to offer only words and promises – often
with no intention of keeping them – he had no choice but to acquiesce.

On 5 September 1999, in the Egyptian resort town of Sharm el-
Sheikh, Egyptian President Hosni Mubarak presided over a ceremony
in which Barak and Arafat signed the Sharm el-Sheikh Memorandum.
It amplified and modified the Wye Agreement, provided a new
timetable for the release of Palestinian prisoners, dealt with economic
issues, defined 13 February 2000 as the deadline for a general framework for peace and 13 September 2001 as the deadline for final status
agreement between Israelis and Palestinians. Most importantly of all,
at least from Barak's point of view, this modified agreement established a timetable which ensured that most of the West Bank land
remained in Israel's hands while the toughest issues were still on the
negotiating table.

However, the following months lacked any real momentum and it
was Barak who behaved as if he had time on his side and it took him
weeks to appoint his chief negotiator for talks with the Palestinians. It
was only after an early November summit in Oslo, officially a tribute
to the late Rabin but which was also to serve as a catalyst for the
renewal of talks between Israelis and Palestinians, that some momentum was given to the talks but with no tangible results. Arafat
demanded that Barak halt the building of new settlements in the occupied territories, and instead of transferring derelict lands to the
Palestinians hand over Arab towns near Jerusalem, a demand which
Barak – because of the proximity to Jerusalem – rejected out of hand.

And while both parties were digging in their heels and making no real progress in their talks, there came, to Barak's relief, a breakthrough on the Syrian track.

Talks with Syria

The breakthrough came in November 1999 when President Clinton and his team, led by Madeleine Albright and special middle East peace coordinator Dennis Ross, detected on one of their visits to Damascus a certain softening of the Syrian position. Previously Syria had insisted that negotiations should be resumed 'from the point where they stopped'. But now, it adopted a more general formula that negotiations might resume 'on the basis of what was accomplished in the past' as a 'starting point' with additional verbal clarification by President Clinton.[26] This was juggling with words, but the opportunity was there and Clinton did not waste it – in a press conference on 8 December he invited Syrians and Israelis for a summit meeting in Washington.

This opened on Wednesday 15 December 1999 in the Rose Garden of the White House and was attended by Foreign Minister Farouk el-Shara of Syria, and Prime Minister Barak. There were face-to-face separate talks between the Americans, Barak and el-Shara and discussions at Blair House, with Secretary of State Albright in attendance, to set a time and ground rules for more formal negotiations on the issues that divided Israel and Syria, including borders, security, terrorism, water rights and diplomatic and economic relations. Also, to consider the sort of agreement Israel and Syria wished to reach. Should it be a DOP? Or a detailed final peace agreement? There was no discussion on the substantive matters which were dealt with only obliquely, and thus all three parties could claim that the two days of talks were an unqualified success though at no time did Barak and el-Shara meet alone. On 16 December, in a five-minute statement outside the West Wing entrance of the White House, President Clinton announced the resumption of peace talks between Israel and Syria.

They met again on 3 January 2000 in the semi-secluded Clarion Hotel and Conference Centre just outside the tranquil town of Shepherdstown, some 70 miles north-west of Washington. The 55-strong Israeli team led by Prime Minister Barak included, among others, Foreign Minister David Levy, Attorney General Elyakim Rubinstein, former Chief of Staff and by now Minister of Tourism Amnon Lipkin-Shahak, dozens of lawyers, military officers and technical experts. Syria's delegation was headed by Farouk el-Shara and numbered between 25 and 30 officials including two deputy foreign ministers, Yusuf Shakkur and Majeed Abusaleh, Syria's former ambassador to the US, Walid Moualem, and several generals and legal advisers. However, the meeting did not go well. The first crisis arose in the early hours of the conference when the Syrians insisted that what the Israelis called the Committee of the Borders and they called the Committee to Demarcate the 4th of June should meet before any other committee did. This crisis was resolved when the American proposal to convene all committees simultaneously was accepted. But even then the thorny issue of Israeli withdrawal from the Golan Heights surfaced again and overshadowed all other matters. The Syrian insistence on a full Israeli withdrawal from the Golan Heights down to the Sea of Galilee was not accepted by Barak who stood firm on his demand that the line should run several dozen metres to the east of the edge of the lake. And in spite of success in some other areas, notably consent by both sides to the opening of full diplomatic relations, establishing trade relations and opening roads, rails and communication links between the two countries, it was still not enough to bridge the gulf regarding the future border between Israel and Syria. There was little progress and when on 10 January the talks stopped and the Americans presented a paper summarizing the results of the talks, the positions in this paper were not much different from the opening positions. The parties dispersed, and although the decision was to convene again on 19 January this never happened. This was because the Syrians were upset that the American paper summarizing the talks was leaked to the Israeli press and they also insisted that Barak should explicitly pledge to withdraw completely from the Golan Heights – an ultimatum which Barak rejected.

In a last-ditch attempt to revive the talks President Clinton proposed a summit meeting to President Assad. Assad agreed. In several telephone conversations and in two meetings with US ambassador Martin Indyik, Prime Minister Barak made his peace offer clear so that Clinton could present it to Assad. Barak was willing to withdraw from the Golan Heights to the 4 June 1967 boundaries if Syria would consent to forgo access to the Sea of Galilee, in exchange for a parcel of land elsewhere. Barak gave Clinton explicit permission to use this offer if he felt certain that Assad would agree to the border modifications.

The Clinton–Assad summit took place on Sunday 26 March 2000 in Geneva. But when Clinton put Barak's proposal to Assad, the Syrian

President – stubborn as ever – rejected it out of hand, insisting that he would not forgo access to the Sea of Galilee. 'I have held barbecues at the Sea of Galilee, swum in its water, sat on its shores and eaten fish from it', Assad told Clinton, 'I have no intention of giving it up.'[27]

The failure of the Clinton–Assad summit had been a heavy blow to Barak and had had a devastating effect on public support for him in Israel. It was in a sense self-inflicted. For since coming to power Barak had talked so optimistically and confidently about the breakthrough with Syria which was, apparently, just around the corner, that when it came to grief the Israelis were deeply disappointed – some even felt betrayed – and lost patience with Prime Minister Barak and his obsession with the Syrians. Barak's poll ratings dropped sharply with fewer and fewer Israelis viewing him favourably.

Out of Lebanon

Barak now had to rearrange his priorities. For the collapse of the Israeli–Syrian peace talks also had unfavourable implications on his plans to withdraw Israeli troops from Lebanon. We should recall that, back in 1985, the Labour–Likud unity government had removed the bulk of Israeli troops from Lebanon where they had remained after the 1982 invasion. Only some 1000 troops were left to patrol Israel's self-declared 'security zone' in southern Lebanon. But whereas these troops were successful in preventing cross-border terror attacks on Israel, they themselves became prime targets of a determined enemy – Hezbullah – which fought a guerrilla war against the Israelis inflicting severe blows on them. Lebanon in the late 1990s turned into an Israeli-style Vietnam.

Barak was determined to withdraw from Lebanon, but he preferred to do so as part of a peace deal with Syria. He thought that he could use Lebanon as a trading card in talks with Assad by which Israel would agree to the continuation of Syrian domination in Lebanon and, in return, Assad would ensure quiet on Israel's northern border and rein in Hezbullah which was armed and encouraged by Syria and Iran. Now, however, with no Syrian partner to agree on such a deal, Barak publicly fixed July 2000 as the date on which he would make a unilateral withdrawal from Lebanon. Perhaps he was still pinning his hopes on Assad's coming forward after all and striking a deal with Israel in order to maintain Syria's hegemony in Lebanon. But it was all wishful thinking. For even Barak's threat – and threat it indeed was – of a unilateral withdrawal in no way moved Assad from his position or if it did the Syrian President gave no indication that it had. Now, realizing that Assad would not budge and concluding that there was no point of remaining in Lebanon and suffering more casualties, Barak brought forward his plans to leave Lebanon and before dawn on 24 May 2000 issued instructions to IDF Chief of General Staff Lt.-Gen. Shaul Mofaz to withdraw from Lebanon.

The hasty but meticulously organized withdrawal from Lebanon, which was dubbed operation Orech Ruach (Operation Stamina), went according to plan and took place under sporadic but sometimes heavy Hezbullah mortar and rocket fire. With the air force and artillery providing covering fire, Israeli troops in armoured personnel carriers and escorted by tanks pulled back from their outposts in southern Lebanon, blowing each one up as they left so that Hezbullah guerrillas could not use them. This task of destruction was completed by Israeli warplanes firing missiles from the air. Towards morning and after a night drive, dust-covered Israeli soldiers yelped with joy as they crossed into Israel at the Good Fence north of Metulla. It was a smooth evacuation without loss, marking a successful end to a sad chapter in Israel's history and allowing Barak to take credit for a solid achievement.

Camp David II

Peace negotiations with Assad having collapsed and the Syrian leader himself disappearing from the scene on 10 June after years of illness, Barak was left – again – with Yasser Arafat – the one and only game in town. Now the idea of convening a Begin–Sadat Camp David-style summit meeting between Barak and Arafat under Clinton's auspices began to take shape. Arafat was not at all keen, for he suspected that at such a summit he would be faced with a Clinton–Barak front and should the meeting collapse he would be held responsible for its failure. Arafat also felt that the gulf between the Israeli and Palestinian position was so wide that it was wiser to try and narrow it by talks at a lower level before convening a summit meeting of leaders, which, if it failed, could increase desperation and perhaps even lead to increased violence in the Middle East. As for Barak – he was a great believer in that the job of leaders is to take hard decisions and that it was for him personally and for Arafat to meet, take the bull by the horns and sort out – once and for all – the Israeli–Palestinian conflict. He thus put increasing pressure on the American President to issue invitations for a summit meeting, which Clinton, keen to seal his own legacy as a Middle East broker of peace, did by calling on Barak and Arafat to come to Camp David to sort out their differences.

At home, in the mean time, the Prime Minister was exposed to growing political pressure by elements fearing that, keen to strike a deal with Arafat, Barak would sell Israel's interests cheaply. Thus, on the eve of Barak's departure to Camp David, three political partners, Yisrael Be'aliya and the religious Mafdal and Shas, resigned from the coalition which effectively disintegrated with support in the Knesset being slashed from 68 to 42. Also, the Sharon-led opposition, smelling blood, lodged a no-confidence motion in Barak's mission, hoping to topple the Prime Minister. Addressing his opponents, Barak reiterated to the Knesset his commitments, namely that in the coming Camp David summit he would fight against a return to the pre-June 1967 lines, for a united Jerusalem under Israeli sovereignty, against a foreign army west of the Jordan river, for blocks of Jewish settlements to remain under Israeli sovereignty and against Israel taking responsibility for the Palestinian refugee problem. When the no-confidence vote was taken the Likud won a majority of 54 to 52, and although this fell short of the 61 members of Knesset needed to topple the government, it was nevertheless a severe blow to Barak on the eve of a most important diplomatic mission. That Monday night, 10 July 2000, Barak departed for Washington at the head of a delegation of 45. In spite of his troubles, Barak was confident that the people of Israel were still behind him; a poll published by *Yediot Aharonot* on 9 July showed that 52 per cent of Israelis said Barak should go to the summit against 45 per cent who said he should stay at home.

The summit opened on 11 July with President Clinton holding separate meetings, first with Arafat and then with Barak, before bringing them together. On arriving for their opening three-way meeting in the afternoon, Barak and Arafat did a little dance at the entrance to the Laurel Cabin at Camp David. It was a stubborn jig as each sidestepped so that the other would be the first to enter the cubicle of decision making. In the end, with Barak's hand on his elbow, Arafat crossed the threshold just ahead of the Israeli Prime Minister. It was a light moment in a summit otherwise riddled with crises. There were two main stumbling blocks which more than anything else bogged the Camp David talks down. The first, Arafat's demand for right of return for Palestinian refugees to Israel proper and the second, the fate of Jerusalem, particularly that of the Temple Mount, holy to both Muslims and Jews.

The refugee question, it is worth mentioning, had been discussed comprehensively and in detail in the so-called 'Swedish channel' in which Israel's Foreign Minister, Shlomo Ben Ami, negotiated with the PLO official, Abu Ala'a, during the two months that preceded the Camp David summit. The Israeli line, in these talks, was to induce the Palestinians to make a historic concession on the right of return, in return for an Israeli consent to transfer to the Palestinians 90–91 per cent of the West Bank. The 'Swedish channel' resulted in an agreement in principle. Its first part was declaratory, consisting of a joint Israeli–Palestinian statement, vaguely worded, presenting a historical recapitulation of the right of return issue in a manner commensurate with the national narratives of Israelis and Palestinians. The other part focused on a mechanism aimed at resolving the refugee problem. The idea was that the Palestinians would forgo the total and sweeping right of return of the refugees and, in return, the international community would contribute $20 billion over a period of 15–20 years to settle all the claims of the refugees. The funds would be given as compensation to refugee households and as an aid grant to countries that would rehabilitate refugees. The Palestinian refugees would be given three options: to settle in the future Palestinian state, to remain where they were, or to immigrate to countries that would voluntarily open their gates to them, such as Canada, Australia and Norway. The Israelis agreed to receive 10,000 Palestinian refugees in Israel. Though the 'Swedish channel' Israelis and Palestinians did not reach a full agreement on the right of return issue, the Israeli impression was that the issue had been more or less resolved. They were, therefore, surprised that in the Camp David talks Arafat and his team had reverted to their traditional position – a demand that Israel agree unconditionally to the right of return of every refugee who so desired.

The parties at Camp David were not successful either in sorting out the Jerusalem problem and had to resort to bridging proposals made by Clinton. He proposed that Israel should have sovereignty over West and much of East Jerusalem and provide for Palestinian sovereignty in some parts of the traditionally Arab eastern sector. Israel would transfer Arab neighbourhoods in northern Jerusalem to the future Palestinian state, allow Palestinian administrative rule in the Old City and Muslim control over the Temple Mount, but with an overall Israeli sovereignty over this site. Later, this proposal was further modified in favour of the Palestinians, suggesting that all Arab neighbourhoods of Jerusalem should go to the Palestinians, the Jewish neighbourhoods to remain under Israeli control and Israeli sovereignty to continue over the Temple Mount. But what looked impossibly generous to President Clinton and Prime Minister Barak – they effectively proposed to divide Jerusalem – looked impossibly meagre to Arafat who, regarding himself as the guardian of the Holy City not just for Palestinians but for *all* Muslims, feared that should he compromise on Jerusalem he would go down in history as a traitor. So he turned down these proposals insisting, instead, that the Palestinians must have full sovereignty over all East Jerusalem, particularly over the Temple Mount.

By Wednesday night, 19 July, after eight days of intensive talks at Camp David, even President Clinton was ready to leave and close down the talks. But at the last minute Barak and Arafat decided to remain at the camp with Secretary of State Albright to continue their talks while the President flew to Okinawa for the G-8 economic summit. Deadlock continued. And when Clinton returned to Camp David on the evening of Sunday, 23 July, he plunged into assembly-line diplomacy and met small teams of Palestinian and Israeli negotiators to tackle each stumbling block. There was some progress, but by Monday night (the fourteenth day of the summit) it became clear that the two unresolved problems of the fate of the refugees and Jerusalem would prevent the conclusion of a deal. With Clinton feeling that it was for Arafat to compromise on these issues, he sent, on Tuesday, 25 July at 1.30 a.m., CIA Director George Tenet to Arafat's cabin to see if he could soften him up on these two remaining problems. But half an hour later Tenet returned empty-handed and told Clinton that Arafat would not budge. At 2:20, Saeb Erekat, one of Arafat's aides, walked into the living room of Aspen Lodge where President Clinton, Secretary of State Albright and National Security adviser Sandy Berger were sitting and read them a letter from Arafat, the gist of which was that the Palestinian leader saw no point in continuing talks on an agreement. With this, the summit ended in failure and a sombre and exhausted Clinton concluded 'with regret' that Israel and the Palestinians were not able to reach an agreement at this time. The war of words started almost immediately as both Barak and Arafat blamed each other for the failure of the summit. President Clinton publicly sided with Barak. He lavished praise on the Prime Minister for his flexibility and chided Arafat for his lack of it. 'The Prime Minister', remarked Clinton, 'moved forward from his initial position more than Chairman Arafat.'[28]

It was, nevertheless, a disappointing moment for Barak who since coming to power had conducted a high-risk strategy in which he had wagered almost everything on achieving peace with Arabs and Palestinians. By now it seemed that he had exhausted his efforts with both Syria and the Palestinians with no major breakthrough on either track.

Disentangling religion from politics

Barak returned to Israel empty-handed – his peace policies in ruins. Now in a challenge to the Orthodox parties that had dropped out of his coalition on the eve of the summit and desperate to demonstrate some solid achievement of his government, Barak turned to his Plan B – a 'social justice programme' – that was a part of his election campaign platform and of which a key element was the disentanglement of religion from politics in Israel.

By now, it is worth mentioning, Israel's religious parties were in such a strong position that successive Prime Ministers, Barak included, had, if they wished to survive in office and promote their national agendas, to agree to excessive religious demands. This situation was the result of the new balance of power in Israel's politics, first manifested in the 1977 election, where the two big blocs, Labour and the Likud, had more or less the same number of seats in the Knesset – a tie – and were thus totally dependent on the goodwill of the religious parties for political support. Not fools, the religious parties realized that it was in their power to crown or topple governments in Israel and they had no hesitation in blackmailing both the Likud and Labour as a price for providing political support. Thus, Prime Ministers were forced to transfer more and more funds to religious parties and institutions and, at the same time, agree to such demands as exempting the growing number of religious students from military service – which inevitably increased pressure on secular Israelis – and accept changes to laws which infringed on the secular character of the state of Israel. Yet – and this was so upsetting – accepting the excessive demands of the religious parties was no guarantee that in critical moments – when support in the Knesset was needed – the religious parties would deliver the goods and support the government.

On 19 August 2000, not much later after his return from the failed Camp David summit, Barak announced, at a meeting with ministers of the One Israel Party, his intention to 'move forward' with the social justice programme and to usher in a period of secular reforms in Israel. The first step, as Barak saw it, was to remove the nationality clause from the identity card that every Israeli must carry which records as

'Jewish' those qualifying as Jewish according to *halacha* – the religious law – or ethnicity for others – Arab, Russian, American or some other non-Jewish designation. By removing this clause Barak thought that a significant step could be made towards severing the connection between the Orthodox establishment, to whom this clause was sacred for it ensured the Jewish character of Israel, and the laws of the state. Barak's intention to remove the nationality clause from identity cards crossed a final hurdle when the Shin Bet, the domestic security service, announced that it would not oppose this move – as it did in the past – on security grounds.

In the mean time, while plans to erase the nationality clause got under way, Barak instructed the Justice and Acting Religious Affairs Minister, Yossi Beilin, to move ahead with plans to eliminate the Ministry of Religious Affairs and incorporate some of its functions into the Justice Ministry, while delegating other functions to the municipalities, the Chief Rabbinate or the Education Department. Barak also instructed the pace to be stepped up in drawing up plans to allow El Al flights and public transportation to operate on the Sabbath and on religious holidays, to impose two years of public service on rabbinical students who were exempt from the draft, and to institute civilian marriages in a shift from the previous practice which only allowed religious marriages supervised by the Orthodox establishment to take place. Barak also instructed steps to be taken to complete Israel's long-evolving draft constitution legislation – a move always opposed by the Orthodox establishment fearing that the laws might conflict with or even discriminate against religious precepts – and to introduce the teaching of English, mathematics and citizenship in all state-funded schools, notably religious schools.

Although after the failure of his peace initiatives Barak lost much of his appeal among Israelis, his 'secular revolution' still had solid backing in Israel, where as many as two-thirds of Israelis declared, according to opinion polls, their support. But Barak's change of track from making peace to implement a secular revolution was soon eclipsed and was eventually halted and dropped altogether by a greater event – a full-blown Palestinian rebellion in Jerusalem and the occupied territories, soon to be dubbed as the *Al-Aqsa intifada*.

The Al-Aqsa intifada

This was touched off by a controversial visit by opposition leader Ariel Sharon, on 28 September 2000, to the Temple Mount, the site of the

Al-Aqsa Mosque in Jerusalem and a place disputed by Israelis and Palestinians. Sharon made the visit in a bid to boost his political support within the Likud where he was challenged by ex-Prime Minister Benyamin Netanyahu who, cleared of corruption charges, was the favourite to unseat Sharon as the Likud leader. But the visit came at a sensitive moment and led to serious Palestinian disturbances which spread throughout Jerusalem and the rest of the occupied territories.

While Sharon's provocative visit was what triggered this wave of riots, deeper causes lay behind the disturbances, most notably the growing frustration of Palestinians towards a peace process that had won them only the shards of an independent state and had not as they had hoped improved their standard of living. From this point of view, Yasser Arafat was right in his objection to the convening of the Camp David summit; he feared– and he would be proved correct – that a failure of the summit might lead to ever growing frustration among Palestinians and hence to violence. Also, it would not be wrong to say that rather than Sharon it was Premier Barak who, by failing to read the political map and insisting on the convening of the Camp David summit, brought on Israel a war which would extract a terrible price.

Two days after Sharon's controversial visit to the Temple Mount, the violent death of 12-year-old Mohammed el-Durra, caught on camera by the television crew of a French news agency and shown throughout the world, provided the Palestinians with a martyr to rally behind and led to more bloodshed. A tit-for-tat vicious circle of violence now developed. On 7 October, a Palestinian mob demolished Joseph's Tomb, a Jewish holy site near the West Bank city of Nablus, and in retaliation an Israeli mob, in Tiberias, northern Israel, vandalized an ancient mosque. Then, on 12 October, two Israeli reservists were lynched by Palestinians after wandering by mistake into the West Bank city of Ramallah where one of their attackers was filmed on television proudly showing his blood-soaked hands. With such horrifying pictures shown on Israeli television Prime Minister Barak ordered immediate military retaliation sending helicopters and tanks to pound Palestinian targets on the West Bank and the Gaza Strip.

On 16 October, in an attempt to stop the bloodshed, President Clinton convened a hurried summit in Egypt, in which Premier Barak and Chairman Arafat participated, in addition to President Mubarak, Secretary General of the UN, Kofi Annan, King Abdullah of Jordan and Javier Solana, the Foreign Affairs Director for the European

Union. The talks inside the Jolie Ville Golf Resort were businesslike at their best and vituperative at their worst. It was a sign of their deteriorating relationship that Barak and Arafat did not make any commitments directly to each other, nor did they put anything in writing. Instead, on 17 October after 28 hours of intensive talks President Clinton squeezed an oral ceasefire plan from Arafat and Barak in which the two leaders committed themselves to taking immediate steps to end the bloodshed. It was also agreed at Sharm el-Sheikh to appoint an American-led fact-finding committee – known later as the Mitchell Committee – to investigate how the war in the territories started in the first place and how it could be sorted out. However, agreements made at the resort of Sharm el-Sheikh were not easy to implement on the ground, and back in the occupied territories the violence flared up as soon as news of a deal spread and was to continue in the days and weeks ahead.

In the mean time in Israel, Prime Minister Barak was fighting for his political survival. His minority government had just 30 seats in the Knesset and could count on the support of only another 10. Barak turned to leader of the opposition, Sharon, to join him in a broad-based coalition, but Sharon set out to exact a high price by demanding a veto over Barak's decisions on peace. Barak felt he could not accept this so, instead, on 30 October, persuaded the ultra-Orthodox Shas Party, which had 17 seats in the Knesset, to give him a 'safety net' for a period of a month. Shas agreed, but extracted a high price for this lifeline. It blackmailed Barak to consider the party's financial demands which ran at about $1 billion and to put on hold the secular revolution to disentangle religion from politics in Israel. While by agreeing – caving in would be a better description – to Shas's demands and dropping his secular revolution Barak could guarantee for himself a few more days in office, he inevitably turned against himself secular Israelis upset by his surrender to the religious.

On 2 November 2000, just before Barak and Arafat were to make yet another separate statement on the implementation of a new ceasefire, a car exploded in Jerusalem's outdoor Mahane Yehuda market, killing two Israelis and ruling out any possibility of announcing the new truce.

The continuing violent uprising of Palestinians in the occupied territories and suicide attacks in Israel proper ended Israelis' romance with peace and their confidence in their dovish Prime Minister, who after rising to power on an enormous wave of optimism and euphoria, had failed both in his attempts with Syria and even more disastrously with the Palestinians. By now Israelis were tired of Barak and some even blamed him for having brought war in his eagerness to make peace. Arrogant and over-confident but by no means a fool and by now lacking not only political but also public support, Barak understood that the game was up and on 9 December 2000 he went public to announce his resignation and called a new election for the post of Prime Minister – though not for the Knesset. He said:

> Out of national and personal responsibility, and in the light of the emergency situation the state is in, the confusion in the Knesset, and the need to continue to work to reduce the violence and to further the chances of peace and negotiations, I have decided to ask again for the public's confidence, and to get a new mandate to lead Israel on the way to peace, security and a new civil–social agenda.[29]

The Clinton Plan and the Taba talks

In the few remaining days before the general election Barak made a last-ditch attempt to strike a deal with Yasser Arafat on the basis of the so-called Clinton Plan. This programme – Clinton's last contribution to resolving the Israeli–Palestinian conflict before leaving office – dealt with the remaining stumbling blocks which had prevented the signing of peace between Israelis and Palestinians. It proposed that the boundary between the future Palestinian state and Israel should be based on the border preceding the June 1967 Six-Day War. Israel would evacuate isolated settlements, annex between 4 and 6 per cent of the West Bank – so as to include those areas where the majority of the settlers live – and, in return, compensate the Palestinians by giving them land elsewhere. The Clinton Plan also addressed security matters and proposed that the Palestinian state should not have offensive weapons, that an international force should be deployed along the border between Jordan and the future Palestinian state and that Israel should have early warning stations in the area. As for Jerusalem – a main stumbling block on the way to peace – Clinton proposed that its Arab neighbourhoods should become part of the future Palestinian state and home to the Palestinian capital, while Jerusalem's Jewish neighbourhoods should form part of Israel. The Holy Basin – an area smaller than three-quarters of a square mile and which includes the Western Wall, the adjacent sacred area and the Jewish Quarter – should go to Israel, while the Temple Mount should form part of the future Palestinian state. As for the Palestinian refugee problem – yet another major stumbling block – the Clinton Plan made five different proposals: rehabilitation of the Palestinian refugees where they lived; absorption into the Palestinian state; absorption into other countries around the world; absorption into the area that Israel will transfer to the Palestinians; and finally absorption of a limited and agreed upon number of refugees in Israel proper. Barak's government accepted the Clinton Plan on 28 December 2000 as a basis for further negotiations and Arafat, in a meeting he held with President Clinton on 2 January 2001, accepted the programme as well.

The road was now open for the renewal of peace talks – a sequel to the Camp David summit – and this took place in the Egyptian resort of Taba in January 2001 between an Israeli delegation led by Foreign Minister Shlomo Ben Ami and a Palestinian delegation led by Abu Ala'a. There was much progress in these talks, but still the gaps between the Israeli and Palestinian positions remained wide and the absence of the imaginative Clinton was acute. The talks ended on 27 January and the possibility of a Barak–Arafat summit to clinch a final deal was pencilled in for 30 January to take place in Sweden. But this never happened. Arafat, as if living on a different planet, launched a fierce verbal attack on Israel and the latter – also failing to seize the moment – continued with her harsh policies in the occupied territories. The last chance of clinching a deal between the Palestinians and a relatively moderate Israeli government, disappeared.

ENTER ARIEL SHARON

The revenge of Israeli Arabs, Russians and religious parties

A general election was held on 6 February 2001 and the victor was Ariel Sharon who swept into power with the largest margin ever in Israel's history – 62.5 per cent as against 37.4 per cent for Barak. Voter turnout, though, was 62 per cent, the lowest ever in Israel's history, a sharp drop from the 1999 election turnout of 78.7 per cent, and a far cry from Israel's voting average of close to 80 per cent. What led to this low turnout was the massive boycott by those who had propelled Barak into the country's top job of Prime Minister less than two years before and who, by now, disappointed with Barak's performance, decided to vote with their feet and not show up at the polling stations.

And thus ironically rather than Sharon winning the election it was Barak who lost it after failing to mobilize a large number of his core voters, mainly Arab Israelis and Russian immigrants.

Indeed, in the Arab sector turnout was only 25 per cent which was a stunning disappointment, though not unexpected, for the Barak Labour camp. The Israeli Arabs who so strongly supported Barak in the previous election were furious with the Prime Minister who, in spite of pledges, failed to appoint an Arab minister to serve in his government and under whose leadership Israeli police shot dead 13 Arab youths demonstrating against Sharon's visit to the Temple Mount, in October 2000. The low turnout in the Arab sector was, perhaps as anything else, a no-confidence vote in the Jewish establishment by the Arab citizens of Israel who showed – by staying in their cafés rather than going to the polling stations – that they did not believe that there was any difference between Barak and Sharon and that they were fed up with the ongoing discrimination against them.

Barak also failed to mobilize another important sector in Israel – the Russian community. Since the great wave of immigration from the former Soviet Union in the early 1990s, the 820,000 Russian immigrant voters became a determining factor in Israel's elections. In the three elections in which the new Russian immigrants participated in 1992, 1996 and 1999 they were the critical mass that toppled and crowned prime ministers. In 1992, they brought Yitzhak Rabin into power, in 1996, their vote led to the Netanyahu victory and in 1999 they helped turn the tide against him with 58 per cent voting for Ehud Barak. While in the 1999 election almost 94 per cent of the eligible Russian voters turned up to vote, this time around between 50 and 60 per cent of them stayed at home. The main reason for that was that unlike previous elections in which the vote was taken for both political parties and for the Prime Ministerial post, this time around the vote was only for the post of Prime Minister. Thus, while in the previous election the immigrants felt that by voting for a party they were strengthening their representation in the Knesset, this time around this did not apply and there was no incentive for them to turn up at the polling stations.

The Russian community was also deeply disappointed with Barak and upset by his dropping of the secular revolution. Being overwhelmingly secular and also being treated badly by Israel's religious establishment which often doubted the Russians' Jewishness, the Russian immigrants were in favour of separation of religious from state affairs. But, as shown, Barak failed to stick to his pledge to carry out this reform programme and he thus turned the Russians against him. Barak's willingness to put Jerusalem on the negotiation table at Camp David was yet another reason why the Russian immigrants turned against him. Israel's Russian immigrant community, it is worth mentioning here, has profound nationalist, right-wing leaning and being, for the most part, immigrants without a Jewish or deeply Zionist identity, they find nationalist symbols important. Jerusalem, for most of them, was regarded as an important symbol and a critical component in forming an identity while in the throes of the traumatic process of integration into Israeli society. Thus, when Barak put this symbol up for sale at Camp David, he frustrated not only the religious sector in Israel, but also the secular Russians. And then there was the *Al-Aqsa intifada* which further eroded support for Barak among Russian immigrants. The reason for this was that the number of casualties among the Russian immigrants was relatively high because many of them dwelt in Galilee, where the Israeli Arabs were rioting, and also in towns and cities with mixed communities such as Ramleh, Lod and Acre, as well in Jerusalem neighbourhoods bordering on Arab villages, where violence was relatively high. Thus, while anxiety over personal safety had been felt throughout the country and among all Israelis, it was stronger among the Russian Israelis. Additionally, Barak's policy of relative restraint in dealing with the Palestinian uprising was seen by the majority of the Russian immigrants as an expression of weakness.

What even further sealed Barak's fate in this election was the *Haredi* – ultra-Orthodox – vote. True, by nature – and it is a fact of political life in Israel – the *Haredim* are in the pocket of the right-wing candidate, but in this election, in particular, the Orthodox rabbis joined together to mobilize their followers to support Sharon and dump Barak as revenge for his attempt at secular revolution and his willingness, as they saw it, to give up Jerusalem and return Jewish land to Arab hands.

On 7 March 2001, Ariel Sharon presented his wall-to-wall coalition between left and right – something Israelis call a National Unity government – to the Knesset, appointing Labour's Shimon Peres, the architect of the Oslo Agreement with the Palestinians, as his Foreign Minister.

The life of the new Prime Minister of Israel, Ariel – Hebrew for lion – Sharon, was closely interwoven with that of Israel's history. He was born Ariel Sheinerman, the youngest of two children of Jewish immigrants from Russia, in Moshav Kfar Malal, a cooperative farming village in Palestine in 1928. Aged 14, he joined the Haganah and he later took part in the 1947 civil war in Palestine, where he was marked out as a brave, charismatic and self-confident leader. He had a natural talent for reading the battle quickly and accurately and for exploiting the terrain to maximize his advantage. Later in the war, Sharon fought against the Jordanian Legion in the battles of Latrun where his force was heavily mortared – 15 out of his 35 men were killed – and he himself was hit by two bullets. In 1953, Sharon established Unit 101, a commando force which he led on 15 October in an attack on the Jordanian village of Kibia in revenge for the killing of a Jewish mother and her two children. Carrying 600 kilograms of explosives, Sharon's team penetrated Kibia, blew up 45 houses, killed 69 Jordanians, half of them women and children, and retreated. By the time the 1956 Sinai Campaign broke out, Sharon was already a brigade commander and he fought against the Egyptians, notably in the bloody battle at the Mitla Pass where he lost 38 of his troops and was later accused of rushing into battle. Some years later, during the June 1967 war, Sharon as a divisional commander, distinguished himself when he planned and brilliantly executed a complex night operation which required meticulous timing and coordination between armoured, infantry and paratroop forces against the heavily fortified defence system of Abu Ageila and Umm Katif. In 1970–71, Sharon – by then OC Southern Command – led a ruthless campaign to root out Palestinian resistance in the Gaza Strip – by killings and expulsions he successfully quietened the area to the delight of then Defence Minister Moshe Dayan.

A few years later, Sharon's name dominated the news when he was the first to lead Israeli forces across the Suez Canal into Egypt during the 1973 Yom Kippur War. After that war, Sharon stood for election to the Knesset and in 1977 his Shlomzion Party won two seats and joined with Begin's Likud Party to form the government in which Sharon himself served as Minister of Agriculture. When Begin was elected Prime Minister for the second time in August 1981, he made Sharon his Defence Minister and it was Sharon who was the brain behind Israel's disastrous invasion to Lebanon. In 1983, in the wake of the Kahan report which investigated Israel's responsibility for the massacre of Palestinians at Sabra and Shatilla and which found Sharon indirectly responsible for the event, he was forced to resign his post. In the coming years, when the Likud was in power, Sharon served in a string of posts in government and with the resignation of Benyamin

Netanyahu as leader of the Likud, Sharon took his place and led his party to victory over Barak.

Sharon was physically large and, in many ways larger than life. Lacking discipline he was impulsive and rebellious, a tough, even brutal soldier and politician, outspoken in his opinions and caring nothing for the conventional rules. Prime Minister Begin once said that 'Sharon's a brilliant general, but a vicious man' which was echoed in what the first Prime Minister of Israel, Ben-Gurion, had once said of Sharon, namely that: 'He's a brilliant soldier but very economical with the truth.'

Managing the Al-Aqsa intifada

By the time Ariel Sharon took over as Prime Minister what began as a series of confrontations between Palestinian demonstrators and Israeli security had evolved into a wider array of violent actions and responses. There had been growing exchanges of fire between built-up areas, sniping incidents and clashes between Jewish settlers and Palestinians and car bombs and suicide bomber attacks in Israeli towns and cities.

Unlike his predecessor Barak who wished to clear the table by making peace with Arabs and Palestinians and put an end to the Arab–Israeli conflict, Sharon – believing peace was unattainable – only wished to contain Palestinian violence – which he himself triggered by his controversial visit to Jerusalem at a sensitive time – and then pursue open-ended interim understandings with the Palestinians. He vowed, though, 'not to negotiate under fire' and, believing that the Palestinians would eventually crack under military pressure, he went on to increase the use of force by dispatching F-16 warplanes and helicopters to bomb the West Bank and the Gaza Strip and by allowing Israeli forces to move deeper into Palestinian-controlled territories; his government also stepped up the policy of assassination of Palestinian activists.

Meanwhile, on 20 May 2001, the Mitchell report was published. We should recall that at the October 1999 summit meeting at Sharm el-Sheikh which was convened by President Clinton to calm down the violence in the Middle East, it was decided to appoint a committee to investigate the causes of the war and offer ways of sorting it out. Chaired by George J. Mitchell, former Member and Majority Leader of the United States Senate, who had achieved success in mediating over the Northern Ireland conflict, the committee visited the region – Israel and the occupied territories – and produced a document which provided for a series of steps beginning with a cessation of hostilities and gradually leading to the resumption of peace talks. The report called on the government of Israel and the Palestinian Authority 'to act swiftly and decisively' to stop the bloodshed, rebuild confidence and resume negotiations. It called on the Palestinian Authority to make clear through concrete action to Palestinians and Israelis that terrorism was unacceptable and to make a '100 per cent effort to prevent terrorist operations'. On the Israelis the Mitchell report called to 'freeze all settlement activity, including the natural growth of existing settlements' and to be more measured and careful in the use of force and try to 'minimize casualties'. The Palestinian Authority was called upon to prevent gunmen from using Palestinian urban areas to fire upon Israeli-populated areas, a tactic which 'places civilians on both sides at unnecessary risk'. The report also called on Israel 'to lift closures, transfer to the Palestinian Authority all tax revenues owed, and permit Palestinians who had been employed in Israel to return to their jobs and to ensure that security forces and settlers refrain from destruction of homes and roads, as well as trees and other agricultural property in Palestinian areas'. Both sides, in the light of damage inflicted to holy places, were called upon to consider a 'joint undertaking to preserve and protect holy places' and to endorse and support the work of Palestinian and Israeli non-governmental organizations involved in cross-community initiatives linking the two peoples.[30]

It was a balanced report with sensible recommendations. Prime Minister Sharon responded swiftly by declaring, on 22 May, a unilateral ceasefire, pledging that the IDF would shoot only in self-defence and would no longer carry out proactive operations. Response from the Palestinians, on the ground, was less than forthcoming and in a Tel Aviv nightclub, on 1 June, a suicide bomber blew himself up, killing 21 Israelis, mostly Russian immigrant teenagers. International pressure was soon mounting on Arafat to declare an immediate ceasefire which he did on 2 June.

A few days later, the Bush administration, which unlike the previous one of Bill Clinton had adopted a hands-off approach to the Middle East conflict, dispatched CIA Director George Tenet to the region to stabilize the situation by turning the ceasefires, declared separately by Israel and the Palestinian Authority, into a signed agreement, restore security cooperation between the parties and create a basis for the implementation of the Mitchell report, leading to political talks. This then led to the so-called 'Tenet Cease-Fire Plan of 13 June 2001' or 'the Tenet Understanding'. The importance of this plan was that together with the Mitchell report, it became the blueprint to end the *Al-Aqsa intifada* and embark on political talks to sort out the dispute between Israelis and Palestinians.

But comprehensive as this plan had been, it was still not enough to stop the violence and bloodshed. Thus, on 9 August 2001, a suicide bomber, with a 5–10 kilogram bomb packed with nails, screws and bolts strapped to his body, blew himself up at the Sbarro Pizzeria in downtown Jerusalem, killing 15 and wounding 130. Israel responded on the next day by seizing the Orient House, the unofficial Palestinian headquarters in Jerusalem and a symbol of Palestinian aspirations for an independent state, and by closing down nine other Palestinian buildings. F-16s fired rockets at police headquarters in Ramallah destroying it, and tanks levelled a Gaza Strip police position. The vicious circle of violence continued when, on 13 August, a suicide bomb attack at the Wall Street Café in Kiryat Motzkin, a Haifa suburb, injured 15 Israelis.

The Palestinians who carried out the attacks in Jerusalem and Haifa came from Jenin, a Palestinian town in the West Bank which was handed over to the Palestinian Authority in 1995 under the interim peace accord agreed at the Oslo peace talks. Jenin now became the target and, on 14 August 2001, Prime Minister Sharon dispatched troops and tanks into this West Bank town – the first major Israeli incursion into a Palestinian-controlled area since the beginning of the *Al-Aqsa intifada*. With helicopters flying above, Israeli tanks and armoured bulldozers destroyed a Palestinian police station and two checkpoints and took up positions outside the governor's residence before withdrawing from the town. Political assassination of Palestinian leaders also continued, and on 27 August 2001 helicopters fired two laser-guided missiles into the West Bank office of Abu Ali Mustafa, Secretary-General of the Popular Front for the Liberation of Palestine, and killed him.

Keen to calm down the situation in the Middle East in order to recruit more countries to the war against terrorism in the wake of the 11 September terrorist attack on New York and Washington by Bin-Laden's Al-Qaida group, President Bush pressurized Israel and the Palestinians to hold talks and stop the violence. On 26 September 2001, Foreign Minister Shimon Peres and Palestinian Authority

Chairman Arafat met in the Gaza Strip International airport and pledged to resume security coordination and exert maximum effort to enforce a ceasefire. But, as before, events on the ground made any attempt to implement a lasting ceasefire impossible. Thus, on 2 October at around 5.30 pm, Palestinians infiltrated into the Jewish settlement of Alei Sinai in the Gaza Strip, opened fire, killed two Israelis and wounded at least 15. In response, Sharon suspended the Peres–Arafat ceasefire and dispatched forces to attack the Gaza Strip. Yet another ceasefire was dead and buried and the tit-for-tat vicious circle of violence continued.

A sheer escalation of this war came in the wake of the assassination, on 17 October 2001, of Israel's Minister of Tourism, Rehavam Ze'evi, by Palestinian members of the Popular Front for the Liberation of Palestine. Ze'evi, a former general, was a right-wing politician and leader of the Moledet ('Homeland') political party which advocated the 'transfer' of Palestinians from the West Bank and the Gaza Strip. His inflammatory rhetoric and his right-wing political views angered the Palestinians who turned him into a prime target. His killing, so the Popular Front for the Liberation of Palestine later stated, was a tit-for-tat retribution for Israel's assassination of the group's Secretary-General, Abu Ali Mustafa, on 27 August. Ze'evi's assassination shocked the nation for although politically many differed with him, this was, nevertheless, the first time in Israel's history that a leading politician was assassinated by Arabs. Prime Minister Sharon, blaming Arafat for encouraging attacks on Israelis, led his Cabinet in issuing the Palestinian leader with an ultimatum, namely to arrest and put on trial the assassins of the Israeli minister. But with Arafat dragging his feet and failing to respond to the Israeli demand, Sharon ordered his forces to invade cities and towns under direct Palestinian Authority control – the forces would later withdraw from there – and he also ordered the bombing of Arafat's private helicopter and he dispatched tanks to surround Arafat's headquarters in Ramallah.

The balance sheet: society and the economy

The Al-Aqsa intifada was a bloody affair overshadowing all other matters of Israeli life. In 2001 alone, there were 1794 terrorist attacks in Israel and in the occupied territories in which 208 Israelis were killed and more than 1563 wounded. The war had a strong impact on society and on relations between Israelis, Arabs and Palestinians. In polls held after six months of war, 58 per cent of Israelis said that their opinion of the Palestinians had changed for the worse. Some 37 per cent reported that this war caused them to adopt more hawkish opinions – as against 13 per cent who said they became more dovish. As for the prospects of peace, 63 per cent of Israelis said that it was impossible to reach a peace agreement with the Palestinians with a majority of 51 per cent declaring that the *Al-Aqsa intifada* reduced the chances for peace. A very large majority of Israelis believed, according to these polls, in the greater use of force, with 71 per cent supporting the assassination of Palestinian leaders who are linked to terrorist acts.[31] For Israelis Arafat was the chief political casualty of this war, completely losing his status as a man of peace even among Israelis from the left, mainly of Meretz, the most prominent Israeli peace camp party. As a result of the *Al-Aqsa intifada*, the centre of gravity in Israel's political map has shifted to the right.

Relations between Jewish Israelis and Arab Israelis deteriorated as the violence and tensions between the two communities grew substantially. In polls, 55 per cent of Israeli Jews reported that their opinion of the Israeli Arabs had become worse. The brighter side of this, though, was that in the process of attempting to understand the motives behind the Israeli Arabs' demonstrations in Israel, many Israeli Jews came to realize that the Israeli Arab riots were a reaction not only to feelings of solidarity with their brethren under military occupation in the occupied territories, but also to historic prejudices and inequalities in Israel itself, where the average income of Arabs in the early 2000s was the lowest of any ethnic group in the country, the infant mortality rate was almost twice as high as for Jews (9.6 per 1000 births, compared with 5.3) and Arab Israelis were discriminated against when it came to social security and other benefits. Perhaps above all, the *Al-Aqsa intifada* increased the sense of frustration within Israeli society towards a peace process which rather than producing security, brought war and devastation.

The Israeli economy suffered enormously as a result of the war and in 2001 Israel found itself deep in recession, perhaps as bad as that which gripped the nation in 1953. In 2001, the number of unemployed reached 258,000, the standard of living dropped by 7.2 per cent, investment in the economy dropped 33 per cent and the economy as a whole contracted 0.5 per cent.

At the time of writing the *Al-Aqsa intifada* continues, the economy is in a terribly bad shape and morale at a low ebb as bombs explode in

Israeli towns and cities. Israel's society is deeply divided, with 40 per cent of Israelis wanting the army to retake land held by the Palestinian Authority and hardliners urging the government to topple Arafat. On the other end of the spectrum, Israel's dovish opposition calls on the government for a unilateral pull-out from the occupied territories and a new round of peace talks.

Appendix I
The Dayan el-Tohami Protocol, 1977

This is the protocol – never before published – of the conversation between Israel's Foreign Minister Moshe Dayan and President Anwar Sadat's emissary Hassan el-Tohami, in Morocco, which shows that, contrary to common belief, no promise was made a priori to President Sadat, before his arrival in Israel a short time later, that he would get the Sinai back.

GENERAL

1. The Foreign Minister [of Israel] arrived in Rabat on a special flight at 19.15, 16 September 1977, accompanied by his bodyguard, the deputy of [Colonel] Dalimi [the liaison officer between Israel and Morocco] and our representative in Morocco . . .
2. On their arrival the visitors were taken to the King's guest house which is situated by his private villa.
3. After a short break Dalimi took Dayan and our representative, at 20.45, to the King's residence to which they were led through a back door used for special and secret guests.
4. The group was received by the Court Minister who then gave Dayan the opportunity to get rid of his disguise and become himself. The group was brought into one of the modern sitting rooms where the King and his entourage were waiting for Dayan's arrival.
5. As Dalimi explained [to us] Tohami had asked to see the King before his meeting [with Dayan] and therefore the King had talked with him before our arrival . . . the participants sat in a half circle

where tea tables were scattered. Two servants waited on them . . .
because Dalimi himself led us [into the meeting room] no one
except for these two servants saw Dayan. The meeting took four
hours without a break and it continued for a short while even when
the King left to see his mother who had come to visit him. . . . From
the beginning there was a relaxed and friendly atmosphere. . . . At
the start of the meeting with Tohami, Dayan gave the King a set of
Canaanite weapons from his private collection.

THE TALKS

The King. He opened by presenting Tohami as someone who enjoyed
the full support of Sadat and who is guided by the supreme aim of
[making] peace and as someone who came [to Morocco] to conduct
constructive, informal and absolutely secret talks. Only [President]
Sadat, his deputy [Hosni Mubarak] and Tohami himself know about the
meeting which could be the start of a new era of direct contacts in which
the two sides [Israel and Egypt] could clarify all the relevant issues . . .
these direct talks are of supreme importance but the USA must not know
about them until a basic agreement has been reached [between Israel
and Egypt]. . . . After Dayan and Tohami had cleared the way then Begin
would come to talk with Sadat. Dayan should refrain from enlarging the
circle of people who know about the secret [talks] and [he should] come
to the next meeting without bringing any other people. If Dayan thinks
it could benefit the process he should bring the head of Mossad [Yitzhak
Hofi] with him. . . . The issue of giving back the [occupied] land to its
sovereign owners is the most important of all. The King acknowledges
(the King looked at Tohami) that the [occupied] land held by Israel is
the only guarantee for [Israel's] security and, therefore, it is necessary
to find, by mutual agreement, other equivalent guarantees. It is necessary to find an acceptable solution for the holy city [of Jerusalem] . . .
so that it would not be an obstacle to peace. The Palestinian [problem]
is the most complicated issue. The King accepted Dayan's view that [the
Palestinians] pose a danger to Israel's future as well as endangering the
King of Jordan. But it is necessary to tackle the [Palestinian] problem
and solve it in a satisfactory way. In fact, the Palestinian [problem] is an
issue [to be resolved collectively by] the Arab states, so they can control
[the Palestinians] . . . the Palestinian problem is basically an Arab problem. . . .

Tohami. Meeting you Dayan here under the roof of the King is a grat-
ifying thing for me. All these years I have thought that I'd meet you on
the battlefield . . . but here we are both in search of peace, thanks to the
efforts of the King and the trust that Sadat has in [Prime Minister]
Begin and you. You are strong and brave leaders and we believe you
would dare to take crucial decisions for the sake of peace. . . . Sadat
did not trust your previous [Labour] government but he does believe
in you. . . . Sadat is very serious about peace . . . we should discuss it
between us without, at this stage, including the USA. At a later stage,
after sorting the matter out, we should tell them. Sadat believes the
time has come to discuss all the issues. He has previously been
approached by [President Nicolae] Ceauşescu [of Romania] who
suggested arranging a meeting [with Rabin's Labour government] but,
at the time, Sadat did not believe this had any value. Now with you he
believes that it is possible to find a solution. . . . But the main problem
is the return of [the occupied] lands. This is a problem of sovereignty,
of national dignity and the continuation of Sadat's [rule]. . . . If Begin
accepted the principle of withdrawal it would be later possible to deal
with all the [other] important issues. It is possible to avert the danger
from the radical Palestinians and it is possible for the Arab states to
look after them. The Palestinians will become a more [negatively]
influential factor if we don't find a solution to their national aspirations
. . . the Palestinian enclave in the east (that is on the West Bank – AB)
could be linked to Jordan where Saudi Arabia and Egypt could
together control the radical [Palestinians] and keep the King of Jordan
on his throne. In the south Egypt would give guarantees and control
the Palestinians in Egypt itself. You [consider] the USA and USSR [a
guarantee for your safety], very well, but it would be better for both of
us to exclude the latter . . . let Begin agree to the principle of withdrawal for the sake of peace between our nations. Without this all our
sincere intentions are doomed because this is the only key for a
brighter future . . . the main issue is the [occupied] territories. . . . Sadat
could negotiate about all the other issues but not our sovereignty over
the land. . . .

The Foreign Minister of Morocco. [To Tohami] What would happen if
Sadat and Begin got on satisfactorily but the Syrian President [Assad]
decided not to join [the peace process?] And don't we have to plan an
Arab stance to prevent such a possibility? To this the King and Tohami
answered negatively, believing that the President of Syria would

follow Sadat's lead with the active support of the King [of Morocco] and [King] Fahad [of Saudi Arabia.]

Moshe Dayan. Considers himself no more than Begin's envoy and, therefore, he would have to bring all the issues to Begin and [he] can't [promise anything] before hearing from Begin . . . we would have to bring before Begin Sadat's demand for Begin's pledge of [an Israeli] withdrawal as a precondition for any further discussions . . . (Dayan turns to the King and Tohami) 'You have to understand that whatever Begin's final decision he would have to bring the matter before his government and the Knesset [for approval]. No Israeli leader . . . could adopt such a decision without the Knesset. These are the rules of our system . . .' (turns to Tohami) 'I can't tell if Begin would accept your request . . . it might be that we would agree, it might be that we would not . . . what would happen to our settlements in the far south [of the Sinai] if we withdrew? Would you let them live there under your sovereignty?'

Appendix 2
Draft Declaration of Principles,
Israel–Syria, 1992

This is the Draft Declaration of Principles (DOP) – never before published – which was prepared in Damascus between May and August 1992. It was offered to the Israelis by the Syrians as a working paper on 31 August 1992. Israelis and Syrians discussed this draft in the Washington talks, concentrating mainly on paragraphs 5(a) and 7.

INTRODUCTION

The peace process is entering its eleventh month without any meaningful advance. And the hopes and expectations which were raised just before the sixth round about what was described as a change in Israeli policy have not – so far – materialized.

We feel that it is about time – if we really want to realize the objectives of the peace process – to spell out clearly and without ambiguity, in an even and balanced document, the basic principles without which no peace can prevail, as well as the obligations and commitments of the two sides in fulfilment of those principles.

The document which we present today observes closely such criteria and aims at enabling the two sides to have before them a constructive and well-balanced text which responds to the basic legitimate requirements of both sides. It is not a response to the two papers presented previously by the Israeli delegation because the said papers were either a mere listing of Israeli demands and preconditions or an inaccurate assumption of 'commonality of views'.

Nor does the proposed document deal with every element relating to the wider Arab–Israeli conflict, due to the fact that these other, no less essential elements, such as withdrawal from the other occupied Arab territories, Palestinian national rights, settlement activities in other occupied territories, and the right of return of Palestinian refugees, are under discussion in other Arab–Israeli bilateral groups and their solutions are essential for the achievement of a really comprehensive peace.

Thus, the draft declaration which we present is a fair and equitable document which does not neglect any of the vital concerns of the parties. It is a real challenge for a peace which is just, comprehensive and lasting.

DRAFT DECLARATION OF PRINCIPLES

1. The objective of peace

Both sides declare their determination to establish a comprehensive, just and lasting peace in the region through the full implementation – with good faith and without delay – of Security Council Resolutions 242 and 338 and the principle of returning Arab land in exchange for peace.

2. Comprehensiveness of the solution

Both sides recognized that for peace to be real and durable, it must be inclusive of all parties to the Arab–Israeli conflict and comprehensive of all fronts. In consequence and although they reckon that the details of issues and problems dealt with by the various groups of the Arab–Israeli bilateral negotiations vary from one group to the other, they nevertheless affirm that the ultimate outcome of the peace process must lead to a comprehensive settlement to all the parties of the Arab–Israeli conflict in such a way as to achieve the above-mentioned peace objective.

3. Security

Both sides acknowledge their mutual right to security and recognize that the security of any party cannot be claimed or guaranteed at the expense of the security of the other party.

4. Seriousness and continuity of the negotiations

Both sides affirm their resolve to pursue their bilateral negotiations with seriousness and positive spirit with the aim of reaching the desired comprehensive settlement at the earliest possible time. In this respect, they express their disposition to persist in these negotiations as long as it is necessary to attain the stated objective and as long as the discussions were characterized by the seriousness and the good faith which both undertook to maintain.

5. Machinery of implementation

In accordance with the first paragraph of this declaration, the two parties shall immediately begin their discussions to examine the machinery and steps necessary to implement Security Council Resolution 242 of 1967, within a precise and agreed timetable. Such a plan of execution must observe the simultaneity of the steps and obligations incumbent upon both parties in accordance with the principle of 'land for peace' and their obligations under the UN Charter and the principles of international law. These steps should include mutually and equally the following, in all clarity:

A. Total Israeli withdrawal from the Syrian Golan occupied in 1967; the evacuation and dismantling of all the settlements which have been established on the occupied Syrian Territory since that date in contradiction to the Geneva Conventions, the principles of international law and UN resolutions.

B. Termination of all claims or states of belligerency between the two sides.

C. Acknowledgement and respect by the two parties of the sovereignty, political independence and territorial integrity of each other and of all states in the area and of their equal right and the right of all States to live in peace within secured and recognized boundaries in conformity with the principles of international legitimacy.

6. Working groups

The two parties shall constitute – within the framework of the implementation of the steps referred to in the previous paragraph – special working groups for military, technical or any other specific purpose as shall be required for the execution of the steps of Resolution 242 mentioned above in paragraph 5.

7. Security arrangements and guarantees

As an expression of their good faith and their obligation to respect the territorial integrity and political independence of each other, the two parties declare their disposition to undertake and accept the necessary measures to guarantee their security in a parallel and reciprocal manner including the possibility of establishing on both sides and on equal footing demilitarized zones or zones with reduced armaments and to obtain from the Security Council, from particular states or from both security guarantees without any prejudice to the sovereignty of any party nor to the principle of equal rights for both.

8. Respect of the international principles and humanitarian conventions

Both sides affirm their obligation to respect the principles and purposes of the UN Charter and international legitimacy. They undertake as well to respect the Geneva 1949 conventions and all international humanitarian conventions and agreements without distinction as to race, sex, language or religion.

9. Registration of the agreement with the UN

The executive steps of Resolutions 242 and 338 detailed above and the obligations ensuing therefrom shall be incorporated in a peace agreement to be registered – after endorsement by the Security Council – with the General Secretariat of the United Nations Organization.

Notes

1 THE ROAD TO STATEHOOD, 1897–1947

1. 'The Basle Declaration, 1897', in Walter Laqueur and Barry Rubin (eds), *The Israel–Arab Reader* (London, 1995), p. 10 (my emphasis).
2. Extracts from Herzl's The Jewish State, in Walter Laqueur and Barry Rubin (eds), *The Israel–Arab Reader,* p. 6.
3. Theodor Herzl, *Diaries,* 2 June 1895 as cited in Yoram Hazony, *The Jewish State: The Struggle for Israel's Soul* (New York, 2000), p. 100.
4. About the SNS's operations, see 'Personal Recollections: Soldiers Diaries, S.N.S., 1938', in Haganah Archive (HA), 80/69/15; also 'Organization and Training of Special Night Squads', Wingate's Papers, HA, 80/69/10, August 1938.

2 THE BIRTH OF ISRAEL, 1948–1949

1. Walter Laqueur and Barry Rubin, *The Israel–Arab Reader,* p. 108.
2. David Ben-Gurion, *War Diary* (Tel Aviv, 1983), entry for 14 May 1948 (Hebrew).
3. Moshe Dayan, *Story of My Life* (London, 1976) p. 96.
4. Abba Eban, *Autobiography* (New York, 1977), p. 125.
5. David Ben-Gurion, *War Diary,* 29 June 1948.
6. Folke Bernadotte, *To Jerusalem* (Tel Aviv, 1952), pp. 132 and 137 (Hebrew).
7. Michael Bar-Zohar, *Ben-Gurion,* (London, 1987), pp. 165-6.
8. David Shipler, 'Israel Bars Rabin from Relating 1948 Eviction of Arabs', *New York Times,* 23 October 1979.
9. David Ben-Gurion, *War Diary,* 15 July 1948.
10. Yitzhak Shamir, *Summing Up: an Autobiography* (Boston, 1994), p. 75.
11. Yitzhak Rabin, *Pinkas Sherut* (Tel Aviv, 1979), p. 65 (Hebrew).
12. Dan Kurzman, *Soldier of Peace, The Life of Yitzhak Rabin 1922–1955* (London, 1998), p. 148.
13. David Ben-Gurion, *From Ben-Gurion's Diary: The War of Independence* (Tel Aviv, 1986), p. 3435.
14. The above quotations are from David Ben-Gurion, *War Diary,* 15 July, 5 July, 10 November and 19 November 1948.

3 YEARS OF CONSOLIDATION, 1950–1966

1. Abba Eban, *An Autobiography*, p. 203.
2. Moshe Dayan, *Story of My Life*, p. 187.
3. Moshe Sharett, *Personal Diary* (Tel Aviv, 1978) (Hebrew), entry for 10 January 1955.
4. Moshe Dayan, *Story of My Life*, p. 187.
5. The above quotations are from Moshe Sharett, *Personal Diary*, Vol. 1, p. 202, line 20; also Sharett's comments about Dayan in his diary Vol. 3, 16 January 1955 (p. 666, comment number 6); also Vol. 3, p. 705, line 22 and Vol. 5, p. 1371, lines 21–4 (respectively).
6. Benjamin Givly to author, Tel Aviv, 27 January 1997.
7. Avraham Dar to author, Atlit, 26 January 1997.
8. Robert Dassa and Marcelle Ninio, Tel Aviv, 24 January 1997, Avraham Dar and Benjamin Givly to author.
9. Ariel Sharon to author, Havat Ha'Shikmim, 1 March 1997 and Jerusalem, 7 April 1991.
10. Letter Sharett to Ben-Gurion, 1 March 1955, Ben-Gurion Archive (BGA), Correspondence file (emphasis added).
11. Moshe Sharett, *Personal Diary*, entry for 22 June 1955.
12. Moshe Dayan, *Diary of Sinai Campaign* (London, 1965), p. 13; Shabtai Teveth, *Dayan, Biography* (Tel Aviv, 1971), p. 441 (Hebrew); Mordechai Bar On 'The Sinai Campaign Causes and Achievements', *Skira Hodshit*, Vol. 33, Numbers 10–11 (15 December 1986), p. 9 (Hebrew).
13. Moshe Dayan, *Diary of Sinai Campaign*, pp. 14-15 (emphasis in the original).
14. Gideon Rafael, *Destination Peace, Three Decades of Israeli Foreign Policy, a Personal Memoir* (London, 1981), p. 31.
15. Yisrael Beer, *Israel's Security, Yesterday, Today Tomorrow* (Tel Aviv, 1966), p. 226 (Hebrew).
16. David Ben-Gurion, *Diaries*, entry for 3 September 1956, IDFA.
17. Shimon Peres to author, the Knesset, Jerusalem, 11 March 1991.
18. Shimon Peres, *Battling for Peace* (London, 1995), p. 130.

4 THE SIX-DAY WAR AND AFTERWARDS, 1967–1973

1. Rami Tal, 'Moshe Dayan, Soul Searching', *Yediot Aharonot*, 27 April 1997 (Hebrew).
2. 'Soviet Official's Comments on Soviet Policy on the Middle Eastern War – CIA Report of Conversation with Soviet Official re June War', LBJ Library, 82–156, doc. 8420. See also the testimony of the Head of the Egypt Department in the Soviet Foreign Ministry, Evgeny Pyrlin, which shows that indeed the false report was released on purpose in order to draw America into the war, in Ahron Bregman and Jihan el-Tahri, *The Fifty Years War: Israel and the Arabs*, (New York, 2000), p. 75.
3. 'Text of Nasser's Speech on the Blockade of Aqaba', *The New York Times*, 26 May 1967.

4. Miriam Eshkol to author, Jerusalem, 30 January 1997.
5. Yitzhak Rabin, *Pinkas Sherut*, p. 173 (Hebrew); also Ariel Sharon to author, Jerusalem, 7 April 1991.
6. Yitzhak Rabin to author, Tel Aviv, 21 March 1991.
7. Meir Amit to author, 26 January 1997, Ramat Gan.
8. About this see Moshe Dayan in a summary of the 1967 War (28 July 1967), Yad Tabenkin Archive (YTA), 15 (Galili), 48/1/3, p. 3 (Hebrew); also Yitzhak Rabin to author, Tel Aviv, 21 March 1991; also Haim Bar-Lev to author, Jerusalem, 19 March 1991; also Ezer Weizman to author, Caesaria, 17 February 1992.
9. Aharon Yariv to the author, Tel Aviv, 27 March 1991; also letter from Yariv to author, Tel Aviv, 2 June 1992.
10. Note from Josef Nevo to Minister Galili in the Wednesday, 7 June, 12.30 meeting of the Cabinet, in YTA, 15/3/326-2.
11. Dayan speaking at a press conference, see reports on 8 June 1967 in the *Financial Times, New York Times, The Guardian*.
12. Yitzhak Rabin to author, Tel Aviv, 21 March 1991.
13. Ariel Sharon, *Warrior, An Autobiography* (London, 1989), p. 463.
14. As cited in Shabtai Teveth, *Moshe Dayan: Biography* (Jerusalem, 1972), p. 334.
15. Letter from Yeshayahu Gavish to author, Ramat Ha'Sharon, 23 September 1991; also Gavish to author, Ramat Ha'Sharon, 5 January 1992.
16. Moshe Dayan, *Story of My Life*, p. 324.
17. As cited in Ahron Bregman and Jihan el-Tahri, *The Fifty Years War*, p. 91 (British version).
18. Interview with former OC Central Command Uzi Narkiss, *Ha'aretz*, 31 December 1997 (Hebrew).
19. Incoming telegram, US Department of State, Summary of Conversation, Secret, June 1967, 3:27, E.O.12356, sec. 3.4., NIJ 94.36, NARA date 7.18.95.
20. Haim Bar-Lev to author, Jerusalem, 19 March 1991.
21. The testimony of Popov Konstantin Ilych, Balashikha, 28 September 1996, in the author's archive.
22. Moshe Dayan, 'What We Stand for and Why', Speech in Armon cinema, 4 May 1970 (Hebrew).
23. Anwar el-Sadat, *In Search of Identity* (London, 1978), p. 219.
24. Interview with Joseph Sisco, Washington, 19 March 1997; also interview with Alfred 'Roy' Atherton who had accompanied Sisco on this visit, Washington, 19 October 1996 in the author's archive.

5 YOM KIPPUR WAR AND THE DEATH OF LABOUR, 1973–1977

1. The above quotations are from an interview with Henry Kissinger, Washington, 24 July 1997, in the author's archive.
2. Interview with General Saad el-Din Shazly, Cairo, 24 February 1997, in the author's archive.

3. About this visit to Moscow, see Mohamed Heikal, *The Road to Ramadan* (London, 1975), pp. 83–90; also Eli Zeira, *The October 73 War, Myth against Reality* (Tel Aviv, 1993), p. 87 (Hebrew).
4. Anwar el-Sadat, *In Search of Identity*, p. 318 (my emphasis).
5. Letter of Anwar Sadat to Brezhnev, as cited in Anwar el-Sadat, *In Search of Identity*, p. 320, and interview with Pavel Akopov, Moscow, March 1997, in the author's archive.
6. Interview with Field Marshal Abdul Ghani el-Gamassy, Cairo, 24 February 1997, in the author's archive.
7. Anwar el-Sadat, *In Search of Identity*, p. 318.
8. Amnon Barzilai, 'Zeira: a Double Agent had Strengthened My Adherence to a Wrong Conception in Yom Kippur', *Ha'aretz*, 28 October 1998 (Hebrew).
9. Anwar el-Sadat, *In Search of Identity*, p. 241.
10. As disclosure of the source of these quotes might expose the identity of the Son-in-Law no references are given here.
11. This document was first published in Ahron Bregman and Jihan el-Tahri, *The Fifty Years War*, pp. 118–19. By exposing this rare document we have managed to confirm rumours of the King's visit to Israel.
12. The above quotations are based on unpublished transcripts, but the reader can find extracts of this crucial discussion in Arie Braun, *Moshe Dayan and the Yom Kippur War* (Tel Aviv, 1992), pp. 39–40 (Hebrew).
13. Interview with Syrian Minister of Defence Mustapha Tlas, Damascus, 3 July 1997; Interview with General Saad el-Shazly, Cairo, 28 September 1996, both in the author's archive.
14. Haim Bar-Lev to author.
15. Yitzhak Hofi to author, Ramat Gan, 21 October 1996.
16. Moshe Dayan, *Story of My Life*, p. 488; Golda Meir, *My Life*, p. 361.
17. Moshe Dayan, *Story of My Life*, p. 494.
18. Matti Golan, *Shimon Peres, a Biography* (London, 1982), p. 143.

6 BEGIN'S YEARS, 1977–1983

1. Eric Silver, 'Begin's Secret Interviews', *The Jerusalem Report*, 21 May 1992; also Dan Pattir, 'With Nicolae Ceauşescu the President of Romania', *Middle East Insight*, May–June 1983, p. 12.
2. Translated from notes in Hebrew taken by an agent of the Mossad, Ben-Porat, in Ahron Bregman's archive.
3. Eric Silver, 'Begin's Secret Interviews', *The Jerusalem Report*, 21 May 1992; also *Yediot Ahronont*, 13 November 1987 (Hebrew).
4. Eric Silver, 'Begin's Secret interviews', *The Jerusalem Report*, 21 May 1992.
5. Mohamed Heikal, the Egyptian journalist, commented: 'Exactly how Tohami presented [his talks with Dayan to Sadat] is unknown, but Sadat understood the message to be that Israel was prepared to withdraw from Egyptian territory.' See Mohamed Heikal, *Secret Channels* (London, 1996), p. 256.

6. Interview with Mordechai Gur in *Yediot Aharonot*, 15 November 1977 (Hebrew).
7. Mohamed Heikal, *Secret Channels*, pp. 256 and 263.
8. Eliahu Ben-Elissar, *No More War* (Tel Aviv, 1995), p. 15 (Hebrew). Ben-Elissar was Director General of the Prime Minister's office and later Israel's first ambassador in Egypt.
9. The above quotations are from Jimmy Carter, *Keeping Faith, Memoirs of a President*, (London, 1982), pp. 347 and 351.
10. Jimmy Carter, *Keeping Faith*, p. 391.
11. Jimmy Carter, *Keeping Faith*, p. 396; Zbigniew Brezezinski, *Power and Principle, Memoirs of the National Security Adviser 1977–1981* (New York, 1985), p. 270.
12. Ariel Sharon to author; Eric Silver, 'Begin's Secret Interviews', *The Jerusalem Post*, 21 May 1992; Dan Pattir, interview with Menachem Begin, *Yediot Aharonot*, 27 November 1987 (Hebrew).
13. Zbigniew Brezezinski, *Power and Principle*, p. 278.
14. The above two quotations are from Zbigniew Brezezinski, *Power and Principle*, p. 287.
15. Arie Naor, *Begin in Power, a Personal Testimony* (Tel Aviv, 1993), p. 221 (Hebrew).
16. Menachem Begin, Speech in the Knesset, *Divrai Ha'Knesset*, 12 August 1982; Ariel Sharon, Speech in the Knesset, *Divrai Ha'Knesset*, 29 June 1982.
17. Amos Amir to author, Tel Aviv, 27 February 1997.

7 THE ROAD TO PEACE, 1983–1991

1. Shimon Peres, *Battling for Peace*, p. 232.
2. Shimon Peres, *Battling for Peace*, p. 307; also Shayke Ben-Porat, *Talks with Yossi Beilin* (Tel Aviv, 1996), pp. 89–90 (Hebrew).
3. George Shultz, *Turmoil and Triumph, My Years as Secretary of State* (New York, 1993), p. 939.
4. Shimon Peres to author, Tel Aviv, 9 July 1997; Yitzhak Shamir to author, Tel Aviv, 21 January 1997.
5. Yitzhak Shamir to author; Moshe Arens to author, Savyon, 26 January 1997.
6. Shimon Peres, *Battling for Peace*, p. 312.
7. Source: B'Tselem, The Israeli Information for Human Rights in the Occupied Territories.
8. General Amram Mitzna to author, Haifa, 27 January 1997.
9. Yitzhak Shamir, *Summing Up*, p. 214.
10. Lawrence Freedman et al., *The Gulf Conflict* (London, 1994), p. 101.
11. Interview with Richard Haass, New York, 21 July 1997, in the author's archive.
12. On this crucial Cabinet meeting, Yitzhak Shamir, Ehud Barak and Moshe Arens to author.

13. Ahron Bregman and Jihan el-Tahri, *The Fifty Years War*, p. 206 (UK version).
14. Yitzhak Shamir, *Summing Up*, pp. 238–9.
15. As cited in Robert Slater, *Rabin of Israel, Warrior for Peace* (London, 1996), p. 505.

8 PEACE AND WAR, 1992 TO PRESENT

1. Mahmoud Abbas (Abu Mazen), *Through Secret Channels* (Reading, 1995), p. 114.
2. Shimon Peres to author.
3. Yair Hirschfeld to author, Ramat Yishai, 25 February 1997.
4. Asher Arian, *Security Threatened, Surveying Israeli Opinion on Peace and War* (New York, 1999), pp. 101 and 104.
5. Yossi Beilin, *Touching Peace* (Tel Aviv, 1997), p. 90 (Hebrew).
6. Shimon Peres to author.
7. All the above, Uri Savir to author, Tel Aviv, 3 March 1997.
8. Yoel Singer, interview, Washington, 21 July 1997, in the author's archive; Yair Hirschfeld to author.
9. Mahmoud Abbas, *Through Secret Channels*, p. 156; Yoel Singer, interview.
10. Mahmoud Abbas, *Through Secret Channels*, p. 152; also interview with a member of the Palestinian delegation, Hassan Asfour, Ramallah, 19 February 1997, in the author's archive.
11. *Draft Declaration of Principles.* Source: Syrian, in the author's archive.
12. Interview with Syrian ambassador Walid Moualem, Washington, 19 July 1997, in the author's archive.
13. Warren Christopher to author, Los Angeles, 23 January 1998.
14. Warren Christopher to author.
15. Mahmoud Abbas, *Through Secret Channels*, p. 177.
16. Mahmoud Abbas, *Through Secret Channels*, pp. 178–9.
17. Shimon Peres to author.
18. In Shimon Peres, *Battling for Peace,* p. 378. Rabin insisted that the letter to Arafat should open with 'Mr Chairman' rather than 'Dear Mr Chairman'.
19. In Walter Laqueur and Barry Rubin, *The Israel–Arab Reader*, pp. 612–13.
20. General Uzi Dayan to author, Tel Aviv, 3 October 1997.
21. Terje Larsen to author, Tel Aviv, 31 March 2000.
22. Note for the Record is to be found in Dan Naveh, *Executive Secrets* (Tel Aviv, 1999), pp. 217–20 (Hebrew).
23. Treaty of Peace between Israel and Syria, 29 August 1998, in the author's archive (emphasis added).
24. Ahron Bregman and Jihan El-Tahri, *Israel and the Arabs, an Eyewitness Account of War and Peace in the Middle East* (New York, 2000), p. 345.
25. Ehud Barak to author.
26. Ahron Bregman and Jihan El-Tahri, *Israel and the Arabs,* p. 350.
27. Ahron Bregman and Jihan El-Tahri, *Israel and the Arabs,* p. 357.

28. Aluf Benn and Yossi Verter, 'Summit Fails; PM says "Dream of Peace Still Lives" ', *Ha'aretz*, 24 July 2000 (Hebrew).
29. Herb Keinon, 'Barak Quits; Election in 60 Days', *The Jerusalem Post*, 10 December 2000.
30. The Mitchell report.
31. Results of the poll as published in *Yediot Aharonot*, 30 March 2001.

Further Reading

For reasons of space, this list is very selective and concentrates on works in English and books as these are more accessible. Details of other relevant material can be found in the bibliographies of the works cited and in the notes of this book.

Abbas, Mahmoud, *Through Secret Channels* (Reading, 1995).

Adan, Avraham, *On the Bank of the Suez: an Israeli General's Personal Account of the Yom Kippur War* (London, 1980).

Alami, Musa, *Palestine is My Country* (London, 1969).

Allon, Yigal, *Shield of David: the Story of Israel's Armed Forces* (London, 1970).

Arens, Moshe, *Broken Covenant* (New York, 1995).

Arian, Asher, *The Second Republic: Politics in Israel* (Chatham, 1998).

Arian, Asher et al. *National Security and Public Opinion in Israel* (Boulder, 1988).

Ashrawi, Hanan, *This Side of Peace* (New York, 1995).

Avineri, Shlomo, *The Making of Modern Zionism: the Intellectual Origins of the Jewish State* (London, 1981).

Avriel, Ehud, *Open the Gates* (New York, 1975).

Baker, James A., *The Politics of Diplomacy: Revolution, War and Peace 1989–1992* (New York, 1995).

Barnaby, Frank, *The Invisible Bomb: the Nuclear Arms Race in the Middle East* (London, 1989).

Bar-On, Mordechai, *The Gates of Gaza: Israel's Road to Suez and Back, 1955–1957* (London, 1994).

Bar-Siman Tov, Yaacov, *The Israeli–Egyptian War of Attrition, 1969–1970* (New York, 1980).

Bar-Zohar, Michael, *Ben-Gurion: a Biography* (London, 1977).

Beckman, Morris, *The Jewish Brigade: an Army with Two Masters 1944–45* (London, 1998).

Begin, Menachem, *The Revolt* (London, 1951).

Ben-Gurion, David, *Israel: A Personal History* (New York, 1971).

Ben-Gurion, David, *Israel: Years of Challenge* (New York, 1963).

Ben-Gurion, David, *Rebirth and Destiny of Israel* (New York, 1954).

Bialer, Uri, *Between East and West: Israel's Foreign Policy Orientation 1948–1956* (Cambridge, 1990).

Black, Ian, and Benny Morris, *Israel's Secret Wars: a History of Israel's Intelligence Services* (London, 1996).

Breecher, Michael, *Decisions in Israel's Foreign Policy* (London, 1974).

Bregman, Ahron, *Israel's Wars: a History since 1947* (Routledge, 2002).

Bregman, Ahron, and Jihan el-Tahri, *The Fifty Years War: Israel and the Arabs* (London, 1998).

Bregman, Ahron, and Jihan el-Tahri, *Israel and the Arabs: an Eyewitness Account of War and Peace in the Middle East* (New York, 2000).

Brzezinski, Zbigniew, *Power and Principle* (New York, 1983).

Bull, Odd, *War and Peace in the Middle East* (London, 1976).

Bulloch, John, and Harvey Morris, *Saddam's War* (London, 1991).

Carter, Jimmy, *Keeping Faith* (New York, 1982).

Churchill, Randolph, *The Six Day War* (London, 1967).

Cobban, Helena, *The Palestinian Liberation Organization* (Cambridge, 1984).

Cohen, Israel, *The Zionist Movement* (London, 1945).

Collins, Larry, and Dominique Lapierre, *O Jerusalem* (Bnei Brak, 1993).

Dayan, Moshe, *Breakthrough: A Personal Account of the Egypt–Israel Peace Negotiations* (New York, 1981).

Dayan, Moshe, *Diary of the Sinai Campaign* (London, 1991).

Dayan, Moshe, *Story of My Life* (London, 1976).

Dayan, Yael, *Israel Journal: June 1967* (New York, 1967).

Eban, Abba, *An Autobiography* (London, 1977).

Eban, Abba, *My Country: the Story of Modern Israel* (London, 1973).

Eban, Abba, *Personal Witness* (New York, 1992)

Eisenberg, Dennis et al., *The Mossad, Israel's Secret Intelligence Service: Inside Stories* (New York, 1978).

Elon, Amos, *A Blood-Dimmed Tide* (London, 2000).

Elon, Amos, *The Israelis: Founders and Sons* (New York, 1983).

El-Shazli, Saad, *The Crossing of Suez: the October War (1973)* (London, 1966).

Engle, Anita, *The Nili Spies* (London, 1959).

Eytan, Walter, *The First Ten Years: a Diplomatic History of Israel* (New York, 1958).

Fahmi, Ismail, *Negotiating for Peace in the Middle East* (London, 1983).

Farid, Abdel Magid, *Nasser, the Final Years* (Reading, 1994).

Fein, Leonard, *Politics in Israel* (Boston, 1968).

Finkelstein, Norman, *Image and Reality of the Israel–Palestine Conflict* (London, 1995).

Fisk, Robert, *Pity the Nation: Lebanon at War* (Oxford, 1990).

Flamhaft, Ziva, *Israel on the Road to Peace: Accepting the Unacceptable* (Boulder, 1996).

Flapan, Simcha, *The Birth of Israel: Myths and Realities* (New York, 1987).

Frankel, Glenn, *Beyond the Promised Land: Jews and Arabs on the Hard Road to a New Israel* (New York, 1996).

Freedman, Robert (ed.), *Israel in the Begin Era* (New York, 1982).

Friedlander, Dov, and Calvin Goldscheider, *The Population of Israel* (New York, 1979).

Friedman, Thomas, *From Beirut to Jerusalem* (London, 1993).

Gabriel, Richard, *Operation Peace for Galilee: the Israeli–PLO War in Lebanon* (New York, 1984).

Gerson, Allan, *Israel, the West Bank and International Law* (London, 1978).

Gilbert, Martin, *The Arab–Israeli Conflict: Its History in Maps* (London, 1974).

Golan, Galia *Yom Kippur and After* (Cambridge, 1977).

Golan, Matti, *The Secret Conversations of Henry Kissinger* (New York, 1976).

Golan, Matti, *Shimon Peres: a Biography* (London, 1982).

Goldmann, Nahum, *The Autobiography of Nahum Goldmann: Sixty Years of Jewish Life* (New York, 1969).

Goldscheider, Calvin, *Israel's Changing Society: Population, Ethnicity, and Development* (Boulder, 1996).

Gorny, Yosef, *Zionism and the Arabs, 1882–1948: a Study of Ideology* (Oxford, 1987).

Grossman, David, *The Yellow Wind* (New York, 1988).

Harkabi, Yehoshafat, *Fedayeen Actions and Arab Strategy* (London, 1969).

Hart, Alan, *Arafat: Terrorist or Peacemaker?* (London, 1984).

Hass, Amira, *Drinking the Sea at Gaza* (London, 1999).

Hazony, Yoram, *The Jewish State: the Struggle for Israel's Soul* (New York, 2000).

Heikal, Mohamed, *The Road to Ramadan: the Inside Story of How the Arabs Prepared for and Almost Won the October War of 1973* (London, 1975).

Heikal, Mohamed, *Secret Channels* (London, 1996).

Hertzberg, Arthur, *The Zionist Idea* (New York, 1977).

Herzl, Theodor, *The Jewish State: a Modern Solution to the Jewish Question* (New York, 1970).

Herzog, Chaim, *The War of Atonement: the Inside Story of the Yom Kippur War, 1973* (London, 1998).

Hiro, Dilip, *Sharing the Promised Land: an Interwoven Tale of Israelis and Palestinians* (London, 1996).

Hirst, David, *The Gun and the Olive Branch* (London, 1977).

Hirst, David, and Irene Beeson, *Sadat* (London, 1981).

Horowitz, Dan, and Moshe Lissak, *The Origins of the Israeli Polity: Palestine under the Mandate* (Chicago, 1978).

Joseph, Dov, *The Faithful City: the Siege of Jerusalem, 1948* (New York, 1960).

Katz, Samuel, *Days of Fire* (New York, 1968).

Kedourie, Elie, *Britain in the Middle East 1914–1921* (London, 1956).

Kimche, Jon and David, *Both Sides of the Hill* (London, 1960).

Koestler, Arthur, *Promise and Fulfilment: Palestine 1917–1949* (London, 1983).

Kollek, Teddy, *For Jerusalem* (London, 1978).

Kornberg, Jacques, *Theodor Herzl: From Assimilation to Zionism* (Indiana, 1993).

Kurzman, Dan, *Genesis 1948: the First Arab–Israeli War* (New York, 1970).

Laqueur, Walter, *A History of Zionism* (London, 1972).

Laqueur, Walter, and Barry Rubin, *The Israel–Arab Reader: a Documentary History of the Middle East Conflict* (London, 1995).

Lewis, Bernard, *Semites and Anti-Semites* (London, 1986).

Litvinoff, Barnet, *The Story of David Ben-Gurion* (New York, 1959).

Litvinoff, Barnet, *Weizmann* (London, 1976).

Lorch, Nethanel, *The Edge of the Sword: Israel's War of Independence, 1947–1949* (New York, 1968).

Love, Kenett, *Suez* (New York, 1969).

Lucas, Noah, *The Modern History of Israel* (New York, 1974).

Luttwak, Edward, and Dan Horowitz, *The Israeli Army* (London, 1975).

Mcdonald, James, *My Mission in Israel* (New York, 1951).

Marlowe, John, *Rebellion in Palestine* (London, 1946).

Masalha, Nur, *Expulsion of the Palestinians* (Washington, 1992).

Medding, Peter, *The Foundation of Israeli Democracy, 1948–1967* (New York, 1990).

Meir, Golda, *My Life* (London, 1975).

Monroe, Elizabeth, *Britain's Moment in the Middle East, 1914–1956* (London, 1963).

Morris, Benny, *1948 and After: Israel and the Palestinians* (Oxford, 1990).

Morris, Benny, *The Birth of the Palestinian Refugee Problem, 1947–1949* (Cambridge, 1988).

Neff, Donald, *Warriors at Suez* (New York, 1981).

Ninio, Marcelle, *Operation Susannah* (New York, 1978).

Nuseibeh, Hazem Zaki, *Palestine and the United Nations* (London, 1981).

O'Ballance, Edgar, *The Arab–Israeli War, 1948* (London, 1956).

O'Ballance, Edgar, *No Victor, No Vanquished: the Arab–Israeli War, 1973* (California, 1997).

Ovendale, Ritchie, *The Origins of the Arab–Israeli Wars* (London, 1984).

Oz, Amos, *In the Land of Israel* (New York, 1983).

Pappe, Ilan, *The Making of the Arab–Israeli Conflict 1947–1951* (London, 1994).

Parfitt, Tudor, *Operation Moses: the Untold Story of the Secret Exodus of the Falasha Jews from Ethiopia* (New York, 1985).

Pasha, Glubb, *A Soldier with the Arabs* (London, 1958).

Patai, Raphael, (ed.), *The Complete Diaries of Theodor Herzl*, 5 vols (New York, 1961).

Pearlman, Moshe, *The Capture of Adolf Eichmann* (London, 1961).

Peres, Shimon, *Battling for Peace: Memoirs* (London, 1995).

Peres, Shimon, *David's Sling* (London, 1970).

Peretz, Don, *Israel and the Palestine Arabs* (Washington, 1958).

Peretz, Don, *Palestinians, Refugees and the Middle East Peace Process* (Washington, 1993).

Perlmutter, Amos et al., *Two Minutes over Baghdad* (London, 1982).

Prittie, Terence, *Eshkol of Israel: the Man and the Nation* (London, 1969).

Prittie, Terence, *Whose Jerusalem?* (London, 1981).

Quandt, William, *Camp David: Peacemaking and Politics* (Washington, 1986).

Rabin, Yitzhak, *The Rabin Memoirs* (London, 1979).

Rabinovich, Itamar, *The Road not Taken: Early Arab–Israeli Negotiations* (Oxford, 1991).

Rabinovich, Itamar, *The War for Lebanon, 1970–1983* (New York, 1984).

Rafael, Gideon, *Destination Peace, Three Decades of Israeli Foreign Policy: a Personal Memoir* (London, 1981).

Randal, Jonathan, *The Tragedy of Lebanon* (London, 1990).

Razin, Assaf, and Efraim Sadka, *The Economy of Modern Israel: Malaise and Promise* (Chicago, 1993).

Reeve, Simon, *One Day in September: the Story of the 1972 Munich Olympics Massacre* (London, 2000).

Reinharz, Jehuda, and Anita Shapira (eds), *Essential Papers on Zionism* (London, 1996).
Riad, Mahmoud, *The Struggle for Peace in the Middle East* (New York, 1981).
Rose, Norman, *Chaim Weizmann: a Biography* (New York, 1986).
Rubinstein, Amnon, *The Zionist Dream Revisited* (New York, 1984).
Rubinstein, Danny, *People of Nowhere: the Palestinian Vision of Home* (New York, 1991).
Sachar, Harry, *Israel: the Establishment of a State* (London, 1952).
Sachar, Howard, *Aliyah, the Peoples of Israel* (New York, 1961).
Sachar, Howard, *A History of Israel* (Oxford, 1987).
Sadat, Anwar, *In Search of Identity: an Autobiography* (New York, 1977).
Safran, Nadav, *Israel, the Embattled Ally* (Cambridge, 1981).
Said, Edward W., *Peace and Its Discontents* (London, 1995).
Said, Edward W., *The Question of Palestine* (New York, 1980).
Samuel, Herbert Viscount, *Memoirs* (London, 1945).
Savir, Uri, *The Process* (New York, 1998).
Schiff, Zeev, and Ehud Ya'ari, *Intifada, The Palestinian Uprising, Israel's Third Front* (New York, 1989)
Schiff, Zeev, and Ehud Ya'ari, *Israel's Lebanon War* (London, 1984).
Seale, Patrick, *The Struggle for Syria* (Oxford, 1965).
Segev, Tom, *The Seventh Million: the Israelis and the Holocaust* (New York, 1993).
Shamir, Yitzhak, *Summing Up: an Autobiography* (Boston, 1994).
Sharon, Ariel, *Warrior: the Autobiography of Ariel Sharon* (London, 1989).
Sheffer, Gabriel, *Moshe Sharett: Biography of a Political Moderate* (Oxford, 1996).
Shimshoni, Daniel, *Israeli Democracy* (New York, 1982).
Shipler, David, *Arab and Jew: Wounded Spirits in a Promised Land* (New York, 1987).
Shlaim, Avi, *The Iron Wall: Israel and the Arab World* (London, 2000)
Shlaim, Avi, *The Politics of Partition, King Abdullah, the Zionists and Palestine 1921–1951* (Oxford, 1988).
Silver, Eric, *Begin: the Haunted Prophet* (New York, 1984).
Slater, Robert, *Rabin of Israel: Warrior for Peace* (London, 1996).
Smith, Charles, D., *Palestine and the Arab–Israeli Conflict* (New York, 1992).
Spiegel, Steven, *The Other Arab–Israeli Conflict: Making America's Middle East Policy From Truman to Reagan* (Chicago, 1985).
Stein, Leonard, *The Balfour Declaration* (London, 1961).
Steven, Steward, *The Spymasters of Israel* (London, 1980).
Stevenson, William, *90 Minutes at Entebbe* (New York, 1976).
Sykes, Christopher, *Cross Roads to Israel: Palestine from Balfour to Bevin* (London, 1965).
Sykes, Christopher, *Orde Wingate* (London, 1959).
Syrkin, Marie, *Golda Meir: Woman with a Cause* (New York, 1961).
Tessler, Mark, *A History of the Israeli–Palestinian Conflict* (Bloomington, 1994).
Teveth, Shabtai, *Ben-Gurion and the Holocaust* (New York, 1996).
Teveth, Shabtai, *Moshe Dayan* (London, 1972).

Touval, Sadia, *The Peace Brokers* (Princeton, 1982).
Tuchman, Barbara W., *Bible and Sword: How the British Came to Palestine* (New York, 1956).
Urquhart, Brian, *Ralph Bunche: an American Life* (New York, 1993).
Vital, David, *The Origins of Zionism* (London, 1975).
Wasserstein, Bernard, *Herbert Samuel, a Political Life* (Oxford, 1992).
Weizman, Ezer, *The Battle for Peace* (New York, 1981).
Weizman, Ezer *On Eagles' Wings* (London, 1976).
Weizmann, Chaim, *Trial and Error: the Autobiography of Chaim Weizmann* (New York, 1949).
Wilson, Harold, *The Chariot of Israel* (London, 1981).
Winer, Gershon, *The Founding Fathers of Israel* (New York, 1971).
Ya'ari, Ehud, and Eitan Haber, *The Year of the Dove* (New York, 1979).
Yaniv, Avner, *Deterrence without the Bomb: the Politics of Israeli Strategy* (Boston, Mass., 1987).
Young, Peter, *The Israeli Campaign, 1967* (London, 1967).

Index

For a name or title starting with Al, El or The, see its second part.

308

DATE DUE

DEC 1 9 2003			
DEC 0 2 2005			
APR 1 3 2007			
GAYLORD			PRINTED IN U.S.A.